TOURISM
CONCEPTS, THEORY AND PRACTICE

TOURISM
CONCEPTS, THEORY AND PRACTICE

Dr. M.R. Dileep
Head-Department of Tourism and Travel Studies
Pazhassiraja College (Calicut University)
Wayanad, Kerala

NEW DELHI

Published and Printed by

Techsar Pvt. Ltd.
4435-36/7, Ansari Road, Daryaganj
New Delhi-110002 (India)
E-mail: tech_info@techsarworld.com
Website: www.techsarworld.com

ISBN 978-93-85909-67-2

Reprint 2024

PREFACE

Begun as an unremarkable recreational activity sometime in the ancient era, tourism had a humble beginning. Several centuries passed and in the due course, it has turned into part and parcel of modern man's social life. Got evolved into a huge economic sector involving billions of people, tourism, of late, has become one of the largest industries and the fastest growing sector in the world. Being a multidimensional and multifaceted activity, tourism is considered an amalgam of industries with diverse products and features.

In fact, tourism as an academic discipline emerged just a few decades back. Rigorous research activities contributed and complemented the once lean tourism literature. Currently, tourism, though on a multidisciplinary platform, has become a full-fledged academic discipline with ample literature and reference materials. As stated before, tourism is a multi-sectoral, and consequently tourism literature also involves diverse topics and themes.

Learning about tourism is indeed an intricate affair. There are many areas to cover and hence a student needs to focus on a specefic aspect to be pursued deep into in order to build up a career. Each area in tourism should be studied in detail. Though there are a number of areas to study in tourism, there are some fundamental aspects to be learnt by every student, professional, working employee and others interested in tourism. Those include principles, policies and practices of tourism.

A student of tourism, air transport, travel and hospitality studies should learn about the relationship between travel and tourism, and the activities and functioning of each of their sectors. Furthermore, it is inevitable to understand the nunances of tourism as an economic and social phenomenon, impacts and benefits, sustainability aspects, IT incorporation, and marketing and promotion. This book is envisaged in a manner to give an insight into the concept of tourism, various types of tourism, travel motivation and demand, industrial elements of tourism, destination and its elements, various organizations functioning in tourism, planning and development of tourism, and benefits and impacts. Moreover, various aspects of sustainable tourism, ecotourism and responsible tourism are also dealt with. An introduction to marketing and information technology applications in tourism is also given. The book ends with a discussion on current status of tourism, contemporary issues in tourism and the future prospects. Indeed, this book, prepared as a comprehensive one with profuse information on tourism principles, policies and practices, is an essential tool for all those who would like to pursue a career in any sector of tourism.

Dr. M.R. Dileep

ACKNOWLEDGEMENTS

God almighty is the true force and I humbly tender my wholehearted gratitude for His immeasurable blessings upon my life and career.

This book is brought to fruition through hard work, patience and perseverance along with the support I received from a large number of people. It is not one or two people helped me in different stages of my academic career and I am obliged to all of them. I am deeply grateful to my colleagues and friends at Pahassiraja College (Wayanad), Kerala Institute of Tourism and Travel Studies (KITTS, Thiruvananthapuram), and Salalah College of Applied Sciences and in other campuses under the Ministry of Higher Education, Sultanate of Oman. I thank all the office bearers and members of Indian Tourism and Hospitality Congress (ITHC), which is the apex body of tourism academicians in India. Also, a large number of my students who are now in different parts of the world in different positions, always encouraged me to do better and I personally thank all of them for their wishes.

The work would not have been successful without the support and prayers of my family members and relatives. I am grateful to all of them for their unconditional support and care, especially my wife, Soorya AN; son, Gautham Krishna; father Mr. Madhavakurup; mother, Mrs. Radhika Devi; father-in-law, Mr. V.K.N. Panicker; and mother-in-law, Mrs. Ambika Devi.

Dr. M.R. Dileep

CONTENTS

1 TOURISM: AN INTRODUCTION

Learning Outcomes

After studying this chapter, you will be able to:

- define tourism;
- distinguish tourists from the rest of travellers;
- understand the complex relationship among various components of tourism system;
- appreciate the multidisciplinary nature of tourism;
- understand how tourism evolved and grew through various centuries;
- identify the factors that contributed towards the evolution of modern tourism; and
- comprehend why tourism is promoted vigorously by countries.

1.1 INTRODUCTION

Tourism, a multidimensional and multifaceted activity with diverse social, cultural, economic and ecological impacts, evolved as one of the largest and most significant economic sectors in the world. In fact, countries, of late are in a race to develop tourism further and attract more and more tourists. There were obstacles at regular intervals, yet tourism has shown utmost resilience and recorded growth consistently for several years. Furthermore, it is poised for incredible progression in the years to come. Tourism has been cited as a 'major force in the global economy', 'engine of economic growth', 'determinant of development', and 'key driver for socioeconomic progress'. This rapidly expanding industry is contributing approximately ten per cent to global GDP (total contribution) and generating employment for 105,408,000 people (3.6% of total employment) directly. In 2014, the total contribution of travel and tourism to employment, including jobs indirectly supported by the industry, was 9.4% of total employment (276,845,000 jobs) (WTTC, 2015). Tourism cannot be considered just an economic activity;

rather it has been described as a *social phenomenon*, and is reported that it can be part of the solution to world problems, such as bridging the gap between the 'haves' and 'have–nots'. As an economic activity, it can help contribute to the alleviation of poverty. In spite of all such benefits, serious debates on the impact of tourism on different spheres, in particular on the physical and human environments of destination, are taking place and attempts in various forms are in progress so as to ameliorate those consequences to the maximum extent.

Certainly tourism is not a new phenomenon that has emerged sometime recently. It existed in different ways in different eras of written history. Yet, the modern form of tourism is something that had a progressive evolution since the end of the Second World War. Moreover, tourism transformed into a significant social activity accessible to most sections of societies across the world. It was not so, some decades back, when tourism was limited to the 'rich' and the 'aristocratic' due to various reasons. History tells that, in the early periods people travelled for a variety of reasons – to satisfy curiosity, to educate themselves, and to fight in wars. Food gathering is supposed to be the earliest reason for travel. The urge to travel has been on the increase since then and it caused the emergence of accommodation sector also. But the concept of tourism emerged just a few centuries ago. The word 'tourist' appeared first in the English language in the early 1800s. Until the last century, the growth of tourism was slow, though 'industrialization' and its repercussions provided much thrust for its evolution during those days. The twentieth century, with its tremendous technological and economic advancements, witnessed incredible developments in tourism, especially in its second half. A detailed history of the development of tourism to the modern form is explained later in this book. Currently, tourism is a huge economic sector involving billions of people. In 2015, more than 1.18 billion tourists travelled internationally, whereas domestic arrival figures were seen to have crossed 7 billion (UNWTO, 2016). This tells about the magnitude of the sector and the forecasts are quite inspiring.

1.2 BASIC CONCEPT OF TOURISM

Tourism has been conceptualized and defined from different perspectives. Moreover, it has been used interchangeably with travel in many cases. Furthermore, it is a multi-faceted phenomenon. These make it difficult to understand the concept of tourism. Having an analysis of various definitions propounded from different perspectives by different authors and authorities would help to unravel the inherent intricacies of this multidimensional phenomenon. Attempts to define tourism can be traced back to many decades. According to available literature, one of the earliest attempts was that of the League of Nations in 1937. The committee of statistical experts of the League of Nations, realizing the importance of collecting tourist statistics and of securing international compatibility, established the definition of the term 'tourist'. It defined *tourist* as any person visiting a country other than that in which he usually resides, for a period of at least 24 hours. The definition gives hints about certain fundamental parameters of tourism, yet, it focuses mainly on international travel, and excludes the concept of domestic tourism. However, the definition encompasses the aspects of minimum duration and the necessity of travel to a distant place from the usual place, which constitutes some of the basic criterion of considering a travel activity as tourism.

According to Hunziker and Krapf (1941), tourism is "the sum of phenomena and relationships arising from the travel and stay of non-residents in so far as it does not lead to permanent residence and is not connected to any earning activity". This definition encompasses more aspects of tourism. A conference of the United Nations held in Rome in 1963, considered recommendations put forward by the IUOTO (Now the UNWTO, United Nations World Tourism Organization) and agreed to use the term *visitor* to describe 'any person visiting a country other than that in which he has his usual place of residence, for any reason other than following an occupation remunerated from within the country visited'. In the definition, two classes of visitors were included; first one being *tourists*, who were classified as temporary visitors staying at least 24 hours, who travel for leisure, business, family mission or meeting. The second were *excursionists* who were classified as temporary visitors staying less than 24 hours, excluding people in transit. This definition recognizes the day visitor, but fails to take into account the domestic tourist. Leiper (1979) points about system aspect of tourism along with another important condition, that the journey would not be for a remunerative purpose. "It is a system involving the discretionary travel and temporary stay of persons away from their usual place of residence for one or more nights, except tours made for the primary purpose of earning remuneration from points enroute". Later in 1981, International Association of Scientific Experts in Tourism (IAEST) and the Tourism Society in Cardiff have refined the concept and held that "tourism may be defined in terms of particular activities selected by choice and undertaken outside home environment. Tourism may or may not involve overnight stays away from home." Rob Davidson (1996) tried to define tourism in the simplest way as "it is about people being away from their own homes, on short term, temporary visits, for particular purposes". Though the definition, is too short to include all aspects some important areas have been mentioned, as far as tourism is concerned, such as travelling to distant places is an essential one, the duration of the travel should be limited and there has to be a purpose behind the travel. "Tourism is the field of research on human and business activities associated with one or more aspects of the temporary movements of persons from their immediate home communities and daily work environments for business pleasure and personal reasons" (Chadwick, 1994).

McIntosh and Goeldner (1990) defined tourism from various perspectives by considering various groups that participate in, and are affected by the tourism industry. The major groups identified were the tourist, the business providing goods and services to tourists, the host community and the government. They stated that, "tourism is the sum of the phenomena and relationship arising from the interaction of tourists, businesses suppliers, host governments and host community in the process of attracting and hosting those tourists and other visitors". From the demand side, tourism can be viewed as "the activities of persons travelling to and staying in places outside their usual environment for not more than one consecutive year for leisure, business and other purposes" (WTO, 1995). Cooper et al. (2000) are of the opinion that this definition is not a strict technical definition, though it does convey the essential nature of tourism. They defined tourism in two perspectives: demand side and supply side. According to them, demand side definition has evolved by firstly attempting to encapsulate the idea of tourism into conceptual definitions and secondly, through the development of technical definitions for measurement and legal purposes. Supply side definitions, according to them, are less well developed, especially the technical definitions. Conceptual interpretation involves a number of aspects including major factors such as short term and temporary movement of people; movement is from the usual environment or places of residence and work to a distant place, along with stay and engaging in touristic activities in the place visited (Cooper et al., 2000; Burkart and Medlik, 1974). Leiper's definition of tourism from the supply side perspective suggests that tourist industry consists of all those firms, organizations and facilities which are intended to serve the specific needs and wants of tourists. Christopher Holloway (1994) believes that defining tourism precisely is all but an impossible task and that, with the advent of twentieth century mass tourist, perhaps the most accurate definition of a tourist is, someone who travels to see something different, and then complains when he finds things not the same. From all the above definitions, it can be clearly stated that, over these years, the definition of tourism has undergone a change and along with the historical changes, tourism has expanded its range and scope.

The analysis of various definitions reveals that tourism is distinguished by a range of factors. It is basically travel from one place to another. The travel has to be from the place of 'usual environment' to a different place. The 'usual environment' essentially includes the place of residence and/or work where the usual day-to-day life takes place. The distance to the place travelling to may vary, preferably a minimum of 35 km as specified by some authors. The total journey should be for more than 24 hours, with a minimum stay of one night in the place visited. The stay should not extend beyond one year, consecutively. The tourist visiting a place has to take part in certain activities which are of touristic characteristics, like, sightseeing. Also, the tourist, during the entire process of travel should not take part in any activity that would enable him or her to earn money as remuneration, directly. Travel takes place due to physical or psychological reasons, or both. These reasons are usually referred to as *travel motivators*.

Table 1.1: Four different perspectives of tourism

The tourist: Tourist seeks various psychic and physical experiences and satisfactions. The nature of these will largely determine the destination chosen and the activities enjoyed.
The businesses providing tourist goods and services: Business people see tourism as an opportunity to make profit by supplying goods and services that the tourist market demands.
The government: The authorities view tourism as wealth factor in the economy of their jurisdictions. The government also considers foreign exchange receipts from international tourism as well as from tax receipts. It takes responsibility in policy making, planning, destination development, identification of new destinations, marketing and promotion, etc.
The host community: Local people usually see tourism as a cultural and employment factor. Tourism results in both beneficial as well as harmful effects on local community.

Source: Goeldner & Ritchie, 2006

Throughout the travel process, a traveller has a variety of needs, all of which constitute the elements that sum up the overall travel experience. Groups of businesses of different nature offer services and products in order to satisfy those various needs. The success of tourism sector depends on the degree of quality of services offered by different business elements. A traveller spends money to buy these services and products which results in an economic activity. The expenditure pattern may vary from one type of tourist to another. Yet, tourist expenditure is indeed the prime reason why destinations intend to attract tourists. Moreover, the tourist will interact with different groups of people ranging from service providers to local community members. This interaction too has significance in the success of any destination. Tourism is a 'people industry' and service delivery by the people involved is very important. *Moments of truth* of a tourist determines the tourist experience. The destination and tourism related businesses and facilities use variety of resources, both natural as well as artificial in order to cater to the requirements of tourists. Consequently, tourists become the consumers of those resources directly or indirectly. Tourism takes place in an open environment and the external environments have influences of different kinds. In fact, tourism is highly sensitive to those external factors.

In the process of developing facilities, infrastructure and superstructure, tourism directly or indirectly causes a wide range of consequences on the environment, culture, society and on the economy. Moreover, the provision of services as well as the behaviour of tourists too can generate consequences. Debates on such consequences are so common across the world, though tourism flourishes at an incredible rate.

1.3 THE TOURIST

In common usage, the term *traveller* is often used instead of 'tourist'. Certainly, the tourist is a traveller. But, are all the travellers tourists? This baffles while learning tourism

Table 1.2: WTO classified list of purposes associated with tourism

Leisure, recreation and holidays
Sightseeing, shopping, attending sporting and cultural events, recreation and cultural activities, nonprofessional active sports, trekking and mountaineering, use of beaches, cruises, gambling, rest and recreation for armed forces, summer camp, honeymooning, etc.
Visiting friends and relatives
Visits to family, relatives or friends, attending funerals, care of ailing persons.
Business and professional
Installing equipment, inspection, purchases, sales for foreign enterprises; attending meetings, conferences or congresses, trade fairs and exhibitions; employer incentive tours; giving lectures or concerts; programming tourist travel, contracting of accommodation and transport, working as guides and other tourism professionals; participation in professional sports activities; government missions: including diplomatic, military or international organization personnel, except when stationed on duty in the country visited; paid study, education and research, such as university sabbatical leave; language, professional or other special courses in connection with and supported by visitor's business or profession.
Health treatment
Spas, fitness, thalassotherapy, health resorts and other treatments and cures.
Religion/pilgrimages
Attending religious events, pilgrimages.
Other
Aircraft and ship crews on public carriers, transit and other or unknown activities.

Source: UN & WTO, 1994

and that necessitates a clear distinction between a tourist and a traveller, though there is no harm in calling one who travels for the purpose of tourism a traveller. This distinction is made for the purpose of measuring tourism as well as conceptualizing a tourist technically from an industrial perspective. The following descriptions about traveller, visitor, excursionist and tourist would help to understand the differences.

Travel is a common phenomenon and the movement can be for any purpose. The basic meaning of travel is movement from one place to another. One of the purposes of travelling is visiting. Hence, in order to identify and distinguish tourist in the whole ambit of travelling, travellers need to be classified into two groups: those who travel for visiting and those for non-visiting purposes. The distinction elaborated by the UN and WTO (1994) in the document titled *Recommendations on Tourism Statistics* is indeed sufficient enough to decipher the much needed differences. It classifies travellers into two as *visitors* and *other travellers*. Visitors are those who make a trip for tourism purposes. According to it, a visitor is "any person travelling to a place other than that of his/her usual environment for less than 12 months and whose main purpose of trip is other than the exercise of an activity remunerated from within the place visited." Here some aspects are specified to distinguish visitors from other travellers. Travel has to be from the 'usual environment', which denotes the place of residence, study or work, to another place. The other aspect specified is maximum duration, which is 12 months at a stretch. Moreover, the travel should not be for a remunerative purpose.

Visitors are further classified into two categories such as 'tourists' and 'same-day visitors'. This distinction is based on the duration of stay at the destination visited. A visitor is called a tourist if the traveller stays at the destination visited for a period of minimum 24 hours. Spending one day in a destination is a parameter in considering a visitor a tourist. Or else, if the duration is less than 24 hours, the visitor is referred to as *same-day visitor*. Tourist can be inferred as any person who travels to a place other than that in which he/she has his/her usual residence, but outside his/her usual environment for a period of minimum 24 hours, not exceeding 12 months and whose main purpose of visit is other than the exercise of an activity remunerated from the place visited. Tourists are defined separately as *international tourist* and *domestic tourist* depending upon the country of visit. If the visit is made to a foreign country, the tourist is an international tourist, whereas the domestic tourist travels to a place within the country of residence, but outside his/her usual environment.

Same-day visitor is also referred to as *excursionist*. It can also be "a breakaway from the usual environment" and the visitor "does not spend the night in a collective or private accommodation in the place visited". As in the case of tourist, the purpose of travelling should also be non-remunerative. The UN conference in Rome states that excursionists are temporary visitors staying less than 24 hours including cruise travellers but excluding travellers in transit. In some areas of the world, excursionists cross borders and the economic impact of such international excursionists is very important to small isolated countries, which receive cruise-ship passengers. This is particularly important for small island countries like Caribbean Islands (people visit during day and are actually accommodated onboard cruise ships). They can also be considered same-day visitors who do not spend the night in a collective or private accommodation in the place visited. The UN and WTO classified various purposes that are considered under the realm of tourism and the same is given in Table 1.2. While we analyze the purposes and other aspects given in it, the following groups are also considered at the time of measuring tourist statistics:

- People travelling for pleasure, for family reasons, for health, etc. (including nationals who live abroad permanently).
- People traveling to attend meetings or for assignments (sports, management). Employees of large organizations on assignments abroad for less than one year are also included.

- People travelling for business (employees of commercial or industrial firms who travel to install machinery or equipment abroad).
- Students and young people at boarding schools or colleges and those who travel or work temporarily during their holidays.
- Visitors from cruise ships even if their stay is less than 24 hours. They can be registered in a separate group, which does not take into account their place of residence. Transit passengers who cross the country in more or less than 24 hours.
- Foreign airlines and ship crews on stopover in a country.
- Musicians or artists on tour, etc.

Table 1.3: Categories of travellers / trips not included in tourist statistics, as per UN and WTO (1994)

Travellers who should not be included in international visitor arrivals and departures:	Trips that should not be included in domestic visitor arrivals and departures:
• Persons entering or leaving a country as migrants, including dependents accompanying or joining them. • Persons, known as border workers, residing near the border in one country and working in another. • Diplomats, consular officers and members of the armed forces when travelling from their country of origin to the country of their assignment or vice versa, including household servants and dependants accompanying them.	• Residents travelling to another place within the country with the intention of setting up their usual residence in that place. • Persons who travel to another place within the country to exercise an activity remunerated from within the place visited.
• Persons travelling as refugees or nomads. • Persons in transit who do not formally enter the country through passport control, such as air transit passengers who remain for a short period in a designated area of the air terminal or ship passengers who are not permitted to disembark. This category includes passengers transferred directly between airports or other terminals. Other passengers in transit through a country are classified as visitors	• Persons who travel to work temporarily in institutions within the country. • Persons who travel regularly or frequently between neighbouring localities to work or study. • Nomads and persons without fixed residence. • Armed forces on manoeuver.

Source: UN & WTO, 1994.

According to Goeldner & Ritchie (2003), the following categories of visitors are not considered tourists:

- Persons arriving, with or without a contract of work, to take up an occupation or engage in any remunerating business activity in the country.

- Persons coming to establish a residence in the country.
- Students and young persons in boarding establishments or schools.
- Residents in a frontier zone and persons domiciled in one country and working in an adjoining country.
- Travellers passing through a country without stopping even if the journey takes more than 24 hours.

1.4 MULTIDISCIPLINARY ASPECTS OF TOURISM

Tourism is a complex process, and is multi-sectoral and multi-factorial. It encompasses many dimensions as it cuts across conventional sectors in the economy, requiring inputs of economic, social, cultural and environmental nature. Multidisciplinary approach refers to collaboration between two or more disciplines to work on a research project while each discipline maintains its own borders, epistemologies, methodologies, and values (Choi & Pak, 2006). By this, it can ensure a broader multilevel view on the application of the intended study, work, planning and development, and it can yield better results compared to a single discipline study. Learning of tourism should come from a wide variety of disciplines and perspectives. Historically, tourism as a discipline has evolved from a number of already established areas like economics, sociology, psychology, ecology, management, history, and anthropology. Explaining the complex nature of tourism needs an evaluation from all those varied disciplines. Economics is one of the major areas associated with tourism. Tourism is largely considered the largest economic sector in the world. The economic contribution of tourism urges destinations and countries to develop tourism. While considering the economic benefits of tourism, the *multiplier concept* is often used to describe the penetration of effects of the expenditure made by tourists deep into the local economy. Assessment of economic contribution in advance is always a prerequisite to the planning and development of tourism, and it is complimented by periodic evaluation of benefits after the implementation of the projects. Tourism is described as an economic sector consisting of an amalgamation of diverse industries offering different products, which are all interrelated. Yet, tourism cannot be explained only from an economic perspective as many other disciples are linked.

Psychological aspects of tourism are also relevant as tourist movement has a psychological perspective. The motivation is often linked with psychological needs and characteristics. Movement patterns, selection of destinations, activities undertaken during the tour and overall tourist behaviour have psychological linkages. Psychological aspects also will come into play in the expenditure made by tourists. After all, tourism is a social process. Tourist's social position has an influence in the decisions made by him/her. Status and prestige are also classified travel motivators. Social interactions with local people, service providers and other relevant stakeholders is always part of tourism. The sociological approach for tourism becomes relevant here having ample interconnection with economics and psychology discussed above. Can tourism be considered separate from political angle? It is virtually difficult as destination survival is often linked to the political factors like political stability, foreign affairs and diplomacy, types of barriers to travel, visa policy, development policy; environmental policy, etc. Moreover, political factors in the tourism markets constitute a major determinant in tourism demand as well.

Environmental studies constitute an inevitable part of tourism. Tourism is often criticized for the impacts it makes on the nature. Tourism planning, sustainable development, waste management, zoning and developmental policies are always looked from the perspectives of environment and ecology. History and anthropology are part and parcel of tourism. These contribute a major group of resources for tourist destinations. Every destination has some historical attractions. Heritage remains of the society are always an attraction for tourists. Cultural and anthropological elements form different tourism types and enhance attractiveness of destinations. All such takes place in the geographical elements. Two main elements are *tourism markets* or tourist generating regions and *destinations* in the tourism system. Economic activities takes place in both these elements. Businesses and industries are spread across destinations mainly. Accessibility is also linked to the geographical elements. Climate is linked to geography and closely associated with tourism in a destination. Climate also causes seasonality. Management discipline has immense importance in tourism. All managerial functions are applicable in tourism organizations. Without proper planning, development and management, tourism in a destination will end up in more impacts than benefits. Another aspect associated with this is *marketing*. Image building, branding, marketing and promotion are equally important for tourism organizations as well as tourist destinations. Legal aspects are of much significance and related to political and social environments. Adequate laws and regulations are important for any tourist destination. Hence, tourism is a diverse area, cutting across large number of disciplines and that necessitates approaching tourism from a multidisciplinary perspective, particularly for planning, development, management, research, sustainable development and even for education and training.

1.5 TOURISM SYSTEM

System is a very common term used in our day-to-day environment. It simply refers to something with different parts and works through coordinated efforts. Webster's unabridged dictionary describes system as *a set or arrangement of things related or connected to form a unity or organization*. In management concept, a system is defined as a set of related components, activities, processes and human beings interacting together so as to accomplish some common objectives. The important aspects of system concept are:

- A system comprises subsystems/parts/elements.
- Each subsystem/part/element has separate function.
- Each part has its own role and relevance in the total system.
- All the parts have interactions and interrelationships with one another.
- The system will have an ultimate objective.

Thus, it can be concluded that a system functions for the accomplishment of its objective. Each part will have separate objectives, which are usually based on the main objective. The accomplishment of objectives of the subsystem/parts/elements will ultimately lead to the accomplishment of the objective of the main system. Numerous examples can be cited for understanding the concept of system. The best example is human body itself.

For better understanding of the complexities and multidisciplinary approaches of tourism, different frameworks can be drawn. One such approach, which is simple and suitable for understanding tourism is the model suggested by Leiper (1990) (Fig 1.1). He considered the phenomenon, tourism as an open system functioning in various environments, such as human, sociocultural, economical, technological, physical, political and legal. As explained above, this system has various parts or elements, which interact with one another in generating tourism. According to it, the following are the elements:

- Tourist
- Geographic elements
  - Traveller generating region (TGR)
  - Tourist destination region (TDR)
  - Transit route region (TRR)
- Tourism industry/business elements.

Tourist is considered the main and most important element of the system. Without the presence of tourists, the system may not function at all. Other human elements in the system also influence the system directly or indirectly. Tourist has direct interaction with some other human elements like professionals involved in service delivery, tour guides, and people from the local community. These interactions are significant in tourism system as positive and healthy interaction is essential for the system futuristically. A poor service delivery can result in customer dissatisfaction. A negative community approach can also adversely affect tourism.

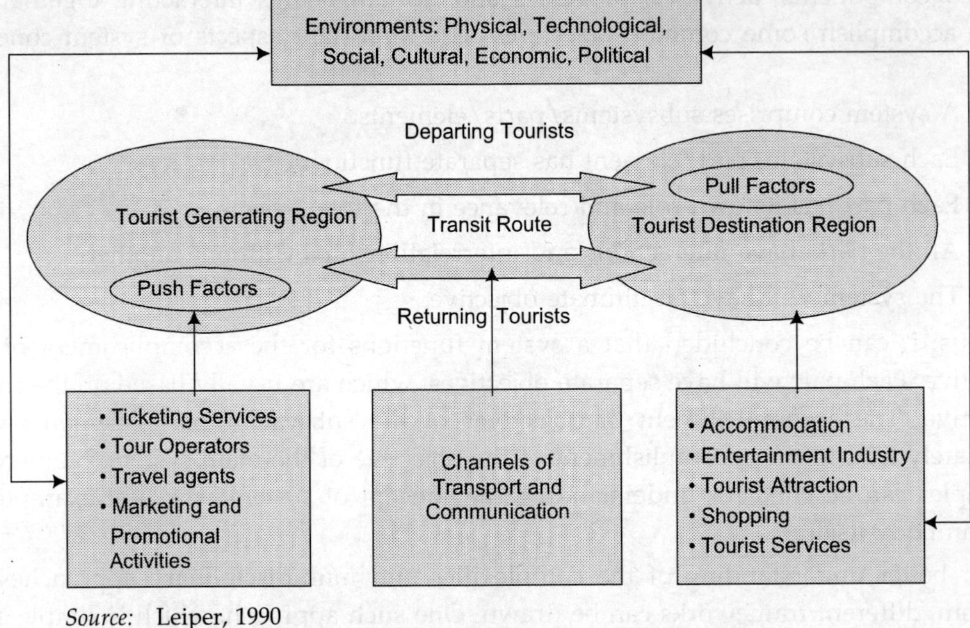

Source: Leiper, 1990

Figure 1.1 Leiper's model of tourism system.

Tourism is ultimately the result of movement of people from one place to another, linked to geographical locations. The various elements acting in the system related to geography are classified as geographical elements. Depending upon the location of the movement of the tourist, these elements are further divided into three groups, such as traveller generating region (TGR), tourist destination region (TDR), and transit route region (TRR). *Traveller generating region* is the area from where the tourists emerge and is represented in the literature as tourism markets. For example, if a traveller from UK is travelling to India to visit various places, then UK will be the generating region. *Tourist destination region* represents the 'end' of tourism, which the tourist ultimately intends to visit. This region attracts the tourists to engage in tourism. In the above example, India is the destination. The area between the traveller generating region and destination region is referred to as the *transit route region*. This not only includes the short period of travel to reach the destination but also includes stopovers; the intermediate places, which the tourist may visit on route.

Tourism industry is the next element in the Leiper's model. As is known, tourism is a multi-sector industry that comprises diverse range of sub-industries. These provide different kinds of products, which are essential for the tourism process. Hotels, restaurants, airlines, travel agencies, etc., are some vital components. Such components may be located in different parts of the system. Hospitality industry is found in the destination region. Transport sector is largely represented in the transit route region.

All the elements of the system interact with each another in various contexts, such as, during the delivery and transaction of the tourism products.

A large number of factors can cause a person to engage in tourism and these can be classified on different bases. When we classify them on the basis of location, some of them can be located in the generating region and some in the tourist destination region. The factors present in the tourist generating region have the capacity to force a person to engage in tourism. For example, income level of a person. If the person has more amount of discretionary income, it may encourage him to participate in tourism activities. Such factors may be referred to as *push* factors. Apart from the factors mentioned above, mobility, educational attainment, paid holiday entitlement, family size, work related stress, etc., may also be included in this category.

On the other hand, a few other factors are seen in the destination region. Leiper says that the 'pull' of destinations energizes the whole tourism system and demand for travel from the generating region. For example, the cultural attractions of a destination can allure a person to visit. In some of the destinations, climate may be a major factor that can attract tourists from anywhere. Such factors are called *pull* factors. Infrastructure facilities, scenic beauty, etc., are some other factors that can be considered pull factors. From this discussion, it can be stated that tourist is the principal element and he/she takes part in the process of tourism due to the integrated effect of 'pull and push' factors. The industrial components located in different parts of the geographical elements offer various facilities and services so as to enable the tourist to satisfy his needs and wants as part of his travel and stay.

1.6 EVOLUTION AND HISTORY OF TOURISM

The history of travel can be traced back to almost the origin of civilization. The origin of word 'travel' is seen in its earliest form of *travail*, meaning painful and laborious effort (Holloway, 2006). *Food gatherers* can be treated as the first 'travellers' and since then, the urge of mankind to engage in travel has been growing. Many milestones were surpassed, and today that activity has grown into a large, diverse industry with plenty of social, cultural and economic dimensions.

Food gathering stage was followed by food production and then, settlement on the river banks. Once man started settling down, he began to apply his mind, and the inborn nature of mankind kept his urge always alive. He began to conquer the world in which travel became inevitable. *Trade* became an important reason in the growth of travel. One of the greatest milestones in the history of tourism is the invention of wheel. It improved the speed of travel and men could cover large distances, which stimulated travel. The increasing trend in travel necessitated to stay and thus the concept of *inns* emerged. It was the sign of beginning of an industry, which was later called tourism.

History provides glimpses of tourist activities held in the ancient period. Invention of money by *Sumerians* (Babylonia) during 4000 BC and the usage of it in business transactions helped travel to grow. *Cuneiform writing* and *invention of wheel* were recorded to have happened during this period. Phoenicians were probably the first real business travellers in the modern sense. Oceans were great mystery for men. Though many ventures to conquer oceans failed miserably, the unending urge for the same continued. Huge sailboats and sailing ships were built. Thus, the sailor stage emerged. The curiosity to experience the outside world really initiated travel among men. Apart from Babylonians, Egyptians also entertained tourism related activities. Greek tourists, during the third century BC, travelled to visit the *healing gods*. The lighthouse of Alexandria was considered one of the seven wonders of the ancient world. Leisure travel reported to have begun during 1500 BC when Egyptians began to travel to visit the pyramids. In Mediterranean, the ancient cradle of western civilization, travel for trade and commerce, religious purposes, medical treatment or education was developed at an early stage. In ancient Greece, people travelled to see the Olympic Games in 776 BC. The evolution of the Olympic Games after 776 BC initiated a stimulus for activities that can be considered equivalent to tourism based upon sporting events. But international travel seemed to be limited due to the Greek Wars. In fact, the emergence of the Roman Empire put an indelible mark in the history of tourism. Tourism as a pleasure activity emerged in this period. Horse-drawn wagons for carriage of goods and people evolved from the battlefields when such were used for military purposes from the 3rd century BC. By the 5th century BC, Athens had become an important destination for travellers visiting major sights like Parthenon. During this period, 'inns' were established in major towns and seaports. Romans created excellent networks of road transportation and communication system to manage their vast empire, which helped 'travel' also. During the era of Roman empire, the state as well as private entrepreneurs created leisure facilities like space for baths and resorts. The construction of Colosseum meant for sports and events is another remarkable example of creating infrastructure. Trade routes were created and travel tendency increased. Business related travel increased in Rome's territories. Roads linking cities to seaside resorts, summer villas and historical sites were constructed which enhanced travel prosperity even for middle class. The capital city became an important urban tourism destination. As part of it, inns, bars, tour guides, and souvenir vendors emerged. Spas had a historical background during the period of the Romans. The practice of bathing in mineral waters during tourist trips for health and pleasure was prevalent. Romans even travelled to outside countries especially Egypt and Greece.

The downfall of Roman Empire brought a setback to tourism development. Declining of the Roman Empire made travel dangerous and less attractive. Pleasure travel remained close to home travel, limiting options to walking, riding horses, being carried on a carrier's wagon (Holloway, 2006). For several centuries (between the 5th and the 15th centuries AD), tourism experienced sluggish growth and was referred to as *dark stage* of tourism. Even in the dark era, tourism related activities could be identified, like emergence of festival and event based tourism evolved as a result of the activities associated with nobility. By the second half of this era, pilgrims to the Holy land emerged. Travel was not comfortable due to the difficult conditions of roads and some highwaymen abounded on some routes.

'Renaissance', originated in Italy after 1350, reached its peak during Elizabethan times. By that time in England, participating in fairs and festivals was important travel motivation for domestic tourists. The social and religious innovative thoughts changed the concept of leisure, to a certain extent, and eventually led to the concept of using leisure time more productively. These changes are reported to have contributed to the rise of the industrial society. The concept of holiday emerged slowly. The word *'Holiday'* originated from Old English *"haligdaeg,"* which simply combined *"halig"* ("holy") and *"daeg"* ("day") into one word. It meant 'holyday'. For most people, this implied a break from work. Religious travels were undertaken during this period (Middle Ages).

By the 15th century AD, the great Renaissance evolved in Europe. Italy became the intellectual capital of Europe and education, politics, economics and others sciences reached to new heights as there were a number of stalwarts in each field in that country. By mid-1600s coaches were operating regularly in Britain, especially between London and Oxford. *Stage coach,* drawn by teams of horses which could be changed at regular points throughout the route, enhanced mobility and comfort. With the improvement of such coaches, one could cover approximately 40 miles a day during summer. Inns served the needs of overnight guests. Also lodging or 'chambers' were available for rent to visitors. In 1815, *'tarmacadam'* road surfacing was discovered which improved the road conditions. In 1832 the *'charabancs'*, public coaches drawn by teams of horses were introduced. By 1820s itself, horse-drawn omnibus was in regular service in main cities of Europe.

1.6.1 Grand Tour

After a long break, Renaissance has come to tourism also. Europe became the hub. People from other parts of the world travelled to Italy, France and other parts of Europe. Started in early 17th century, it is considered a direct result of the freedom and quest for learning emerged as a result of Renaissance. Diplomats, business people and scholars engaged in travel. It started as a tour seeking education, travelling to major cultural centres of Europe. It was a traveller's circuit to key destinations and places in Europe, mainly by the wealthy aristocratic and privileged classes in pursuit of education, culture and pleasure (Page, 2007). These tours lasted long, even up to three years. Such 'travel' then was referred to as *'Grand Tour'*. Oxford English dictionary defines grand tour as a tour to the principal cities and places of interest in Europe, formerly said to be an essential part of the education of the young man of 'good birth' and 'fortune'. The grand tour can be defined in terms of class, which would determine the places visited and the mode of travel. The reasons for undertaking the grand tour were also diverse: career, education, culture, literary, health, scientific, business and economic. Sooner, the grand tour expanded to include leisure travel as well, where pleasure seeking young men travelled to France and Italy, mainly to cities like Paris, Venice, and Florence. British travellers also ventured into other destinations in Europe. This *aristocratic* grand tour had been in Europe for a long time and gained popularity by eighteenth century when the emerging middle classes also joined the trend.

The grand tour gradually faded as other nations of the world also rose to this status in accordance with European nations. The emergence of industrial revolution led to different changes in the various spheres of human life. Manually produced things turned to be industrial mass products using machines. The rate of productivity increased. Employment rate was also increased. People started working with machines, and continuous work with machines gave way for monotony, which forced them to take rest away from the working atmosphere. This stimulated travel tendency of human beings to indulge in recreation and leisure. This was how industrialization helped tourism to grow. The scientific inventions and applications revolutionized the lifestyle of men. The eighteenth century saw the development of seaside resorts and by 1815, a service began operating between London and Gravesend which initiated travel to distant resorts.

Introduction of the steam engine, railways, steam ship, etc., made travel easier and faster and stimulated travel among people. Rising personal income due to rapid industrialization also energized travel propensity among men. By late 18th century, coastal areas emerged as new form of visitor attractions mainly in European and North American countries. There was a wide belief about the use of seawater for health reasons and sea coasts were gaining prominence for leisure and recreation activities. During this period, people travelled in masses and visited many places such as Greece, Rome, France, Italy and so on. But they moved in a cluster rather than in an organized group. In 1841, as secretary of South Midland Temperance Association, Thomas Cook organized an excursion for his members from Leicester to Loughborough, at a fare of one-shilling. The success of this venture, involving 570 people, encouraged him to arrange similar excursions using chartered trains and by 1845, he was organizing such trips, on a commercial basis. In such an organized tour, the organizer took care of the travel arrangements, accommodations, transport at destination and return to the homeland. The concept of organized tourism started flourishing and by 1855, Cook had extended the field of operations to the continent, organizing the first 'inclusive tour' to the Paris exhibition that year. He also made administration of travel easier by introducing the *hotel voucher* (1867) and in 1873 the *circular note*, a precursor to today's traveller's cheque.

The invention of photography further stimulated growth of tourism. The first regular cross channel steamship was introduced in 1821, on the Dover-Calais route. In 1872, Thomas Cook first organized 'round the world tour'. As tourism grew in the later years of the century, the organizers of travel became established institutionally. Thomas Cook and Sir Henry Lunn were two of the best-known names of the period, but many other well-known companies were also established. In the United States, American Express initiated money honours and travellers cheques. The development in the transport sector saw people moving in large numbers. The concept of mass tourism, thus, evolved into a major force in tourism.

During the late 19th century and early 1990s, imperial trade of many European countries created more demand for business travel. The growing rail transportation was another factor that pushed tourism forward. In the opening years of 20th century, travel continued to expand, encouraged by the increasing wealth, curiosity and consistent developments in the transport sector. The First World War slowed the growth of international tourism, particularly. By 1920s, many cruise liners successfully carried cruise tourism, focusing on business and pleasure activities. But, then the depression occurred in industrial economies during 1920s and 1930s, limiting the scope of both international and domestic tourism. In fact, the First World War generated different impacts in expanding worldwide travel. The road networks were improved. Different mass communication methods were experimented. In the United States, the use of motor cars for private holidays increased.

In Britain, in 1921, four major rail companies emerged such as London, Midland and Scottish Railway (LMS), London and North Eastern Railway (LNER), Great Western Railway (GWR) and Southern Railway (SR). The arrival of airlines posed a threat for long distance rail transportation, but in the early periods it was used mainly for mail carrying purposes. During the 1930s, *holiday camps* were introduced aiming at the growing low-income market for holidays. Resorts and hotels proliferated along the seasides of England. The government started initiatives in tourism business and in 1929, the British Government established British Travel and Holidays Association and by the outbreak of the Second World War, the British government recognized tourism as a means for foreign exchange earnings. Billy Butlin built the first holiday camp in 1936. It became a trend and as per an estimate, by 1948, one in twenty holiday makers stayed at Butlin Camps. During the same era, *second homes* were developed as a widespread phenomenon in some countries. Aviation too started to impact travel by then.

The Second World War also slowed down the growth of international tourism. Yet, with the technological breakthroughs in aircraft design achieved during and after the War, air services proved a viable alternative to shipping for international travel. Access to new forms of transport, particularly road-based in the inter-war periods opened up more non-rural areas for tourism. The post-war period saw growth in income leisure time and opportunities for international travel. The end of world wars caused many changes in the political equations the world over. Advances in aircraft technology and surplus aircraft in the immediate post-war years aided rapid expansion of air travel. Air travel became faster, safer and more comfortable. Boeing 707 was successfully introduced for commercial purposes in 1958 which encouraged international travel further. Apart from the emergence of aircraft with jet engines, 1950s experienced the emergence of chartered tourism using small aircraft. A further technological break-through in air transportation occurred in 1970, when the first wide-bodied jet (Boeing 747s), capable of carrying over 400 passengers, appeared in service. Transportation improvements were observed in terms of speed safety and comfort. Introduction of jet aircraft, wide-body jets, evolution of high-speed trains, emergence of larger aircraft, arrival of cruise tourism, etc., stimulated tourism. Development of new forms of accommodation establishments, like self-catering, second home, etc., also contributed in tourism's growth. Increased availability of information and forced development of destinations by governments are some other factors. The advent of developments in information technology caused revolutionary changes in tourism. The second half of the last century has seen tremendous growth in tourism and has been considered a social right in this modern world. The most critical change that took place between tourism in the past and the present is that it has been transformed from being an activity preserved for the rich to a mass phenomenon.

1.7 EVOLUTION OF INDIAN TOURISM

In India, during the early periods, a sophisticated agricultural economy made the export of cash crops an important trade link. Manufacturing of iron ore into steel for weaponry was another item of trade by the later Vedic period. Therefore, people always wanted to find a route to India. The sea route was found by the great sailors. The incidence of *Christopher Columbus* landing on the shores of America, and proclaiming as landed in India, reveals the amount of interest they had to discover sea route to India. Tools and textiles were other renowned Indian products. Trade became an important reason to travel to India.

The epics like *Ramayana* and the *Mahabharata* show different events in which intensive travel was involved. The various kingdoms and dynasties ruled India also gave much importance to travel. The invasion of Alexander the Great was a milestone in the history of Indian tourism, which stimulated travel among countries. Instances of various foreign visitors to India can be traced from Indian history and the best examples are Hiuen Tsang's and Fahien's visits from China. The emergence of Buddhism really stimulated intra-and inter-regional travel. Inns had proliferated throughout India by that time and people travelled to many places related to Buddhism. Other religions also contributed in initiating travel to religious places.

Table 1.4: Important events in the history of tourism

4000 BC	Invention of money by Sumerians (Babylonia)	1936	First Butlins holiday camp opened.
5 – 15th cent. AD	Dark era of tourism	1944	Chicago convention and formation of ICAO
1763-1773	Renaissance stage of tourism	1945	IATA was established.
1749	Dr. Thomas Nugent published a guidebook, "The Grand Tour".	1947	International Union of Official Travel Organizations (IUOTO) was formed.
1820	Introduction of regular steamboat services	1949	First package tour was organised by Vladimir Raitz to Corsica with 32 passengers on a DC3 aeroplane.
1822	Robert Smart of Bristol, England announced himself as the first steamship agent, booking passengers for steamers to various Bristol Channel ports and to Dublin, and Ireland.	1950	Vladimir Raitz established mass charter air movement.
1830	First passenger train service begins, between Manchester and Liverpool.	1954	Boeing 707 passenger aircraft introduced and came into commercial transportation in 1959.
1840	The first steamship was built for leisure cruises by Cunard.	1969	Boeing 747 Jumbo Jet introduced; capable of seating 500 passengers.
1841	Thomas Cook organized the first modern tour.	1970	On 27 September, the IUOTO Special General Assembly Meeting in Mexico City adopts the Status of the World Tourism Organization (WTO).
1867	Thomas Cook introduced hotel voucher.	1975	WTO began its legal existence.
1872	Thomas Cook first organized 'around the world tour'.	1978	Deregulation of air transportation began in the US.
1873	'Circular Note' was introduced by Thomas Cook.	1980	From 1980 onwards, September 27 was celebrated as "World Tourism Day".
1988-89	The Savoy, Claridges and Carlton hotels were opened in London.	1991	Gulf War begins
1903	Airplane's first flight at Kitty Hawk, North Carolina by the Wright brothers.	2002	2002 is declared International Year of Ecotourism.
1908	Automobiles entered the travel scene in the US when Henry Ford introduced his famous model.	2003	WTO became a United Nations specialized agency.
1920s	Chartered flight appeared in tourism.	2005	Introduction of the Airbus A380, capable of carrying up to 800 passengers.

The diversity of attractions in India has deservedly won high praises and even extravagant encomiums from travelers, since times immemorial. Though dominated by pilgrimage tourism, travel and tourism has been integral to Indian tradition and culture (Bezbaruah, 1999). *Atithi devo bhava* (guest is god) and *vasudhaiva kutumbakam* (the world is one family) were the essence that enriched the guest-host relationship. There are remarkable examples of travel for fun, recreation, spiritual and learning in Indian history and even in our classics, the *Ramayana* and the *Mahabharata*. Buddhism, one of the greatest religions in the world, born in India, always encouraged travel, mainly for the purpose of learning, teaching and disseminating its principles, values and ethics.

India was attracted by many travellers from across the world. Kashmir was one of the major attractions at that time as many travellers visited Kashmir and praised lavishly about its enchanting natural beauty. For example, Hiuen Tsang, the well known Chinese pilgrim who travelled across India and Central Asia for 16 years in the 7th century AD, was captivated by the valley to spend two years over there. Marco Polo (Yule) and Fahien, two great travellers of medieval history also travelled to India and spent a few years in this country to learn its inherent cultural and natural vibrancy. Ibn-e-Batuta, the famous traveller covered more than 14,000 kilometres in India. Pilgrimage, pleasure and religion were the three major travel motivators of that time. India had travel facilities of high order, as supported by historians. When Alexander the Great reached India, he found well-maintained roads, rest houses, police stations and wells. When Alexander established democratic government in Esphesus, around 0.7 million tourists were sent to visit India, to enjoy acrobats, jugglers and magicians (Akhtar, 1990).

India had every reason to attract a traveller. Max Muller, the world famous Orientalist mentioned

> "If we were to look over the whole world to find out the country most richly endowed with all the wealth, power and beauty that nature can bestow – in some parts, a veritable paradise on earth – I should point to India. If I were asked under what sky the human mind has most fully developed some of its choicest gifts.... I should point to India" (Muller, 1882).

History reveals that since ancient times, rulers of various kingdoms in India in different periods built luxurious palaces, enchanting gardens, marvellous temples, grand forts, tombs and memorials and all of them complemented to the rich cultural heritage of this land. These still remain the backbone of Indian tourism. In addition, this vast land is rich with flora and fauna of varied kinds, and the topography and climate varies from one region to another, altogether adding value to the attractions of this country.

The concept of *domestic tourism* existed right from the Vedic age. India had rigorous tourism activities from early periods. *Tirath yatra*, Kumbha Mela at Prayag, Ujjain, Yatra to Puri, Amarnath, etc., are some of them. During the Medieval and British era, leisure tourism was enjoyed more by the kings and the affluent. This continued in British era as well. Shalimar Garden and Nishat Garden in Srinagar, summer hills like Shimla, Ootacamund, Darjeeling, Mount Abu, etc., are examples of destinations where leisure tourism flourished. These places later became famous tourist destinations.

Even before India gained independence from British rule, authorities took initiatives to develop and promote tourism in the country (IEMR, 1977). *Sargent Committee*, appointed by the Government of India in 1945 to study the tourism development in the country, submitted its report in 1946. This marked an important milestone in the history of Indian tourism and offered a range of means and measures for the development of tourism in the country. It was followed by the appointment of *Traffic Committee* to suggest means for promoting tourist traffic to India. In the light of the recommendations of both the committees, in 1949, a unit called *Tourist Traffic Branch* was created in the Ministry of Transport, along with setting up of two regional tourist offices in New Delhi and Bombay to promote tourist inflow to the country. The main objective of tourism development during this period was to attract foreign tourists. In 1950, a central tourist advisory committee was appointed. Sooner, *American Tourist Promotion Group* was formed to attract tourists from USA and in 1952, the first overseas tourist office was opened in New York.

The expansion of national tourism organization further continued. During 1955-56, the Tourist Traffic branch in the Ministry of Transport was expanded further and renamed as Tourist Division. This was followed by another major milestone in the history of Indian tourism by forming the Tourist Department in 1958. Soon after, working groups such as *Tourist Promotion Committee, Simplification of Frontier Formalities Committee*, and *Hotel Standards and Rate Structure Committee* were set up to suggest methods for promoting inward tourist traffic and removal of bottlenecks in the inflow of tourists to the country. Indeed, the efforts reaped benefits in the post-independent periods as the foreign tourist influx to the country registered a compounded growth rate of 24.5% between 1951 and 1960 (IEMR, 1977). The industry too has grown considerably.

Another important initiative of the Government of India after independence was the formation of an ad-hoc committee on tourism under the chairmanship of L K Jha in 1963, which submitted a 15 point plan for organizational changes and other measures to increase tourist arrivals. In 1965, in the light of Jha Committee's suggestions, a coordination committee was appointed. Later, Ministry of Transport reorganized as Ministry of Transport and Civil Aviation included Department of Tourism as well. Later, Ministry of Tourism and Civil Aviation was formulated, followed by the formation of ITDC in 1966. These initiatives paved the way for tourism development in the country. Tourist arrivals in India registered a compounded growth rate of 8.1% between 1961 and 1970 and 12.2% between 1971 and 1976. During this period, world tourism progressed at an annual growth rate of 6.4%. Majority of the foreign tourists to India were from Western Europe (40%) and North America (14%). Western Europe had been consistently the top most generating region for tourist flow to India.

Ironically, tourism was not given due attention in the 'planning' provisions of the country. Initial planning attempts were marginal and intensively diverted towards the tourists, rather than making a balancing attempt to envisage the volume and nature of benefits derived by various sectors of the national economy from the much publicized tourist flow as well as the benefits derived by the tourist centres or areas visited by the tourists. Tourism planning had a humble beginning in the second Five-Year Plan with a provision of Rs. 3.37 crore (out of Rs. 4800 crore). In the third plan, allocation for tourism was Rs. 5 crore, which was raised to Rs. 8 crore later. Fourth plan also saw a meager allocation of Rs. 36 crore. Though the planning provisions were limited, efforts to improve the infrastructure went on. It was only in the fourth plan, the economic significance of tourism was fully realized. Provision for developing accommodation, transportation and recreational facilities were entertained in it. By 1975, the government set up a number of youth hostels, bringing the total number to 14. During the fifth plan period, five more tourist bungalows were constructed. Fifth plan had given more importance to tourism development. Integrated resort development agenda was initiated at Kovalam, Goa, Gulmarg, Kullu and Manali, along with youth hostels, forest lodges and the like. The focus of sixth plan was to optimize the use of the existing capacity and to increase substantially tourist accommodation in the public well as private sectors. The seventh plan agreed in principle to accord tourism the status of industry. Its main focus was to promote domestic tourism vigorously and to diversify overseas tourism. The first *National Tourism Policy* was announced in 1982, which focused on areas such as promotion of domestic tourism and intra-regional tourism (among South Asian nations); improvement of infrastructure mainly for cultural tourism; travel circuit approach; conservation of natural and cultural heritage; promoting ITDC; HR development by setting up of exclusive training and education institutions (like Institute of Hotel Management and Catering Technology and Indian Institute of Tourism and Travel Management); promotion of island, beach tourism, sports tourism, youth travel; cultural, wildlife, adventure and social tourism, as well as employment generation.

The dearth of adequate and quality accommodation was always an important issue for tourism in India. Way back, the Sargent Committee had raised the issue and urged the need to set up adequate accommodation facilities urgently. Jha Committee also pointed out the increasing need for quality accommodation. Even in 1956, recommendation was there from the authorities to construct 5000 rooms or 8500 beds in the following three years. *Star categorization* was introduced in 1958 by the Hotel Standards and Rate Structure Committee. The hotel Review and Survey Committee set up in 1967 also highlighted the issue and its report estimated that India required an additional 10,433 rooms in one to five star category by 1973 against the available 7013 rooms in 1968. The efforts resulted in hotels and similar accommodation establishments, and also to enhance the quality of accommodation supply. But tourist arrivals continued to grow consistently and hence the gap between demand and supply of accommodation widened. While foreign tourists prefer hotels and resorts, domestic tourists go for variety, including hotels, choultries, friends and relatives' residences, cottages, camping sites, youth hostels and motels. In 1975, there were 201 classified hotels with 13,022 rooms and the figures changed to 427 with 31,402 rooms by 1984. The growth was reportedly attributed to some incentives offered by the government in the form of tax sops and creation of hotel development fund. Other components of tourism industry too had experienced growth during the period. For example, the number of travel agents increased significantly during the period and by 1982, there were around 203 agents, of which 122 were approved by Department of Tourism, Government of India.

Wildlife tourism, a form of tourism gained prominence during 1970's. Realizing the importance of it, an amount Rs. 60.20 lakh was earmarked for wildlife tourism promotion in the fourth plan. This resulted in the arrangement of more amenities for tourism in wildlife destinations. Major Wildlife Sanctuaries and National Parks were created during this period.

The periods of 1980s and 1990s saw rigorous promotion of tourism in India. Different schemes were introduced like Destination India Programme, Destination South India Programme, Gandhi Tours, Buddhist Destination, Beach Resort Complexes, Discover India and Tourist Complexes along with promotional campaigns undertaken through the national carriers such as Air India and Indian Airlines. Subsequently, state governments also came up with different schemes. Kerala is a good example with commendable efforts to promote tourism during the period. In 1986, Kerala gave tourism the status of industry. Consequently, tourist arrivals too have grown significantly across the state, along with substantial infrastructure development.

Following the spur in tourism development in the 1980s, the next decade experienced a vast change in Indian tourism. Before nineties, cultural tourism was the predominant component of inbound tourism. Golden triangle consisting of Delhi, Jaipur and Agra constituted the core of it, along with Bombay and Aurangabad in the west. Authorities focused on developing different products to attract all types of tourists. Beach tourism emerged as a major component. The cultural base became more strengthened by fairs and festivals that were taken as part of tourism. Adventure tourism involving winter sports, trekking, heli skiing, etc., sprang up to the main stage during this period. Many more tourist circuits emerged, e.g., Buddhist Circuit. Air transportation has seen incredible change mainly due to the change in air policy to involve private carriers as well. Department of Tourism came up with the thrust of developing more exotic and exciting destinations. Business and MICE tourism emerged as innovative products. Efforts were taken to provide world class facilities for attracting more international conventions and conferences to India, as part of business tourism promotion. India Convention Promotion Bureau (ICPB) was formed with this objective. The year 1991 was celebrated as *India Tourism Year*, which further stimulated tourism development activities. The National Policy of 1992 marked new directions for tourism development. State governments were encouraged to develop tourism and a few states like Tamil Nadu, Kerala, Karnataka, Andhra Pradesh, Rajasthan and Goa responded suitably. *Incredible India*, an innovative tourism promotion campaign was designed and implemented to market India at the international level by the beginning of this century. The campaign focused on aggressive marketing and promotion of India's tourism products in the popular western tourist markets, along with new markets like Australia, New Zealand and far eastern countries.

The efforts taken by the national and state level authorities resulted in the growth of tourism significantly. By 2006, around 44,47,000 foreign tourists visited India. The number of foreign tourist arrivals in 1951 was just 16,829 and in 1975 only 4,65,275. By 2015, number of foreign tourists visiting India went up to 80.16 lakh. This shows consistent increase in tourist arrivals to the country after independence. Infrastructure too has grown significantly. For instance, the number of rooms in 1975 was 7085 whereas it went to 97,770 in 2004. Along with the phenomenal growth in tourist arrivals and tourism industry, the product range in India also expanded incredibly over the last fifty years. In the fifties, international tourism in India revolved around cultural attractions, but now it has expanded to include a range of innovative products including backwater tourism, medical tourism, rural tourism, ayurveda tourism and business tourism, in addition to other nature based tourism forms. The socioeconomic contribution of tourism development in the country is commendable. It benefits the country by being a fast earner of foreign exchange, generating employment opportunities and contributing significantly in the local economy through expenditure by the tourists.

1.8 REASONS FOR THE GROWTH OF TOURISM

From a humble beginning centuries ago as an activity limited to the 'rich and the aristocratic', tourism has evolved as the most significant economic sector in the world. The rate of growth augmented in the post-world war era. A number of reasons contributed in its phenomenal growth. Of them, consistent enhancement of the economic circumstances of various societies across the world is a major one that resulted in increased discretionary income level. The urbanization, penetration of economic development into many more countries after the end of colonization, and the emergence of new economic giants are other related factors that facilitated the growth of tourism. Another most significant factor was the phenomenal evolution of transport technology and the rising of air transport as the leading transport mode across the world. The contribution of air transport in tourism is remarkable and both share a symbiotic relationship. Since 1960s, more and more countries started developing and promoting tourism, lured by the potential economic gains. This created more destination choices for both *wander lust* and *sun lust* categories. Business tourism had a sudden rise once globalization and liberalization began its march into every nook and corner of the world. Advent and advancements in information technology too influenced tourism greatly to surge ahead. Changes in the socio-demographic factors like increased education level, better health, decreasing household size, increased life expectancy, and rise in the number of women and elderly travellers too have complemented the evolution of tourism substantially. The following constitute some of the major factors of growth of tourism:

- Increased political stability and peace among sovereign nations after the second world war.
- Increased dynamism in attractions and product development.
- Consistent advancement in aviation technology and corresponding increase in comfort, speed, and safety of air transport.
- Changing attitude of local population towards tourism.
- Increase in accessibility, and affordability of transport.
- Increased government involvement for tourism development.
- Changing demographic patterns and early retirement possibilities.
- Better health status of people and increase in life expectancy.
- Spread of economic development to many more countries.
- Rising income opportunities and increase in discretionary income.
- Increasing rate of urbanization.
- Rising social status of tourism.
- Globalization, liberalization and spread of international trade resulted in increased level of business tourism.
- Phenomenal rise of tourism as a leading recreational activity.
- Increasing amount of leisure time.
- Favourable visa and other policies related to international travel.
- Advancements in information and communication technology.
- Escalating lure of tourism and related industries' marketing and promotion.
- Emergence of new economic giants.

1.9 WHY IS TOURISM PROMOTED?

As stated before, tourism has been developed and promoted intensively by the sovereign countries across the world. Certainly, there exists a hyper-competitive environment among those nations. Every nation is trying hard to have increased market share. Undoubtedly, the economic benefits it can bring is the prime cause of tourism development. Tourism contributes nine per cent of World's GDP and is regarded as an engine of 'economic growth'.

International tourism acts as an export, to be precise an 'invisible export' consisting of transaction of intangibles. While tourists from foreign countries visit, they make expenditures on various items and through this process foreign currency enters into the host country's economy. This gives tourism the status of 'fast earner of foreign currency'. This direct contribution has a significant bearing in the 'balance of payments' of a country. In 2015, India received foreign currency equivalent of Rs. 1,26,211 crore by the visit of 80.16 lakh foreign tourists. Usually, countries try to maximize their travel receipts through promotional and marketing strategies. In the case of domestic tourism, tourism expenditure helps in redistribution of income and to a certain extent it is treated as an 'export' between the local regions. Government receives revenue through tourism in various forms, particularly from taxes, VISA fee, entry fee, and surcharges. Taxes are levied directly, e.g., through luxury tax in accommodation units, and indirectly, e.g., through the provision of various imported items.

Tourism is a highly labour-intensive sector. Regions and countries with higher unemployment rates obviously depend on tourism for creating employment and income opportunities. Each and every business sector of the tourism industry amalgam generates

Table 1.5: Reasons of developing tourism in India

India Tourism Policy 2002 states that:

Tourism is seen as a priority sector because it is:

- able to maximize the productivity of India's natural, human, cultural, and technical resources, thus leading to sustainable development;
- labour-intensive and cottage or small industry based, providing employment that is of a high quality thus contributing to higher quality of life;
- capable of being primarily focused on rural areas with appropriate and relatively low cost programmes;
- has extensive forward and backward economic linkages that build overall income, employment (especially for women, youth, and disabled persons bringing greater social equity, and justice), investment, and raises central, state, and local government revenue;
- able to deliver significant levels of hard currency as an export industry; and
- able to promote understanding, peace and contribute to national unity and regional stability.

There is great potential for creating enormous number of new jobs through travel and tourism. The employment potential is the highest in the tourism sector as compared to any other sector and India has the potential to more than three times its travel and tourism jobs. The tourism industry has a very strong linkage to socioeconomic progress of the country. It has a very high revenue capital ratio. It is estimated that an investment of Rs. 1 million creates 47 direct jobs and 11 indirect jobs, which far surpasses the employment potential from agricultural and industrial sectors.

Source: Tourism Policy, 2002, Ministry of Tourism, Government of India.

employment in a significant manner. Income generation and employment generation possibilities are indirectly present, since many other sectors are linked to tourism industry in one way or another. According to a press release dated 28th May, 2015 of World Travel and Tourism Council (WTTC), tourism industry in 2014 supported 277 million jobs (directly and indirectly), which is 9.4% of world employment. As tourism investment increases, dynamism will be visible in investment of other industrial sectors as well. The benefits are deep rooted in the economy and come in direct, indirect and induced manners. The 'multiplier effect' becomes relevant in this context, particularly for income multiplier. Apart from the economic benefits, tourism causes a range of sociocultural benefits as well. Page (2007) has made an attempt to list the reasons why tourism is gaining increased social significance.

- Tourism is a discretionary activity, which denotes that it is not associated with a basic need to survive.
- Tourism is of growing economic significance for countries of all kinds.
- Many governments consider tourism as a sector that can create employment opportunities of various kinds.
- Tourism is increasingly becoming associated with quality lifestyle as it is considered giving rest, relaxation and an opportunity to do something different in a new environment.
- Tourism is now increasingly seen as a basic right in many developed countries, especially in the west.
- In some of the less developed countries, it is promoted as a possible solution to minimize poverty.
- Holidays are a defining feature of non-work for many workers.
- International travel is becoming more accessible in the developed and even some developing countries due to an array of reasons, such as the emergence of low cost carriers.
- Consumers spending on discretionary items such as travel and tourism is increasingly considered a less costly item in household budgets, particularly in developed countries.
- Technological advancements enhanced travel prosperity tremendously; particularly the spread of the Internet made the booking of travel-related products very easy.

All such benefits and contributions are discussed in detail in the following chapters. Hence tourism, as such, is a priority for nations and regions for development.

1.10 CONCLUSION

Currently, tourism is the fastest growing economic sector and one among the top three industries in the world. Conceptually, it is a social process emerged by the movement of people from their usual environment to a different place for specific purposes other than for remunerative activities. This phenomenon has been evolved through many centuries and now it has occupied a prominent position in the social life of people of almost all societies across the world. In fact, all social, cultural, technological and economic developments that occurred after the end of Second World War spurred the growth of tourism to a modern form in which all sections of the societies take part. Of late, countries are engaged in a stiff competition to attract more and more tourists and that creates a hyper competitive business environment. The existing trend points to the fact that tourism is poised for further growth tremendously in the years to come as well.

Key Terms

Domestic tourism
Excursionist
Geographical elements
Grand tour
Inbound tourism
Industrialization
International tourism
Outbound tourism
Push factors
Pull factors
Renaissance
Same-day visitor
Stay
Tourism system
Tourism industry
Tourist generating region
Tourist destination region
Trade
Travel
Tourism
Tourist
Visitor

Review Questions

Short Answer Type Questions

1. Define tourism.
2. Write the parameters to consider the traveller a tourist.
3. "All the travellers are not tourists". Comment on the statement.
4. What are the classified purposes in tourism?
5. What do you mean by multidisciplinarity of tourism?

6. What do you mean by geographical elements of tourism system?
7. Write about different elements in tourism system.
8. Discuss how the elements in tourism system are interrelated.
9. Where can tourism industries be located in various geographical elements as per the Leiper's model of tourism system.
10. Discuss how various factors present in tourism generating and destination region influence people to take part in tourism.
11. Write a brief account on the instances of tourism in the ancient period.
12. What do you mean by Grand Tour?
13. Give a brief account on the evolution of tourism during Roman era.
14. Write how world wars contributed to the growth of tourism.
15. Discuss the tourism development activities after independence in India.
16. Write about infrastructure limitations in tourism in the tourism history in India.
17. Give a brief account on the reasons of growth of tourism, particularly after the Second World War.

Essay Type Questions

1. Elucidate the significance of tourism economically and socially.
2. Explain the concept of tourism. Discuss how to identify tourists from other groups of travellers.
3. Write an essay on the evolution of tourism through centuries. Discuss how various inventions and discoveries influenced its development.
4. Discuss the concept of tourism system using Leiper's model of tourism system. Elucidate the complex interrelationship among various elements of the system.

2 CLASSIFICATION OF TOURISM

Learning Outcomes

After studying this chapter, you will be able to:

- understand how tourism is classified;
- comprehend different types of tourism;
- identify the nature and characteristics of various categories of tourism; and
- understand various tourism terminologies.

2.1 INTRODUCTION

Being the most dynamic economic sector in the world, tourism witnesses the emergence of new forms of tourism every now and then, with the primary objective of remaining competitive in this hyper-competitive tourism environment. Indeed modern tourism is manifested in different phenomena, connections and relationships and all these are the basis for classification. It is not one or two ways in which tourism can be classified; rather the classification can be done in several ways. Moreover, all forms of tourism seen in the international tourism sector can neither be brought under classification nor be discussed in this chapter. Some of them are used just by industry practitioners to ensure differentiation as part of marketing, whereas some others are just as competitive weapons used by destinations. Compared to three decades ago, the current tourism research encompasses a number of newer types of tourism forms, along with the evolution of tourism related research and development of the discipline of tourism. Basis of classification of tourism can be diverse with each group having separate characteristics and purposes. Tourists certainly form a heterogeneous group and tourism in a destination too is heterogeneous. Yet commonalities can also be identified. Some of the most significant classifications are discussed here along with a brief on some of the major tourism types seen in international tourism.

International and domestic tourism constitute the most fundamental classification of tourism based on the origin and destination of the tourists. The following types can be seen in this classification:

Tourism

- International tourism
  - Inbound tourism
  - Outbound tourism
  - Inter-regional tourism
  - Intra-regional tourism
- Domestic tourism
  - National tourism
  - Regional tourism
  - Inter-state tourism
  - Intra-state tourism

2.2 INTERNATIONAL TOURISM

According to the origin and destination, there are two main ways to describe the movement of tourists from one place to another: international and domestic. *International tourism* includes travel from one country to another for the purpose of visiting and spending minimum one night in the destination visited and does not extend more than one year. The destination is a foreign country to the tourist and the travel involves crossing the borders of countries. International tourism differs from domestic tourism as it focuses on those who cross a country's border. Border crossing can be either by land, sea or air. The host countries always prefer to proliferate international tourism as it is considered similar to export trade. This category of tourism is one that has the most economic significance, particularly since it helps in the generation of foreign currency and plays a major role in the balance of payments of the destination country. The expenditure made by an international tourist in any destination generates ripple effect in the economy. Hence, international tourist is a visitor, whose stays in the country he visits exceeds 24 hours, thus spending at least one night in the visiting country. For example, if an Indian travels to visit the places in Singapore for a short term, and comes back to India after the visit, then he/she can be called an *international tourist* and the phenomenon arisen by the process can be called *international tourism*.

2.3 DOMESTIC TOURISM

Domestic tourism is the term used to describe tourism activities that take place within a country by the visit of its citizens. In other words, the country of origin and destination is the same. It does not involve crossing of international borders as part of travel. According to World Tourism Organization, "domestic tourism comprises the activities of a resident visitor within the country of reference (either as part of a domestic tourism trip or part of an outbound tourism trip)" and "a domestic tourist is any person residing in a country who travels to a place within the country, outside his or her usual environment for a period not exceeding 12 months and whose main purpose of visit is other than the exercise of an activity remunerated from within the place visited" (UNWTO, 2012). *Domestic tourists* are those people who travel within their own country for tourism purposes. Historically, domestic tourism is a major activity and it is the earliest form of tourism. Earlier, domestic tourism was a limited category, having fewer motivations, like visiting for pilgrimage and visiting friends and relatives. According to Scheyvens (2007), domestic tourism has evolved on a large scale recently. Increase in disposable income, introduction of labour rights associated with leisure and vacation, governmental policy about the deregulation of air travel, emergence of low-cost carriers, advent and growth of information technology and the like are some of the major reasons that spurred the growth of domestic tourism in the last 50 years or so. Domestic tourist is a visitor who spends at least 24 hours in the destination that he/she visits and the destination is situated in his/her own country. Domestic tourism represents the lifeline of tourism industry and it helps in redistributing domestic currency spatially within the boundaries of a country. For example, an Indian from Tamil Nadu visiting Goa to enjoy a holiday and returns home after the visit.

Domestic tourism has different levels. *National level* domestic tourism, despite the size of the country, is the most significant category as it helps in redistribution of income at the national level, along with the multiplier effect being generated at particular sites which tourists visit. Inside the nations, some regions can be distinguished without actual boundaries. There can be different forms of tourism existing inside these regions as well, and that marks the existence of regional level tourism within a country. For instance, in India itself, tourist movement can be seen within the south Indian region, north Indian region and the like. It can also be considered *inter-state tourism.* State level tourism is growing well in India. A domicile of a state's visiting attractions inside the same state represents *state level tourism*. Similarly, tourist movement from one state to another state is also a major tourism category in India.

2.4 INBOUND AND OUTBOUND TOURISM

Inbound and outbound tourism are two forms of international tourism. *Inbound tourism* generally refers to the incoming of tourists from another country. According to the UNWTO, it "involves non-residents travelling in the given country" (UN & WTO, 1994). Simply, it is the flow of foreign tourists travelling to a destination country (or international arrivals). If a foreigner arrives in India for visiting various places, then he is called an inbound tourist in relation to Indians. Thus, the phenomenon arising out of the visit by a foreigner in one's country can be termed inbound tourism. The foremost choice of travel mode among inbound tourists is by air, closely followed by road, and, then by water and rail. While their primary purposes are leisure, recreation, and holiday; secondary reasons include health, religion, and visiting friends and relatives. Business, conference- and profession-related arrivals account for a further one-eighth of global inbound traffic (UNWTO, 2013). Incoming tourism is another term used in this context. *Incoming tourists* are those who visit a country which is not their country of residence for the purposes of tourism. If a tourist comes from Germany to the UK, then he is an outbound tourist for Germany and inbound tourist for the UK. Simply inbound tourism or incoming tourism involves visits to a country by non-residents. In fact, countries are interested more in inbound tourism particularly due to its ability to bring in foreign currency and the role it can play in the balance of payments of a country, in addition to other economic benefits. Tour operators are still a major determinant in ensuring regular inbound tourism to a country.

2.4.1 Outbound Tourism

Outbound tourism refers to the process just opposite to inbound tourism. According to World Tourism Organization, it involves "residents travelling to another country"(UN & WTO, 1994). The term *outbound tourist* refers to tourists leaving their country of origin for another, i.e., the residents of a country travelling to a foreign country (or international departures). This category does not involve the tourism activities taking place inside a traveller's own country and the goods and services acquired within the generating country, for or after the trip. *Outgoing tourism* is another term used to refer to the tourism in the same context. 'Outgoing tourists' are those who leave their own country to visit another country. Thus, if a tourist from the UK goes on summer holiday to Germany or Spain, he/she is an outgoing tourist. When an Indian is travelling to visit a country, say Singapore, the phenomenon and activities arising out of that are included in outbound tourism. Here, one thing to be noted is that, a tourist is referred to an outbound tourist in relation to the origin country, and the same tourist turns to be an inbound tourist in the destination country. When an Indian travels to Singapore for a visit, he is an outbound tourist to India, and an inbound tourist for Singapore. Outbound tourism was more from European countries and USA for a long time, yet the latest trends show that outbound tourism has strengthened greatly in Asia and Middle East regions as well. China has now surpassed USA as the number one outbound tourist country in the world.

Table 2.1: UNWTO definitions of basic tourism types

Domestic tourism comprises the activities of a resident visitor within the country of reference either as part of a domestic tourism trip or part of an outbound tourism trip.
Inbound tourism comprises the activities of a non-resident visitor within the country of reference on an inbound tourism trip.
Outbound tourism comprises the activities of a resident visitor outside the country of reference, either as part of an outbound tourism trip or as part of a domestic tourism trip.
Internal tourism comprises domestic tourism and inbound tourism, that is, the activities of resident and non-resident visitors within the country of reference as part of domestic or international tourism trips.
National tourism comprises domestic tourism and outbound tourism, that is, the activities of resident visitors within and outside the country of reference, either as part of domestic or outbound tourism trips.
International tourism comprises inbound tourism and outbound tourism, that is, the activities of resident visitors outside the country of reference, either as part of domestic or outbound tourism trips and the activities of non-resident visitors within the country of reference on inbound tourism trips.

Source: UN and UNWTO, 2008.

2.5 INTRAREGIONAL AND INTERREGIONAL TOURISM

Defining a region is difficult as the concept of a region is inherently volatile. Demarcating a region depends on the reference of a particular geographical area in a specific context. It means that the term region is used to refer to a particular area as per the context of the usage. The term *region* may refer either to an area within a country or to a group of countries. According to UNWTO, countries, states, provinces, and other administrative regions or political groupings of nations can be regarded as regions (WTO & UN, 1994). For example, Gulf Cooperation Council (GCC) is a region based on a socio-political background. Region can be a continent or be used to refer to a vast area extending beyond a continent. Inside a country, there can be different regions based on cultural reasons, geographical reasons and the like. Similar parameters can be used in international tourism as well. In international tourist statistics, *regional tourism* is usually referred to show the movement of tourists inside a region and between regions. When UNWTO publishes its annual statistics, the Asia-Pacific region is shown as a single region. This region extends beyond the continent demarcation as it encompasses all countries in the Asian continent except west Asian countries along with countries belonging to other continents, like Australia and New Zealand. The same is the case with the Middle East. It is a transcontinental region with a sociocultural demarcation. Tourism is often cited according to these regional considerations. Interregional and intraregional tourism are more often used in the context of international tourism, particularly in the context of measurement of global tourism, based on the parameters associated with economic, social, cultural and tourist movement patterns. *Interregional tourism* can be referred to as the tourism that takes place between two regions whereas *intraregional* is all about tourism taking place within a region. For instance, tourism among countries situated within Europe is intraregional tourism and movement of tourists between countries belonging to Europe and America is interregional tourism. While tourism inside the Middle East is intraregional, tourism between the Middle East and Asia is interregional. Within a country also interregional tourism can be specified, like between northeast India and south India and so on. Countries also have joined together to promote intraregional tourism, like ASEAN tourism.

2.6 LEISURE AND BUSINESS TOURISM

These are the two predominant categories of tourism, i.e., leisure tourism and business tourism. Both are growing at a tremendous pace, yet the latter gathered momentum in the recent years as a result of vibrancy emanated in the international business environment.

Leisure tourism refers to tourism that takes place due to movement of people for the purpose of pleasure, in one way or the other, and to spend their free time. 'Leisure tourists' travel for the purpose of leisure, so they are likely to be on holiday or taking a short break. The reasons for engaging in leisure tourism are so diverse. Leisure is a common term used to signify the free time when people are not otherwise engaged like working, sleeping, and other similar activities of routine nature. During leisure time, they are relatively free to make a choice, in terms of space or time. Leisure and recreation are connected to each other. *Recreation* is all about the activities people engage in leisure and both the terms are often used interchangeably. During leisure time, people may try to have experience and undertake activities they like. Those who engage in recreation feel refreshed. The modern era is featured with increased leisure time and greater access to facilities, and that results in increased indulgence in recreational activities by more and more people. Furthermore, amount of leisure time of employees has significantly improved, especially in the post-war era, as industrialists and entrepreneurs started considering it essential for enhancing productivity of employees. Of late, tourism has turned to be one of the most prominent recreational activities.

In fact, increase in leisure time itself is a major reason in the growth of tourism worldwide. Engaging in leisure tourism may involve reasons such as wish to indulge in recreational activities, entertainment, relaxation, health purposes, social reasons, and the like. Leisure tourism has prevailed since the ancient times and has gained much significance since the end of Second World War, mainly due to the changes in the socio-economic circumstances. Leisure tourism industry aims to provide enjoyable and memorable touristic experience and operates in an increasingly competitive and dynamic business environment. The leisure industry contains a wide range of organisations and facilities that can provide recreational and enjoyable tourist experiences. This sector may include sports and physical recreation facilities, arts and entertainment, countryside recreation, varying attractions including natural and manmade. The market segments also consist of varied categories like independent travellers, families, retired people, couples, groups, school groups, special interest groups, and visit friends and Relatives (VFR).

On the other hand, business tourism is all about travel with a business or a profession related purpose or reasons that do not directly result in earning money. Though the main purpose is business related, the leisure aspect also forms an inevitable part of it with a varying degree. In this, travel has to be away from the usual environment to a distant place with the primary purpose of work or business interest. People travelling to a place to attend a meeting, conference or an event associated with their business is the core of business tourism.

In a broader spectrum business tourism covers off-site face-to-face meetings with business partners, incentive trips as part of rewarding and motivating employees or as part of sales promotion, and the travel for participating in large-scale conferences, conventions, exhibitions, and trade shows (UNWTO, 2013). The leisure element, usually, gets involved automatically in the travel when the traveller travels, stays, purchases various tourism related products and services and also involves in some sort of recreational activities in free time away from the work. This aspect was pointed out by Rob Davidson (1996) that business tourism, can involve a substantial leisure element. For instance, even the conference delegates, visitors to trade fairs and individual business travellers may participate in trips to local attractions and/or places of entertainment, and experience local cuisine as a way of relaxing at the end of day after the busy hours. In many a cases, business tourists may bring their families along for vacation. In such cases, the stay in the destination may extend for some more days after the business part of the trip is over. The industrial elements that cater to the needs of the business travellers are also the same as those of leisure tourism. They also need accommodation services, transport system, entertainment options, and the like.

MICE (meetings, incentives, conventions and exhibitions) tourism is the core of business tourism. In tourism literature it is also expanded as meetings, incentives, conferences and events. At times, both the terms are used interchangeably. People travelling for the purpose of attending various business related meetings, conferences, conventions, exhibitions, and trade fairs along with the incentive travel constitute MICE tourism. This broad term is used to embrace MICE markets, as well as sports, concerts, festivals, among others (Getz, 2008). Event is often linked with MICE tourism. Essentially, event tourism focuses more onto visiting, attending or participating in events of various kinds than the other categories like incentives. But in event tourism non-business, non-professional categories like sports and festivals too have a considerable share. MICE tourism in the world, particularly in Asia has been growing more rapidly than in other parts of the world (UFI, 2007). A number of MICE related associations are also there, like Convention Industry Council, Destination Marketing Association International, International Association of Exhibitions and Events, International Congress and Convention Association, Meeting Professionals International, and Professional Convention Management Association. In India, India Convention Promotion Bureau (ICPB) is there to promote MICE tourism. Business tourism and leisure tourism have been explained further through their comparison in Table 2.2.

Table 2.2: Comparison between business tourism and leisure tourism

Business tourism	Leisure tourism
Choice of the destination is not in the hands of the traveller; it depends on the venue of the event.	Though it can be influenced, the ultimate choice regarding the destination is made by the traveller.
Primary purpose of travel is business, professional or related activities.	Primary purpose is to participate in leisure activities.
Higher level of spending power as the trip may be sponsored, and it is less price sensitive.	Spending capacity depends on travellers, discretionary income, and is more price sensitive.
The travel decision is usually taken by others.	Decision to travel is personal, with or without the influence of family/peer groups.
Traveller is the ultimate consumer, need not be the customer always.	Leisure traveller is usually the customer as well as the consumer.
Decision making may take less time.	Decision making time varies from medium to long duration.
Customer satisfaction primarily depends on the accomplishment of the intended business related purposes.	Satisfaction is more of a degree of the accomplishments of anticipated leisure reasons.
Accommodation preferences are different, in a way that helps the traveller to carry out his task, e.g., business tourist may prefer a hotel location with transport connectivity inside the city.	Leisure tourists, accommodation preferences are varied which enhances tourist experience.
Travel may take place more on working days.	Travel may take place more on holidays.
Business travellers do not depend on tour operators, and travel arrangements are done differently.	Substantial amount of leisure tourists still depend on intermediaries though the share of online based arrangement is increasing.
Usually, frequent and more experienced travellers.	Frequency and experience of leisure tourists are widely varied.
Duration of total journey depends on completion of business-related task.	Journey duration varies from short breaks of two or three days to a few weeks.
Less seasonal.	Seasonal fluctuation in demand is high.
Destinations are usually urban centres.	Along with urban centres, non-urban centers/rural regions too have substantial share.

2.7 MASS TOURISM AND 'NICHE' TOURISM

Number of tourists visiting a place has much significance. On the positive side, it increases economic benefits of the destination; whereas on the other side, it is a determinant of the impact created by tourism over there. Mass tourism is the most used term in this context. Other forms of tourism with a specification about the maximum number of tourists include a range of tourism types like, *ecotourism, niche tourism, sustainable tourism,* etc. Some of them are usually referred to as Special Interest Tourism (SIT).

2.7.1 Mass Tourism

Mass tourism refers to the movement of a large number of organized tourists to popular holiday destinations for recreational purposes. Usually, it involves travelling of large number of people, predominantly during the seasons. Simply, it is all about the movement of large number of visitors to one place and most of them use standardized package products which causes mass consumption. This type of tourism depends heavily on industry through intermediaries such as tour operators, travel agents, and it is relatively cheaper through package deals. Poon (1993) defines 'mass tourism' as a large-scale phenomenon, packaging and selling standardized leisure services at fixed prices to a mass clientele. According to Kelly and Nankervis (2001), it is "sometimes referred to as *mainstream* tourism, that is, large-scale movement of people to and from leisure travel destinations, often making use of tour packages incorporating travel, accommodation and sightseeing". Many of the destinations, particularly the new and emerging destinations depend on mass tourism operators greatly in order to get established in the international market. Some destinations are also called *mass tourism destinations* as they are visited regularly by large number of tourists with massive tourism infrastructure and facilities. The term is also used to refer to large-scale tourism commonly, without a specification about the necessity of involvement of intermediaries. The popular forms of leisure tourism pioneered in successful international destinations are also called *mass tourism*. Due to the mass consumption of resources and usage of attractions and facilities, mass tourism is notorious for negative impacts on environment, society and culture, particularly.

2.7.2 'Niche' and Special Interest Tourism (SIT)

Tourism being a consumer activity is constantly being developed by the tourism industry and the associated businesses, as marketing is used to develop new innovative ideas, products and services as well as destinations. This has led to the development of 'niche tourism' and products focusing on specific interests and activities. Both the terms are used interchangeably. 'Niche' in the parlance of marketing represents relatively a small group or specific segment of the market defined by the special needs or interests. 'Niche' market need not be a small group always as some of such products can attract large number of people. Marketers may go for special products as part of niche marketing, provided the economic viability of the product is ensured. Individual consumers in the 'Niche market' are usually identifiable by the same specialized needs or interests, with a strong desire for consuming the products being offered. Niche tourism is also defined from this perspective, with a specific market segment. It offers a well-defined product matching the exclusive needs and interests of that specific market segment. Niche tourism is often associated with diversity and innovation while offering tourism products and is considered to be more sustainable due to the nature of visitors as they are deeply interested in experiencing the tourism with necessary concern towards environment. Tourists, unlike in the case of mass tourism, on the other hand should be able to have meaningful and authentic experience through this type of tourism.

Special Interest Tourism (SIT) is also presented in the same way as niche tourism. In this category, the activity of interest dominates the destination choice of the tourist, i.e., holiday choice is inspired by specific motivations, and correspondingly the major determinant in tourist satisfaction is the level of experience the tourist can have from the place visited based on the specific need or interest he/she had prior to the visit. Brotherton and Himmetoglu (1997) distinguish special interest tourists (activity focused) from general (destination focused) and mixed interest tourists. It clarifies that the common definitional element of special interest tourism is the specific interest-based motivation (history, wildlife, rock climbing, ethnic tourism, art, and heritage). Experiencing or enjoying a special interest related to unusual hobbies, activities, themes or destinations is the prime motive. SIT involves a wide range of tourism types: culinary/cuisine tourism, wine tourism, sports tourism, art tourism, photography tourism, film tourism, and adventure tourism.

Some examples of SIT are discussed in detail below.

- **Bird watching tourism:** Seeing birds in their natural habitats is a passion for many. That too, when it is for seeing rare species in remote locations, the experience turns euphoric and memorable. Some are more interested in this activity and this leads to the emergence of bird watching tourism. Simply, viewing birds in their natural habitats is known as bird-watching or *avitourism* (Moss, 2004). Here the purpose of travel is observing birds. Participated mainly by people with keen interest and knowledge about birds, the tourists need to have good fitness levels. Age group of customers vary, from youngsters to senior citizens. Many countries have thriving bird watching societies, which promote and sponsor trips to destinations where there is an abundance of bird life.
- **Bicycle or cycle tourism:** Experiencing a physical activity as part of holidays, than just visiting places and staying in posh accommodation, is on the rise. Bicycle tourism, also called *cycle tourism* is one such type of tourism in trend, in which

cycling plays a significant part of the holiday experience. It includes activities undertaken by those "on vacation for more than 24 hours or one night, and for whom the bicycle is an integral part of this trip" (Ritchie, 2010). Such tourists usually prefer to have long rides to countrysides and remote locations with limited tourism infrastructure. Usually, they travel in rather small groups and have a *backpacker* kind of attitude towards tourism and its services. The trip is all about leisure combined with adventure and/or physical experience. Moreover, the duration of the trip varies from a few days to many months at a stretch.

- **Golf tourism:** Golf tourism is more of a type of sports tourism, but varies due to its inherent characteristics combined with the leisure element and size of the segment that makes it a 'niche'/special interest tourism. Availability of golf courses of international standards becomes a prerequisite for developing golf tourism. Playing golf is the prime motive, yet having it in a different location clubbed with exquisite leisure enabled this tourism segment to grow very fast. US is one of the leading locations of golf tourism, along with countries like Portugal, the UAE, Scotland, Spain, France, South Africa, Scotland, Britain, Morocco, and Ireland that are in the forefront of golf tourism. The market for this includes mainly the healthy and high spending traveller in the age group above forty.
- **Skiing tourism:** Skiing tourism is a form of winter tourism as well as sports tourism. It is defined as travelling to participate in the activity or sport of gliding or moving over snow on wood, plastic, or metal curved upward in the front, attached to shoes or boots (Saur, 1999). World over, there are plenty of ski resorts with downhill, heli-skiing as well as with cross-country ski trails. Usually, there are exclusive ski areas that offer facilities and services for skiing, snowboarding, ski running and other possible winter sports. Keen interest in skiing is the prime motivation of such tourists. Climate is the ultimate requirement for providing skiing tourism options.
- **Adventure tourism:** Adventure tourism can be a 'niche' tourism category when it is offered exclusively for those keenly interested people with necessary skills and knowledge. On the other hand, commercial adventure tourism operations and tours have evolved typically following the discovery and promotion of suitable locations by intrepid individuals or specialized activity groups (Buckley, 2006). Adventure tourists are those who participate in sports or adventurous activities whilst on holiday. In the parlance of real adventure tourism, the activities included are adrenalin pumping, taking place in outdoor real environments. The environments can be unusual, exotic, remote or in a wilderness setting. There are a large number of adventure tourism activities and the participants, whether novice or experienced, may require sufficient personal fitness to engage in both real and perceived risks, including injury during adventures.

According to Teagasc Fact Sheets (2006), the adventure tourism types/activities can be classified under three headings such as getting wet, getting high, and getting faster. They are listed below. The nature of level of required physical activity associated with adventure can vary from low to high level with varying risk factors. But the term is used loosely to attract certain types of customers by tour operators and some other industry elements.

Table 2.3

Getting wet	Getting high	Getting faster
• Surfing	• Flying	• Archery
• Canoeing, touring, rental and expedition services	• Gliding	• Karting
• Kite surfing	• Paragliding	• Mountain biking and expeditions
• Wakeboarding	• Ballooning	• Paintballing
• Skateboarding	• Rock climbing	• Land boarding
• White-water rafting	• High rope	• Rallying
• Water-skiing	• Microlighting	
• Diving	• Zorbing	
• Windsurfing		
• Kayaking		

Source: Teagasc Fact Sheets/ Maria Heneghan, 2006

2.8 CULTURE RELATED TOURISM TYPES

Culture and its intrinsic elements have been the major attraction types since times immemorial and they constitute one of the foremost categories of travel motivations. A wide variety of tourism types are included in this category. The major ones are discussed here.

2.9 CULTURAL TOURISM

The quest for seeking something different, particularly to understand, experience and appreciate features of other cultures has been a major reason behind travel and that forms the base for cultural tourism. It is one of the oldest forms of tourism. The tourism existed during Roman era, and the phenomenal leisure tourism that occurred in Egypt millennia ago had ample cultural elements. Even the 'Grand Tour' had its foundation on cultural tourism. Tourism and culture have always been closely linked in almost all successful tourist destinations in the world. For instance, Europe has always been an important destination for those attracted by its rich cultural and historic legacy. Cultural tourism is defined as "the movement of persons to cultural attractions away from their normal place of residence, with the intention to gather new information and experience to satisfy their cultural needs" (Richards, 1996). A wide range of attractions are involved in this category and that includes any element of culture, with both tangible and intangible dimensions. For such reasons, *cultural tourism* can be considered a broad category involving a number of other tourism types. Craik (1997) also opines the same that cultural tourism "has become an umbrella term both to identify specially organized culture based tourism experience and to provide unity and add depth to a diverse range of culture-related aspects of tourism more generally".

The attractions that form the backbone of cultural tourism include the remains of the historical past, the features of heritage, museums, art and art forms, architecture, visual arts, concerts and performances, cuisines, etc. As stated above separate tourism types like heritage tourism, history tourism, ethnic tourism and the like can be seen. Cultural elements are being used to attract tourists since ancient times and still used to promote destinations to enhance their competitiveness and attractiveness. Many of the destinations use cultural elements as a means of developing comparative advantages in an increasingly competitive tourism marketplace, and to create local distinctiveness against the unification of culture in this globalised era. While an array of negative impacts of tourism on culture is identified, cultural tourism can have positive aspects and it can preserve dwindling remains of history and heritage. Many dying art forms and features are now getting revived through tourism.

2.10 HISTORICAL TOURISM

History is something that fascinates people. It has always been a matter of attraction for tourists and the post-world war era gave much scope for it when the social, economic and political changes were phenomenal world over. Historical tourism has grown and now, even the places where wars took place form an attraction. Historical tourism is often denoted as a form that is centered on the narratives of a particular site, place, or a region (Grozeva, 2009). According to Weston (2011), historical tourism "ultimately reminds us both of the powerful ideality of history and the fundamental material reality of the past and our kinship with all those separated from us by time, place and culture, or by the rudimentary fact of their not being us". For a country and its people, the remains of history form a matter of pride and people would love to show these to the visitors. For a visitor historical remains give ample scope for satisfying the need for learning something about the past, understanding the evolution of people and civilizations and the like. Destinations are now in a process to identify the historical tourism attractions and to develop and promote them as part of the product diversification agenda to enhance the attractiveness and competitiveness of the destination.

2.11 INDIGENOUS TOURISM

Indigenous tourism is often promoted by destinations with the intention to promote authentic experience as part of tourism. When the authenticity of tourism is not preserved and the indigenousness is exposed as just a product to attract people, the very essence of the purpose of indigenous tourism is lost. *Indigenous tourism* is defined as "tourism activities in which indigenous people are directly involved either through control and/or by having their culture serve as the essence of the attraction" (Butler and Hinch, 1996). Tribal tourism is part of it and is promoted as a form of tourism to have authentic experience with culture of tribal societies and its features along with an intimate and positive interaction with the culture. This kind of tourism should not lead to any impact, yet the same should be able to contribute towards the preservation of the cultural values while generating economic benefits. Many tribal areas have succeeded in adding tourism to their economic development in a way that affirms the tribal community and improves quality of life. Australia develops and promotes **aboriginal tourism** as well as **tribal tourism** with the distinction of having authentic experience. Australian Tourism Commission (ATC) argues that "aboriginal tourism experiences are varied, but a common thread is the inclusion of insights about the cultural knowledge, lifestyle, and beliefs of Australia's indigenous people". It categorizes the essential aspects of aboriginal tourism into four: it is "concerned with culture and biodiversity, asserts prior informed participation of all stakeholders, and active decision making processes accorded to indigenous and local communities, recognizes indigenous person's special connection to land and waters, and recognizes customary proprietary knowledge held on a community and individual basis". (ATC/Breeze Robertson, 2011). A tourist visiting an aboriginal tourism site can have a variety of indigenous experiences and activities. These have to be owned and operated by the local people in order to ensure maximum economic benefits to them.

2.12 FILM-INDUCED TOURISM

Movies, TV programmes and popular artists too have the ability to drag tourists to visit places, architecture and events associated with them. This resulted in a kind of tourism movement called *film-induced tourism*. It is viewed as a form of cultural tourism and represents the growing demand for locations which are popular due to their presence in films and TV programmes. In general, films can influence in creating or enhancing the image of a destination that can eventually result in visitation (Butler, 1999). Iconic films can induce travellers to visit the physical properties like scenery and landscape, and their associated themes, storylines, events and actors, shaping the audiences' feelings, emotions and attitudes towards places; and such visit experiences are enhanced in memories by associating them with actors, events and settings (Iwashita, 2006). Various types of film induced tourism are given in Table 2.4

Table 2.4: Film-induced tourism types

On location

- Film tourism as primary travel motivator: The film site is an attraction in its own right, strong enough to motivate visitation.
- Film tourism as part of a holiday: Visiting film locations (or studios) as an activity within a larger holiday.
- Film tourism pilgrimage: Visiting sites of films in order to 'pay homage' to the film; possible re-enactments.
- Celebrity film tourism: Homes of celebrities; film locations that have taken on celebrity status.
- Nostalgic film tourism: Visiting film locations that represent another era.

Commercial

- Constructed film tourism attraction: An attraction constructed after the filming purely to attract/ serve tourists.
- Film/movie tours: Tours developed to various film locations, *on location tours.*
- Guided tours at specific on-location set: Tours to specific sites, often on private land.

Mistaken identities

- Film tourism to places where the filming is only believed to have taken place: Movies and TV series that are filmed in one place that is created to look like another; often in other countries for financial reasons; known as *runaway productions.*
- Film tourism to places where the film is set, but not filmed: The films have raised interest in a particular country, region or place, where the story is based, not where it was actually filmed.

Off-location

- Film studio tours: Industrial tours of working film studios, where the actual filming process can be viewed, e.g., Paramount Studios.
- Film studio theme park: Usually adjacent to a studio, specifically built for tourism with no actual filming or production taking place.

One-off events

- Movie premieres: Particularly those outside traditional sites.
- Film festivals: Many cities hold film festivals that attract film buffs and fans for the event.

Armchair travels

- TV travel programmes: The successor to travel guidebooks and written travelogues.
- Gastronomy programmes: Many cooking shows take the viewer to various places around.

Source: Adapted from Beeton, 2005

2.13 LITERARY TOURISM

This is an innovative category of cultural tourism, with special focus on the production and consumption of places, landscapes, museums, historical buildings, and graves associated with published creative writings and/or their authors. Travellers belonging to this category visit places associated with literary works or figures; these vary from self-identified, dedicated, and knowledgeable "pilgrims" as fans of an author or novel, to those who have more moderate passing interests (Robinson & Andersen, 2003). Visiting book festivals is also an element of this. Author and fiction-related literary tourism opportunities exist along with opportunities arising from literary festivals and book shops. This could include following the route taken by a fictional character, visiting particular places associated with a novel or a novelist, places and events from fictional texts as well as the lives of their authors such as their home or visiting a poet's grave. Some scholars regard *literary tourism* as a contemporary type of secular pilgrimage. At times, imaginative geographies are created, such as "Shakespeare's England" or "Wordsworth's Lake District." The extent of literary tourism links with the popularity of the writings of the author. There are also long-distance walking routes associated with writers, such as the 'Thomas Hardy Way'.

2.14 MUSIC TOURISM

Music is a passion for many and the quest for travelling to see music concerts, festivals, places where musicians lived, sites of music history or for pure aural pleasure is on the increase. Music and tourism are variously related and sites related to music events too are turning out to be domestic as well as international tourist attractions. In the case of music tourism, the prime motivation is the affection towards music. Western countries are promoting music tourism aggressively. For instance, UK takes vigorous steps in this direction. A promotional document of the UK says that "Music tourists already spend over £1bn and an increase in this sector could again help achieve the target set. Overseas tourists are gold dust. They comprised just 6% of the total population of music tourists in 2012, but accounted for 20% of music tourist expenditure. Support comes from across the political spectrum for the music industry to push strategies to help grow music tourism. Music tourism is already successful at drawing tourists into every corner of the UK". It also includes that total direct and indirect expenses generated by music tourism in 2012 was £2.2 billion, and the amount spent directly by 6.5 million music tourists was £1.3 billion (UK Musica & Visiti Britain, 2012).

2.15 ETHNIC TOURISM

Ethnic tourism means experiencing first-hand the authentic practices in other cultures, particularly that of the indigenous communities. It means that the visit is driven with a serious quest for experiencing the difference authentically. While Smith (1977) defines it as tourism "marketed to the public in terms of the 'quaint' customs of indigenous and often exotic people", Van den Berghe (1992) opines it as the search for authentic encounters with other ethnicities, involving complex relations and a division of labour among three groups: tourists, tourees (natives who modify their behaviour to meet tourism demands), and middlemen (brokers who mediate tourist-touree encounters). Anything related to such culture can become part of ethnic tourism like involvement in ethnic events and festivals, watching traditional dances and ceremonies, shopping for handicrafts and other souvenirs, interacting with them to learn about the culture, living with ethnic communities in their habitats, engaging with them in their traditional jobs, participating in their cultural performances, visiting ethnic villages and the similar. Examples of communities where ethnic tourism can take place include *Amish* communities of the United States, the *Maori* of New Zealand, Australia's *Aboriginal* communities, and the tribal communities in different regions in India, like, in Assam, Meghalaya, and Andaman and Nicobar Islands. *Souvenir* is a major item to be marketed through this kind of tourism. Care has to be taken in minimizing the commercialization, acculturation, and the tendency of staged authenticity, along with other impacts.

2.16 PILGRIMAGE TOURISM

Pilgrimage is one of the earliest reasons of travel and has continued to be a major one even in the modern world. Traditionally, it applies to journeys with a religious purpose, but it can also refer to *secular travel* with particular importance for the pilgrim (Morinis, 1992). Pilgrimage tourism involves travelling to sacred places, indulging in spiritual tours, serious and meaningful journeys to places with some importance for the pilgrim. In fact, pilgrim tourism in a particular place can be something that has been developed over a period of time, not something that has been developed one fine morning. India is famous for pilgrimage tourism as India is the birthplace of a number of religions. Buddhist pilgrimage tourism is one that attracts many tourists from far and wide. Government of India recently has started PRASAD (Pilgrimage Rejuvenations and Spiritual Augmentation Drive) with the aim to promote sustainable pilgrimage tourism in the country, to strengthen measures for safety, security and proving quality tourism services in pilgrim cities, to bridge infrastructure gaps in pilgrimage destinations. This involves integrated development of pilgrimage destinations to provide complete religious and spiritual tourism experience. In its initial phase, 12 cities were identified for implementation which include Varanasi, Amritsar, Ajmer, Mathura, Gaya, Kanchipuram, Velankanni, Dwarka, Puri, Amravati, Kedarnath and Kamakhya.

2.17 RED TOURISM

The remains of a blood-spattered revolution are also something of attraction for the new generation. Red tourism is based on the same. Red tourism is a form of Communist heritage tourism, which involves authorized tours to revolutionary sites, such as memorial museums, halls, and/or monuments (Li et al., 2010). It is all about visiting sites of historical significance to the revolutionary activities of the Communist movements in various countries. The revolutionary transformation of the world through Communist movements of twentieth century was a remarkable social phenomenon and that left numerous sites and monuments, which now attract millions. China is in the forefront of red tourism tapping millions of visitors every year. Russia too has entered into the scene and now there is a tie-up between both Russia and China to have a symbiotic relationship on red tourism.

2.18 YOGA TOURISM

Yoga, the holistic health care system, evolved in India since the ancient times. It has now turned to be one of the USPs of Indian tourism as well. Yoga is part of the grand heritage of India. *Yoga* means union, yoke, or to connect. A yoga practitioner seeks to connect with self, others, and surroundings. According to Kelly and Smith (2009), Yoga tourism is a journey of self with transformative capacities on physical, psychological, spiritual, and social awareness. Yoga is getting deep rooted in other societies as well particularly due to its magnanimous capacity to pursue a healthy lifestyle for people. Yoga tourists may visit places where real yoga is practised, along with places where indigenous wellness systems are in place.

2.19 INDUSTRIAL TOURISM

Industries too have the ability to attract tourists and that created a novel kind of tourism called *industrial tourism*. Simply, it can be defined as the tourism that involves movement of people with the purpose of visiting operational industrial sites. These industrial sites are not aimed at any sort of tourism activities which denotes that the core activity at the site has to be non-tourism. The sites can include production sites that make unique indigenous products, branded and exclusive products, technological products, beverages and food varieties, unique souvenirs and the like. This is also considered a form of *cultural tourism*. There are two forms in this:

- Visits to industries where productive activity is actually happening, to watch and/or learn processes that are actually alive, in motion, and in real time.

  Examples:

  - BMW plant in Munich offers an incredible industrial visit experience.
  - The Chantiers de l'Atlantique shipyard in Saint-Nazaire, France, has been built around 600 vessels and more than 110 cruise ships and ocean liners (including the RMS Queen Mary 2) since it opened in 1861.

- Visit to industrial heritage centres or industrial archaeology/architecture, which is founded on a long dead and later recreated heritage.

  Examples:
  - New York's Brooklyn Navy Yard opened in 1801 and was used to build warships.
  - Manchester with Ancoats, (once known as the *workshop of the world*, includes impressive mills and complexes), Castlefield (includes the site of the 79AD Roman fort of Mamucium; the 1761 Bridgewater Canal – the world's first true canal system; and world's first passenger railway location); and Bolton Museum, Aquarium and Archive.

2.20 ALTERNATIVE TOURISM

It is natural to look for alternatives when the existing ones turn to be perturbing due to the consequences. The ill-effects of haphazard tourism development imposed the need for creating alternative forms and a number of alternative tourism types emerged with the intention to minimize the negative impacts of tourism. Certainly, alternative tourism emerged as a rejection of mass tourism as this causes impacts of varied nature. It involves tourism that respects the values of local people and nature, favouring encounters and exchanges and building experience (Smith & Eadington, 1994). The definition of alternative tourism is rather vague, yet the concept relies more on minimization of impacts and ensuring equitable development of tourism.

Table 2.5: Alternative tourism characteristics

- The attempted preservation, protection and enhancement of the quality of the resource base which is fundamental to tourism.
- The fostering and active promotion of development, in relation to additional visitor attractions and infrastructure, with roots in the specific locale and developed in ways that complement the local attributes.
- The endorsement of infrastructure, hence economic growth, when and where it improves local conditions and not where it is destructive or exceeds the carrying capacity of the natural environment or the limits of the social environment whereby the quality of community life is adversely affected.
- Tourism which attempts to minimize its impact on the environment, is ecologically sound, and avoids the negative impacts of many large-scale tourism developments undertaken in areas that have not previously been explored.
- An emphasis on not only ecological sustainability, but also cultural sustainability, that is, tourism which does not damage the culture of the host community, encouraging a respect for the cultural realities experienced by the tourists through education and organized 'encounters'.

Source: Wearning and Neil, 1999.

Alternative tourism, of late, is used to refer to any type of tourism with similar principles and characteristics. Some of the alternative types of tourism are discussed below.

2.20.1 Geotourism

This is another 'niche tourism' category with a focus on geological features. National Geographic has been promoting this type of tourism internationally. According to National Geographic, Geotourism is the "tourism that sustains or enhances the distinctive geographical character of a place: its environment, heritage, aesthetics, culture, and the well-being of its residents. It is *environmentally responsible* committed to conserving resources and maintaining biodiversity; *culturally responsible* committed to respecting local sensibilities and building on local heritage; and *synergistic* bringing together all elements of geographical character to create a travel experience that is richer than the sum of its parts and appealing to visitors with diverse interests". According to another definition, "Geotourism is knowledge-based tourism, an interdisciplinary integration of the tourism industry with conservation and interpretation of abiotic nature attributes, besides considering related cultural issues, within the geosites for the general public"(Sadry, 2009). This, in addition to the tourism perspective, acts as a vehicle to foster geo-conservation and an understanding of geological heritage.

2.20.2 Green Tourism

The concept of Green Tourism had come into prominence even before the sustainable tourism concept gained significance. In general, greening of tourism is in trend and it involves enhancement of efficiency in energy, water, and waste management systems while improving the employment potential and ensuring social, cultural and environmental sustainabilities. According to the World Tourism Organization, *green tourism* consists of "tourism activities that can be maintained, or sustained, indefinitely in their social, economic, cultural and environmental contexts" (UNWTO, 2012). According to Dodds and Joppe (2001):

- the green tourism concept involves environmental responsibility (protecting, conserving, and enhancing nature and the physical environment to ensure long-term health of the life-sustaining ecosystem);
- local economic vitality (supporting local economies, businesses and communities to ensure economic vitality and sustainability); cultural diversity (respecting and appreciating cultures and cultural diversity so as to ensure the continued well-being of local or host cultures);
- and experiential richness (providing enriching and satisfying experiences through active, personal and meaningful participation in, and involvement with, nature, people, places and cultures).

Currently, this term is less used comparatively, though the concept sustains through some other forms of tourism.

2.20.3 Responsible Tourism

Responsible tourism is a 'buzzword' in tourism, with almost same principles as sustainable tourism, yet with increased focus on equitable distribution of economic contributions especially among the local community. According to the Cape Town Declaration (Conference on Responsible Tourism in Destinations held in 2002), the characteristics of responsible tourism include:

- minimize negative economic, environmental, and social impacts;
- generate greater economic benefits for local people and enhance the well-being of host communities, improving working conditions and access to the industry;
- involve local people in decisions that affect their lives and life chances;
- make positive contributions to the conservation of natural and cultural heritage, to the maintenance of the world's diversity;
- provide more enjoyable experiences for tourists through more meaningful connections with local people, and a greater understanding of local cultural, social and environmental issues;
- provide access for physically challenged people; and
- be culturally sensitive, which engenders respect between tourists and hosts, and builds local pride and confidence.

2.20.4 Sustainable Tourism and Ecotourism

Emerged against the pressure of a holistic alternative to haphazard tourism development, *sustainable tourism* is the most prominent category of tourism in terms of minimizing social, cultural and environmental consequences of tourism. It is defined as the type of tourism that is "economically viable, but does not destroy the resources on which the future of tourism will depend, notably the physical environment and the social fabric of the host community (Swarbrooke, 2002). *Ecotourism* is another category with almost similar characteristics, but travel has to be limited to natural areas. (The details of the above three concepts are discussed later in this book).

2.20.5 Urban and Rural Tourism

- **Rural tourism and village tourism:** Increasing urbanization is a major reason in the evolution and growth of rural tourism. Many of the city dwellers prefer to enjoy holidays in the countryside and engage in various adventurous and other physical activities. Escape from cityscape is something enjoyable for many.

Increasing rate of urbanization has led to the growth of rural tourism as a counterbalance to urbanization (Hall et al., 2003). Countryside has been an attraction for a very long time. Up to the 1940s, tourism in the countryside remained relatively a small-scale and passive activity. In the post-Second World War period, both the nature and scale of rural tourism and the socioeconomic structure of the countryside that plays host to tourists have undergone fundamental transformation. There is no universally accepted definition for rural tourism. It is essentially an activity that takes place in the countryside. Indian tourism, in its guidelines towards rural tourism, defines *rural tourism* as "any form of tourism that showcases the rural life, art, culture and heritage at rural locations, thereby benefiting the local community economically and socially as well as enabling interactions between the tourists and the locals for a more enriching tourism experience ...... it is experience-oriented, the locations are sparsely populated, it is predominantly in natural environment, it meshes with seasonal and local events and is based on preservation of culture, heritage and traditions." (Incredible India.org). In rural tourism it is important to maintain 'rurality' (natural/traditional/non-urban environment) and social, cultural, economic and environmental sustainability of the place.

Village tourism too has the same concept, with a limited space for tourist activities. The geographical space where this occurs is purely in a village environment and the appeal of the village is derived from a combination of physical, historical, and nostalgic attributes and the prospect of encountering a community in microcosm. Through this, the traveller experiences a different way of life while discovering something of the regional character of a nation. Compared to this, rural tourism

Table 2.6: Farm tourism and agritourism

Farm tourism	Agritourism
Being one of the five categories of rural tourism (Roberts & Hall, 2001), farm tourism includes "all tourism and recreation activities connected with a [...] farm or any agricultural, horticultural, fishery or agribusiness operation." (Prezbórska, 2003). Usually, it is used in the specific space context of farms and plantations. The following are the activities in farm tourism: • accommodation; • farm visitor centres, galleries and museums; • farm shops for produce and crafts; • guided walks and farm trails; • educational visits; farm activities, such as mustering, fruit picking, horseriding and fishing; and • food and beverage outlets (IEMSS/ Coombera and Limb, 2004)	This happens in the agricultural settings. It is "the practice of touring agricultural areas to see farms and often to participate in farm activities" (Merriam Webster's Dictionary). This term is used interchangeably with many others, such as 'agricultural tourism', 'farm tourism', 'agritainment', and 'farm visits' (Colton & Bissix, 2005).

is a wider term, including the whole countryside which is more a village concept. Moreover, the experience of the tourist essentially includes the nuances of host guest relations in a village environment. According to Allerton (2003), a village tourist attempts the discovery of a village in the context of exploration beyond the boundaries of developed sites, experiencing the life of the host society as lived, which is different from his/her social environment. *Farm tourism* and *agritourism* are also often considered rural tourism forms and both are used interchangeably.

- **Urban tourism:** Urban tourism essentially has the opposite characteristics of rural tourism. Urban certainly includes a wide variety of options for tourism. Cities themselves act as platforms for sightseeing due to their diverse features and constructions. There is no exact definition for urban tourism, yet it is widely viewed as tourism that takes place in cities and towns with multiple options for tourists. Nowadays, tourism occupies a substantial amount of space within urban destinations via tourist-historic urban cores, museums of all kinds, urban waterfronts, theme parks, and specialized precincts (Edwards et al., 2008). Host tourist interaction is minimum, compared to village tourism. As shopping tourism and business tourism gained increased significance, urban tourism started growing at a tremendous pace. The core of shopping tourism is basically the shopping spaces which are primarily more available in cityscapes than in rural setups. Most of the cities have ample heritage features as well. Some of the big cities in the world have wonderful monuments and museums. These become another major element of touristic attractions. Cities are indeed major tourist centres across the world as well. MICE tourism too has ample significance in urban tourism.

2.20.6 Space Tourism and Astro-Tourism

Just more than a decade ago, the first tourist had an incredible sojourn into space and that marked the beginning of space tourism. It was in 2001, Dennis Tito, an American businessman and former JPL scientist, had a recreational trip to space with a reported cost of USD 20 million. This successful trip caused some others to follow space tourism and that caused the origination of space travel propensity, all of a sudden. Mark Shuttleworth, the second space tourist, had a journey in the very next year and wandered in the space for eleven days, at almost the same cost. Now, a number of enthusiasts are in the queue to visit space. NASA has been publishing various reports on space tourism. Travelling to space is a costly affair and many reports say that in the short run, space tourism will gain important status due to the use of short sub-orbital flight. Space tourism has to include the market for the product and the means of transport along with the destination. Page (2007) opines that in the long run, enhanced space tourism possibilities will emerge due to the availability of short earth orbital flights using reusable spacecraft and the making of space hotels located around earth's orbit. It is forecast that in future space tourism options will not only include the ability to travel to destinations in space, but also activities such as orbital flight or the ability to stay in space based hotels or stations (Cooper et. al., 2008). Astro tourism also has a similar intent but with a different concept. Fayos-Solà and Marín (2009) define *astro tourism* as the "tourism using the natural resource of unpolluted night skies for astronomical, cultural, or environmental activities". Space-India opines that astro tourism offers travellers the unique opportunity to satisfy their curiosity and learn truths about the mysterious skies (space-india.com). Space camps to NASA, archeo-astronomy, star parties, astrophotography, etc., are some of their astro tourism programmes.

2.20.7 Visiting Friends and Relatives (VFR)

Visiting family and friends is a significant reason for travel and it is one of the listed purposes of tourism as per UNWTO. This involves visits to relatives or friends, attending funerals, care of invalids and the similar. This type of travel may help in strengthening social networks, sustaining relationships and social life at a distance. Its relevance increases when people are geographically dispersed as part of modern lifestyle. VFR tourists, visiting family or relatives, are unlikely to spend as much on tourism as they do not use accommodation facilities. It generates repeat visits to a destination. Having strong bounds to destinations' residents, the VFR market is generally more resilient than other segments (Godfrey & Clarke, 2000). According to McIntosh, et al. (2003), the primary activities of this segment include socializing, dining at home and entertainment, and the secondary activities include dining out, recreation, shopping, sightseeing and urban entertainment. Living in a rural environment can also be included in this if the visit is made to a village area. Though traditionally, this was not highlighted in tourist statistics due to little industry significance from the point of view of low level of expenditure by them, currently it has given increased relevance, especially since it is a major source of tourists in many destinations.

2.20.8 Types of Nature Tourism

Nature tourism is a broad category and includes any type of tourism using nature and its elements as the primary attraction. Nature-based tourism encompasses all forms of tourism where relatively undisturbed natural environments form the primary attraction or setting (Buckley, 2009). In general, it consists of any form that features nature as its primary setting or attraction. Its activities represent a broad spectrum of passive to active behaviours; consumptive and adventurous; as well as non-consumptive contemplative activities. Even ecotourism can be treated as nature tourism adhering to sustainability principles. This is with a large market share of leisure tourism in the world. The major types of nature tourism include:

- Nature tourism
- Ecotourism

- Coastal tourism
- Marine tourism
- Beach tourism
- Forest tourism
- Wildlife tourism
- Wilderness tourism
- Island tourism
- Desert tourism
- Safari tourism

Some of the various types of nature based tourism are discussed below.

2.20.9 Coastal Tourism, Marine Tourism and Beach Tourism

Coastal regions attract tourists in large quantity and this phenomenon has existed since several centuries. The tendency of people flocking to coastal regions to unwind, relax and feel refreshed has been there since ancient times. Historically, the movement of

Table 2.7: Coastal and marine tourism activities

Coastal recreation/tourism activities	Marine recreation/tourism activities
• sand-dune surfing	• SCUBA diving
• beach volleyball	• snorkeling
• tidal-pool exploration	• yachting
• kite-flying	• waterskiing
• land yachting	• wakeboarding
• fishing	• boat based fishing
• skimboarding	• sea animal watching
• horseriding	• scenic boat cruising
• sand-castle building or sand sculpting	• sea-kayaking
• radio-controlled boating	• surfing, surf-ski paddling, kitesurfing
• wildlife watching	• board sailing (windsurfing)
• shell-fish gathering	• dragon boat paddling
• beach combing	• stand-up-paddle boarding
• sunbathing (baking)	• swimming
• picnic and barbecues	

Source: ICMTS/www.coastalmarinetourism.org

people to coastal areas evolved along with the advancement in transportation. With the development of modern transport, coastal areas have become readily accessible, with the coastlines and islands drawing large number of tourists to their shores. The coastal area refers to the border area between the land and sea/ocean and *coastal tourism* represents the tourism activities in and around that region. Europe was the hub of the evolution of coastal tourism and later that spread to every nook and corner of the world.

Marine tourism, on the other hand, takes place in the sea, not on the coast or beach. According to Orams (1999), marine tourism includes those recreational activities which involve travel away from one's place of residence and which have the marine environment (waters that are saline and tide affected) as their host or focus. Hence, marine tourism is present under the sea, in the sea or on the sea. Variety of activities can be included in marine tourism. Some of them are listed in Table 2.7.

Beach tourism, in concept, is same as coastal tourism. *Beach tourism* is a major category of tourism in many of the western developed countries. This type of tourism is focused more on established beaches that lure and attract tourists from far and wide. The 3S' concept, representing the "sun, sand and sea", and now "surf" also, is all about beach tourism. Happening against a beautiful background, beach tourism involves visiting beaches, relaxing and engaging in recreational activities in and around the accessible beaches. Sun bathing is a common phenomenon seen widely in beach tourism. The spectrum of beach tourism has been broadened to include a wide variety of recreational activities.

2.20.10 Forest Tourism, Wildlife Tourism and Wilderness Tourism

Forest tourism is a broad term in which the prime focus of tourism are the forested landscapes. It includes various forest types. People explore forests with varied objectives, yet learning and watching the features and living beings over there are the prime motivators. In fact, forest is home to large variety of flora and fauna along with tribal settlements. All are highly fragile and hence, tourist movement into forests needs extreme care, or else the irrevocable impacts of such movements may damages to varied dimensions. Today, the scenic beauty of all the forest biomes is highly valued. The presence of unique flora and fauna makes specific sites ideal for creating national parks and protected areas serving to conserve forest ecosystems while encouraging use. *Wilderness tourism* is more about movement into an undeveloped land with minimal human imprints. Wilderness areas include protected and unprotected natural areas (with some amount of wilderness), national parks, wildlife sanctuaries, estates, and national forests. This has emerged mainly out of a quest for escape from the city life and to interact with nature in its pure form (Nash, 2001). *Wildlife tourism* has some "consumptive" aspect as well, historically, as human-wildlife encounter of varied forms can be seen in it. *Consumptive wildlife tourism* encapsulates extractive recreational activities (such as hunting), while *non-consumptive wildlife tourism* pertains to viewing and/or encountering wildlife (Higginbottom, 2004). In wildlife tourism, fauna has more significance. Animals and other varieties form the prime attraction. Nowadays, even in wildlife tourism, recreational activities like hunting are increasingly being discouraged/banned. All these nature related tourism categories are widely classified as ecotourism as well, though, practically, many of them fail to adhere to strict principles and guidelines of ecotourism and sustainable tourism. Unplanned, uncontrolled and mass movement can cause more harm than benefits.

This category also includes island tourism and safari tourism.

- **Island tourism:** Islands are romantic and that gives a perfect setting for a rather hedonic holiday. "Their appeal may relate to the very feeling of separateness and difference, caused by their being physically separate...and given peoples' desires for the different while in pursuit of leisure, different climates, physical environments and culture can all be expected to enhance the attractiveness of islands as tourism destinations" (Butler, 1993). It is difficult to locate a specific definition for *island tourism*, yet it can be defined simply as diverse tourism activities taking place in islands. It will have a range of recreational activities, services and facilities for the visitors and tourist attractions can also be varied. Beaches are usually the major attractions in island tourism, but many of the islands also have a good variety of other attractions.

- **Safari tourism:** Safari tourism is a kind of expedition over landforms to explore the culture, geography, scenery, and wildlife. Originally, *safari tourism* focused on consumptive tours through game hunting. But of late, this mainly includes trips to observe and photograph wildlife, hiking and sightseeing. Many of the African countries are famous for safari tourism. Safari experience includes guided, self-driven, walking, hiking, fly-in, elephant back, river-boating, primate, horseback, balloon, night game-viewing, photographic, and mobile tented journeys. A safari offers a unique opportunity to see and understand wildlife roaming, often in protected parks, living the way nature intended. Apart from this, the term safari is used for variety of other types of journeys as well. Desert safari is very common in Arab countries, particularly in the GCC countries. This is usually a four-wheeled car trip over sand dunes deep into the deserts. Animals are also used in safari for going into adventurous regions. Camel safari, elephant safari, etc., are common in many countries. Walking safari trips are also there. Accommodation in such categories is more ecofriendly, but with limited facilities. Many a times accommodation can be in the form of tents.

2.20.11 Food Related Tourism: Food, Culinary and Wine Tourisms

In modern tourism, food is also an attraction that belongs to the special interest category. Dining out is a growing form of leisure where meals are consumed not out of necessity but for pleasure. In the same, the environment around and the occasion also become an integral part of the leisure experience. *Food tourism* is a broad term that primarily aims at the consumption of food, though other aspects related to food are also present. It has been defined as "a visit to food producers with a strong interest in tasting that food and an even stronger motivation to learn about the production process from raw materials to the final product" (Buiatti, 2011). Experiencing food is the major reason of such travel. Hence, any travel to places which are famous for special/indigenous food is part of food tourism. Having the food with all its true spirit and essence and visiting places where food preparation takes place is an important part of it. In fact food tourism is not just to taste food somewhere; rather it has to be linked to the land the same is famous for. Food is an important part of the culture and identity of a land and its people. Switzerland is mostly popular for its chocolate and cheese, each of which is enough reason to visit, hence Switzerland is a noted food tourism destination. While Croatia welcomes tourists who like meat, cheese, noodles, beer and fruit spirits; Jamaica is visited by people for jerk chicken, Appleton Estates rum, Red Stripe beer, and tropical fruit varieties.

Culinary tourism is another term used in this context. The word "culinary" derives from the Latin *culina,* meaning kitchen, thus limiting the scope of "culinary tourism" to food-related activities. Culinary tourism is also referred to as *food or gastronomy tourism* (OECD, 2012). It is concerned with the desire to experience a particular food or region where a specific food is produced (Hall & Sharples, 2003). It includes any tourism experience in which a person learns about, appreciates, consumes or experiences food and drink that reflects the local cuisine, heritage, or culture of a place. Culinary tourists are also *food motivated tourists* inspired by the interest in tasting food varieties, participating in food festivals, and the like. The culinary tourist is a type of a special

Table 2.8: Tourism types based on the vehicle/medium of transportation

- Rail tourism (using tourist trains and rail tourism packages)
- Charter tourism (journey by charter flights, and packaged tourism)
- Cruise tourism (not as a transport, but luxury trip-based tourism for several days in sea with off-shore excursions)
- Automobile tourism (using cars)
- Coach tourism (packaged tourism by coaches/buses)
- Cycling tourism (using bicycles, trips in countryside, mainly)

interest tourist whose interest in food is the primary reason influencing his travel behaviour and at the same time, eating and drinking being ultimately cultural affairs (Murcott, 1986). The culinary tourist is also a cultural tourist. The main difference is, visiting to observe food manufacturing is seen associated more with food tourism than culinary tourism. It denotes that food tourism is a broader term encompassing more elements.

Wine tourism is one of the fastest growing segments of tourism in the world. It is also a type of food tourism, but the focus is more on wines and other beverages only. It includes visitation to vineyards, wineries, and wine festivals/events as a main travel reason or secondary motivation. In many cases, an attribute of wine tourism is wine tasting in cellars or vineyards (Hall et al., 2000). Major wine tourism destinations in the world includes The US, Argentina, Chile, Mexico, Central America, the Caribbean, South Africa, New Zealand, Australia, Canada, Portugal, Spain, and France. Wine Roads, Special Wine Events and Festivals, Experiential Wine Programmes, Wine Villages, and Winery Tours are some of the trends in wine tourism, of late.

2.20.12 Health, Wellness, Medical, and Spa Tourism

Health has been a major reason for travel for quite a long period of time. As the concern of longevity increased among all sections of the society, seeking options for physical and mental well-being, physical fitness and treatments has become a major trend in the entire travel domain. Many authors use this as an umbrella term, which includes medical and wellness tourism. Simply, *health tourism* is travelling for the purposes of improvement and/or maintenance of health. Travellers may have several other aims and desires as well, like being outdoors, visits to attractions or events, culture, entertainment, various activities, and similar others. The service providers consider these additional aims and include the above in their products (Tuman/Tartu Ulikool, 2013).

Wellness tourism products range from meditation retreats, life coaching holidays, alternative therapies, day spas, to cosmetic surgery, and some of the medical and dental procedures in luxurious environments. While distinguishing wellness from health, Muller and Kaufmann (2000) regarded *wellness tourism* as a subset of health tourism. Wellness tourism is more subjective, with a preventive intent. Wellness tourism can be travel to seek wellness in a distant place or can be for the maintenance of wellness while on some other trip. Wellness tourism is more holistic in nature and the domains of it include wellness of both mind and body, not just for body treatment.

Medical tourism emerged as an area in tourism literature recently. It is all about people travelling across international borders with the intention of receiving some form of medical treatment. This treatment may span a full range of medical services, but it usually includes dental care, cosmetic surgery, elective surgery, and fertility treatment. The healthcare sector prefers medical travel, but the tourism industry and its marketers, in general, favour it as medical tourism. At the same time, healthcare professionals argue that tourism generally implies leisure, and thus "travel" should be preferred to "tourism" (Whittaker, 2008). Yet, from the demand perspective, medical tourism is regarded as temporary movement of people for either physical or mental treatment or seek to improve or change health through either surgical or non-surgical medical measures. The common elements in the gamut of medical tourism are:

- Cosmetic surgery (breast, face, liposuction)
- Dentistry (cosmetic and reconstruction)
- Cardiology/cardiac surgery (bypass, valve replacement)
- Orthopaedic surgery (hip replacement, resurfacing, knee replacement, joint surgery)
- Bariatric surgery (gastric bypass, gastric banding)
- Fertility/reproductive system (IVF, gender reassignment)
- Organ, cell and tissue transplantation (organ transplantation; stem cell)
- Eye surgery
- Diagnostics and check-ups. (OECD, 2010; Lunt et al./OECD)

Spas were one of the earliest tourist attractions. Even during the Roman era, spa based travel was in trend. Currently, spa related facilities are created to attract tourists. Harmsworth (2004) claims that "the spa market is one of the fastest growing leisure sectors, where societal trends and aspirations find instant reflection in the developments on both the demand and supply sides. The market is very fragmented, each segment catering to different customer needs, which continuously change in line with social and lifestyle changes." In fact, spa tourism can be considered part of health tourism. Also it is being treated as a section of wellness tourism. In a spa attraction, variety of facilities and services are arranged so as to encourage the renewal of mind, body, and spirit. Becheri (1989) has classified spa tourists into four categories: people looking for relaxation, people wishing to delay their ageing, people wanting a short break on a weekend, and people concerned with illness prevention. Lately, alternative and traditional wellness practices like yoga, massage of various types, and some other alternative holistic health systems, that emphasizes relaxation and alleviation of the mind, body, and spirit; are also used in spa tourism.

2.20.13 War Related Tourism: Military Tourism and Battlefield Tourism

Military tourism is all about visits to historical battlefields, war monuments, and cemeteries. It also describes the type of tourism undertaken by off-duty military personnel seeking 'rest and relaxation'. Military tourism is gaining prominence as remains of historically significant military/defence related sites, monuments, military stations and war locations are increasingly been converted into attractions as part of consistent efforts to be dynamic in the competitive tourism environment. USA, with immense defence related remnants from the recent history, is advancing in this area. On the other hand, *battlefield tourism* has emerged as an important form of tourist activity that has expanded beyond age-old battlefields and museums to include new experiences such as re-enactments, alternative histories, and the addition of sites that have some association with military activity (Prideaux, 2007). People's interest in visiting battlefields, to remember war heroes; to rekindle memories of loved ones who fell in battle; to ponder on the feats of those who they will never know; and to gloat on victory or lament over defeat; is on the increase. Now countries are promoting such kind of travel, as an addition to the existing tourism paradigm.

2.20.14 Sports Tourism

Sports is a major attraction for visiting any destination. The trend began during the ancient Olympic Games and is continuing with increased momentum since a few decades back. Sports tourism can include either passive or active involvement in competitive sports. This type of tourism considers sports as an attraction and has three major domains such as hallmark events, health and fitness, and outdoor recreation (Hall, 1992). Travel occurs to observe and/or physically participate in football games, golf tournaments, and events like Olympics, Football World Cup, etc. Broad components of sports tourism are:

- *sports participation travel*: travel for the purpose of participating in sports, recreation, leisure or fitness activity;
- *sports spectatorial travel*: travel for the purpose of spectating sports, recreation, leisure or fitness activities or events (Pitts, 1997); and
- *celebrity and nostalgia sports tourism*: visits to the sports halls of fame/famous sports related attractions and venues, and meeting sports personalities.

Olympic tourism is a segment of sports tourism. Major cities are keen to hold Olympics as it can generate positive images of host cities as potential destinations through event-related media coverage featuring the destination. Also people from almost all the countries participating in it flock to the city, where Olympics is being held. The economic effects generated not only during the event, but post the event is also a possibility due to the awareness generated and image created. The visitors category involves participants in the sports activities as well as other visitors whose main purpose is not participation

2.20.15 Dark Tourism (Thano Tourism)

Some travellers are attracted to the negative images of places that have suffered disasters. The disasters can be either manmade or natural. Travel motivations in this category include remembrance, education, curiosity or entertainment. The traveller encounters spaces of death or calamity that have perturbed the public consciousness. Many a

Table: 2.9: Some other types of tourism

Enclave tourism

Some of the resorts provide all tourist facilities and services inside their own premises and the tourist can have the intended experience within it. This forms a kind of enclave that is entirely self-sufficient with little contact with the world. Therefore, tourists are segregated from the local community, and tourism that occurs in such environments is called *enclave tourism.* This is highly concentrated, with little possibility of decentralization, form of tourism development and entirely enclosed and self-contained (physically, socially, economically). Usually, large scale multinational agencies set up such kinds of self-sufficient resorts. Enclave tourism is happening on large scale in major tourist destinations, usually in locations with abundant natural beauty.

Pro-poor tourism

Tourism that can provide net benefits for poor people is referred to as pro-poor tourism (Ashley et al., 2001). It is developed to benefit the economically poor and can also be used to benefit local communities. It is to ensure that tourism growth contributes to poverty reduction, and not classified as a specific product or sector of tourism, but promoted as an approach to tourism development.

Senior tourism

A tremendous increase in the number of senior citizens throughout the world, has made this group an attractive niche market, called senior tourists, for tourism with its own particular needs. It is characterized by its size, buying power, improved health status, and differing tourist behaviours. The extended health status and lots of spare time after retirement along with good finances to spend for travel created senior tourism and is increasingly been identified as a niche tourism type by almost all destinations.

Sex tourism

One of the most debated and with extreme sociocultural impacts, sex tourism is in fact in trend in some destinations, though without referring to it in that way. Sex related services in various forms are being offered either openly or secretly in many destinations. Women, children and even men are used in this sector in a highly commercialized way. The magnitude of this is stunning and plenty of immoral activities including women and children trafficking are happening the world over.

Shopping tourism

Shopping at locations away from usual environments is in vogue and increasing at a good pace. The ever increasing shopping phenomenon clubbed with leisure pursuits paved the way for shopping tourism. However, many tourists have recently begun to travel to destinations, particularly overseas, with the purpose of experiencing new shopping opportunities that may be unavailable at home. It has grown from perusing street stalls to visiting specialty shops, large shopping centres, or outlet malls.

Social tourism

Social tourism was earlier considered "the relationship and phenomena in the field of tourism resulting from participation in travel by economically weak or otherwise disadvantaged elements in society" (Hunzicker, 1951). But in its modern form, social tourism includes the social movement for visiting with the primary objective of benefiting either or both the host or the tourist populations (Minnaert et al., 2011). Primarily, this refers to the initiatives that aim to include people into tourism who would otherwise be excluded, and results from participation in travel by economically weak or 'otherwise disadvantaged elements' in the society (Hall, 2000).

Contd...

Volunteer tourism

Oxford dictionary online defines voluntary tourism as a "form of tourism in which travellers participate in voluntary work, typically for charity: at *the core of voluntourism is the desire to help others*". It is viewed as the activities engaged in by tourists who "volunteer in an organized way to undertake holidays that might involve aiding or alleviating the material poverty of some groups in society, restoration of certain environments, or research into aspects of society or environment" (Wearning, 2001).

Youth tourism

According to the UNWTO, "youth travel includes all independent trips for periods of less than one year by people aged 16-29 which are motivated, in part or in full, by a desire to experience other cultures, build life experiences and/or benefit from formal and informal learning opportunities outside one's usual environment". Such travellers have a preference for budget accommodation, emphasise on meeting other travellers, independently organised, flexible travel schedules and longer rather than brief holidays (Haigh, 1995). This segment, with a growth rate of more than the general tourism sector, is estimated to represent almost 190 million international trips a year and by 2020, (UNWTO and WYSE Travel Confederation, 2011). There will be almost 300 million international youth trips per year.

destinations now identify such sites and create space for people to visit. Examples of such sites can include New York's Grand Zero; Peace Memorial Park in Hiroshima; Genocide Memorial, Rwanda; and the Auschwitz Memorial and the Auschwitz-Birkenau State Museum.

2.20.16 Backpacker Tourism

This category of tourism is based on the nature of tourists and their behaviour in the destination in terms of using tourist services and facilities. Such tourists are self-organized tourists with flexible itinerary and interested more into the local culture and features of the destination. Usually, they stay longer in the destination, like for some months, and tend to experience the local lifestyle. Their recreational focus may include nature, culture, or adventure, and go for authentic experience, preferably. Such kind of movement of tourists, commonly referred to as *backpacker tourism*, gained momentum during the last three decades or so. In general, backpacker tourists tend to:

- use budget accommodation,
- involve in longer rather than very brief holidays,
- be predominantly under 40 years of age,
- have flexibility in their itineraries, and
- show a willingness to be involved in social and participatory holiday activities. (Pearce et al., 2009).

Backpacker tourism usually gives a fillip to rural tourism and helps in cultural exchange. Negative impacts are argued to be less for this category.

2.21 CONCLUSION

Tourism is highly diverse, encompassing a large variety of tourism types. It is classified in a number of ways, of which some are fundamental to be understood by each and everyone associated with tourism. International tourism, domestic tourism, inbound tourism, outbound tourism, etc., belong to this category. A few of the terminologies are in fact umbrella terms which comprise varied tourism types. For instance, nature tourism and cultural tourism include a number of similar tourism forms. Some of the terminologies emerged as part of the dynamism in the sector in order to remain competent in the market. Tourism types like social tourism, sustainable tourism, etc., are conceptually significant categories that need thorough understanding to practise. Tourism is poised to grow further and it is expected to have more and more types added regularly. It will strengthen the discipline of tourism as well.

Key Terms

International tourism
Inbound tourism
Outbound tourism
Inter-regional tourism
Intra-regional tourism
Domestic tourism
Leisure tourism
Business tourism
Mass tourism
Niche tourism
Special interest tourism
Cultural tourism
Historical tourism
Indigenous tourism
Film-induced tourism
Pilgrimage tourism
Rural tourism
Alternative tourism
Urban and rural tourism
Sports tourism
Military tourism
Forest tourism
Nature tourism
Ecotourism
Coastal tourism
Marine tourism
Beach tourism
Forest tourism
Wildlife tourism
Wilderness tourism
Island tourism
Desert tourism
Safari tourism
Food tourism

Review Questions

Short Answer Type Questions

1. Distinguish between international tourism and domestic tourism.

2. Distinguish between outbound tourism and inbound tourism.
3. What do you mean by inter-regional tourism?
4. Discuss the nature and characteristics of leisure tourism.
5. Differentiate leisure tourism from business tourism.
6. What is MICE tourism?
7. What are the features of business tourism?
8. What is mass tourism?
9. 'Mass tourism is often blamed for negative impacts of tourism'. Comment on the statement.
10. What is niche tourism?
11. Discuss the characteristics of special interest tourism.
12. Write brief account on some of the special interest tourism (SIT) types.
13. Discuss adventure tourism.
14. Give a brief account of cultural tourism.
15. Differentiate between historical tourism and ethnic tourism.
16. What do you mean by indigenous tourism? Discuss some of its types.
17. Discuss the significance of films on tourism.
18. Write the types of film-induced tourism.
19. Explain how rural areas can be used for tourism.
20. Write about different industrial tourisms.
21. What do you mean by alternative tourism? Write in short on some of its types.
22. Differentiate between farm tourism and agritourism.
23. Distinguish between urban tourism and rural tourism.
24. Elucidate space tourism and astro tourism.
25. Write short notes on coastal tourism, marine tourism and beach tourism.
26. What are the different types of tourism in forest areas?
27. Write brief notes on different food tourism types.
28. What are the war tourism types?
29. Discuss sports tourism.
30. What is dark tourism?
31. What do you mean by backpacker tourism?

Essay Type Questions

1. Explain how to classify tourists geographically.
2. Write an essay on nature tourism and its types.
3. Write an essay on evolution of health tourism and its types.

3 TOURISM MOTIVATION AND DEMAND

Learning Outcomes

After studying this chapter, you will be able to:

- define 'travel motivation';
- understand different types of travel motivators;
- identify the factors that determine travel tendency of a population;
- understand the concept of tourism demand; and
- learn how to measure tourism demand.

3.1 INTRODUCTION

Intrinsic and inherent causes behind movement of people from one place to another, from a tourism point of view, have been a matter of investigation for scholars since long. Yet, understanding why people choose to travel and become tourists is a complex issue. A number of studies from different perspectives were undertaken in this area. It is accepted that a range of motivating factors prompt people to travel. There are thousands of destinations in this world. Millions of people are travelling. Different people choose different destinations. Although there are many alternate destinations, the perspective of the traveller to choose a specific destination is usually circumscribed by a number of factors like attitude, time, family responsibilities, finance, education, and physical health. Such factors may also be influenced by travellers' personality type, value and the like (Bhatia, 2006). Understanding tourist motivation may help to explain why certain places are developed as successful tourist destinations and continued to grow and pass through various stages in its lifecycle (Page, 2003).

Basically, motivation refers to all the forces operating within a person to cause him or her to engage in certain kinds of behaviours different from others. The question of 'why' when applied to the human activities brings the concept called motivation. It is needed for all activities of mankind. A motive can be defined as a person's basic predisposition to reach for or strive towards a particular goal or combination of goals. Motivation is usually closely linked with the purpose.

The basic questions of motivation as applicable in various fields can similarly be applied to travel and tourism as well. Travel motivations have their roots in *psychological* and *sociological* factors that are difficult to analyze especially on a mass scale. A significant amount of travel is motivated by specific objectives involving business, education, pleasure, health, culture, religion and personal emergencies. Travel for tourism encompasses a wide range of human emotions and motivations. Here, tourism or *travel motivators* can be defined as the basic reasons why people engage in tourism. Understanding travel motivators is crucial for all stakeholders in tourism sector, particularly for marketers. The UNWTO has specified the following two critical aspects of the need for understanding motivation, decision making and consumer behaviour in relation to travel and holiday-making:

- First, it helps businesses and organizations in the public sector to plan for visitor activities.
- Second, in an increasingly competitive sector, it is essential for destinations, businesses and other operators to be able to understand what types of visitors and market segments they are attracting and wish to attract. (UNWTO, 2011)

Apart from the above, knowledge of travel motivation is also required in all marketing activities and it also influences the nature of tourism development. A clear understanding of travel motivation is essential to the successful promotion of any tourist destination. Tourism marketers should first identify the travel motivation of prospective patrons or clients and then present the travel product that will best fulfill those desires and motivations (McIntosh and Goeldner, 1990). Moreover, it is useful to understand why some people do not travel and the barriers of travel.

3.2 TRAVEL MOTIVATION THEORIES

As stated before, learning about what motivates people to travel is important for tourism planners, developers and marketers. There are a number of studies that classify travel motivation. Hills (1965) concluded that the motive of many vacation makers is in a response to psychological depletion and is an opportunity to allow the tourist to replenish and restore; if the traveller finds what they want they will come back enriched, regenerated and recharged. According to Gray (1970), all tourists can be classified into two categories of distinct motivations such as *wander lust* and *sun lust*.

- **Wander lust**: Here the travel is to satisfy curiosity, to experience the strange and unfamiliar. It is all about "innate human need to temporarily leave familiar surroundings to experience different cultures and places" (Pike, 2008). It describes the desire to exchange the known for the unknown or familiar with unfamiliar, to leave familiar things and to go and see different places, people and cultures or architecture of the past in places famous for their historical monuments and also past associations.

- **Sun lust:** It can be described as the search for a better set of amenities than are available at home. This consists of travel for "specific purpose for benefits not available at home, such as winter/sun holidays or visits to a larger city" (Pike 2008). This category generates a type of travel which depends on the existence elsewhere for better amenities and facilities for a specific purpose than are available in the home country/place of the traveller.

Examples for wander lust can be cultural tourism, anthropological tourism, etc., where people travel to see different things. In the case of sun lust, travelling to a resort for participating in skiing can be taken as an example.

In 1972, Erick Cohen attempted to classify tourists based on the degree to which they seek familiarity and novelty. Tourists may vary considerably which may have association with personality, roles, sociological aspects, and the like. He proposes a continuum of possible combination of novelty and familiarity and, by breaking up the continuum into typical combinations of these two. The classification is as follows.

- **The organized mass tourist:** This type of tourists is less adventurous, and anxious to maintain its own environmental bubble during the tour. These tourists travel as part of a package tour and are highly organized throughout the tour. They go for readymade package tours off the shelf and interaction with the local community will be low or nil.
- **The individual mass tourist:** These tourists have somewhat similar characteristics of organized mass tourists, but have more flexibility and scope for personal choice. This category of tourists uses similar facilities as used by organized mass tourists. The tour is also part of an organized package holiday, but they may also wish to visit other sights not included in package tours. Moreover, tourists tend to interact a little with the local culture/society.
- **The explorer:** These tourists try to get off the beaten track. They organize trips themselves with comfortable accommodation and reliable transport facilities. As they prefer independent tours, they make their own arrangements. Since they do not wish to remain in environmental bubble, they prefer to experience the social and cultural vibrancy of the destination.
- **The drifter:** These tourists prefer to be away from familiarity, do not seek any contact with other tourists and make attempts to mingle more with local community and wish to live with them. Being adventurous with no fixed itinerary, they, while being spurned all connections with tourism industry, would like to immerse themselves with local culture.

Plog (1974) developed a theory within which the US population could be classified as a series of interrelated psychographic types. These types range from two extremes.

- The word *Psychographic* derives from '*psyche*' or '*self-centred*', meaning the centring of one's thoughts or concerns on small problem areas of one's life. Poised to be nervous and non-adventurous, they would be attracted more by destinations at maturity/declining stage. These persons tend to be conservative, preferring safe destinations.
- The word *Allocentric* derives from the root word '*allo*' meaning varied in form. They are more confident and willing to experiment with life. They may explore new destinations. Their interest patterns are focused on varied activities. Such a person is outgoing and is characterized by a considerable degree of adventure and willingness to reach out and experiment with life.

Plog found that the US population was normally distributed along a continuum between these two extremes. Other groups have been identified between allocentrics and psychocentrics. Most people fall in mid-centric classification.

- Mid-centric: There are a large number of people falling between the allocentric and the psychocentric types of tourists. This type of tourists is called mid-centrics. These tourists are not particularly adventurous, but they are receptive to new experiences.

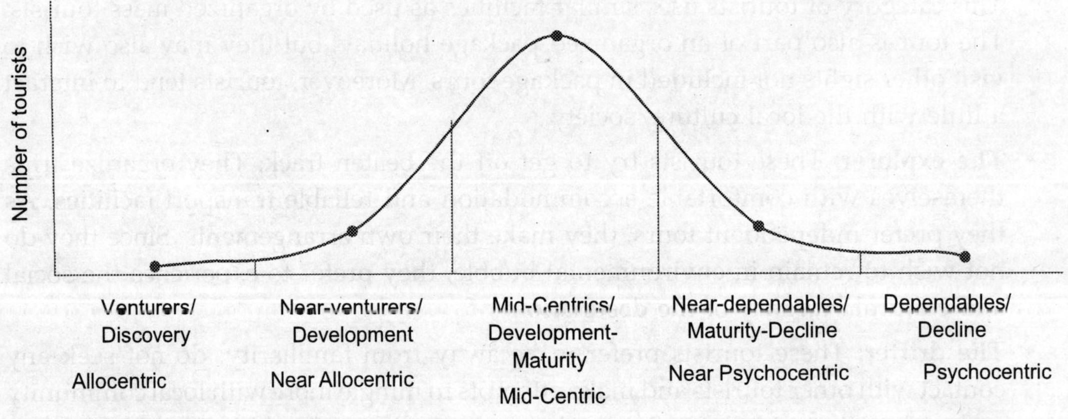

Source: Plog, 1974

Figure 3.1 Plog's theory of travel motivation.

Table 3.1: Sample list of travel motivators as per Plog (1974)

Allocentric motivators	Near allocentric motivators	Mid-centric motivators	Psychocentric motivators
Education and cultural motives	Religious pilgrims or inspiration	Relaxation and pleasure	Prefer familiar travel destinations
Study of genealogy	Participation in sports events and sports activities.	Satisfying personal contacts with friends and relatives.	Like commonplace activities in destinations
Search for the exotic	Travel as a challenge	Health-change in climate, sunshine, spas, etc.	Prefer relaxing sun-and-fun spots
Satisfaction and sense of power and freedom	Business travel, conferences, meetings, conventions	The need for change for a period of time	Prefer low activity level
Gambling	Theatre tours, special entertainment	An opportunity to escape from life's problems	Prefer staying at familiar hotel chain
Development of new friendships in foreign places	A chance to try a new lifestyle.	The real or imagined glamour of the destination	Dining at restaurants offering cuisine of their home country
Sharpening perspectives		Appreciation of beauty-natural beauty	Prefer familiar rather than foreign atmosphere
Political campaigns, government hearings		Sensual indulgence: food, comfort, to sexual enjoyment, rest, etc.	Prefer purchasing complete tour packages featuring a full schedule of activities.
Vacation or second homes and condominiums.		Shopping	
		Joys of transportation: cruise ship, etc.	
		Pleasure of pre- and post-travel	

Source: Plog, 1974.

Dann (1981) pointed out that there are seven elements within the overall approach to motivation. These are as follows:

- **Travel is a response to what is lacking yet desired:** Travellers are motivated by the desire to experience phenomena, which are different from those available in their home environment.
- **Destination 'pull' in response to motivational 'push':** Destinations have attracting capacities, and some force factors exist in the personal environment of an individual.
- **Motivation as fantasy:** In normal family atmosphere, it is difficult to undertake behaviours which are not culturally sanctioned and fantasies about destinations may motivate them to engage in tourism.

- **Motivation as classified purpose:** A group of different types of purposes behind engaging in travel are listed and a person may be motivated by any one of them. The purpose may include visiting friends and relatives, enjoying leisure activity, study, etc.
- **Motivational typologies:** This approach is internally divided into two. First one is behavioural typologies such as the motivator's 'sun lust' and 'wander lust' as proposed by Gray (1970). Second one is the typologies that focus on dimensions of the tourist role.
- **Motivation and tourist experience:** This approach is characterized by the debate regarding the authenticity of tourist experience and depends on beliefs about types of tourist experience.
- **Motivation as auto-definition and meaning:** This suggests that tourist motivations can be better understood by the way in which the tourists define their situations rather than simply observing their behaviour.

Every motivation is based on some human need with varying importance as suggested by Maslow in his theory, Maslow's Need Hierarchy. Though it was not based on tourism, the same needs can be identified from tourism motivation point of view as well. An attempt of that kind is shown in Table 3.2.

A popular classification of travel motivators is the grouping of various travel motivators under four major categories such as physical, cultural, interpersonal and status and prestige by the Mexican scientist, Ramumbo. These are called *Ramumbo travel motivations*. Same type of classification is done by McIntosh and Goeldner, as well. Brief discussions on these four categories are as follows.

- **Physical motivators:** These are related to physical relaxation and refreshment to mind, health purposes, sports and pleasure. This group of motivators is linked to

Table 3.2: Maslow's theory : 'Needs' connected to tourism

Psychological/ Physical	Relaxation	Relief of tension, 'sun lust', physical relaxation and activities
Safety	Security	Keep oneself active and healthy Tour guide service in unfamiliar locations
Belonging	Love	Family togetherness, enhancement of kinship, relationships, facilitation of social interaction, interpersonal relations, searching the roots, etc.
Esteem	Achievement, status	Social recognition, professional development, show one's importance to other, ego enhancement
Self-actualization	To be true to one's own nature	Self-discovery, satisfaction of inner desires, learning.

Source: Adapted from Mill & Morrison, 1992.

those activities which will reduce tension. Health tourism, sports tourism, etc., come under this category.

- **Cultural motivators:** Those identified by the desire to see and know more about other cultures, to find out about natives of a country, their lifestyle, music, art, folklore, dance, etc. Cultural tourism, anthropological tourism, etc., come under this category.
- **Interpersonal motivators:** This group includes travellers with the desire to meet new people, visit friends or relatives, and to seek new and different experiences. In this category, travel is considered an escape from routine relationships with friends and neighbours or the home environment or it is used for spiritual reasons. Religious tourism, VFR, etc., come under this category.
- **Status and prestige motivators:** These include a desire for continuation of education (i.e., personal development, ego enhancement, etc). Such motivators are seen to

Table 3.3: Crandall's list of travel motivations

- Enjoying nature, escaping from civilization: to get away from civilization for a while, and be close to nature.
- Escape from routine and responsibility: change from daily routines and responsibilities of everyday life.
- Physical exercise: to keep in shape.
- Creativity: to be creative.
- Relaxation: to relax physically, so the mind can slow down for a while.
- Social contact: tourism could do things with companions, to get away from other people.
- Meeting new people: talking to new and varied people to build friendships.
- Heterosexual contact: to meet people of the opposite sex.
- Family contact: to be away from family for a while to help bring the family together.
- Recognition, status: to show other tourists could do it, so others would think highly of the tourist.
- Social power: to have control over others, to be in a position of authority.
- Altruism: to help others.
- Stimulus seeking: for the excitement because of the risks involved.
- Self-actualisation (feedback, self-improvement, ability utilisation): seeing the results of your efforts using a variety of skills and talents.
- Achievement, challenge, competition to develop skills and abilities due to the competition; to learn what he/she is capable of.
- Killing time, avoiding boredom: to keep busy to avoid boredom.
- Intellectual aestheticism: to use mind to think about personal values.

Source: Crandall, 1980.

be concerned with the desire for recognition and attention from others in order to boost the personal ego. This category also includes personal development in relation to the pursuit of hobbies and education. (McIntosh and Goeldner, 1990)

UNWTO specifies that "travel motivation is becoming increasingly characterised by a search for leisure, emotional recharge, authenticity, fulfilling experience, outdoor activities/adventure, and a general desire to participate and explore, rather than merely relax. In particular, there is a need to 'get away from it all', and to use travel and holidays as discovery of place, cultures and of self" (UNWTO, 2009). There are a number of other travel motivations as well. All are relevant and useful for understanding tourist motivations. As stated earlier, there are different approaches in tourism motivation and the above illustration gives a clear picture on the tourist/travel motivators in general. The following, as pointed out by Page (2007), are some of the significant inferences with regard to the learning of tourist motivations.

- Tourism is a combination of products and experiences that meet a varied range of needs.
- Tourists are not always conscious of their deep psychological needs and ideas, and even when they do not know that they are, they may not reveal them to researchers, family and friends.
- Tourism motives may be multiple and contradictory, with some working in harmony and others working in direct opposition (i.e., "push" and "pull" factors).
- Motives may change overtime and be inextricably linked together.

Though there are multiple theories, and with contradicting views, every destination needs to understand specific motivations with regard to them. That becomes crucial in planning and development, and for marketing to compete internationally.

3.3 DEMAND FOR TOURISM

Comprehending *tourism demand* is crucial as it influences growth, development and change in tourism businesses and destinations (Page, 2003). Though tourism has grown in size and magnitude, still only a very small population engages in international tourism. It denotes that international tourism remains an unobtainable luxury for many. Assessing the demand is an inevitable task of destination managers. Measured in different ways, demand is manifested using diverse approaches. In fact, further development in a destination also needs to be based on the trends in demand. Marketing and promotion activities require up-to-date information on the tourists visiting the destination. In order to understand the socioeconomic significance of tourism, demand measurements are also relevant.

Simply, demand can be considered the desire of people for particular goods or services. The definition of demand varies according to subject perspectives. Economists consider demand to be the schedule of the amount of any product or service that people are willing and able to buy at a specific price in a set of possible prices during a specified period of time. Psychologists' view on demand is different. They look at demand from the perspective of motivation and behaviour. Tourism demand has been defined in numerous ways. It can be defined as the relationship between individuals' motivation to travel and their ability to do so (Pearce, 1995). Mathieson and Wall (1982) define *tourism demand* as the "total number of persons who travel, or wish to travel, to use tourist facilities and services at places away from their place of work and residence". Page (2007) argues that tourism demand is about using tourism as a form of consumption to achieve a level of satisfaction for an individual, and involves understanding their behaviour and actions, and what shapes these human characteristics. The consumption is all about satisfaction of tourists' needs, and desires, and such factors are shaped mainly by various socio-economic determinants of tourism demand. McIntosh and Goeldner (1990) have come up with a different definition. According to them, demand for travel to a particular destination will be a function of the propensity of individuals to travel and the reciprocal of the resistance of the link between origin and destination areas. Propensity can be thought of a person's predisposition to travel. In other words, how willing is the individual to travel, what type of travel experience he or she prefers, and what types of destinations are selected. Resistance relates to the relative attractiveness of various destinations, i.e., a function of several other variables such as distance, cost of tourist services at destinations, quality of services at destinations, effectiveness of advertising and promotion, seasonality, etc. Resistance is inversely related to demand. While analyzing tourist motivation from the perspective of consumer decision making process, three distinctive elements which condition the demand are identified, and they are:

- **Energizers of demand:** These factors promote an individual to decide on a tour, i.e., they collectively create the motivation to travel.
- **Effecters of demand:** The factors that may enhance or suppress the energizers that promotes decision to take a tour.
- **Filters of demand:** There are some social, economic and psychological factors that determine the choice of particular destinations. Some of such factors can hinder the demand, despite the presence of a wish to go for a tour, i.e., they have the ability to filter the inappropriate.

Generally, tourism demand is represented by using the number of tourists. From that perspective, it can be suggested that there are three basic components, which constitute the demand for tourism (Page, 2003; Cooper et al., 1993).

These are explained below:

3.3.1 Effective or Actual Demand

This is the actual number of participants in tourism or the number of people who are travelling. This shows the quantity of tourism participation. This component is one of the most widely measured all over the world and is the easiest of all.

3.3.2 Suppressed Demand

This component comprises category of people who do not travel due to circumstances from their personal side or the industry side in general. Based on two major elements associated with the circumstances, suppressed demand can be distinguished into two, such as *potential demand* and *deferred demand*. In potential demand, the person does not engage in tourism due to factors of his/her circumstances, like health problems, etc. This category will travel at some time in the future if they experience a change in their circumstances. For example, if travel tendency was suppressed by health reasons and if it is changed in the future, travel may occur. The category of deferred demand consists of people whose demand has been postponed because of the problem in the supply or the industry environment. For example, terrorist attacks in a destination, bad weather conditions, etc. If the conditions change, this category may be turned into effective demand category.

3.3.3 No Demand

Be it anywhere, there will be a category of population who do not like to travel or are unable to travel due to some reasons. They give rise to a 'no demand' category (Page, 2003; Cooper et al. 1996).

3.4 INDICATORS OF TOURISM DEMAND OF A POPULATION

We have to represent demand in a quantifiable term. As stated before, number of tourists are considered most commonly. But that is also not specific as in most of the cases, the number of tourists shown in tourists statistics is not the exact number of individuals, rather it can be the number of trips instead. The description given by Cooper et. al., (2000) throws some light on this. According to them, *travel propensity* is the most useful indicator of an effective or actual demand. Travel propensity is a term, which refers to the penetration of tourism trips in a population. In other words, it is related to the tendency of the population to engage in tourism activities. There are two forms of travel propensities described below.

3.4.1 Net Travel Propensity (NTP)

This measures the travel propensity among individuals in the population, i.e., it refers to the percentage of the population that takes at least one tourism trip in a given period of time. It does not consider the number of trips undertaken by a person.

3.4.2 Gross Travel Propensity (GTP)

The measurement is done on the 'trips', not on 'individuals'. Thus, the term refers to percentage of trips taken by the population in a given period of time. If a person is taking three trips in a particular period of time, then 'three' will be the number considered for finding out gross travel propensity (Cooper et al., 2000).

Travel frequency can be found out from these, by dividing gross travel propensity by net travel propensity. Due to suppressed demand and no-demand categories, net travel propensity can never be 100%, but in societies with high travel tendency, the gross travel propensity can go beyond 100%, even up to two or three times.

3.5 DETERMINANTS OF TOURISM DEMAND

The demand for engaging in tourism depends on different factors associated with a tourist's personal side or from the supply side. The person may be motivated to travel, but the ability to do so depends on various factors. Such factors can be called *determinants of demand* for tourism and they are present in both the living environment of the person as well as the destination environment. Cooper et al. (2000) have identified lifestyle and life cycle factors. *Lifestyle factors* arise as part of his or her life and also as part of his or

Table 3.4: Determinants of tourism demand

Economic Determinants	Social-Psychological Determinants	Exogenous Determinants (Business environment)
Discretionary income	Demographic factors	Availability of supply of resources
GNP/per capita income	Travel preferences	Economic growth and stability
Cost of living	Motivation	Technological advancement
Tourism prices	Benefits sought	Accessibility
Private consumption	Perception of destination	Political and sociological environment
Transportation cost	Images of destination	Levels of development
Cost of living in relation to destination	Awareness of opportunities	Natural disasters
Exchange rate differentials	Attitudes about destinations	Epidemics
Promotional expenditure	Cognitive destinations	War and terrorism
Marketing effectiveness	Amount of travel time	Social and cultural attractiveness
Physical distance	Amount of leisure time	Degree of urbanization
Relative prices among competitive destinations	Paid vacation	Special factors
	Past experience	Restrictions, rules, laws
	Life span	Barriers and obstacles
	Physical capacity, health, wellness	
	Cultural similarities	
	Affiliation	

Source: Uysal, 1998

her engagement with various activities for supporting his or her life to be a successful one. This includes level of income and employment, amount of holidays/free times, the level of educational attainment, and a person's ability to be mobile (mobility). *Life cycle factors* are the factors that automatically evolve during the lifespan of a person which may either discourage or encourage the travel propensity of a person. The age group in which the person belongs to (domestic age), household size, race and gender are the major life cycle factors. Other determinants of tourism demand and travel propensity, most of which connected to the country of origin, mainly include factors such as level of urbanization, economic development, political and technological factors.

Certain personal factors are predominant. If the educational level is more, it can lead to increased tourism demand. The same is the case of mobility. Demographic factors like age, gender, and religion also matter. Very aged and infants have lower travel propensity. Youngsters can travel more. Increased income level causes increased disposable/discretionary income and that can lead to increased travel tendency. Same is the case with employment. If free time is more together with adequate provision for paid holidays, then the tendency to travel will also be more. Large family size limits travel and the stage of family life cycle is also relevant. Retired families with good health conditions have increased travel propensity these days. Tourism is *price elastic* product, primarily, and less cost of travel can attract more mass tourists. The cost of products and services is also important. Competitive price availability can inspire inflow of tourists. Weak currency tempts to have more financial complications and can affect travel.

There are many geographical factors that influence travel demand. Seasonality is a serious determinant of a destination's tourism demand. Seasonal variations can help in increased inflow of tourists. Accessibility is a significant factor. Increased accessibility, location and less distance can be favourable. Availability of a range of natural and cultural attractions is definitely an important factor for a tourist destination for maintaining its demand. Increased urbanization and economic development can be catalytic in tourism growth. Regarding a destination, its image, both organic and induced, and the way marketing communication activities are done also act as determinants of demand. It can be induced and enhanced by quality marketing communication and promotion by the destinations. The channels used for marketing communication too play a part in it. Technological developments in the origin country as well as in the destination country are advantageous. Safety and security is of increased relevance particularly as the world is suffering from terrorism. Quality of the services offered by the industry also contributes. Having travel formalities favouring tourists can attract more visitors. Government policy and regulations with regard to Visas, health checks, and insurance come under the category of political factors. Regulations on supply and tourist movements, transport regulations and bilateral agreements for air travels are also determining factors in tourism demand.

3.6 MEASURING DEMAND FOR TOURISM

The measurement of demand for tourism is a relatively recent activity. The scientific measurement of tourism demand assumes great importance in view of the fact that the countries benefiting from this activity need to know how it affects their economy. Nowadays, visitors' attitudes, behaviours, purchasing patterns, etc., are also considered for measurement since all these have much importance for planning, developing, managing and marketing of various elements in tourism industry. Countries usually adopt different methods for the measurement of demand for tourism. Both international and domestic tourism are measured separately since both give different dimensions of contributions to the society. The importance of measurement of tourism demand is of different kinds. Some of the major reasons, according to Page (2007), are given below.

- To understand why and how significant tourism is for destinations, regions as well as countries, in terms of the scale and value of visitors. The revenue generated due to visits of tourists and multiplier values are commonly considered for measuring the economic contribution of tourism.
- Generally, international tourism is considered for measurement. Since it acts as an invisible export and a fast earner of foreign exchange, tourism has an important role in the balance of payments of a country.
- To assist the tourism industry and government in making policies, planning, and anticipating the type of facilities and services required for tourism to grow and prosper. The demand statistics is necessary for forecasting and predicting the future and such activities will help the developers to make plans and policies.
- To assist in understanding what type of marketing is needed to reach tourists as consumers and what factors can persuade them to visit a country or destination. The statistics about visitors, their characteristics, activities engaged, facilities used, product purchasing behaviour, etc., are important for the marketers. The marketing strategies can be developed on the basis of such facts and promotional activities can also be designed based on them.
- To help the tourism industry to make decisions about what type of action is required to develop and promote tourism business and further develop it in this area.
- For understanding the trends: The statistics on tourist arrivals can give information about the trends, fashions and changes in the case of tourist arrivals. This is also necessary for the authorities engaged in planning and development.

3.7 PROBLEMS OF MEASURING TOURISM DEMAND

Measuring tourism demand is an arduous task, particularly since it is not easy to conduct surveys on tourism. In general, there are a number of reasons that limit measurement of tourism demand. The following are the major issues faced while measuring tourism demand:

- Tourists are a transient and highly mobile population. Data collection is not that easy.
- Interviewing such mobile populations is often undertaken in a strange environment like at ports, or points of departure or arrival, where the possibility of disruptions can be high.
- Other variables such as weather can influence the responses (Latham, 1989).
- Tourist markets are located far away from destinations and hence doing household surveys, etc., is difficult.
- Chance of double/multiple counting is high as tourist is a mobile customer, and can cause duplication of data.
- While on tour, tourists are in the consumption phase and hence data gathering mechanism can be a disturbance for them.
- Tourists experience measurement is accurate after the completion of the tour, but getting them available for data collection has remote chances after the holidays.

Data collection, analysis and presentation, the various stages in demand measurement, need knowledge, experience and expertise. There is a need for a dedicated team with ample expertise for doing it. In tourism, dedicated teams under the aegis of the following are often seen involved in the measurement of its demand:

- Specialized organizations, like market research companies.
- Tourism consultants
- National tourism organizations
- Public sector agencies
- Destination management organizations
- Industry/professional associations
- International organizations at regional as well as global level.

3.8 TOURIST STATISTICS

In general, tourism demand is measured and presented in the form of *visitor arrivals* and the amount spent. The first category involves counting the number of people who arrive at a destination, the number of nights or days they spend. This category is extremely useful for the industry in general. Accommodation sector relies much on the data for the number of nights. The expenditure made by tourists is also of much significance for the destination and some other stakeholders of tourism. Another category of measurement is *information about the visitor*. Hence, altogether, three types of tourist statistics can be identified in the tourism sector (Bhatia, 2006; Cooper et al. 2000). They are volume, value and visitor profile statistics. A brief account on each of them follows.

3.9 VOLUME STATISTICS

This is the most used quantified form of tourism demand. Measurement of this, which shows the volume of tourist arrivals, takes place at various levels across the world, such as at local, state, national, regional and global levels. Though it is assumed as a measurement of the number of people who visit a destination, it is actually the number of trips, not individuals included in the statistics. If a person is taking three trips in a year to a country, then in this statistics, it will be counted as three.

Table 3.5: International tourist arrival statistics (World and regions) (Millions)

	2000	2003	2004	2005	2010	2014
World	683	689.3	763	803	949	1133
Europe	393.3	396.2	41.4	438	488.9	581.8
North Europe	43.7	44.2	47.9	51	62.8	71.3
Western Europe	139.7	136.1	138.9	142.6	154.4	174.5
Central/Eastern Europe	69.2	68.3	78.6	87.8	98.4	121.1
South/Med. Europe	140.8	147.7	150.9	157.9	173.3	214.9
Asia & the Pacific	109.3	119.3	152.6	155.3	205.4	263.3
North-East Asia	58.3	67.6	87.6	87.5	111.5	136.3
South-East Asia	35.6	36.3	47.4	49.3	70.5	96.7
Oceania	9.2	9.0	10.2	10.5	11.4	13.2
South Asia	6.1	6.4	7.5	8.0	12.0	17.1
Americas	128.2	113.1	125.7	133.2	150.1	181
North America	91.5	77.4	85.8	89.9	99.5	120.4
Caribbean	17.1	17.0	18.2	18.8	19.5	22.4
Central America	4.3	4.9	5.8	6.3	7.9	9.6
South America	15.3	13.7	15.9	18.2	23.1	28.6
Africa	27.9	30.8	33.2	37.3	49.5	55.7
North Africa	10.2	11.1	12.8	13.9	18.8	19.8
Sub-Saharan Africa	17.7	19.7	20.4	23.4	30.8	35.9
Middle East	24.4	30.0	35.4	38.0	54.7	51.0

Source: UNWTO-Tourist Statistics (Highlights) 2015.

Total number of trips can be taken by multiplying the number of individuals by the average number of trips taken per individual (for a population). This is the easiest to obtain, but it fails to include the volume of days/nights since it is important for the accommodation sector. Hence, sometimes number of tourist nights are also considered for finding out volume statistics. Then the above given equation will be changed as:

Total tourist nights = Number of tourist trips × Average length of stay (nights stayed)

3.10 VALUE STATISTICS

Value statistics is also called *expenditure statistics* and it provides the basic information on the economic contribution of tourism to a region. Tourist receipt is a very common type of economic information provided as part of this statistics. Usually, such receipts are shown in two forms such as direct and indirect. Expenditure made by tourism forms the base for value statistics. All the expenditures by tourists will be considered in this statistics except payments made to international airlines.

3.11 VISITOR PROFILE STATISTICS

This type of statistics, also called *characteristics statistics*, measures the characteristics and/or behaviour of the visitors and of the visit. This statistics is important for the marketing and promotion activities. With regard to the visitor, the details like profile of them including age, sex, group, type, nationality, occupation and income are gathered. On the other hand, the profile of the visit is also collected which can include the details about origin and destination, mode of transport tourists are using, purpose of visit, length of stay, accommodation used, activities engaged, etc. All these help in understanding tourist behavior and visitor profile statistics is very much relevant for marketing and promotion, in addition to the significance for planning and developmental activities.

Table 3.6: Foreign exchange earnings (FEEs) (in crores) from tourism in India

2001	15083	2008	51294
2002	15064	2009	53700
2003	20729	2010	64889
2004	27944	2011	77597
2005	33123	2012	94487
2006	39025	2013	107671
2007	44360	2014	12330

Source: Ministry of Tourism, India Tourism Statistics, 2014, Government of India.

3.12 METHODS OF MEASUREMENT

Measuring international tourist statistics is easier compared to domestic as they have to pass through entry and exit points. Different methods can be used to gather data. Some of them are listed below.

- Volume statistics can be obtained using counting procedures at the entry and exit points of a country.
- Records of international carriers can also be used for compiling international volume statistics
- Registration at accommodation establishments can give volume statistics, and to some extent, visitors profile statistics also.
- Sample surveys can be conducted for obtaining visitor profile statistics and value statistics.
- Foreign exchange statements can be utilized for getting value statistics of international tourism.
- Survey of suppliers can be conducted for the value and visitor profile statistics.
- The demand statistics can be taken from the records of government related formalities like visa, emigration, foreigner's registration, etc.

Domestic tourism demand can be measured using different survey techniques:

- Sample surveys can be undertaken in the households (*household survey*) for getting visitor profile statistics and value statistics, mainly.
- Surveys can be done while tourists are on their course of journey (*en route survey*). Care has to be taken to choose strategic points of time to approach them.
- Surveys can be done with tourists while they are in the destinations as well. Care has to be taken not to disturb them and different methods can be used like questionnaires and interviews.
- *Registration at accommodation establishments* can give volume statistics, and to some extent, visitors' profile statistics also.
- Sample surveys can be done with other suppliers of tourism products.

Demand measurement is undertaken by almost all destinations and countries, and statistics are published regularly, usually on annual basis. International organizations too undertake demand measurement and publish statistics on regular basis. UNWTO and WTTC take the lead role in compiling the country-wise statistics and publishes it annually. In India, all state governments and Ministry of Tourism, Government of India measures and publish tourism statistics regularly.

3.13 CONCLUSION

There are many reasons that prompt people to travel. It is important for those involved in tourism development and supplying tourism products to understand the reasons why people engage in tourism. These factors are commonly referred to as *travel motivators*. In fact, a number of theories related to tourist motivations and still research is going on in this area. *Tourism demand* is a term used to indicate the quantity of tourism that occurs in a tourist destination. There are a number of factors that determine tourism propensity of a population. Some of the factors like income, availability of free time, educational level, mobility, household size, etc., are the factors related to a person, and level of urbanization, economic development, etc., are the factors present in a region or a country that determine tourism demand. Tourism demand in a destination is generally measured as *tourist statistics* (three types). While volume statistics assess the trips taken by tourists, value statistics focuses on the expenditure by the visitors. The third type, visitor profile statistics measures the characteristics of tourism. Various methods, like sample surveys, are used to measure the above statistics. Due to the peculiar nature of tourists as consumers, the measurement of various aspects of tourism demand is not very easy.

Key Terms

Motivation	Gross travel propensity
Travel motivator	Tourism demand
Wander lust	Effective demand
Sun lust	Tourist statistics
Allocentric motivators	Volume statistics
Mid-centric motivators	Value statistics
Travel propensity	Visitor profile statistics
Net travel propensity	Tourism measurement

Review Questions

Short Answer Type Questions

1. What do you mean by travel motivator?
2. Distinguish between 'sun lust' and 'wander lust' category of visitors.
3. Discuss various approaches to classify travel motivators.
4. Discuss how to classify travel motivators on the basis of interrelated psychographic types, as suggested by Plog.

5. Write some examples for allocentric and mid-centric travel motivators.
6. List Remumbo's travel motivators.
7. Explain the concept of tourism demand.
8. Discuss the elements of tourism demand.
9. What is travel propensity? Explain how to indicate travel propensity of a population.
10. Enumerate the factors that determine tourism demand of a population.
11. List some of the factors related to a country or a region that determine travel propensity.

Essay Type Questions

1. Discuss the reasons why destinations should measure tourism demand.
2. Explain various types of tourist statistics.
3. Discuss the importance of tourism demand measurement.
4. Elucidate the reasons why tourism measurement is considered difficult.
5. What are the methods that can be used to measure tourism demand.

4

TOURISM INDUSTRY

Learning Outcomes

After studying this chapter, you will be able to:

- understand the nature and characteristics of tourism industry;
- identify the components of tourism industry;
- explain the role of government in tourism development and promotion;
- comprehend the role and functions of intermediaries in tourism;
- explain what are travel agencies and tour operators;
- understand the relationship between tourism and transportation;
- understand various modes of transport and their role in tourism; and
- explain the meaning of accommodation and different types of accommodation units.

4.1 INTRODUCTION

Many argue that tourism, instead of treating it as an industry, has to be considered an economic sector representing a wide range of businesses and other economic entities. Yet, along with its growing significance, tourism is increasingly being represented as an industry. Moreover, tourism has gained official industry status in many countries, including India. It was during the seventh five year plan (1985-90), tourism was accorded industry status in India. Moreover, the concept of product is also relevant as tourism offers products for tourists to consume, which can help to satisfy the needs and wants of tourists who are the ultimate consumers. Hence, considering tourism as an industry has gained much more significance in this era of modern tourism. Furthermore, this is a rather diverse sector with complex interactions and interrelationships among various sectors in it. Also, for understanding its complexity and the inherent characteristics, it is better to consider tourism as an industry.

4.2 TOURISM INDUSTRY: THE CONCEPT

Tourism industry is defined from different perspectives. Some of the definitions focus on the range of businesses involved in it. For instance, Leiper (1990) suggests that *tourism industry* is defined as the range of businesses and organizations involved in delivering tourism products. According to Leiper's system model, tourism industry is one of the elements of that system and it is an amalgam of diverse elements with necessary interactions and interrelationships. Riley et al. (2002) opined that tourism industry in general, can include a number of industries, like hotels and resorts, transport, tour operators, travel agencies, tourist attractions, conference business, tour guides, tourist information services, souvenir shops, beach vendors, relevant government offices, NGOs and educational establishments. Complex linkages and interrelationships exist among those different individual components of the tourism industry. Each sector has its own role and relevance in this composite tourism industry. A more explicit way of describing tourism is to consider it as '... representing the sum of those industrial and commercial activities producing goods and services wholly or mainly consumed by foreign visitors or by domestic tourists' (Ritchie and Goeldner, 1994). Tourism demand is first created and then satisfied by the concentrated marketing efforts of a diverse range of organizers, by providing tourists the needed products. These altogether constitute the world's largest and fastest growing industry (Holloway, 2006). It is important for all the components of the industry to play their respective roles well in order to make tourism successful. The industry is featured with some common characteristics that are unique to some extent. Some of them are:

- Service orientation
- Fragmentation of supply
- Labour intensive
- High fixed costs of service operations.
- Heterogeneity
- Dominant role of intermediaries
- Seasonality and fluctuating demand
- Immovability
- High level of interdependence
- Rigidity of supply
- Price elasticity

As an industry, tourism is highly service driven. It consists of industries with service orientation, predominantly. Transport services and hospitality industry, the major two industry elements are classified as service sectors. The experience a tourist gains from the phenomenon of tourism is intangible in nature. There are also some tangible elements that contribute to tourism, yet the majority has significant service orientation. Fragmentation of supply is another feature. Tourism industry is a combination of diverse industries. Each of them produces discrete products and are located at different geographical locations. Airlines are predominantly located in the *transit route region* (TRR). While accommodation sector is mainly in the destination, outbound tour operator is situated in the origin region/tourism market. As a result of this geographical fragmentation of the supply, it is a challenge for any destination to achieve coordination and integration of all components across all sub-sectors of the tourism industry. Tourism sector, primarily being a service-oriented sector, needs a large workforce to perform. United Nations World Tourism Organization reiterates the need for large amount of human resource requirements in tourism sector. According to them, "Tourism industries are largely labour intensive and provide jobs to many people. They include not only well trained professionals, but also a large number of workers with difficulties to find a job elsewhere, such as newcomers to the labour market (young people and migrants), women with family responsibilities who can only work part time, and workers with little qualification in general" (UNWTO, 2011). Tourism is one of the largest employment providers and according to World Travel and Tourism Council, Tourism, directly and indirectly "now supports nearly 277 million people in employment - that is 1 in 11 jobs on the planet" (WTTC, 2015).

Many of the tourism industries are characterized by *high fixed costs* and *low variable costs*. A firm which has large proportion of fixed cost in comparison with the total cost is said to have high fixed cost. Hotels and airlines, for instance, are featured with high fixed costs. This gives an opportunity to go for flexible pricing as well. *Breakeven* of all these organizations is usually at a much higher level of output and takes a long period in order to break even. *Heterogeneity*, another feature of tourism industry, represents the diversity included in the industry as well as the degree of variability of the industry in delivering services and other offerings at different times. Hospitality, attractions, transport, travel organizers/intermediaries and public sector agencies are the five fundamental sectors in tourism. Each of them has different products. Moreover, each of these sectors has a number of sub-sectors as well. For instance, hospitality involves two main segments such as accommodation and food and beverage. Consumers have varying attitudes and behaviours and likewise the products are also diverse. The other aspect of heterogeneity, the *degree of variability* in product offering and service performance is also relevant and is discussed in the section of product characteristics. *Intermediaries* have significant role in tourism. Traditionally, tour operators or wholesalers and travel agents have an important role in product design, pricing, distribution and promotion. Moreover, due to the distance involved in accessing the products to consume, the distribution system gained much significance. Furthermore, there is a need for coordination among various supply elements as they are geographically fragmented. Some of the destinations need interventions of intermediaries for regular inflow of tourists. Small scale businesses also depend much on tour operators for their businesses to survive. The advent of the Internet has led to many changes and the sector is facing disintermediation at a fast rate, yet tourism intermediaries remain key players in tourism sector world over.

Seasonality affects the industry severely in off season when tourist arrivals are very low. All these factors influence both supply and demand, and consequently production, distribution and consumption are affected. In addition to the economic aspects of seasonality, it has considerable impact on environment, society and culture as well. Due to *inseparability* and *perishability*, products have time limit as well. Therefore, the suppliers face severe challenges in managing the business. Ensuring cash flow and managing the expenses including salary, is a difficult task for the financial managers in the off seasons. In addition, the demand fluctuates according to changes in business environments as well. Tourism is a sensitive industry and hence small changes can affect businesses significantly. For instance, a severe fluctuation in the currency rates in destination region and generating region can even affect demand badly. Spread of a communicable disease too can affect demand. *Immovability* is perhaps a unique characteristic of tourism industry. The industries and their products cannot be moved in order to make consumption possible. Instead, the consumer has to travel and consume the product where it is located. A destination is composed of immovable natural and cultural attractions. Beaches, mountains, lakes, monuments and similar elements are to be enjoyed by tourists in locations where they are situated. Moreover, many other tourism industry elements are also immovable.

Tourism industries have high level of *interdependence*. The dependency and interrelationship among tourism industries may vary, but the same needs to be taken into consideration. The supply of one (for example, hotels in a destination) depends on the supply of another (such as air travel) and they complement each other. A change or an issue in one industry can affect the supply and delivery of service in the other sector. For example, a crisis due to a cyclone can affect a destination, which will impact demand for the destination and consequently all tourism industries in destination will also suffer. Similarly, the airline services to the destination will also face crisis. Overall, tourist satisfaction is usually the result of the sum of all levels of satisfaction in individual service delivery points and hence if the tourist receives a poor service from one individual industry, it can affect the overall tourist experience. Many of the industries in tourism cannot easily and quickly adjust to the increase in demand. Demand variation can occur at different occasions, but the supply capacity remains same in the short run. A hotel, for example, cannot add or remove rooms in line with a sudden demand variation. Implications of this are diverse. A decrease in demand can create supply issues as over capacity can cause wastage of resources. Many a times, the price reduction strategy is applied which affects the profit level. When demand increases, supply cannot be increased and therefore revenue maximization cannot be attained. Price levels may be increased depending on the increasing demand, yet, additional production requirement cannot be managed. This is applicable in industries like hotels, resorts, airlines, etc. In the long run, supply capacity can be modified depending on the emerging circumstances. Most of the tourism products are highly *price elastic*. Leisure tourism depend much on the discretionary income and consequently, price is a sensitive factor. In general, lowering of price can boost the demand and vice versa. Marketers have to consider this factor seriously as travellers are susceptible to price inducements and to other marketing efforts in respect to choices relating to destination, place and type of accommodation, and timing of the trip.

4.3 BUSINESS ENVIRONMENTS

Every business is influenced by a number of factors inside and outside the firm. Tourism, being a sensitive and international sector, the influence on environments is indeed very significant. Environment is a term usually used to represent all such factors that have some influence on a business or on an industry. Any variation in these factors may influence the businesses either positively or adversely, and the intensity of the influence depends on a number of factors including nature of the environmental factors, type of factors, quantum of variation in the factors and relationship of the factors with the business or the industry. According to Morrison (2006), "the business environment includes an array of dimensions, including economic, political, legal and technological factors. While only a few decades ago these external aspects were seen as centring to the home country of the business, the environmental horizons of the business have now widened to take on a host of international forces, which interact with national and local factors". In general, environmental factors are classified into two: *internal* and *external* factors, especially in the context of business organizations. Here, internal represents all such elements or factors that exist in an organization or industry and over which the industry has considerable control. For instance, organizational resources constitute an internal environment and it includes different types, like, financial, human and physical resources. Their significance in effective and efficient performance of the business is extremely high and the control over them for managers or authorities is relatively high as most of them can be changed, modified or increased as per the requirement.

External environment factors exist outside the organization or the industry and they too have significant influence. Organizations or the industries do not have any control over these factors. In the context of business environments, external environments may have two different kinds of factors: *task environment factors* and *general environment factors*. The former may include variety of factors that are related to competitors, suppliers, regulatory agencies and the like. The general environment factors influence all or major similar firms in the same manner. Demographic, economic, legal, technological, political or socio-cultural are such factors. Usually, *uncertainty* is a feature of external factors. Industries can forecast possible level of fluctuations, as accurate forecast is indeed extremely difficult. Businesses are usually alert on such fluctuations and authorities have to comprehend their nature in terms of complexity, dynamism and uncertainty. The degree of influence depends on a number of factors including number of possible external factors that influence the business, nature of the business, etc. Companies usually undertake different kinds of measures to analyze environments. Businesses and the industry usually analyze the environmental factors to see the strengths, weaknesses, opportunities as well as threats during crucial occasions, like, for strategic development. Understanding business environments is essential, especially in this hyper dynamic business environment. Political, economic, social and technological (PEST) analysis is considered a prerequisite for designing strategies.

Economic factors such as economic environment of a business have crucial influence in the case of most businesses. They are largely associated with the national economic system, and in the case of tourism, it is even associated with international economic circumstances. The economic health of a country has an impact on the travel and tourism industry. A country that has a strong economy can afford to invest in tourism, in terms of new infrastructure, supporting the industry through the public sector, and mounting promotional campaigns. Economic policies of the government, overall economic circumstances, economic growth of the country, capital markets, financial institutions, currency fluctuations, financial position of the country, financial crisis, global financial environment, etc., are the major economic environmental factors. *Currency fluctuation* is a major issue in tourism. If the destination currency loses its value, the inflow of tourists can go up and at the same time outbound tourism becomes costlier for the people of that country. *Inflation* also has the same impact. If inflation happens beyond a certain limit, then the cost of tourism products will increase which can adversely affect inbound tourism.

Legal factors include laws, regulations and similar aspects that influence businesses. Legal systems, legal protection for local/indigenous businesses, crime and law, law abiding tendency, and human rights regulations have some impact in managing businesses. Labour factors can control, limit, guide, dampen or even boost business growth. Usually, every country has a number of laws like companies act, factories act, employees welfare act, industrial disputes act, pension and provident fund act.

Political factors and terrorism are related to various aspects associated with political circumstances in the country. Some are related to the ideologies of the ruling parties and some others are related to the peaceful environment existing in the country. Political stability in the country, approach of the political parties to the industry, nature of political system and systems governance, political risks, national security, authority centre, corporate influence in politics, and the influence of foreign political factors have some role in successful management of businesses. Political favour always encourages tourism. Favourable VISA rules always result in increased inflow of tourists. The devastating terrorist attacks on New York's World Trade Centre on 11 September 2001 also had an impact on the worldwide tourism industry, as people were afraid to fly, particularly American tourists. The result was a decline in visitors to Britain, and a decline in worldwide travel for leisure and for business. In October 2002, terrorists bombed a resort in Bali, killing over 200 people. The tourism industry in Bali was ruined. It recovered only two years later.

Sociocultural factors include social values, customs, social stratification, social class migration, class structure, religious values, customs and traditions, desires and expectations of people, behaviour patterns, accepted behaviour norms, social institutions, and the like. These are not written laws or rules. Adherence of the values and beliefs is also a factor. Indeed, it is essential for businesses to understand the social and cultural environment.

For any industry, there will be *competitors* in the market, some direct while some others indirect. These competitors can be the businesses with products and/or services similar to or those that can be substituted in the place of some particular products. Competition can be not only from direct competitors, but also from substitute products, new entrants and 'competitive industry structure'. The issue of the substitute products is that it can easily replace another product when such a need arises. Any time, new entrants can emerge. Different situations which are likely to overcome the entry barriers, emergence of an existing one as a competitor by diversifying their products, and possible emergence of large firms with vertical integration strategies may emerge. The competitive structure is related to the quantum or nature of competition prevailing in the market, whether monopolistic, oligopolistic, or pure competition.

Technological developments challenge the businesses to utilize them to reap benefits. Latest IT advancements benefit as well as challenge the businesses. The pace of development in technology is amazing and that gives challenging times for the businesses. But the opportunities they provide are marvellous and become imperative to adapt to the latest technologies. Those who utilize the opportunities of latest technologies reap increased benefits, compared to those who are hesitant. Changes and advances in technology, national level adoption of technology changes, education and training, research and development capabilities, patents, technology transfer from outside to inside, and technology infrastructure creation are some other factors that influence tourism industries.

Demographic factors such as population size, its growth, age composition, population distribution, average family size, family life cycle, etc., influence businesses. These may change over time and may vary from country to country or region to region. Such changes can cause changes in consumer interests, buying behaviour, etc.

Physical forces include the geographical and ecological environments of a place. This has more influence in this age of sustainable development, especially in ecologically sensitive areas. Climatic conditions can affect the performance of the businesses as well. Climatic disasters, like cyclones, torrential rain and the consequent floods, Tsunami, volcano eruptions, etc., can dampen tourism. In addition, raw materials availability for many businesses may depend on the climatic conditions.

International factors are those that exist at the global level or in minimum two countries or more than that. Economic recession, regional wars, international organizations, rules, laws, human rights issues, regionalism, etc., can affect tourism in diverse ways.

4.4 COMPONENTS OF TOURISM INDUSTRY

Tourism industry consists of both private and public sector agencies. A symbiotic relationship exists between public and private sectors and effective partnership between them is crucial in the success of a tourist destination. The diversity in nature and functionalities of sub-sectors of the industry invite special attention. The major components of tourism industry are:

- Destinations and attractions
- Government organizations
- Intermediaries
- Transportation
  - Air transport
  - Land transport
    - Road transport
    - Rail transport
  - Water transport
- Accommodation
- Entertainment and recreation
- Shopping
- Hospitality
- Infrastructure

4.5 DESTINATIONS AND ATTRACTIONS

Destination is defined from different perspectives. Simply, *destinations* are the *raison d'etre'* of travel. Generally, it is viewed from a geographical perspective, and according to it destinations are specific areas, which travellers choose to visit and spend significant amount of time. Attractions form the core of a destination. Any facility, event or specialties that attract visitors to a particular place can be called *attraction*. Attractions have the ability to 'pull' the tourists to that particular destination. Attractions are the indispensable parts of tourism and are seen in the destination region of the tourism system. Attractions come in many forms and all such can be classified mainly under two headings, natural and manmade. *Natural attraction* comprises a variety of attractions and in this world of modern tourism, natural attractions have much importance. Beaches, lakes, mountains, wildlife, forests, valleys, rivers, landscape, spas, etc., are some of the natural attractions. Each destination will have different attractions or will have a combination of many attractions. Manmade attractions are usually the facilities, events or constructions, which are artificial, built/organized either solely for tourism purpose or some other purposes, but being used as an attraction for tourism purposes. Sports facilities, museums, forts, theme parks, zoos, etc., can be considered manmade tourism attractions. (Destination and attractions are discussed in detail in Chapter 6).

4.6 GOVERNMENT ORGANIZATIONS

In general, Governments act as a catalyst in tourism development and promotion. Yet, multiple roles are played by the government, directly and indirectly. Being a facilitator for tourism development and growth, Governments have other responsibilities as well, like immigration activities, negotiating aviation rights, visa regulations and so on. Such responsibilities are usually undertaken by different departments functioning under the government, not by the tourism authorities directly. Government's direct involvement in tourism helps in developing tourism by acting as a facilitator and promoter. On the other hand government also has to give attention to minimize environmental damage, cultural erosion and social 'impacts' that may be a result of tourism development. There are many other reasons why government is involved in tourism. The major reasons are:

- Foreign exchange earnings and their importance for the balance of payments.
- Employment creation and the need to provide education and training.

Table 4.1: Peter's inventory of tourist attractions

Cultural: Sites and areas of archeological interest, historical buildings and monuments, places of historical significance, museum, modern culture, political and educational institutions, and religious institutions.

Traditional: National festivals, arts and handicrafts, music, folklore, native life and customs.

Scenic: Wildlife, beaches, flora and fauna, mountains, resorts.

Entertainment: Participating and viewing sports, amusement and recreation parks, zone and oceanarium, cinemas and theatres, night life, cuisine.

Other attractions: Climate, health resorts or spas, unique attractions.

Source: Peters, 1969.

- Large and fragmented industry requires careful coordination for development and marketing.
- Maximizing the benefits to the host community.
- Spreading the benefits and costs equitably.
- To build image of the country as a tourist destination.
- Market regulation to protect consumers and prevent unfair competition.
- Provision of public goods and infrastructure as part of the tourist product.
- Protect tourism resources and the environment.
- Regulate aspects of social behaviour, for example, gambling.
- Monitor the level of tourism activity through statistical surveys (Cooper et al., 1993).

Worldwide, governments see their main role in relation to tourism as promoting a general economic environment favourable to the industry's development. The governmental agencies have lead roles in national and regional tourism development. government, through its various agencies, pursues the development and maintenance of tourism at the regional and national levels. Generally, government's involvement in tourism takes place in the following ways:

- Stimulating the economic growth
- Provision of infrastructure
- Fiscal revenue
- Border controls
- Spatial redistribution
- Protection of resources
- Regulatory safeguards
- Managing of exogenous events
- Stimulating social benefits
- Minimizing market failure (Pike, 2008).

The government has to provide also opportunities for lower income group of people so as to partake in tourism and recreational activities. In some countries, *social tourism* is promoted with this objective. They also interact with different tourist organizations at both national and international levels. Government has to offer a comprehensive regulatory framework within which tourism can operate competitively. Also in many a cases, government has to intervene in the process of tourism development. According to Davis et al. (1993), the functions of the state can be classified into five such as developer and producer; protector and upholder; regulator; arbitrator; and distributor. Coordination is another major role of government. Usually, every country has an apex body for developing tourism called National Tourist Office (NTO). Under them, various other agencies function. Government takes up a number of functions in the parlance of tourism and the major ones are:

- Initiates dynamism in the tourism sector and provides a new series of innovative products.
- Minimizes seasonality and ensures tourist arrivals in low seasons as well.
- Raises standards of tourism services and facilities.
- Generates research data/measures tourism.
- Develops indigenous entrepreneurship to promote equitable distribution of economic benefits.
- Promotes social tourism.
- Creates infrastructure.
- Planning and development.
- Ensures that visitor facilities are accessible.
- Attains and maintains regional and international recognition.
- Contributes intellectual leadership to tourism development.
- Provides opportunities for discussion and debate on tourism related issues.
- Provides training and development activities for working professionals to meet the standards of international tourism.
- Makes provision of data and information to various stakeholders on various aspects of tourism, as per the needs of the users.
- Ensures visitor management measures to avoid crowding and deterioration of quality of the destination.
- Creates image, marketing and promotion.
- International representation and creation of understanding with other countries.

As part of its functional duties, government also takes up the responsibility to encourage and facilitate the industry by providing of financial and other aids. Furthermore, policies are periodically assessed by the authorities to give direction to tourism development. In general, government itself develops infrastructure for the development of tourism. This may be initiated through public agencies. ITDC is an example for the same. Tourism is a sector vulnerable to crisis of various sorts, ranging from simple epidemic to terrorist activities. The effects of crisis on tourism necessitates serious concern. In such situations, government has to come up with urgent actions to ameliorate the issues and rejuvenate the sector to remain competent. In addition, it is a sector where political factors have to be favourable for growth and development.

Government is vested with the responsibility to initiate a conducive business environment for the industry to grow and develop. Regular research is inevitable for any sector to develop. Market researches pave the way for the industry to plan, develop strategies and market efficiently. Public agencies usually undertake periodic surveys in tourism. Marketing, promotion and brand building are also undertaken by the tourism authorities. Usually, the government takes up measures to ensure quality in offering tourism related services and products, and coordinate with various efforts of the sector to maintain quality and competitiveness. Promoting *tourism sustainability* is another task entrusted with the authorities, with support and assistance of international organizations, like UNWTO. While developing, tourism has to be considered a tool for preservation of cultural features, natural resources, social values and customs, and also to bridge the gap between the "haves and have-nots" as tourism is considered an effective solution to alleviate poverty.

4.7 NATIONAL TOURISM ORGANIZATION (NTO)

National Tourism Organization/National Tourist Office (NTO) is established for the promotion and development of tourism at the national level. NTOs usually have a statutory obligation to promote tourism. The world's first NTO is New Zealand Department of Tourist and Health Resorts, established in 1901 (NZTPO, 1976, in Pike, 2008). The trend continued and many famous destinations followed New Zealand in establishing NTOs. The first statutory legislation on tourism was made in 1969 in Britiain by the enactment of Tourism Act and it caused the formation of National Tourism Board of Scotland, Wales and England as well as British Tourist Authority. Good number of NTOs were formed during 1950s and 1960s. In the US, tourism promotion seriously began in 1961 when International Travel Act was passed.

NTOs have a position within the framework of tourism authority at the national level, which may be inside or outside the Ministry of Tourism of a country. It usually has a separate constitution, enacted by law and a board of directors appointed from outside government. This helps to have independence from the political system. Public money is the major source of funds for most of the NTOs. Some NTOs perform only marketing functions such as:

- Marketing and promotion: International and Domestic
- Development of products and human resources
- Planning and research: market research, planning and development
- External relations: public relations, corporate affairs, and organizational liaison.

Apart from NTOs, destinations may have *destination marketing organizations* (DMOs). (These are discussed in detail in another chapter).

4.8 INTERMEDIARIES

Intermediaries are the persons or agencies involved among the producers/suppliers and the final consumers. Be it any industry, a major task of intermediaries is to transform goods or services from a form that consumers do not want, to a product that they do want. Though the activities may differ, the role of intermediaries has much significance for some crucial tourism sectors. In tourism, it is possible to buy its components like, accommodation, transport, excursions, etc., directly from the producers. Here middlemen are not necessary. Yet, tourism involves middlemen transactions as well. In such cases, intermediaries become the link between the suppliers of tourism products and their potential customers and thus form the distribution system or the channels of distribution. The presence of intermediaries generates many benefits for the customers and the producers. The promotion expenses of the suppliers are reduced by the involvement of intermediaries. A traveller, by purchasing a package tour, can avoid search and transaction cost thus saving money, effort and time. Presence of intermediaries helps tourists to minimize uncertainties and confusions. Usually, tour operators, acting as intermediaries tend to offer lower prices.

According to Cooper et al. (2000), the benefits of the intermediaries for various elements of tourism system are:

Principals

- They can sell their services in bulk and through it, they transfer the risk of selling to the tour operator.

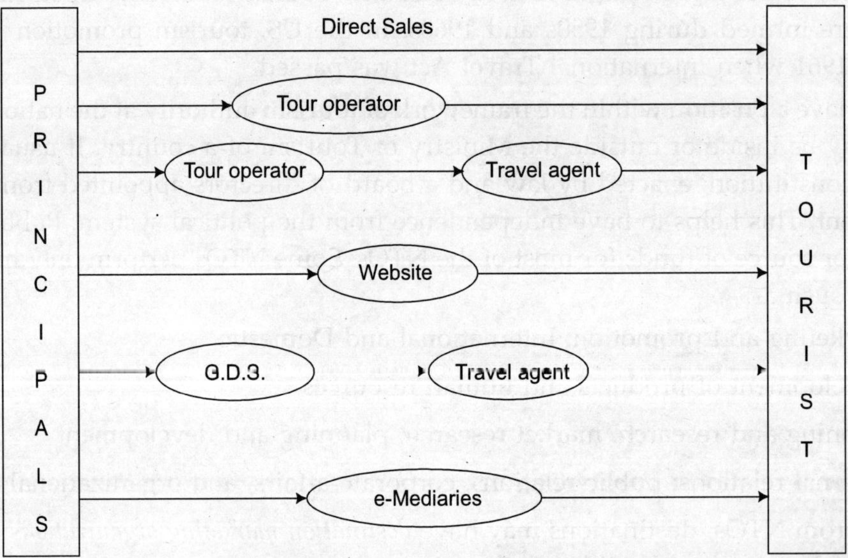

Figure 4.1 Travel distribution channels.

- They can reduce cost of marketing and promotion by focusing on travel trade, instead of consumer promotion.

Consumers

- They can minimize search and transaction costs, by being able to purchase inclusive packages.
- They can minimize uncertainties of travel due to specialized information and suggestions from intermediaries.

Destinations

The network of tour operators at the national and international levels enables destinations to reduce marketing and promotion costs. This is more relevant in the case of developing countries.

In addition to tour operators, intermediaries in tourism also include retail agents, GSAs, travel agents, e-mediaries and travel brokers. In certain cases, independent travellers put their own itinerary together. They can purchase the key components from suppliers, or from the outlets of suppliers or via retail travel agents. Direct purchase is more relevant in domestic tourism. Suppliers can establish their own outlets for their products. But, having own outlets is not easy for all kinds of suppliers. In main cities and centres, outlets are possible, but not everywhere. For example, airline companies have their own branches in big cities of the world, but sales mainly happen through general sales agents (GSAs) and retail travel agents. When we consider the complete range of products in tourism, you can identify a large number of intermediaries. For the airlines sector, the sales are happening through different channels. Airlines may have own offices/branches in major cities, yet in other areas, GSAs will be acting as representatives of airlines, and they may issue tickets, or may do it through IATA recognized travel agencies. In village areas, sub-agents without IATA recognition help customers in getting tickets. Electronic ticketing provision has changed the airline product distribution system significantly. The most common way of distributing foreign holiday travel is through inclusive tours packaged by tour operators and sold by travel agents. Some holiday packages are marketed directly to the public by the wholesalers. Computer Reservation System (CRS)/Global Distribution System (GDS) has also been introduced in the tour operation sector. In fact, travel agencies and tour operators, being the main intermediaries, are the major constituents in the distribution system of the tourism industry as well.

Intermediaries have a range of roles in the tourism sector. They are not just distributors of products of the principals. In fact, they perform a variety of value added functions, and of them the major functions are:

- Providing information on types and availability of services.
- Contacting current and potential consumers.

- Arranging reservation and other travel facilitators.
- Assembling services to meet travellers' needs.
- Preparing tickets and/or providing confirmation.
- Arranging extensive marketing data to tourism suppliers through databases containing targeted consumer behaviour information.
- Minimizing costs of acquiring new customers.
- Initiating repeat use of supplier channels.
- Marketing excess inventories.
- Risk taking by buying or booking large quantities of services in advance and then reselling them to individuals and groups (Cook et al., 2002).

Online intermediation is a new trend called *reintemediation*. A range of online intermediaries are emerging. Online travel agents like Expedia have significant share in the distribution of travel products. Almost all tourism products are now sold online. A brief description about travel agent and tour operator, the major intermediaries in tourism, is given below.

4.9 TRAVEL AGENT

Travel agent is defined as an intermediary selling the wholesome travel products or parts of products or a combination of the parts to the consumer (Goeldner and Ritchie, 2006). A travel agent can be viewed from marketing perspective as well as from legal perspective. In the former case, it is an agent like a middleman, acting on behalf of clients, making arrangement with suppliers of travel products and receiving commission from the clients. On the other hand, on legal terms, it is an agent of the principals, like airlines, cruise companies, etc., to sell their products. According to Page (2003), the tasks performed by travel agencies include:

- Making reservation
- Provision of travel information
- Planning itineraries
- Calculating fares and charges
- Producing tickets
- Advising clients on destinations, resorts, transportation and other tourism products
- Communicating with other clients
- Arranging travel facilitators
- Maintaining accurate records of reservation
- Acting as middleman when customer's complaints occur.

Traditionally, travel agents were the main distributors of airlines products. The major types of travel agents, according to Cook et al. (2006), are:

- **Independent agencies:** Small agencies, unaffiliated to large organizations and privately owned, traditionally serving customers from walk-in locations or over telephone.
- **Agency chains:** Wholly owned, mega agencies that have large number of branch offices in many countries.
- **Agency channel-franchisees:** Semi-independent agencies affiliated with each other through franchisee organizations.
- **Consortium-affiliated agencies:** Independent agencies who link together through a consortium to gain competency.
- **Specialty agencies:** They offer limited services like cruise.
- **Corporate travel agencies:** Agencies offer services mainly to business clients. They may have branch offices at major client locations.
- **Corporate travel departments:** The department of a corporate agency functions as a travel agent for the organization (for its employees' travel requirements).
- **Home based agencies:** Agents who conduct services from their houses, mainly using electronic technology. This may be independent or affiliated with some organization.
- **Internet agencies:** Travel agencies which transact through the Internet.

Traditional travel agencies are facing challenges from the Internet. The sector is now adopting diversification strategies along with specialized services in order to remain competitive.

4.10 TOUR OPERATOR

A tour operator puts together the tour components and sells the tour package through his or her own company, retail outlets and/or through approved retail travel agents (Goeldner and Ritchie, 2006). According to Laws (1997), tour operator is "a company specializing in packaging the elements of inclusive holidays for sale to clients". Though it fulfills a number of roles, the basic role is to organize and package different elements of the tourism experiences, offer them for sale to the public through different channels, and to operate the tour as per the pre-set itinerary (Page, 2003). These definitions reiterate the significance of tour operation.

Another definition, as suggested by Yale (2001), says that a *tour operator* is "a person or a company who purchases different items that make up an inclusive holiday in bulk, combines them together to produce package holidays and then sells the final products to the public either directly or through travel agencies". Usually, such packages are

Table 4.2: USTOA: Top ten reasons to book a package tour

The United States Tour Operators Association's Top 10 Reasons to Book a Tour in 2013 were:

Affordability

By buying in bulk and negotiating special rates for various services like accommodation and transportation, achieve substantial economies, which is passed on to the consumer. Besides, tourists can have additional savings when the packages include select meals, hotel tips and sightseeing.

Peace of Mind

A properly planned package and the tour operated by a professional team will bring peace among tourists since it minimizes the uncertainty, trust about the proficiency of the operator, presence of escort or other assistants in emergency. Also payment for the package is made in advance which makes tourists more comfortable.

Unparalleled Access

As part of a tour group, tourists don't have to wait for services as these have been arranged in advance.

"E Factor"

Tourists, nowadays prefer to go beyond the tourist hotspots and experience the history, culture, and distinct tastes of a destination. Professional tour operators provide some exotic experiences in addition to the usual stuff. This adds to the tourist's experience.

Variety

There are a large number of itineraries to choose from and even customized packages to suit peoples' requirements. Diversity of offerings makes the tour operation business more attractive.

Guaranteed Accommodations

Getting quality accommodation service and confirmation of the same is essential. Tour operators ensure this.

Convenience

All elements of a tour are available at convenience for the tourist since the tour operator is responsible for arranging them.

Insider Knowledge

Details about the attractions and places to be visited are arranged with the support of local experts which enhance the quality of the tourist experience.

Freedom

Nowadays, itineraries are created with more flexibility that provides enough time to explore particular points of interest on one's own. Local tour guides can assist in this context.

Protection

The association ensures protection from financial issues, in case if something like bankruptcy or insolvency occur, to the member tour operator and hence, booking a tour will not end up in a loss to the potential tourist. "In addition to protecting consumer's vacation, these operators must meet strict requirements of ethics and integrity in their tour offerings and advertising."

Source: UTSOA, 2013.

Table 4.3: Elements of a package tour

Basic elements
• Aircraft seat
• Accommodation at the destination
• Return and transfer from airports to the accommodation
• Services of a tour operator
• Insurance
Optional add-ons
• Car hire
• Excursions
Alternative forms
• Multi-destination packages, i.e., visiting more than one destination
• Optional extension of the package to expand the itinerary
• Linear tours by coach operators

Source: Page, 2003.

called *all inclusive* packages, which consist of elements like international travel, domestic travel, accommodation, sightseeing, etc. Usually, the tour operator gets the services in negotiated rates from the suppliers. They work with all segments of the tourism industry to negotiate rates, block space and coordinate varied services to conduct the tour smoothly at an inclusive price.

4.11 TYPES OF TOUR OPERATORS

Different types of tour operators like *inbound* (handling incoming foreign tourists), *outbound* (handling outgoing tourists), *domestic operators* (handles tours within the country), *mass market operators* (those who concentrate on mass markets), and *specialist tour operators* (specialist to certain places/types of destinations) are there in the market.

4.11.1 Inbound Tour Operator

Inbound operator handles a foreign tourist since its arrival at the entry point. The major operation commences with the transfer from the arriving airport to the hotel. The duty of an inbound tour operator ends with bringing back the tourist to the exit port after the visit.

Their operations mainly include 'meet and greet' during arrivals, and transfers, and arrange accommodation services, excursions/sightseeing trips, optional trips, and specialised services. Their focus remains on foreign markets and developing products and services to cater to the tourist requirements. Usually, an itinerary is followed, though in certain cases the duties are limited to arranging certain facilities. At times, inbound

Table 4.4: External factors that impact tour operation business

Foreign exchange rates	Interest rates at home and abroad
Inflation at home and abroad	The cost of aviation fuel
Unemployment rate in tourist market	Political changes in home and abroad
Outbreaks of diseases	Natural disasters
Wars	Terrorist activities
Airport delays and aircraft accidents	Fashion
Weather and climatic conditions in home and abroad	General negative image and publicity

Source: Yale, 2001.

operators act on behalf of tour operators situated in the tourist market country. Some of them act as *ground handling agents*, to arrange accommodation and transport facilities along with 'meet and greet' services.

4.11.2 Outbound Tour Operator

An outbound operator serves tourists belonging to their domestic or regional market to visit foreign countries. The focus of marketing is the local market. They may design and operate their tours, working with partners at the destinations or may go for already designed tours of inbound operators located at the destination. Outbound operation is more arduous as matters related to international travel also have to be dealt with.

4.11.3 Domestic Tour Operator

Domestic tour operators develop, market, organize and operate tours for the people of the same country to visit places within the country. Both management and marketing of tours are relatively easier since the travel takes place within the country and the source market is also the same country. Some of them perform duties similar to those of outbound operators whereas some others operate in a way akin to that of ground handling agents. Bigger firms usually undertake both the functions. Coach tours are also common in this category.

4.11.4 Mass Market Tour Operator

Mass market operators organise tours to established destinations and the focus is on groups having more number of tourists. Package tours are the main products and the profit is earned from volume sale as margin from each sale is less. Moreover, the commission received from the suppliers is also more.

4.11.5 Specialist Operators

Unlike mass tourism, specialist tours are not designed for established destinations or attractions, rather they are initiated for people with specific motivation to experience something different in their life or as part of a passion. Distinguished tourism products are consumed in this category. This category is dominated by small- or medium-scale operators. Adequate knowledge about the attractions, mastery of the necessary skills for operating such tours, etc., matter in remaining competitive in the special interest tour operation sector.

Other types of tour operators, as described in Table 4.5, have gained prominence over the years.

Table 4.5: Types of tour operators

Coach tour operators: Coach tour operator use buses/coaches for conducting tours, usually within a country.
Rail tour operators: Some operators conduct tours using rail transport. Domestic tours are more suitable for such kind of tours, though there are international rail based tours also.
Ferry tour operators: Some operators use ferries for transporting tourists from origin point to their destination.
Charter tour operators: Mass tour operators may use charter flight services for conducting tours. Either they hire a charter flight or may adopt a part charter arrangement.
Skiing operators: Skiing is a passion for many, and organizing tours to skiing destinations is a trend that began many decades ago.
Cycle tour operators: Tours using bicycles are in vogue nowadays. Cycle tourism is spreading to almost every part of the world. Usually, these tours are organized in countrysides.
Safari operators: Safaris are organized to different geographical terrains, like forests and deserts. Automobile vehicles are used in certain cases. Animals like elephants and camels are used for safaris in some locations.

4.12 TRANSPORTATION

Accessibility is one of the primary elements of tourism. Tourism is the outcome of the travel and stay of people. The provision of adequate, safe, comfortable, fast, convenient and cheaper public transport is a prerequisite for mass-market tourism. In most cases, tourism has been developed in areas where extensive transportation networks are feasible and have the potential for further development. Tourism demand has stimulated rapid development of transportation. Development in technology has been helping the transport sector to develop and expand. Transportation encompasses different modes of travel. The importance of this sector in relation to tourism is mainly in the following ways:

- **Reach the destination:** Transport provides the means of travel to the destination from the tourist's place of origin, and back again.

- **Internal transportation:** Transport provides the means of travelling in and around the destination after reaching there.
- **Inter-destination transportation:** Tourist can travel from one destination to another using various transport modes.
- **Attraction:** Transport can be a main feature of a tourist trip when the form of transport itself is one of the main reasons for taking the trip.

4.13 MODES OF TRANSPORT

On the basis of the medium in which transportation activities take place, transportation can be classified into three: *land based, air based* and *water based.* Each form has its own relevance and importance.

- **Land transport:** There are a variety of land based transport forms in the global tourism sector. *Road transportation* is one of the most important forms and in the last century, it has grown tremendously. It involves a range of different forms of transport. Bus (including coaches), cars, rental cars, taxi services, etc., are the major road transport modes. The developments that took place in automobile sector during 1920s revolutionized the holiday and recreational habits. Road transportation became the primary mode of transport, and it still remains a major one. *Rail transportation* is another major category. Rails are being used in different forms. Trains are perceived to be safe, inexpensive and offer convenience of movement within the carrying unit. In the USA, railways do not have much relevance, but the rest of the world relies much on railways. Rail transportation is considered a highly environment friendly form of transport. Technological developments has impacted rail transportation also; it provides luxury, safety and speed. Though many other forms of transport emerged with more speed, safety and comfort, yet railways remain an important mode of transport. Independent/free tourists rely on railways more than others. *Passenger rail transportation* is a component in travel anywhere in the world and it is the most important transportation mode especially in countries like India, South Korea, Japan, and China.
- **Air transport:** The last sixty years have seen the transformation and growth of air transport from its infancy to becoming giant. Throughout the 20th century, air transportation has been experiencing technological advancements and various factors helped in managing the air transport industry to become a popular and mass transportation mode. Equipment manufacturers, airports, air navigation, air traffic control and airlines are the fundamental components of transport (Holloway, 1996).

- **Water transportation:** Transport by water-borne vessels of all kinds continues to play an important role in this industry. Reaching a destination by sailing has been an important method of transport since the first primitive boat was built. Cruises, luxurious ships exclusively used for leisure purposes, are gaining increased significance in tourism. In fact, *cruise tourism* is one of the fastest growing segments in international tourism. Boats, ferries, houseboats, canoes, hydrofoils, etc., are also used for tourist transportation. Inland waterways include rivers, lakes, fiords and canals and inland transportation is often associated with sightseeing rather than as a means of transport from one place to another.

4.14 ACCOMMODATION AND HOSPITALITY

'Accommodation' is one of the most vital components of tourism. *Stay* is an activity which necessitates to have accommodation and eating (food and drink) facilities. People living away from home, whatever the need be, they need to stay somewhere that provides all the comforts of home. Here, the concept of accommodation and catering becomes relevant. Thus, accommodation and catering sectors become the most essential components of tourism industry. Accommodation provides the base from which tourists can engage in the process of staying at a destination. The development of accommodation has accompanied the growth of resorts, areas of tourism activity and the demand to visit specific areas. The accommodation sector comprises widely differing forms of sleeping and hospitality facilities which can be conveniently categorized as either *serviced* or *non-serviced*. In serviced sector, services including catering and housekeeping are provided. Hotels, motels, guest houses, etc., come under the category of serviced accommodation. In the other category, such services are not offered. Apartments, villas and campsites come under the category of self-catering, and mostly non-serviced. Accommodation sector, particularly hotels and resorts, provide facilities for business travel, like facilities for meetings, recreations and entertainment. Moreover, they can be appealing to tourists as well and provide ancillary services and products. Accommodation sector is often seen categorized, nationally and internationally. In fact, there is a fine distinction between classification and grading in accommodation industry. *Categorisation* refers to the division of accommodation into categories or groups based on type. Classification of tourist accommodation involves separating accommodation units based on the physical amenities and features which they may or may not possess. Classification often involves units on the physical amenities and features they have, like bedrooms (single, twin, double, triple), air conditioners, bathroom facilities, TV and the Internet, stocked bar, etc. Classification derived is often used for grading and many countries' hotel standards are government regulated. Grading provides qualitative judgements regarding amenities and facilities of accommodation units. A number of grading systems are used throughout the world,

Table 4.6: Types of accommodation establishments

Hotels and similar establishments

- Hotels, motels, roadside inns, beach hotels, residence clubs.
- Boarding houses, hostels, tourist residences and similar accommodation arranged in rooms and providing limited services.

Supplementary accommodation establishments

- Holiday dwellings, including collective facilities, under common management, such as apartment hotels and cluster of houses or bungalows arranged as dwelling type accommodation and providing limited services.
- Tourist camping establishments, e.g., caravans, trailers, mobile houses, etc.
- Social tourism accommodation establishments, e.g., youth hostels, tourist dormitories, holiday homes, etc.
- Other types like health establishments, holiday work camps, etc.

Private or special tourist accommodation

- Homes rented from private individuals.
- Accommodation provided without charge by relatives or friends.
- Own dwellings.
- Other private accommodation.

Source: Eurostat/McIntosh & Goeldner, 1990.

although the star (or other symbol) grading system is probably the most common. Under a star grading system, accommodation with only 1 star would be of the most basic quality whereas an establishment with 5 stars would offer the highest level of luxury and service.

Hospitality refers to the friendly reception and treatment of strangers. In tourism industry, hospitality is considered an important element and is usually connected with accommodation industry. In hotels, guest service is an important area which requires skills. A skilled employee, working in hotel industry, engaged in guest services can deliver service in connection with hospitality. But in general, hospitality can be considered a mix of many aspects of tourism such as friendly reception of tourists, extending positive attitude towards tourists' needs and wants and maintaining a conducive atmosphere by all the direct and indirect stakeholders of tourism, by which tourists can get satisfaction from the visit. Hospitality industry is also referred to as the *hotel/accommodation industry*.

Accommodation plays a vital role in the overall economic contribution which tourism makes at the local, regional and national levels. Finding out the share of accommodation sector in revenue generation in comparison to total tourism is difficult, but as a very general rule, perhaps 33% of the total trip expenditure is allocated to this sector (Cooper et al., 1993). The demand for accommodation industry products is highly volatile and fluctuates on seasonal and periodical bases. Perishability of the accommodation products

Table 4.7: Typology of tourism accommodation

Primary Accommodation		Secondary (Supplementary) Accommodation	Intermediary Accommodation
Hotels	Motels	Traveller bungalows	Eurotel
International hotels	Roadside motels	Traveller lodges	Aparthotel/Apartotel
Residential hotels	Suburb/Perimeter motels	Dak bungalows	
Commercial hotels	Tourist cabin	Forest lodges	
Resort hotels	Resort properties	Rest houses	
Summer resorts	Motor hotels	Circuit houses	
Warm winter resorts	City motor hotels	Holiday and conference centres	
Cold winter resorts	Highway hotels	Hostels	
Year round resorts		Youth hostels	
Health resorts		Bed and breakfast establishments	
Transient hotels		Paying guest accommodation	
Budget hotels		Railway retiring rooms	
Convention hotels		Dormitories	
Activity based hotels		Sarais (inns)	
Sports hotels		Dharamshalas	
Ski hotels		Self-service accommodation	
Boatels		Holiday houses	
Pilgrim hotels		Caravan/camping sites	
Airport hotels		Camping grounds	
Hotels on wheels		Tents	
Hotels for children		Rotels	
Lotel		Yachts	

Source: Kamra, 2000.

is an important concern for the marketers. Accommodation can act as a catalyst for a range of additional sales opportunities within the tourism and hospitality business. Upselling and yield management are two concepts in practice nowadays in the accommodation sector.

4.15 FOOD AND BEVERAGE

Food is an inevitable component of tourism and hospitality. Strange food items are always an attraction to visitors and hence cuisine sector has an importance in tourism. Tourists' needs vary greatly—some may wish to try local dishes, some may prefer something already familiar to them, and some may have special requirements. This difference stimulates the growth of the catering industry worldwide. India is famous for its variety of cuisines like Punjabi, South Indian, etc. Beverage (drinks) is also an inevitable component of international tourism. Food and drink have to be made available to tourists. Diverse range of catering establishments have emerged in this industry. Within the food service industry, three distinct market segments are identifiable. These are:

- **Restaurant market:** Restaurants and similar food service units.
- **Travel and lodging market:** Restaurants and other food units within the accommodation industries.
- **Contract feeding market:** Food vendors and catering services attached to large establishments and are usually subsidised or for welfare purposes. They function on the basis of contracts undertaken between the parties.

The following are some important catering establishments.

4.15.1 Restaurant and Cafe

There are places where tourists have an opportunity to mix with the local population while having a meal. Menus will be supplied to visitors to choose items they wish to consume. Waiters are there at the service of the visitors. The restaurant industry has been growing tremendously during the last several years.

4.15.2 Fast-food Establishments

The concept emerged during the late 1970s and has revolutionized the eating habits of people worldwide. Many fast food establishments have emerged all over the world and international chains have started their own outlets in major cities.

4.15.3 Pubs

Pubs were established as the centres of relaxation and drinks. Initially, it offered only snacks, but later, meals were added. The sale of alcoholic drinks proliferated pubs throughout the world.

Apart from these, the following are also part of food and beverage sector:

- Food processing technology
- Kitchen and catering equipment

- Restaurant supplies and related services
- Food products and beverages
- Ingredients and seasonings

4.16 ENTERTAINMENT AND RECREATION

Entertainment is an essential component in tourism. Usually, a destination will have some kind of entertainment and recreational activities, and such facilities will be a part of the total attractions of that place. Tourists spend a good share of their total expenditure on entertainment. An entertainment centre itself will be an attraction for tourism and the best example of it is the Disney World. Cinemas, fairgrounds, night clubs, zoos, race courses, theme parks, etc., come under the category of entertainment related attractions. Theme parks, developed from the idea of amusement parks, are now mushrooming everywhere.

4.17 SHOPPING

In any kind of tourism, shopping is an important component. Shopping, recently, is not just a laborious activity to buy essential goods; rather, it's increasingly being considered as a recreational activity as well. *Hedonistic shopping* is a trend visible in the parlance of tourism. Shopping is not restricted to the shops in the home city alone as curious shoppers fly across borders, travel to far away cities with the ambition of joyous shopping. Consequently, big cities are in a mad rush to lure hedonistic shoppers by seriously engaging in *mallification*, generating exclusive retailing options and by organizing shopping festivals. The pleasure of relaxed shopping coupled with travel, stay and sightseeing has made way for a new segment in tourism called *shopping tourism*. According to Timothy (2005), shopping tourists "are consumers who enjoy shopping as a leisure-time activity". Traditionally, shopping was part of tourism, but that remained mainly for buying products like souvenirs, which provide memories of the holiday they had.

In order to ensure shopping tourism, retailing amenities and options coupled with restricted forward and backward leakages are inevitable. In modern tourism, retailing has become a determinant in the competitiveness of a tourist destination. Correspondingly, many destinations are trying to ensure as many retailing options as possible. Retail centres of various kinds focused at floating population in order to be in a position to generate different shopping experiences as per the needs of the shoppers. The latest trend is of two kinds, one is that the shoppers travel and engage in holiday with the main purpose of shopping, and the other is travellers on holiday with other travel motivators and engage in hedonic shopping as well, apart from the traditional shopping of souvenirs. Economic significance of tourism related retail business lure destinations to integrate maximum retailing opportunities intended at the tourists so that tourists spend maximum while in the destination. United Nations World Tourism Organisation (UNWTO) in its survey on shopping tourism reveals that about 50% of tourists in Venice come specifically for shopping as well as cultural and leisure activities. In New York, shopping is reported to be the single most popular activity among all types of visitors. Almost 25% out of every dollar spent by visitors in NYC is spent on shopping.

Visitors traditionally purchase something from a destination, mostly, which is unique and indigenous. Souvenir trade is the vital component of tourism shopping. The items purchased from a destination give cherished memories of the tour, especially the souvenirs. The souvenir trade includes handicrafts, wood carvings, handloom items, pottery items, natural products, jewellery, fabrics, metalwork, metalware, stonework, embroideries, carpets, rugs, shawls, etc. Emporiums, shops, boutiques, cooperative outlets, governmental handloom and handicraft outlets, etc., are parts of souvenir trade. In certain cases, shopping itself becomes the major attraction. Now the scenario has changed and shopping itself has become a major motivation, thus shopping tourism has become a new sector. For example, the Dubai shopping festival lasts for one month and attracts plenty of tourists from the world over. Shopping is an activity by which the local trade and local community can draw maximum benefits from tourism.

4.18 INFRASTRUCTURE

Infrastructure represents all forms of constructions above or below ground needed by an inhabited area. It is mainly in the form of transportation, utilities and other services. In relation to tourism, infrastructure consists of those essential services catering to the needs of the tourist. These include accommodation and food, local transport, information centres and the necessary items to support tourism activities like roads, public utility services, and parking facilities. Usually, such amenities will vary according to the nature of the destination. Proper planning and other management principles have to be incorporated at the time of infrastructure development in a tourism destination. Improper approach can lead to degradation of environment and natural beauty, congestion, crowding, etc.

4.19 CONCLUSION

Tourism industry consists of several elements which vary in nature, size, and activities. Almost all the components share some common characteristics like seasonality, pricing flexibility, perishability, dominant role of intermediaries, etc. Attractions are factors that are inherent in a destination which 'pull' the tourists to visit. Manmade and natural are two categories of attractions. Government or the public agencies that are vested with the authority of tourism at the national as well as state level play a critical role in tourism development and promotion. Intermediaries have an important role in tourism as a range of middlemen are involved in its process. Travel agency and tour operator constitute the chief intermediaries. Travel agents act on behalf of clients for making arrangements with travel product suppliers and on the other hand, they act as agents of the principals. A tour operator basically organizes and packages different elements of the tourism experience and offer them for sale to the public using different marketing tools. Transportation is a major component of tourism industry. Transport and tourism are inseparable and the former developed hand-in-hand with the latter. A good transport network is essential for the success of a tourist destination. Accommodation industry is another vital sector in tourism. Quality accommodation is a prerequisite in success of any tourist destination. The industry consists of serviced and non-serviced categories and both have diverse range of industrial units. Food and beverage is another essential component of tourism industry. This offers food and beverage services to the guests. The above two categories together are commonly known as the hospitality industry. Shopping, infrastructure, entertainment and recreation are the other sectors of importance in the tourism industry.

Key Terms

Tourism industry
Tourism product
Attractions
Tourist destination
National tourist office
Intermediaries
Middlemen
Travel agency
Tour operator
Distribution system
Transportation
Accessibility
Internal transportation
Local transport
Land transport
Water transport
Rail transport
Air transportation
Bus
Scheduled services
Coaches
Charter services
Airport services
Car rentals
Customer service
Water transport
Ocean liners
Cruises
Ferry services
Accommodation
Serviced accommodation
Supplementary accommodation
Food and beverage
Entertainment and recreation
Shopping industry
Hospitality
Infrastructure

Review Questions

Short Answer Type Questions

1. Write a brief account on tourism industry.
2. Explain major characteristics of tourism industry.
3. Discuss the role of attractions in tourism.
4. Explain the role and responsibilities of government in tourism development.
5. What is an NTO? What are its functions?
6. Explain why intermediaries are so important in the tourism process.
7. What are different types of travel agencies?
8. What are the major functions and activities of intermediaries?
9. Who is a travel agent? What are the functions of a travel agent?
10. Explain the functions of a tour operator.
11. What do you mean by transportation?
12. Discuss how transportation is classified.
13. What are the various modes of air transport?
14. What are the various modes of road transport?
15. What are car rentals? Discuss the role of car rentals in tourism.
16. Discuss the importance of rail transportation in tourism.
17. What are the components of air transport?
18. Explain the relevance of cruises in tourism.
19. Write a short note on accommodation industry.
20. Explain the classification of hospitality industry.
21. Explain the significance of accommodation industry in tourism.
22. What do you mean by souvenir industry?
23. Give a brief account of tourism infrastructure.

Essay Type Questions

1. Write an essay on tourism industry. Discuss the role and relevance of each component of industry in tourism.
2. What is transportation? Discuss its various components. Elucidate the interrelationships between tourism and transportation.
3. Discuss the role and relevance of government in tourism. What are the steps that should be taken by government to promote sustainable development of tourism in that country?

5

TRANSPORT AND TOURISM

Learning Outcomes

After studying this chapter, you will be able to:

- elucidate the relationship between air transport and tourism;
- understand the various elements of air transport system and the functions of each of them;
- comprehend the role and operations of airlines and airports;
- explain the regulations and agreements applicable in air transport for its smooth and efficient functioning; and
- Understand water and land transport forms connected to tourism and their importance.

5.1 INTRODUCTION

Transport enables the visitor to consume the products and experience what he purchased or going to purchase. In fact, travel is the most fundamental element of tourism. Travel is often used synonymously with tourism. Both concepts involve participants' mobility, while the latter is linked to the motive of pleasure, recreation, health, knowledge gain, socialization, and hedonism, among others (Wall, 2000). Tourism, over the years, has become one of the largest industries in the world, along with the evolution and growth of transport. Among amenities, accessibility and attractions, the most vital components of tourism (Goeldner & Ritchie, 2003), accessibility is all about transportation and associated facilities. *Transport* simply means to carry people or goods from one place to another whereas *transportation* refers to the means or system for the same. Generally, transportation is classified into three: air based, water based and land based, on the basis of the medium in which it takes place. *Surface transportation*, simply, is anything that moves overland. Broadly, surface transportation involves road transportation and rail transportation. From a tourism point of view, it covers cars, coaches, buses, rental cars, taxi services, rail services, etc. (Gee et al., 1997). Transport can enhance tourism experience or damage it. Tourist usually uses different forms of transport during the course of his travel. Earlier, travel was assumed as a passive element in the process of tourism; but now in this busy modern technology filled environment, transport plays a very active role and even a minor interruption can contribute to the dissatisfaction of tourists. This illustrates that the quality of the transportation and the experience gained while using it constitute an important aspect in the overall tourist experience. It is of paramount importance to integrate various modes of transport to ensure seamless travel experience without major service interruptions.

5.2 TOURISM AND TRANSPORT: THE INTERRELATIONSHIP

Tourism and transport are inseparable and complimentary to each other. Transport bridges the gap between the origin and destination in tourism. According to Boniface and Cooper (2002), transportation has developed hand-in-hand with tourism. The developments in transport stimulated the growth of tourism. Tourism development, on the other hand, demanded further developments in transport. The role of transportation is basically related to accessibility and transportation renders tourist destination accessibility to their markets. The lack or insufficiency of accessibility will certainly lead to issues for tourism. Tourism and transportation are inextricably linked and as global tourism increases, additional demand will be placed on the transportation sectors (Goeldner and Ritchie, 2003; Holloway, 1996). Transport, one of the most significant factors that has contributed to the tremendous development of tourism in the world, basically offers essential link between tourism origin and destination areas (Page, 2005). The transport sector has grown in a tremendous manner by which external environments force the transport operators to offer more enjoyable and satisfying transport products to the tourists. Hence, the transport service has much relevance and importance in the context of tourism experience. From the geographers' point of view, from a spatial expression, tourist transport is a vital link between tourist generating and destination regions. Geographers typically analyze travel as a response to satisfy human desire for movement and spatial outcome of such journeys. For a geographer, transport facilitates the process of movement that has economic and budgetary costs. The economists analyze tourist transport system based on demand and supply issues associated with the use and provision of different modes of transport and implications for the future. Transport geographers consider policy management and planning issues associated with the provision of transport. Marketers have identified the importance of a more consumer oriented focus for tourist provision. Without adequate transport network, tourism would not exist as it is a part of tourism infrastructure. An integrated transport network with convenient transfers between different modes of transport is essential with reasonably priced travel options. Within the destinations, tourists need a choice of transport to transfer between port of arrival and their final destination. Both public and private investment is involved in tourism and the transportation industry is a major segment of the tourism industry particularly in terms of employment and revenue generation. Many estimates suggest that up to 40% of the leisure time is spent on traveling. Hall (1991) is of the opinion that the evolution of tourism in Australia is inseparable from the development of new forms of transport and a clear relationship exists between transport development and tourism development.

In most cases, tourism has been developed in areas where extensive transportation networks were in place. Increasing rate of tourism demand has stimulated the rapid development of transportation. Cooper et al. (2000) interpret tourism product as everything that the visitor consumes not only at the destination, but also en route to and from the destination. From that perspective, transport constitutes some key elements of the product. In certain cases, transport itself is treated as products. For instance, *Palace on Wheels* of India, the *Orient Express*, etc.

World Tourism Organization reports that air and land (road and rail) are the most widely used means of transport by the international tourists (WTO, 2005). In 2014, more than half of all overnight visitors travelled to their destinations by air (54%). The next largest share is of surface transport, about 41% (road 39% and rail 2%). Hardly 5% of the international travellers used water transport for reaching the destination. The share of air transport has been increasing steadily over the years.

Many studies reveal that transport sector is greatly influenced by intermediaries like tour operators. The advent of information technology has remarkable contribution in changing the scenario by giving more freedom to travellers to access transport products. Investments in public transport provide social and economic benefits for both residents and tourists alike. Investment in transport infrastructure is a long-term proposition and is unlikely to yield tangible benefits in market led economics in relation to tourism; yet, without tourism, it would not be able to develop.

5.3 AIR TRANSPORT

It was a dream of people to fly from one place to another in a comfortable manner till the beginning of 20th century. But, the last century turned dramatic with regard to flying, as mechanized flying was born, grew and became a huge industry with so much economic, social and cultural contributions. Now, flying conjures diverse images of leisure, recreation, connectivity, business productivity, social contact and cultural exchange. The emergence of aviation was dramatic and phenomenal over a period of ten decades. In fact, aviation is a combination of different types of air transport sectors. Air transport is a segment in the whole gamut of aviation and is the most significant mode of transport, growing at an incredible rate. The significance increases along with the distance to be covered. Simply, it is the mode of transport using aerial vehicles for the purpose of moving people, cargo and mail from one place to another. The predominant view of air transport is related to the service of *common carriers*, which are used in the context of public transport. In the parlance of tourism, no other mode of transport offers such ease of access to international tourism destinations, such rapid transfer between major cities at the continental or global scales, or such a wide range of opportunities for travellers to encounter and experience new places (Ben-Daley, 2010). Currently, air transport is the predominant mode of transport and as per the latest statistics, more than fifty per cent of the international travellers use air transport. William E. O' Connor (2001) opines that air transport is an intermediate product as most of the people use it as a means to achieve some other purpose. For example, tourists may fly to a destination with an objective of a happy vacation; the air trip is largely or entirely a means to achieve this objective.

The following, in general, are the broader categories of aviation:

- Civil aviation
  - Commercial air transportation
  - General aviation
- Military aviation

Table 5.1: ICAO definitions of commercial air transportation

Commercial air transport operation

An aircraft operation involving the transport of passengers, cargo or mail for remuneration or hire. It can be classified into scheduled and non-scheduled operations.

Scheduled air transport (international)

A scheduled international air service is a series of flights that has all the following characteristics:

- it passes through the airspace over the territory of more than one State;
- it is performed by aircraft for the transport of passengers, mail or cargo for remuneration, in such a manner that each flight is open to use by members of the public; and
- it is operated, so as to serve traffic between the same two or more points, either in accordance to a published timetable, or with flights so regular or frequent that they constitute a recognizably systematic series.

Non-scheduled air transport

It is a commercial air transport service performed as other than scheduled air services. A charter flight is a non-scheduled operation using a chartered aircraft. The following are the categories:

- Passenger charter flights
- Cargo charter flights
- Combined passenger-cargo flights
- Non-scheduled non-charter flights for the carriage of individually ticketed or individually billed traffic (sometimes referred to as on-demand air taxi service).

Source: ICAO, 2009.

Civil aviation is one of the two major categories of flying, representing all non-military flying involving both general aviation and scheduled air transport. Civil aviation encompasses two major categories such as commercial air transport and general aviation (GA). Commercial air transportation, which is all about the transport of passengers, cargo or mail for remuneration or hire in a professional manner, is the most prominent. It includes both scheduled and non-scheduled categories of air transport. Charter airlines, major airlines, regional airlines and low cost carriers are all components of commercial air transportation. General aviation includes all other civil flights, private or commercial.

Table 5.1 presents definitions of commercial air transportation as given by the International Civil Aviation Organization (ICAO, 2009).

5.4 EVOLUTION OF AIR TRANSPORT

Air transport has grown tremendously in a short span of time. The last fifty years have seen the transformation and growth of air transport from its infancy to becoming giant. It didn't occur all of a sudden; rather, the experimental flight of Wright brothers that took place in 1903 at Kitty Hawk, North Carolina was the end result of many attempts and developments over several years by a number of people. Many dreamt of flying freely in the sky and to travel to distant places. Many mythological stories had specific mention about flying and vehicles used for flying. Yet, the real flight in a controlled way with the help of an engine became possible only in 20th century. In fact, even in 18th century people could fly, but it was using a hot air balloon. In 1783, a flight in the air became possible in a hot air balloon, which was designed first by the Montgolfier brothers. It had practical difficulty as the balloon could only travel downwind. In the next year itself, a steerable balloon was invented by Jean-Pierre Blanchard and that was the first human-powered dirigible air vehicle. In the following year, in 1785, he crossed the English Channel. Later in 1799, Sir George Cayley came up with the concept of an airplane, as a fixed-wing flying machine with separate systems for lift, propulsion, and control. There were a number of similar developments prior to the historic event of the experimental flight of Wright brothers. It was on 17th December 1903, using the flight *Flyer One First Flight* by Orville Wright, with the help of Wilbur Wright flew a distance of 39 metres (120 ft) for a duration of 12 seconds. This was an important milestone in the history of travel as well as tourism. Modern tourism, to a great extent, depends on air transport. Time is important for all, and people want to reach places in the shortest span of time. Any issue associated with tourism certainly will affect international travel and, vice versa as well. The technological advancements happened during the world wars really helped the growth of air transportation. The following constitute the major impacts of the world wars on air transportation.

The first scheduled passenger flight debuted in Europe on August 25, 1919, with a route between London and Paris, and jet passenger service was inaugurated on May 2,

1952, with a flight between London and Johannesburg, South Africa (Cook et al., 2002). In fact even before that, there was an airline that undertook service for a short period. The first airline service, in 1914, carried only one passenger as the flight was a single capacity carrier. It was on new year day, the first service of the first airline started off a new form of commercial transportation, scheduled passenger air transport, from St. Petersburg in Florida, USA. It was organized by St. Petersburg-Tampa Airboat Line, the first scheduled passenger airline service in the world. The service did not last long as it was wound up within four months. The first passenger was none other than the then Mayor of St. Petersburg, Abram Pheil. Pan American World Airways are the pioneers in the international air transport history. It was found in 1927 by Juan T Trippe, a First World War naval pilot with a fleet of two Fokker F-7 Trimotor air planes. In the United States, passenger service did not begin until April 17, 1926, with an inaugural 6.5 hour flight between Los Angeles and Salt Lake City. The advancement in technology and the corresponding development of jet engines was a major milestone in the history of air transport. It caused tremendous improvement of speed and long route flights by enabling flights to fly farther without refueling, enlarged seating capacity, improved comfort, etc. Also, it resulted in improved economics of long distance air services and improved freight carrying capacity.

Civil aviation had a landmark period during the mid 1940s. Chicago Convention (1944) became a milestone year in global civil aviation. The system of bilaterally negotiated 'traffic rights' between nations, which was applied generally before the war, was reaffirmed by the 1944 Chicago Convention, and the same gave birth to International Civil Aviation Organisation (ICAO) as a UN agency in order to guide and regulate global civil aviation. International Air Transport Association, with the objective of smooth and efficient commercial air transportation, was formed in April, 1945. Jet aircraft were introduced in 1950s, but wide bodied aircraft were used widely in commercial transportation from 1970s only. Example for wide bodied aircraft are DC-10, Boeing 747 and Lockheed Tristar 1011. The airlines' quantum leap came with the introduction of the Boeing 727, the narrow-bodied jet that made nonstop transatlantic routine flights. Propeller aircraft had flown at about half the speed of the net. When the jet age arrived, international travel was fast and soon became relatively inexpensive (Lundberg and Lundberg, 1993). 1980s saw further improvements in air technology with the introduction of such aircraft as DC-9-80 and Boeing 757 and 767. These flights too were fuel-efficient. By 1989, the market for airplanes was growing each year by one and one-fourth times the size of the total aircraft market in 1960. Introduction of Boeing 747-400 had dramatically shifted travel patterns, with increased seating capacity of 410. During 1990s, new kinds aircraft were introduced like MDII, Airbus, A-340 and Boeing 777.

Currently, commercial air transport carries millions of passengers. The following trend analysis report of the ICAO reveals the current status of commercial air transportation.

Table 5.2: Scheduled air transport: International and domestic

Sl. No.	Year	No. of passengers (Millions)	Freight in tonnes (Millions)
1	2005	2700	47.0
2	2011	2865	48.1
3	2012	2998	47.4
4	2013	3132	48.5
5	2014	3303	50.4

Source: ICAO, 2014.

"The total number of passengers carried on scheduled services had risen to 3.5 billion in 2015, a 6.4 per cent increase from the previous year. The number of departures reached approximately 34 million globally, and world passenger traffic, expressed in terms of total scheduled revenue passenger-kilometres (RPKs), posted an increase of 6.8 per cent with approximately 6562 billion RPKs being performed. The aviation industry, composed of some 1400 commercial airlines, 4130 airports and 173 air navigation service providers (ANSPs), continued to play a critical role over 2015 in fostering the growth of tourism and trade. Over half of the world's 1.1 billion tourists are transported by air today, while aircraft carry 35 per cent of world trade by value." (ICAO, 2015)

5.5 AIR TRANSPORT INDUSTRY

Air transportation is a complex process and understanding the same requires to analyze it under different headings. Civil aviation business is composed of a number of elements, as follows:

- airports;
- air navigation and traffic control services;
- airlines; and
- aircraft and manufacturers.

5.6 AIRPORTS

Basically, an airport is the place where aircraft can take off and land. At the very minimum an airport consists of a runway, but other components are hangars and terminal buildings. Apart from these, an airport may have a variety of facilities and infrastructure including fixed base operator services, air traffic facilities, etc. Of late, an airport is not only a centre of movement of people and cargo; but also it is central in the development, operation and economics of the airlines, and a necessity for the socioeconomic development of a society. Number of airports has been on the rise consistently, with much potential for further remarkable developments as a result of the incredible growth in passenger and cargo transportation. The recent spur in the growth of air transport was remarkable. For instance, the volume of travellers using regular air transport had doubled from 1990 to 2000 (Kazada and Caves, 2000). As per an estimate of CIA of the US (2013), there were 41,821 airports in the world until 2013. But this figure includes all the aerodromes of all sizes and nature. The number of airports in commercial aviation is much less. According to the ICAO, the aviation industry consists of some 1,400 commercial airlines, 4,130 airports and 173 air navigation service providers (ANSPs) (ICAO, 2015). Table 5.3 gives the list of top ten airports in terms passenger and cargo movement.

Table 5.3: Top ten airports (2013)

In terms of passenger transportation		In terms of cargo transportation	
Airport	**No. of passengers**	**Airport**	**Cargo (metric tonnes)**
Atlanta (ATL)	94,431,224	Hong Kong (HKG)	4,166,303
Beijing (PEK)	83,712,355	Memphis, TN (MEM)	4,137,801
London (LHR)	72,368,061	Shanghai (PVG)	2,928,527
Tokyo (HND)	68,906,509	Incheon (ICN)	2,464,384
Chicago (ORD)	66,777,161	Dubai (DXB)	2,435,567
Los Angeles (LAX)	66,667,619	Anchorage, AK (ANC)	2,421,145
Dubai (DXB)	66,431,533	Louisville, KY (SDF)	2,216,079
Paris (CDG)	62,052,917	Frankfurt (FRA)	2,094,453
Dallas/Fort Worth (DFW)	60,470,507	Paris (CDG)	2,069,200
Jakarta (CGK)	60,137,347	Tokyo (NRT)	2,019,844

Source: CIA, 2013.

Simply, airport is a space where flights can land and take off, with facilities for loading and unloading options. One runway or helipad (for helicopters) is inevitable for an airport. Yet, it exists with a range of other facilities and services as well, in addition to the roads and runways to take off and land. It provides all infrastructure needed to enable passengers and freight to transfer from the surface to air modes of transport and to allow aircraft to take off and land (Graham, 2003). Hangars and terminal buildings are common components in an airport. Additionally, an airport may have a variety of facilities and infrastructure, including fixed base operator services, air traffic control, passenger facilities such as restaurants and lounges, and emergency services. A military airport is known as an *airbase* or air *station*. The terms airfield, airstrip and aerodrome may also be used to refer to airports of varying sizes. International Civil Aviation Organization (ICAO) has clearly stated the concept of an airport. The following would help to understand it better. In many a cases, the term aerodrome is used for referring to an airport. According to ICAO, *aerodrome* is "a defined area on land or water (including any buildings, installations and equipment) allocated wholly or in part for the arrival, departure and surface movement of aircraft". (ICAO Definitions-UVS International). This is a broader definition for all sorts of airports and airstrips. Even general aviation landing facilities are included in this. *Airport* is a subset of aerodrome as all airports are aerodromes whereas all aerodromes are not airports. The distinction is based on the basic necessities required for calling an aerodrome an airport. For an airport, all necessary infrastructure and facilities are required as per ICAO specifications. Young and Wells (2004) specify that commercial airports, be it anywhere in the world, should satisfy a set of international technical standards intended to ensure aircraft safety and interoperability across national boundaries. ICAO defines an international airport as "any airport designated by the contracting state in whose territory it is situated as an airport of entry and departure for international air traffic, where the formalities incident to customs, immigration, public health, agricultural quarantine and similar procedures are carried out." (ICAO Definitions-UVS International). An airport infrastructure offers many services and activities. The major ones include:

- Ground handling
- Baggage handling
- Passenger terminal operations
- Airport security
- Cargo operations
- Airport technical services
- Air traffic control
- Aircraft scheduling for takeoff, landing, etc.
- Airport access (Page, 2005).

Ownership of airports may be in state hands, under the control of local authorities, or in private ownerships (Holloway, 1996). In India, majority of the airports are controlled by Airports Authority of India, a government agency. It was set up in 1995 by merging the International Airports Authority of India and the National Airports Authority. Currently, AAI manages 126 airports which includes 11 international, 89 domestic and 26 civilian enclaves at defence airfields. In Britain many regional airports are in local authority hands, while seven of the major international airports are owned and operated by BAA, a private corporation formed by denationalization out of the former state run agency.

The British Airports Authority in 1987 sold London's Heathrow, Gatwick, and Stansted airports and the four main Scottish airports to private interests. Privatisation of airports was also proposed in America like in the case of JFK, New York and Los Angeles international airports. Airports have to generate income in order to meet the expenses and now being businesslike, airports have to generate profit as well. The following are the major revenue opportunities for airports:

Table 5.4: National plan of integrated airport systems (NPIAS): definitions of airport categories

Commercial service airports are publicly owned airports that have at least 2500 passenger boardings* each calendar year and receive scheduled passenger services. The definition also includes passengers who continue on an aircraft in international flight that stops at an airport in any of the 50 States for a non-traffic purpose, such as refuelling or aircraft maintenance rather than passenger activity.
Non-primary commercial service airports are commercial service airports that have at least 2500 and no more than 10,000 passenger boardings each year.
Primary airports are commercial service airports that have more than 10,000 passenger boardings each year.
Cargo service airports are the airports that in addition to any other air transportation services that may be available, are served by aircraft providing air transportation of only cargo with a total annual landed weight** of more than 100 million pounds. An airport may be both a commercial service and a cargo service airport.
Reliever airports are airports designated by the FAA to relieve congestion at commercial service airports and to provide improved general aviation access to the overall community. These may be publicly or privately owned.
General aviation airports are public-use airports that do not have scheduled service or have less than 2500 annual passenger boardings. In this category, national represents those general aviation airports that support the national and state system by providing communities with access to national and international markets in multiple states and throughout the United States. Regional supports regional economies by connecting communities to statewide and interstate markets. Local supplements communities by providing access to primarily intrastate and some interstate markets. Basic links the community with the national airport system and supports general aviation activities (e.g., emergency services). Unclassified provides access to the aviation system.
*Passenger boardings: It refers to revenue passenger boardings on an aircraft in service in air commerce whether or not in scheduled service.
**Landed weight: The weight of aircraft transporting only cargo in intrastate, interstate, and foreign air transportation.

Source: FAA, 2015.

- Landing fee
- Airport ATC charges
- Aircraft parking
- Passenger charges
- Freight charges
- Aircraft handling services
- Rent or lease income for airport tenants
- Income from duty-free shops, etc.
- Parking fee, etc.

5.7 STRUCTURE OF AN AIRPORT

Ideally, an airport can be divided into three sections:

- Landside
- Airside
  - Runways to land and takeoff
  - Taxiways to reach from the gate to the runway for takeoff and from runway to the gate after landing
  - Aprons: parking areas of aircraft away from terminals
  - Ramp area where aircraft park near to a terminal to load passengers and cargo
  - Air traffic control tower
  - Support services and facilities
- Terminal: the main building acts as an interface between airside and landside and through which passengers and cargo are processed to be able to avail air transport services.
  - Departure area: Major activities/components include baggage screening, airline check-in and boarding pass collection, passport control/immigration clearance, security check–in, concourses, commercial services, and gate waiting area.
  - Arrival area: Arrival gates and passage, baggage claim areas, passport control/immigration clearance services, customs clearance, commercial area.

Airports cause a variety of impacts on the society and environment. Some of them are:

- Effects on people who live close to airports and under flight paths.
  - Noise pollution.
  - Water pollution: Runoff from aircraft, airfield deicing operations, fuel leaks, spills, and solid and liquid waste contribute to water pollution in and around the airport.
- Emissions that effect the built and natural environments: Aircraft emits a number of pollutants that alter the chemical composition of the atmosphere, changing its radiative balance and hence influencing climate. The emissions include carbon dioxide (CO_2), nitrogen oxides (NO_2) particles (mainly soot) of sulphur oxides, carbon monoxide, and various hydrocarbons (Graham, 2003).
- Increased land use for development of airport and evacuation of people along with other impacts, like soil erosion.

- Additional congestion on roads, etc., as a result of additional passengers travelling to the airports
- Waste and energy management concerns due to improper handling of waste and excessive consumption of energy.

5.8 NAVIGATION AND AIR TRAFFIC CONTROL

Air navigation services constitute a system that makes air transportation a smooth and safe affair. Air navigation facilities are used for the provision of air navigation services. Air navigation facilities denote any facility or system which provides a pilot with information to enable him/her to reach the destination, smoothly, safely, and in time. It mainly consists of air traffic control (ATC) units and associated telecommunication radio beacons, satellite systems, and other aids to landing, weather forecasts, airports, computer terminals, etc. The technical services, which are provided on the ground to assist and control aircraft while in the air and in landing or takingoff, are key in the operation of aviation services. Air traffic control has the function of guiding aircraft into and out of airports, giving pilots updated automatic recordings, detailed information on ground conditions, climate details, runways in use, and the state of navigation aids. Pilots get information on what height and direction to fly. ATC ensures the efficient and safe movement of air traffic through the following services:

- **Separation assurance:** Safety of flights ensured by keeping aircraft separate from each other, as well as from other hazards.
- **Flight information:** It provides continuous flight information services to aircraft in flight.
- **Search and rescue services:** It offers services by notifying and alerting appropriate agencies about aircraft in need of search and rescue.

5.9 AIRLINES

Airlines provide various types of air based transportation services. It can be defined as "an industry which consists of a vast network of routes that connect cities in different parts of a country/world, and over the network a large number of airlines carry passengers and cargo on scheduled services" (Wells, 1998). They are basically organizations that run regular/occasional services for carrying passengers and goods using aircraft. Other components like airports are the facility providers for the operation of services by the airlines. Both private as well as state owned agencies run airlines. *National carriers* are the airlines operated under governmental authorities, directly or indirectly. Low cost carriers (LCCs) brought a new trend of 'no-frills' with reduced rates and limited services in the scheduled airline sector and currently they are running successfully in most of the countries. Majority of the airlines in the world are privately owned. USA is the most important country in the case of air transportation, followed by European countries. Some European airlines, such as SAS in Scandinavia, are partly state-owned, but in the UK, all airlines are now in the private sector, since British Airways was privatized in 1987 (Holloway, 1996). Airlines operate different types of services like scheduled, non-scheduled and air taxis. A brief account of each of them is following.

5.9.1 Scheduled Services

Scheduled services operate on defined routes, domestic or international, for which licences are granted by the government or other authorities concerned. Operations are based on a published schedule of flights. The airlines are required to operate on the basis of their published timetables, regardless of passenger load factors. These services may be publicly or privately owned, though the trend is more on privatization particularly in developed countries. Public airlines are recognized as the national flag-carriers. Scheduled services are currently seen in two ways: full service carriers (FSC) and low cost carriers (LCC).

Full service carriers (FSC): They are also called *legacy airlines* as well as *common carriers*. These airlines offer full basket services to passengers. The services include meals, beverage, lounge, entertainment, etc. They employ more people and cover larger geographical area due to the hub and spoke agreements with smaller airlines. Different types of aircraft are used. Examples include Air India, Emirates, Singapore Airlines.

Low cost carriers (LCC)/Low cost airline (LCA)/ No-frills airlines: This is a model of service with limited options for passengers, and became prevalent since deregulation in 1978. They don't offer majority of inflight services like, food or beverage. Usually, they use single type of aircraft and employ leaner number of people compared to FSCs. In order to avoid delays and to reduce turnaround time, LCAs usually offer point-to-point services and connecting flights are not encouraged. Examples: South West and Jet Blue Airways in USA; Ryanair and Easyjet in Europe; Air Asia and Tiger Airways in Europe.

Some of the business strategies adopted by LCCs are discussed in Table 5.5.

5.9.2 Charter Services

Charter services represent the air service that does not operate on regular schedules. Charter services, at times referred to as *supplemental airlines*, in which the flights, without published schedules, are chartered as paid by a tour operator or any middlemen for a fixed charge. Responsibility of the airline is to operate the aircraft. Selling of seats and

Table 5.5: Business strategies of LCCs

- Limited Inflight services: Airlines do not offer food on board. Some of them sell snacks, bottled water, and drinks on a fixed price.
- More seats, mainly through lesser leg space, lack of business or first class, and by saving food storage space.
- Disintermediation: LCCs usually sell tickets via online sources, mainly their websites and save intermediary commissions.
- Less employees: LCCs usually have less number of employees compared to FSCs, particularly inflight service crew size is much smaller.
- Less turnaround time due to variety of reasons.
- Similar aircraft in fleet: This helps immensely in maintenance and in using spare parts along with the use of crew.
- Earnings from inflight marketing and sales: LCCs promote onboard shopping.
- Low baggage allowance.
- Dynamic pricing: highly flexible pricing strategy depending on the demand.

other responsibilities are usually vested with middlemen. The flights are chartered as paid for completely by a tour operator or other middlemen for a fixed charge. These airlines have only limited schedules and lease or charter aircraft to large groups or to other airlines. Sometimes major airlines charter aircraft to handle passenger overload. A number of scheduled airlines own charter subsidiaries as well. British Airways operates a charter service under the Caledonian brand, and in 1992 took over Dan-Air, a joint charter and scheduled service operator, partly to reinforce charter operations. Lufthansa operates charter subsidiary Condor (Holloway, 1996).

5.9.3 Air Taxis

Air taxis, used particularly by business travellers, are privately chartered aircraft accommodating between four and eighteen people. They have advantages like convenience and flexibility and routes can be tailor-made for passengers. Small airfields close to industry or office locations can be used. Very small aircraft as well as helicopters are used for air taxi services. In Britain alone, there are around 350 airfields suitable for air taxis. A range of aircraft are used, from helicopters like the *Bell Jet Ranger*, or the piston-engined *Piper Twin Comanche* (each seating three to four people) to *Embraer Bandeirantes* that are capable of carrying 18 passengers up to 300 miles.

5.9.4 Commuter Airlines

These are the airlines that operate on short routes to enable passengers to connect cities within major airports. Airports are away from cities, particularly large cities. Commuter airlines usually enter into special partnership agreements with major airlines, called *code share agreement*. By this, smaller airlines can share the name and code of larger airlines.

5.9.5 Cargo Services

Airlines provide cargo services as well. Exclusive cargo airlines/flight services extend cargo services. Air Cargo includes air freight, mail and the several types of expedited small package services. Though many airlines specialize in carrying cargo, much of the cargo is transported by the regular passenger airlines (O' Connor, 2001). The "cargo mix" consists of various commodities being carried by air.

Air Cargo

Mail

Small packages (air express)

Air Freight

Emergency

Routine perishables

Routine surface-divertible (O' Connor, 2001)

Pickup and Delivery Services

Airlines sometimes provide 'pickup' and 'delivery' services of the cargo which means pickup service for the customer to the airport and from destination airport to the recipient. Usually, shippers arrange this like in the case of mail, postal departments undertake pickup and delivery service. In certain cases, airlines contract with surface transport operators to facilitate pickup and delivery.

Table 5.6 differentiates between freight forwarders and cargo agents.

Table 5.6: Freight forwarders and cargo agents

Air Freight Forwarders
They are the intermediaries. *Consolidator* is the common term used in some areas, instead of forwarder. They act on behalf of airlines and their principal function is to consolidate small shipments into one large shipment and then offer the large shipment as one entity to the airline (O'Connor, 2001). William O' Connor also argues that the air freight forwarder is an "indirect carrier" as it accomplishes the air haul indirectly by using the facilities of the airline instead of using own aircraft and it has the legal responsibilities of common carriers without actually performing the line haul. Here, the forwarder is responsible to the consignee for safe delivery of the cargo into the hands of the recipient and charges the consignee in accordance with its own set of rates.
Cargo Agents
Cargo agents accept cargoes and send them at regular airline rates, adding a charge for the services offered by them. They do not act as consolidators.

5.10 AIRCRAFT AND EQUIPMENT MANUFACTURERS

An aircraft, a device used for travelling through air, helps in connecting people and places, along with transporting cargo and goods. *Airplane*, another term used instead, is defined by National Aeronautics and Space Administration (NASA) as "transportation devices which are designed to move people and cargo from one place to another. Airplanes come in many different shapes and sizes depending on the mission of the aircraft" (NASA-www.nasa.gov). Aircraft manufacturers produce aircraft of various kinds. Within the former category, the world market is dominated by three manufacturers; Boeing, which has built 7000 aircraft during its lifetime and holds by far the biggest share of the aircraft market; the Airbus Industries consortium of companies in Germany, France, Spain and Britain (British Aerospace), which is now the second largest manufacturer; and Mc Donnell Douglas. Aircraft engines are manufactured separately, and again three companies dominate the market: Pratt and Whitney, Rolls Royce and General Electric. The aircraft market is effectively controlled by two US companies and one European. Some commonly used aircraft with flight range, equipment code and passenger capacity are furnished in Table 5.7.

In small aircraft manufacturing segment, British Aerospace plays a prominent role in the market, with popular aircraft such as the 146 Regional Jet, the ATP (Advance Turbo-Prop) and the Jetstream. The smallest aircraft, with seating capacity of 19, are mainly twin turboprops; while the largest aircraft can seat up to 50 or more, and tend to be more of jets. The demand for smaller aircraft has rapidly increased to fill the need for feeder services from rural airports into 'hub' airports, from where connections are made for long-haul or intercontinental flights.

Table 5.7: Aircraft: range and capacity

Type of Aircraft	Flight range (in miles)	Passenger Capacity
Airbus A-320	4026	150-180
Airbus A350-1000	7900	366-440
Airbus A-380	8400	544–853
Boeing 727	3060	250-380
Boeing 737 MAX 9	3515	180-220
Boeing 747	5500–6500	430–452
Boeing 747-8	8900	410-605
Dettavill and Twin Otter	745	20
McDonnel-Douglass DC-9	2400-3000	70-131
Lockheed L-1011 Tristar	2200	90-139
McDonnel-Douglass DC-10	5998	246-330

5.11 AIR TRANSPORT REGULATIONS

International air transportation requires complex negotiations and agreements among nations and carriers. Over flight privileges must be obtained by all countries for international air transportation. Scheduled routes are assigned on the basis of agreements between governments of the countries concerned. National governments approve and licence the carriers which are operated on scheduled routes both domestically and internationally. Furthermore, there were some technical reasons to be solved in the ever expanding air transport and burgeoning competition towards the end of Second World War. A number of summits and conventions were held for evolving strategies and

Table 5.8: ICAO: "Freedoms of Air"

First Freedom of the Air - the right or priviledge, in respect of scheduled international air services, granted by one State to another State or States to fly across its territory without landing.

Second Freedom of the Air - the right or priviledge, in respect of scheduled international air services, granted by one State to another State or States to land in its territory for non-traffic purposes.

Third Freedom of the Air - the right or priviledge, in respect of scheduled international air services, granted by one State to another State to put down, in the territory of the first State, traffic coming from the home State of the carrier.

Fourth Freedom of the Air - the right or priviledge, in respect of scheduled international air services, granted by one State to another State to take on, in the territory of the first State, traffic destined for the home State of the carrier.

Fifth Freedom of the Air - the right or priviledge, in respect of scheduled international air services, granted by one State to another State to put down and to take on, in the territory of the first State, traffic coming from or destined to a third State.

"So-called Freedoms"

Sixth Freedom of the Air - the right or priviledge, in respect of scheduled international air services, of transporting, via the home State of the carrier, traffic moving between two other States. Unlike the first five freedoms, this is not incorporated as such into any widely recognized air service agreement such as the "Five Freedoms Agreement".

Seventh Freedom of the Air - the right or priviledge, in respect of scheduled international air services, granted by one State to another State, of transporting traffic between the territory of the granting State and any third State with no requirement to include on such operation at any point in the territory of the recipient State, i.e., the service need not connect to or be an extension of any service to/from the home State of the carrier.

Eighth Freedom of the Air - the right or priviledge, in respect of scheduled international air services, of transporting cabotage traffic between two points in the territory of the granting State on a service which originates or terminates in the home country of the foreign carrier or outside the territory of the granting State (also known as *consecutive cabotage*).

Ninth Freedom of the Air - the right or priviledge of transporting cabotage traffic of the granting State on a service performed entirely within the territory of the granting State (also known as "stand alone" cabotage).

Source: ICAO/Manual on the Regulation of International Air Transport (Doc 9626, Part 4), www.icao.int.

measures aiming at the future. The Warsaw Convention held in 1929 first established common agreement on the extent of liability of the airlines in the event of death of or injury to passengers, or loss of passenger baggage. Then at the Chicago Convention on Civil Aviation held in 1944, the government representatives participated in discussions decided to promote world air services and to reach an agreement on standard operating procedures for air services between countries. The Chicago Convention laid the foundation for regulations of international air transport. The "**freedoms of air**", also referred to as **bilateral agreements**, have become the most significant outcome of the convention. The freedoms are given in brief in Table 5.8. A number of strategies and measures were evolved during the last four decades to beat competition. The introduction of net inclusive tour basing fares for tour operators; variable pricing techniques such as Advance Purchase Excursion (APEX) tickets and standby fares; and more recently 'frequent flyer' programmes, in which passengers collect additional free miles based on the mileage they chalk up with a carrier, have all helped to stimulate demand and fill aircraft seats.

Some strategies have been discussed here that support air transport regulations.

- **Open sky policy:** Open sky policy, which means unrestricted access by carriers into the sovereign air territory of a country, was an important policy change that happened in the western countries. It resulted in the emergence of new airlines and increased competition. Instead of a simple three-tier structure, which includes economy, coach, and first class, there are multiple prices and airlines change these prices hundreds of thousands of times each day to meet customer needs, maximize load factors, and to increase revenues through their yield management systems (Cook et al., 2002).
- **Hub-and-spoke system:** To overcome the increasing pressure from passengers, to increase flights to all cities without increasing fares, airlines introduced "hub-and-spoke system" (Foster LD, 1994). It is an operational arrangement by airlines in which passengers are transported to an intermediated point, called, *hub,* to board planes to their final destination. Here a hub-and-spoke refers to a *bicycle wheel*. Hub symbolically refers to a major city from where passengers can board in flights to other destinations. Each spoke represents one route from hub to one of the destinations. For example, if one wishes to travel from Bombay to Cape Town in South Africa in British Airways, it may not have a direct flight (point-to-point) from Bombay to Cape City. In this case, the passenger will board an aircraft to London first and from there, he can board another flight to Cape Town. From London, which is the hub, similar services will be offered to many destinations situated in different parts of the world. For making this successful, many airlines have entered into cooperative contracts, called *inter-line agreements* that enable passengers to travel on a connection involving different carriers while paying a single point-to-point fare, called 'joint fare'.

To accommodate the price-sensitive passenger, an increase of discount seats would ensure that the passenger will stay with the airline for long. Many major airlines engage in interline agreements. Some airlines have more than one hub. Delta Airlines, for example, has six major hubs: Atlanta, Dallas/Fort Worth, Salt Lake City, Cincinnati, Los Angeles, and Orlando. Airlines operating on major routes between 'hub' airports within a country are known as *trunk route airlines*, while those operating from smaller, often rural airports into these hubs are referred to as *regional feeder* or *commuter airlines*. The main purpose is to serve the needs of commuting business people, many of whom regularly use these routes. By utilizing the hub-and-spoke system, airlines are able to increase operating efficiency through scheduling arrivals and departures using the existing fleet. Major hub cities are given in Table 5.9.

- **Code sharing agreements:** Code sharing is another strategy followed by airlines world over. "International airlines penetrate markets by using code sharing agreements, a form of market sharing by which two or more airlines share a flight by using a single airline code, although segments of the flight are flown separately" (Lundberg and Lundberg, 1993). Regional/commuter airlines on spoke routes typically operate on a code share basis. In a *code share agreement*, a regional/ commuter airline will share the same two-letter identification code of a major airline in the computer reservation system. For example, British Airways offers a flight from Seattle to London via Chicago, but United Airlines flies the Seattle-to Chicago segment and only the final leg, Chicago to London, is flown by British Airways. Foreign airlines are eager to tap the US market, without having to stretch themselves to service many points in this country. The airline for the final destination, the airport or city whose code appears on the ticket, accepts responsibility for most of the consumer related problems that may arise on these segmented flights. *Banking flights*, another strategy, is the process of coordinating flight schedules to maximize the use of ground crews and equipment.

Table 5.9: Major carriers and hub cities

Carrier	Hub Cities
Air Canada	Montreal, Toronto, Vancouver
American Airlines	Dallas/Fort Worth, Chicago, San Juan, Nashville, Raleigh/Durham, Miami
America West	Phoenix, Las Vegas
British Airways	Heathrow (London), Gatwick
Continental Airlines	Houston, Denver, Newark
Delta Airlines	Atlanta, Dallas/Fort Worth, Salt Lake City, Los Angeles, Cincinnati
KLM	Amsterdam

Source: (Cook et al., 2002)

5.12 SURFACE TRANSPORT

Surface transport, one of the most common and major forms of transport, has experienced considerable growth since the beginning of the last century. Rail transportation though, has not shown considerable progress in the second half of the last century, still is a major mode of transport. An understanding of the evolution, growth, current scenario and future prospects of both forms of transport is important for a tourism student.

5.13 ROAD TRANSPORTATION

Road transportation is one of the most important forms of tourism transportation and during the last century, it has grown tremendously. It involves a wide variety of modes of transportation. Bus (including coaches), cars, rental cars, taxi services, etc., are the major road transportation modes. The advent of automobiles in 1920s and the motor car revolutionized the holiday and recreational habits. Road transportation became the primary mode of transport (Sinha, 1997). Road transportation is still one of the most attractive modes of transport and according to Cooper et al. (2000), in the context of tourism, attractions of road transportation in comparison with railways and other forms of transport are:

- Control of departure times.
- Ability to carry baggage and equipment easily.
- Ability to use vehicle for accommodation.
- Control of the route and the stops en route.
- Maximum privacy.
- Low perceived pocket expenses.
- Liberty to use the automobile once the destination is reached, etc.

5.13.1 Bus

Bus, considered as a shortened version of *omnibus*, a Latin word meaning 'for everyone', is a large road vehicle which can carry a number of persons, from around twenty to fifty or even more. Omnibus is the first organized public transport system that existed in France during 1800s. It is also claimed that a bus route was first operated in 1824 in UK, from Manchester to Pendleton in Salford. Omnibus also started service in the second half of 17th century in New York in the US. The world's first motorized bus, a Benz truck modified, was made in Germany in 1895.

Diversity is the feature of bus travel, it varies from one area to another. Bus travel is not just used by low budget tourists. Generally, buses are used for urban as well as sub-urban scheduled travel. In such cases, comfort level may not be that high. The advantage of a bus is that it can reach more destinations than railways. A variety of buses are in use the world over. Type of buses usually varies according to the usage. Commuter buses, double decker, school buses, trolley buses, motor coaches, tour coaches, mini buses, midi buses, articulated trams and road trains are the different types of buses used for passenger services. A coach is basically a bus that is designed and equipped for intercity services, charter or excursion tours (Foster,1994). Coaches are comfortable buses and they are used for regional or cross-country journeys. Younger generation is particularly attracted to coach travel (Holloway, 1994). The coaches are graded on the basis of different aspects, e.g., leg room space, onboard amenities like kitchen, toilets, air conditioning, cloakroom, etc. Coach travel offers a wide range of tourist services including the following:

- Express coach routes, both domestic and international.
- Private line services.
- Tour and excursion operations.
- Transfer services.

It is an important question as to why many people prefer bus tours than other forms. According to Lundberg and Lundberg (1993), people chose bus tours due to a variety of reasons such as:

- Value for money.
- Easy access.
- Convenience.
- Easy and quick to organize.
- Comfortable group size.
- Total experience, including social aspects.
- Bus journey provides better interpersonal relationships.
- Continuous sightseeing (one can see much more of the region he/she is travelling through).
- Tourist can understand the cultural and social vibrancy more through bus journeys.

Recreation vehicles (RVs) entered into the travel scene in USA and Canada. Corollary to the growth of automobile travel, RV camping sites were also developed in western countries. Coaches and tour services in domestic and intraregional tourism became predominant, particularly in Europe. Also, there are some reasons why many people do not prefer bus tours as they are time consuming (less speed), have less moving space inside, are tiring, lack sleeping facilities, etc. Different types of bus services are offered as part of road transportation. According to Foster (1994), generally bus transportation is divided into four categories:

- Intercity bus service (inter-state, and regional as well).

- Coach tours.
- Charter coach tours.
- Airport transportation.
- General bus service (public and private bus services).

Coach tours are package tours in which motor coach transportation is an important component. The tour range is from hours to days. In India, private concerns mainly operate coach tours. Some public sector agencies also operate such coach tours. For instance, India Tourism Development Corporation (ITDC), Kerala Tourism Development Corporation (KTDC), etc., organize coach tours as well as charter services.

5.13.2 Automobiles

In the parlance of tourism, automobile is an important mode of transportation and automobiles informally represent cars and allied vehicles, in the international context. The advent of cars provided families in particular a new freedom of movement, increased opportunities to take day excursions as well as longer trips. Accessibility to interior resorts improved. Car ferry services flourished in Europe. *Camping* and *caravan* holidays boomed. Many tourist destinations in the world still depend on private motor vehicles. Tour operators offer self-driven car packages. Vehicles used as part of recreational business are also referred to as *recreational vehicles* (RV). RV, Motorised caravans or motor homes offered camping facilities. Railways too adopted to meet the needs of the tourist, introducing motor rail services for motorists which allowed the tourists to take their cars with them by rail on longer journeys. The credit of love affair with the automobile in North America goes to the pioneering genius, Henry Ford, who ushered in the age of mass automobile travel with his famous model *T car*. Between 1908 and 1923, 15 million Ford cars were sold. The factors why people chose automobiles for tourism are listed below (Sinha, 1997):

- Control of the route and stops en route.
- Control of departure times.
- Ability to carry baggage and equipment easily.
- Low expenses due to travelling with three or more persons.
- Freedom to use vehicle once the destination is reached.
- Driving itself is a recreational activity, which many are fond of.
- Better sightseeing while travelling, etc.

5.13.3 Car Rental

Car rental has gained much significance now, particularly for business travel. Rental industry provides a critical link between service for business and pleasure travellers worldwide. *Business travellers* constitute the largest segment, over 70% of all the vehicles. (Goeldner and Ritchie, 2003). Rental car sector is growing in an amazing manner, and is being used for business as well as vacation purposes. Car rental companies have expanded services like vallet delivery, parking services to avoid shuttle buses, offering on the board computerized navigation system, drop boxes for return of keys and rental forms and equipping service personnel with hand-held computers to complete rental transactions to the point of return (Cook et al., 2002). Car hire companies can be divided into two: the large international companies with franchise operators and small, generally locally based independent companies (Holloway, 1994). Large corporations have additional advantages including contacts with airports and railways (with a desk at terminals); link with airlines and hotels to increase sales; car rental services (CRS) linkage and link with travel agencies and tour operators. The major companies in US are Herts, Avis, Budget, National, etc. Rental cars are even available at airports in many cities. CRS accessibility is available through major CRS agencies like Sabre, Galileo, etc. In India too, the practice of car rental has caught up. Car rental services are available in almost all the major towns and cities. The range and type of car rentals vary from place to place.

5.13.4 Taxi and Limousine Service

Taxi and limousine play an important role in tourism. Taxicab is a public transport vehicle for single or small group of people and they are available for hire. The concept has existed since early periods using the then available vehicles. Taxi service is basically intra-city in nature and it is a vital component of travel industry. It is subject to licensing and rate regulation by the authorities.

Limousine is an expensive luxury car driven by a chauffeur. Limousine service acts as a unique market niche, competing with both taxis and coaches. It is usually long, black or white in colour. The specialty of this car is that it has a typical portion between the driver compartment and the rear passenger compartment with a sliding glass so that conversations of passengers can be kept private from the driver. Airlines often contract with limousine services for passengers. Corporates also engage in such contracts.

5.13.5 Recreation Vehicle

Recreation vehicle segment is a strong component that needs mention in the case of land based transportation in the beginning of this century. Slide-out technology was introduced in RVs during 1990s and later, advanced further. Slide-out is available in livingrooms, dining rooms, bedrooms and kitchen. At the touch of a button, a portion of the room and other objects in it, like a couch or a table slide outward up to about 3.5 feet. Motor homes, travel trailers, fifth wheel trailers and even fold camping trailers are some of the examples of slide-outs.

5.14 RAIL TRANSPORT

Rail transport is the transport of passengers and goods by means of vehicles designed to run along railroads or railways. The train consists of individual boggies linked together with an engine. Rail transport is considered a mass transportation mode and one of the most energy efficient carriages. They make highly efficient use of space since they travel on two parallel rails and carry hundreds of passengers together along with carrying goods. *Passenger rail transportation* is a component of travel in many locations in the world and it is the most important transportation mode especially in countries like India, South Korea, Japan, China, etc., though in the US, it does not have much importance and relevance as in other countries (Goeldner and Ritchie, 2003). The railways played a major role in the first half of the last century, but as ownership of private cars increased, the tourist traffic on the railways fell (Holloway, 1994). Interior destinations could not be accessed by rail. Inconvenience, time consuming and continuous fare hike made railways unattractive. But the fuel crisis that took place during the early 1970s gave a sigh of relief for railways. Package tours on railways increased, but by mid-1980s, the trend again reversed. High-speed trains began to operate from 1960s onwards. The highest railway line was built in China in 2005, the *Qinzang railway* through the Tanggula mountain pass.

Channel tunnel rail service was introduced for passengers as well as freight movement by mid-1990s in Britain and shuttle services for passengers and cargo service began through it. It offered regular rail services from London to other parts of UK, Paris, Brussels, etc. In 1989, the community of European Railways announced plans for transcontinental high-speed rail networks, extending some 21,000 miles, to be in place by 2015. France is also in the midst of massive programmes of railway expansion. By 2025, they will be able to bring all the major cities within reach of Paris by high-speed trains travelling at 186 km per hour or more. Germany too is making plans to introduce faster trains. The Netherlands, Belgium, Italy, Sweden and Denmark all have similar plans. Both Germany and Japan have developed *magnetic levitation* (MAGLEV) trains capable of speed over 300 mph.

Though many other forms of transport emerged with more speed, safety and comfort, still railways are an important mode of transport. The following are the reasons why many people prefer train services:

- Affordable cost.
- Relatively higher safety.
- The ability to move around the coach.
- Personal comfort.
- The ability to look out of the train.
- Arriving at the destination relaxed.

- Environment-friendly form of transport.
- Centrally located termini.
- Decongested routes.
- More interaction with fellow passengers.
- Better bathrooms and other facilities.
- Freedom to engage in simple recreational activities while travelling.
- Pantry services.
- More luxury for higher payment.
- Speedier than many other forms of transport (Cooper et al., 2000; Sinha 1997).

Rail transportation was a major mode of passenger traffic in Europe, but as discussed earlier, the importance declined after the advent and growth of automobiles. The automobile has overtaken rail transport in every sense and the developments and growth in air transportation too contributed a great share in the declining importance of rail transport in USA. The declining role of rail services caused the authorities to think of strategies and measures to revamp the rail transport system in USA, during the second half of the last century. When railway systems suffered financial issues and, in 1970, under the Rail Passenger Service Act, US Congress created the National Railroad Passenger Corporation (NRPC) to subsidize and oversee the operation of intercity passenger trains. The original brand name of NRPC was *Railpax*, but it was changed to AMTRAK. High speed trains (around 180 miles per hour) are operated in France, Britain, Italy, Japan, Germany, Sweden, Korea, and Spain. Introduction of high-speed rail service between London, Paris, France, etc., was an important milestone in the history of rail transport (Cook et al., 2002). *Eurail pass* was first introduced by Austria, Belgium, Denmark, France, West Germany, Italy, Luxembourg, Holland, Norway, Portugal, Spain, Sweden and Switzerland. The *Orient Express* is the most famous luxurious or scenic trains in the world. This runs from London to Istanbul in Turkey. The *Blue Train*, another classic train, travels between Cape Town and Johannesburg.

High-speed trains in France are known as *Trains a Grande Velocita* (TGV). Passengers in high speed trains increased tremendously. In 1994, an important TGV train was introduced, connecting London with Paris in three hours and London with Brussels in three hours and fifteen minutes through English-French Channel Tunnel. EPS is a state owned British company which runs *Eurostar* in conjunction with French Railways and Belgium railways. Eurostar trains are moderately expensive and technologically advanced. They travel at a speed up to 300 km per hour. By far the best known and most widely used international rail pass is Eurail pass, which can be used in 16 European countries: Austria, Belgium, Denmark, France, Germany, Greece, Hungary, Ireland, Italy, Luxembourg, the Netherlands, Norway, Spain, Portgual, Sweden and Switzerland. Eurail Pass was a real stimulation in the development of rail transport in Europe. It is used as a marketing tool to attract international visitors. Unlimited travel throughout Western

Europe except Britain for different time periods is allowed for the pass holders. Some countries in Europe introduced separate passes for attracting tourists to their countries. For instance, *Britail Pass* in Great Britain, *Swiss Pass* in Switzerand, and *German Rail Pass* in Germany.

Among the specialized trains, probably the fanciest and certainly the most glamorous train in history, the Orient Express, has been revived. The original Orient Express ran from Paris to Istanbul and was a favourite of royalty and the *haut monde*. There are really three Orient Expresses: the *Nostalgic Orient Express* that runs occasionally between Paris and Istanbul, the route of the original Orient Express; the *Venice Simplon Orient Express* that runs between Boulogne and Venice twice a week and between Paris and Venice three times a week; and the *English segment of the Venice Simplon Orient Express* that runs from London to Folkstone. The Eurotunnel, nicknamed "the Chunnel", will provide underwater rail service between France and England. The Chunnel, a $13.44 billion Anglo-French venture, is really three tunnels! In an emergency, passengers can be evacuated through cross-passages set at 400-yard intervals.

Asia is one continent where rail transport is an important mode of transport, particularly South Korea, Japan, India, etc., South Korea is one country which has good rail network and has introduced high-speed trains as well. In Asia, Japan is much advanced in rail transportation. It had introduced high-speed *bullet trains* between Tokyo and Osaka. Japan's bullet trains, which began operations in 1964, pioneered super-fast rail service and arguably provide the best overall rail service in the world, measured by frequency of trains and on-time performance.

Indian Railways (IR) have a well established computer based reservation system and Indian Railways Catering and Tourism Corporation (IRCTC) has launched on-line ticketing facility for the passengers. A new project for issuing monthly and quarterly season tickets through automated teller machines (ATMs) has been launched in some important cities in India. *National Train Enquiry System* has been started in order to provide upgraded passenger information and enquiries. Information systems for the freight, *Freight Operation Information System* (FOIS), has been made available in around 250 locations throughout India and an intranet, *Railnet*, has been developed for easier communication and assistance for administration among different regional headquarters and others. IR has improved private participation particularly for infrastructure development. Optical fibre based communication system has been adopted for more efficient and improved telecommunication systems on Indian railways. India became the first developing country and the 5th country in the world to roll out the first indigenously built state-of-the-art high horsepower three-phase electric locomotive when the first such loco was flagged off from Chittaranjan Locomotive works. Indian railways have been earning/winning many recognitions and appreciations for a long time. For instance, *Darjeeling Himalayan Railways* attained World Heritage Status from UNESCO and *Fairy Queen*, the oldest functioning steam engine in the world, found a place in the

Guinness Book of World Records. As part of adhering to social obligations, IR offer many concessions and other benefits to the weaker sections of the society like, senior citizens. Metro rail service is an important transport mode in major cities in India. Indian Railways have been playing a vital role in the development of tourism in India, by direct and indirect ways. Indian Railways is one of the cheapest modes of transport available in India, which can be used for tourist transportation also. Apart from this, Indian Railways are directly involved in tourism by various schemes and luxury trains exclusively for tourism in collaboration with state tourism agencies. Illustrations of important tourism luxury trains and schemes are as follows:

5.14.1 Palace-on-Wheels

Palace-on-Wheels is a palatial train, which gives royal experience, and passes through the golden triangle of Indian tourism. It gives a delightful experience; the traveller will feel like an erstwhile monarch, travelling in royal splendour. Fully air conditioned, the train comprises 14 deluxe saloons, equipped with class amenities to enhance the pleasure of travelling. The Rajasthan Tourism Development Corporation and Indian Railways jointly run the *Palace-on-Wheels* tour programme. In the past 20 years of operations, it has been rated as one of the best rail journeys in the world. The passenger coaches were originally

Table 5.10: Palace on wheels: tour itinerary

Days	Destination
Day 1	Delhi (departs)
Day 2	Jaipur
Day 3	Sawai Madhopur/Chittorgarh
Day 4	Udaipur
Day 4	Jaisalmer
Day 5	Jodhpur
Day 6	Bharathpur/Agra
Day 7	Delhi

Table 5.11: Tour tariff (As per 2017 status)

Tariff – Per Person Per Night, Rates are given in US dollars		
Occupancy	**April and September**	**October to March**
Single occupancy	650	865
Double occupancy	500	650
Triple occupancy	450	575
Half fare for children between 5 and 12 years of age		

Source: Official website of Indian Railways/luxury trains.

meant to be personal railway coaches of the erstwhile rulers of princely states of Rajputana, Gujarat, the Nizam of Hydrabad and the Viceroy of British India. They have rich and traditional interiors. A new metre gauge air conditioned *Palace-on-Wheels* was introduced in 1984 and had 13 salons, 2 restaurant cum kitchen cars, one bar-cum-lounge and 4 service cars. Later, a new broad gauge *Palace-on-Wheels* was constructed and has been running since 1996. Now, it has 14 salons, all interconnected, and the interiors of the salons reflect the aesthetics of the former royal states of Rajasthan. Apart from accommodation, the train has many other facilities for a luxurious journey like bar, lunge, CD/MP3 players, attached toilets, posh pantry, luggage collection, attendant, newspapers, security, etc.

The *Palace-on-Wheels* tour package consists of seven nights/eight days covering the major tourist attractions in Rajasthan along with Agra. The journey starts from Delhi cantonment (every Wednesday at 1630 hrs).

5.14.2 The Deccan Odyssey

The *Deccan Odyssey* consists of six luxury train cruises which passes through Maharashtra, Gujarat and Rajasthan. The train consists of 13 fully air-conditioned deluxe salons, each a combination of 4 twin bedded chambers with channel music, intercom, CD/MP3 player, attached toilets, running hot and cold water, etc. The train provides facilities for physically challenged persons, luggage collections, attendant, meals, mineral water, newspapers, magazines, security, wine/bar, group photograph, etc. Maharashtra Splendor, Indian Odyssey, Jewels of Deccan, Maharashtra Wild Trails, Hidden Treasures of Gujarat and Indian Sojourn are the luxury tourist trains under the Deccan Odyssey now.

Table 5.12: The Deccan Odyssey/Maharashtra splendor: Tour itinerary

Days	Destination
Day 1 (Wednesday)	Mumbai
Day 2 (Thursday)	Nashik
Day 3 (Friday)	Aurangabad (Ellora Caves)
Day 4 (Saturday)	Ajanta Caves
Day 5 (Sunday)	Kolhapur
Day 6 (Monday)	Goa
Day 7 (Tuesday)	Sindhudurg
Day 8 (Wednesday)	Mumbai

Source: Official website of Indian Railways/luxury trains

The tariff is almost similar to that of *Palace-on-Wheels* and this presidential suite is available for USD 12,579 for single occupancy. Indian passengers can pay in equivalent rupee amount against US$ at the exchange rate prevalent at the time of payment. The tariff is inclusive of travel, sightseeing, entrance fee, etc.

5.14.3 The Royal Orient

The Royal Orient is a luxury train that cruises through some of India's most culturally fascinating states such as Gujarat and Rajasthan. Like *Palace-on-Wheels* and *Deccan Odyssey, Royal Orient* is also rated amongst the most wonderful train journeys in the world and it takes you to palaces and forts steeped in legends of heroism and chivalry, their palaces and imposing forts that give a special experience. The tour departs from Delhi and the itinerary includes: Delhi cantonment, Chittaurgarh, Udaipur, Junagarh, Veraval, Sasangir, Dilwara, Ahmedabad and Jaipur.

5.14.4 The Fairy Queen

The Fairy Queen, finds mention in the Guinness Book of World Records. It offers an idyllic weakened trip between Delhi and Alwar (Rajasthan). The trip includes picturesque town of Alwar in Rajasthan and the Sariska Tiger Reserve and gives fond memories of a once-in-a lifetime experience. *The Fairy Queen* is the oldest working broad-gauge steam locomotive in the world and was built in the year 1855 by a British firm for East India Railways. The train has only a first class (non-a/c) chair car having forty seats and a pantry car for onboard catering. The tariff for round trip package is Rs. 12,375/- for each passenger (all inclusive except alcoholic drinks). Foreigners can pay equivalent amount in USD.

5.14.5 Indrail Pass

Apart from the luxury trains, Indian Railway also offer one railway pass scheme (*Indrail pass*), as part of promotion of international tourism to India. To explore the splendour of multifaceted India, Indrail Pass provides excellent value and enhances the diagram of holidays from abroad. It enables a tourist to travel wherever he likes and whichever trains he likes within the validity period. A separate foreign tourist quota has been provided in all classes and almost all trains for the facility of the tourists. Reservation facility is available against Indrail from any reservation office of Indian Railways. The pass holder is not required to pay any reservation fee, super fast charge or surcharge for the journey. Indrail passes can be purchased from India tourist bureaus at major railway stations and certain recognized travel agents in Delhi, Madras, Mumbai and Calcutta and from abroad—general sales agents of Indian Airlines and Air India. These passes can only be purchased by foreign nationals and non-resident Indians on payment of US dollars, pound sterling and other convertible foreign currencies.

5.15 WATER TRANSPORTATION

Water transportation is one of the earliest forms of transport, and still plays an important role in travel and tourism sector. Hence, getting an idea about water transportation is crucial for a beginner in tourism studies. Transport by water appears to have been in vogue from very early times. Reaching a destination by sailing has been an important method of transport since the first primitive boat was built (Holloway, 1996). Travel by water offers many unique advantages, though air transport has the leading role in international transportation. Cruising in particular, is enjoying a popularity boom that has not been seen since the heyday of the 'between wars' period. Cruises offer the advantage of total relaxation, and an all-inclusive price that allows the passenger to be carried from one destination to another in comfort and safety, and without the need to constantly pack and unpack. Different forms of water transport other than cruises too have advanced during the last fifty years. Short-sea (ferry) vessels have achieved new standards of comfort on many routes. They attract tourists not just in order to travel from one point to another, but to enjoy a *mini-cruise* which provides food and entertainment that a few years ago was available only in luxury cruise liners. Technological developments benefited in reducing high operating costs. In the mean time new forms of water-borne transport have been developed like hovercraft, jetfoil and the twin hulled catamaran ferry.

Water transport, one of the earliest forms of travel, still is an attractive transport mode in the parlance of tourism, though type and nature of travel has changed dramatically over the years. As with any other forms of transport, water transport services now offer more comfort and luxury. Over the years, safety and speed have increased. Water transportation consists of a wide variety of carrying units/vessels. A brief account of the commonly used such vessels is given below.

5.15.1 The Ocean Liners

Line-voyage services are those offering passenger transport on a port-to-port basis. Until 1950, these shipping lines occupied a prime position in international transportation. But the advances in air transport caused the decline in travel by ship. From 1950s onward, advances in air transport enabled fares to be reduced, especially on popular routes across the Atlantic, to a point where it became cheaper to travel by air than by ship. Most of the remaining passenger-carrying vessels operating around the world are built essentially to carry cargo. By 1957, air transport started to overtake sea transportation in Atlantic (Holloway, 1996). The ships built for operating in the 1950s failed to meet the needs of the post-war market; insufficient cabins with private bathrooms were available to meet the needs of the American market in particular, and the vessels' specifications and size made them inflexible and unsuitable for routes other than those for which they were built. Currently, a number of ocean liners operate efficient services now. Cunard Line's transatlantic services, P & O's services to the Far East and Australia, Union-Castloe and British India Lines' service to South and East Africa are some major route services, though the importance has decreased considerably.

5.16 CRUISE TOURISM

Cruise tourism is a 'buzzword' in tourism sector nowadays. Of all the segments of international travel, cruises, the most luxurious form of water transport, are the fastest growing. Cruise based holidays are in fashion among tourists in the modern world. Cruise industry is relatively young in comparison with the ocean liners, which had a grand history. Passenger ships were forerunners of the present-day cruise ships. The cruise ship is not only important as a means of getting from one place to another, but also comprises the tourists' accommodation and the source of their meals and entertainment. The cruise market has been on expansion and the nature of market is also changing. It caters to all types of needs, ages and purchasing abilities. Advances in marine technology and changes in demand have enabled recent cruise ships to be built for a purpose, in a variety of sizes. There are a number of famous identified cruise routes in the world. New and bigger cruise ships are being built, some of which sail to northern ports in summer and the Caribbean and Mediterranean during the winter (Lundberg and Lundberg, 1993). Large cruises on the average accommodate some 1000 passengers, while small vessels carry fewer than 100 passengers and are sometimes called *mini-cruisers* or *ultra-yachts* (Gee et al., 1997).

Florida is an important region for the cruise tourism. The port of Miami, known as the 'Capital of Cruise World' and the home to 21 cruise ships, is the largest and busiest cruise port in the world. Fort Lauderdale, Port Canaveral, Tampa, Los Angeles, etc., also serve as home ports for some cruise lines. New York City and Boston are also important embarkation points in relation to cruise tourism. The expansion in cruise sector causes addition of new fleet and new ports of call. The last two and half decades have seen tremendous expansion in the cruise sector and it has grown at an average annual growth rate of 8.4% (Goeldner and Ritchie, 2003). As per an estimate, the average length of a cruise was 6.5 days during 2000. The growth of cruise sector is expected to continue and many new ships are scheduled to come for operation in the next few years. It serves as home for many of the US based cruise industries. Cruises mainly offer a *resort type* experience. In the US travel and tourism sector, cruise industry has an important role. Most of the cruises are there for three, four or seven days in length, though voyages of more length have been observed. Provided there is sufficient demand, optimum profits can be achieved by employing larger vessels, and the trend in the 1980s and 1990s has been too build ships in the range of 50,000 to 60,000 tonnes, with some exceeding 70,000 tonnes, and carrying an excess of 2000 passengers.

The major cruise destinations are Caribbean countries, Mediterranean area, Alaska, the Panama Canal and North European region. Caribbean has the largest share among them, attracting half of the cruise passengers worldwide. Caribbean cruises, by contrast, enjoy year-round market demand, although the winter period, when the climate is more temperate than in summer, has the greatest market demand. Recent trends reveal that African destinations and some destinations in Asia are also emerging as popular destinations for cruise tourism. The transit of the Panama Canal still remains as one of the most famous attractions and the cruises through it either begin or end in San Francisco, Los Angeles or Ft. Lauderable. An estimate says that around more than hundred ships have been introduced in North America since 1990. In cruise sector, as in the case of rest of the travel and tourism sector, consolidation is taking place. Large cruise companies are acquiring some smaller companies, and mergers as well as tie-ups are taking place. *Carnival*, world's largest cruise company recently acquired Cunard and Costa Cruise Lines. Royal Caribbean International (RCI), the second largest player also acquired Celebrity Cruises recently. Shorter, less expensive cruises continued to do well. Cutting prices and offering a variety of cruises—rock 'n' roll cruises, chocolate cruises, and golf tours, in which passengers disembark at several different ports to play golf.

Cruises offer a variety of services as part of the cruise tourism product. Accommodation facilities vary from sleeping rooms with berths, for as many as three or four persons to lavish bedrooms built as staterooms. A variety of sports and game options such as tennis, jogging, aerobics, pumping iron or perfecting a golf swing, in most cruise ships are also offered onboard. Fully equipped gyms, health spas, and athletic counsellors are also a part of many cruises. Food is offered throughout the day in a variety of forms, from seven-course meals to theme event dinners. Cruises provide different entertainment options too like, full-scale musical productions, individual cabaret performances, discos, gambling, and so on.

Some of the major cruise routes (Holloway, 1996) are:

- The Caribbean, Bermuda and the Bahamas, including the coast of Central and South America.
- The Mediterranean, divided between the Western and Eastern sectors.
- The West Coast of North America including Mexico, the USA (including Alaska) and Canada.
- The Pacific islands and Far East.
- The Baltic Sea, Northern capitals and the North Cape.
- West Africa and the Atlantic islands of the Canaries and Madeira.
- Round the world.

Cruises are classified according to the size, comfort level, services offered, etc. According to Gee et al., (1997), cruises are classified as resort cruises, deluxe or luxury cruises, and adventure or exotic cruises. The features of each category of cruises are as follows:

Resort Cruises

- Large vessels, which can accommodate 1000-2000 plus passengers.
- Food and beverage are plentiful.
- Warm climate places are usual destinations.
- Markets are highly segmented.
- Shipboard activities include entertainment, aerobics, and bingo.
- Short itineraries: 3 to 7 days.

Deluxe or Luxury Cruises

- Capacity varies from 125 to 950 passengers.
- High level of personal service is offered.
- Cabins are usually suites.
- Dining facilities are elegant and stylish.
- 14 days or longer itineraries, with some as long as a month.
- Entertainment consists of classical music, shows and educational lectures.

Adventure or Exotic Cruises

- Likely to explore narrow inlets and allow passengers to wade ashore.
- Onboard interpretation activities.
- Usually older and smaller ships are used.
- Ports of call are unusual.
- Basic dining services with substantial fares are available.
- Tourist-type shopping and sightseeing are less important than discovering new places and experience.
- Passengers are older, educated; most are professionals.

Many forecasts reveal that cruise sector has a bright future. The growth in the industry shows impressive gains with lot of scope for future growth. High satisfaction levels among cruise passengers, which should create a high percentage of repeat cruisers, and potentially large foreign markets are the two major factors that contributed in the growth of cruise tourism. Incentive travel market is an important segment for cruise tourism.

5.16.1 Ferry Services

The term *ferry* is one which embraces a variety of forms of short-distance water-borne transport. Ferries are the boats for transporting persons and automobiles across a comparatively small body of water. Ferry boats, or ferry liners, found in many parts of the world, transport travellers on fresh and salt water. In India, these services are very famous, particulary in remote areas. Kerala is an example where regular ferry services are operated in lakes. In the United States, ferry boats have been used to cross Lake Michigan and for transport between Alaska and the state of Washington, as well as in other locations. Modern ferry boats permit travellers to combine the use of a motor vehicle with a trip over large stretches of water by carrying campers and trailers on the boat. Ferry services are usually used by passengers in combination with some form of land transport, for example, coach, train or car, which carries them to the ferry ports from their places of origin and to their final destination after the sea cruising. There are plenty of famous ferry routes including English Channel routes, north sea routes, Irish sea routes, etc. Ferry companies have been developing new routes and to tap regional markets and to offer greater choice.

5.16.2 River Boats

River boat is a boat used on rivers or to ply on rivers. River boats, featuring staterooms, restaurants, and entertainment, provide a popular means of travel in many countries, including England, France and the former Yugoslavia. Similar services are operated in India in major rivers.

5.16.3 Paddle Wheelers

Paddle wheeler is basically a ship or a boat propelled by paddle wheels, driven by a steam engine. Though it is on old technology, paddle wheelers have returned to some rivers in America. Paddle wheelers were in service from 1811 onwards in major rivers like Mississippi, Missouri and Ohio.

5.16.4 Houseboats

Houseboat is a boat that has been designed or modified to be used primarily as human dwelling and cruising. Houseboats have become increasingly popular in the United States. They can be rented, usually on a weekly basis. Indian backwaters are famous for houseboats. Houseboats of Kashmir are world famous. Kerala is another destination, where large houseboats are used. Based on houseboat cruises along network of rivers and lakes, a new kind of tourism called *backwater tourism* has evolved in Kerala.

5.16.5 Canoes

Canoes are long, narrow and light boats pointed at both ends, moved by a paddle. They are popularly used in water touring, speed competitions, and white-water sports, or navigate through rapids in the boundary water areas between Minnesota and Canada, and in parts of Maine. Canoe rental firms also operate on rivers. In India, canoes are used for transportation of goods as well as for short passenger trips.

5.16.6 Submarines

Submarines are basically transport modes, which can be operated completely submerged in water. They are also defined as vessels capable of operating under water for sustained periods. Submarines are the underwater equivalent of hot-air balloon rides. The speed is moderate, neither too fast nor too slow. It neither goes very far nor is very fast. Submarines offer an exciting new experience.

5.16.7 Barges

Barges are flat-bottomed boats used to transport goods on inland waterways or large, roomy boats elegantly furnished and decorated to carry passengers down rivers and canals. Barges are usually not powered, being pushed or towed by a tugboat instead. River barges move at a snail's pace and usually carry from 4 to 25 passengers on major rivers in North America and Europe. *Sail cruising, bareboat charters, yatch cruising,* etc., are some other forms of water transport being followed in connection with tourism. Different modifications were made to traditional forms and extra services possible are incorporated in such transport forms to make them attractive.

5.16.8 Hovercraft, Hydrofoils and Wave-Piercing Catamarans (WPC)

Hovercraft is a vehicle that is capable of moving over land or water while supported on a cushion of air made by jet engines. It rides on a cushion of air just above the surface of water, and its ability to travel over land as well as water avoids the usual capital costs associated with dock facilities, as the craft can simply be beached on any convenient and obstacle-free foreshore. It produces more sound and cannot operate in rough weather. *Hydrofoil* is a boat equipped with a device which raises the hull out of the water when the boat is moving, enabling to travel fast and economically. Recent models have been powered by jet engines and are operating in some parts of the world. *Catamarans* are sailing boats with two parallel hulls. WPCs are twin-hulled vessels large enough to accommodate cars, travelling at speeds up to 40 knots (comparable with hovercrafts) and these have been operating on cross-channel services since 1991.

5.16.9 Inland Waterways

Lakes, rivers and canals constitute the inland waterways. These have great potential for recreation and tourism. Along the waterways, tourists travel at a leisurely pace on various types of boats. The major waterways of the world have long attracted the tourist. The Nile River in Egypt, has provided inland waterway cruising for many years. The Rhine, the Mississippi, the Danube, Yangtze and Li rivers, etc., also experience inland waterway tourism. Inland waterways in particular—lakes, rivers and canals—provide exceptional opportunities for recreation and tourism, and in Britain the renovation of former canals, derelict locks and similar water sites have added in recent years to the many opportunities for river and lake recreational travel. Waterways are often of international importance, either because they border or run through more than one country or because other nations wish to use them for trade; a number of these waterways have been internationalized. In India, inland navigation facilities had attracted people towards river valleys from very early periods.

5.16.10 Mini Cruisers

Similar to cruises, *mini cruises* are also in trend. Generally, they are operated along the Pacific Coast from Alaska to California and Atlantic coastal areas from marine to Caribbean. The common characteristics of the travellers using mini cruises (Gee et al., 1997) are as follows:

- Many travel in non-family groups.
- Passengers are predominantly old married couples with fairly high income.
- Many have previous cruise travel experience.
- They are relatively high spenders on shore for hotels and food, which benefits other sectors of the travel industry.

5.17 CONCLUSION

Transport is an inevitable component of tourism. Its evolution is the cardinal reason for the growth of tourism. All forms of transport are significant in tourism. Yet, the share of air transport is increasing and currently, more than fifty per cent of tourists use air transport for reaching destinations, followed by land transport. In water transport forms, cruise is gaining significance due to its inimitable leisure tourism potentials. Certainly transport technology is in a path of further advancements and it will influence tourism to surge ahead.

Key Terms

Transport	Passenger
Air transport	Scheduled airline
Civil aviation	Charter airlines
Commercial aviation	Deregulation
General aviation	Bilateral agreements
Airport	Freedoms of air
Airline	Hub-and-spoke system
Air navigation	Code share agreements
Tourism	Land transport

Coaches
Rail transport
Water transport
Cruise tourism

Review Questions

Short Answer Type Questions

1. Elucidate the role of transport in tourism.
2. How has tourism contributed in the growth of transportation?
3. Classify transport forms.
4. Define aviation and air transport.
5. What are the types of aviation?
6. What do you mean by civil aviation?
7. What are the purposes for which general aviation is used?
8. Differentiate between scheduled and non-scheduled services.
9. Explain the use of charter flights in tourism.
10. What do you mean by bilateral agreements?
11. Write a note on freedoms of air.
12. What is a code-share agreement?
13. Explain the structure of an airport and its functions.
14. Explain how airports cause pollution.
15. What are navigation services?
16. What are airline operations?
17. What do you mean by 'open sky policy'?
18. Write a short note on deregulation.
19. Discuss the significance of land transport in tourism.
20. Discuss the various land transport used in tourism.
21. Write short notes on any two special tourist trains.
22. Discuss the various water transport means used in tourism.
23. Write a short note on the types of cruises.

Essay Type Questions

1. Explain the contribution of air transport in the growth of tourism.
2. Discuss the role and relevance of rail transport in tourism.
3. Write an essay on air transport and its components.
4. Write an essay on cruise tourism.

6

TOURIST DESTINATION

Learning Outcomes

After studying this chapter, you will be able to:

- understand the concept of tourist destination;
- explain the various elements of a tourist destination;
- understand the lifecycle of a destination;
- elucidate the relationship between destination elements and tourist arrivals;
- explain attractions and their various types;
- comprehend the evolution and growth of tourism in a destination; and
- understand DMO and its role and functions.

6.1 INTRODUCTION

Destination is a common term used in different contexts. The Oxford Dictionary defines it as "the place to which someone or something is going or being sent". Traditionally, destination is used for referring to a place where something is going or sent, or someone is going or being sent. The use of the term for the visit had become common and later the place where people liked to visit started to be called *tourist destination*. Now, destination is used to refer to the specific area in which travellers choose to visit and spend a significant amount of time. This views destination from a geographical perspective, but of late the aspect of space is also missing when we refer to some tourist destinations. In cruise tourism, there is no specific place where a tourist spends time. In space tourism, the location is not on the earth, but it takes place in the outer space. Virtual tourism concept is based on simulation and hence location and place have no significance. Though such concepts are emerging, the traditional concept of destination is still valid with diverse facets. While treating destination as a place, there is no exact boundary, shape and size for considering a place as a tourist destination. It depends on the context. A country can be called a destination. The same can be used for a continent

Table 6.1: Top ten destinations in India and the world

Top ten destinations (countries—foreign tourist arrivals) in the world	Top ten destinations (states—foreign tourist arrivals) in India
France	Tamil Nadu
USA	Maharashtra
Spain	Uttar Pradesh
China	Delhi
Italy	Rajasthan
Turkey	West Bengal
Germany	Kerala
United Kingdom	Bihar
Russia	Karnataka
Mexico	Haryana
Source: UNWTO statistics, 2014	Source: India Tourism Statistics, 2014

as well. A region inside a country can also be called a destination. Hence, there is no unanimous consent on the geographical aspect of a destination.

6.2 DESTINATION: CONCEPT AND DEFINITIONS

Basically, a destination is a geographical concept that is primarily defined by visitors from outside the location although many places seek to make themselves destinations for visitors in order to be able to benefit economically for tourism (Cooper and Hall, 2008). Gunn (1994) pointed out that *destination zone* is the geographic area containing a critical mass of development that satisfies travellers' objectives. Though traditionally, destination is considered a place where people spend their holidays, it is now viewed from different perspectives as well. From visitors' perspective, destination is an area where they choose to visit and spend their holidays and the resulting impacts of their activities. On the other hand, developers perceive destination as "managing demand for tourism and its impacts on the destination" (Laws, 1995). In the tourism system concept, destination is the final point of visit which denotes that they are not simply transit or stopover points.

Destinations can be naturally attractive like wildlife sanctuaries or they can be designed with manmade or artificial attractions like amusement parks, historical complexes or holiday villages. People and their customs and lifestyle including fairs, festivals, music, dance and ornamentation can also be staged as attractions. Destinations and attractions sometimes cover a vast area. More than the site or event, the attraction of a destination lies in the image that the potential tourist has of a particular place. In fact, the image of a destination depends on a variety of factors like attitude of host population, civic amenities, natural surroundings, accessibility, food, etc. The image is neither constructed nor deconstructed overnight. It tends to build up over time. No destination can be popular unless it is accessible and offers services and amenities that tourists demand. Essential services are accommodation and food, backed up by local transport, activities and entertainment.

Any place with potential can become a destination once destination-oriented developments take place. The following are some of the essential actions to be undertaken as part of it:

- convert resources with potential into attractions;
- provide appropriate transport to, from and within the destination;
- provide an appropriate range of tourist accommodation facilities; and
- ensure successful integration of tourist related developments into the changing activity patterns of the place on a long-term sustainable basis (Howie, 2003).

The selection of a destination by a tourist depends on the purpose and motivation for travel. A destination and its attractions must have *pull* capacity to induce travellers to visit. Some destinations are more prone to the impacts of tourism, both positive as well as negative. Care has to be taken at the time of development for maximizing the benefits and minimizing the negative impacts. The people residing in and around a destination also have a role in making it successful. In recent years, environmental, cultural and social aspects have emerged as important dimensions for developing a destination.

6.3 COMMON CHARACTERISTICS OF DESTINATIONS

Though geographically, destinations can vary in size, from a small resort to a region within a country, the whole of a country or even larger area of the globe (Holloway, 2006). They share certain common characteristics, for example, Khajuraho is a destination with a limited area and at the same time, India as a whole can also be considered a destination. It is the area where a good majority of the industry components are situated. For example, accommodation industry, food and beverage sector, attractions, etc., are located in the destination region. According to Cooper et al. (2000), the following features can be identified in most of the destinations:

- Destinations are amalgams.
- Destinations are cultural appraisals.
- Destinations are inseparable, that is, tourism is produced where it is consumed.
- Destinations are used not just by tourists, but by many other groups.

Destination as a product has been defined as *an amalgam* of some fundamental components, like attractions, facilities and accessibility. There are other components also that have much significance in the era of modern tourism. The success in attracting tourists depends on the quality of these essential components. *Attractions* - whether they be artificial features, natural features or events—provide an invitation to visit. A range of amenities, support facilities and services are required by a tourist at a destination. *Accommodation* and *food and beverage* sector of the destination not only provide physical shelter and sustenance, but also create the general feeling of being welcomed and a lasting impression of the local cuisine and produce. Apart from these, a range of retailing businesses are there in a destination. *Infrastructure* and *superstructure* are the alternative ways of looking at the components of a destination. Infrastructure represents all forms of construction above or below ground needed by an inhabited area. It is mainly in the form of transportation, utilities and other services, normally shared by tourists and visitors alike. Whereas superstructure is normally a private sector activity and it includes accommodation, built attractions, retailing and other structures.

Destinations are *cultural appraisals* as well. "Cultural appraisal is a process of learning about domains or constructs of a culture.... It's also about recognizing and respecting cultural strengths as an important focal point for developing appropriate interventions ..." (EdCaN-learning resources-Australia). Tourists visiting a destination can learn about the culture of the local population and vice-versa. When it comes to cultural tourism, the destination is a living cultural area, open for learning and respecting the cultural features. *Inseparability* is a core feature of tourism as tourists are inevitable in the process of tourism. Without tourists, the phenomenon of tourism does not evolve. The products are consumed in the place of production and immovability of the products is a core feature of tourism products. Moreover, most of the amenities and facilities enjoyed by the tourists are shared by the local people as well. It means that the infrastructure is meant for both guests as well as hosts. Superstructure is meant primarily for tourists. There are also some other features that make destinations unique from other products. The feature of *intangibility* is a crucial one to the destination. Tourist gains an experience from tourism over there. *Perishability, seasonality, fragmentation of industry* and *complementarity* are the other characteristics that can be attributed to tourist destinations.

6.4 FUNDAMENTAL ELEMENTS OF TOURISM IN A DESTINATION

Tourism is complex with diverse elements. Each element is interrelated, and the quality as well as performance of each of them contributes in the success of the whole process of tourism. Pertaining to the most significant element of tourism, the destination, which is the *raison d'être* of tourism, a framework of a few A's can be identified. Each 'A' in it represents each element that is essential in the context of a tourist destination. The most discussed framework is 3A's, which involves Attractions, Amenities and Accessibility. Yet, in contemporary tourism, in its most advanced form with increased economic significance, enhanced international interaction, information and communication technology integration, as well as with the need for competitive survival in the hyper competitive globalised environment. It is inevitable to identify more elements so as to make sure of getting a comprehensive knowledge of tourism. A number of basic elements can be identified, categorized into a framework of 7A's, such as:

- Attractions
- Accessibility
- Accommodation
- Amenities
- Ancillary services
- Activities
- Awareness.

6.5 ATTRACTIONS

Tourists like to visit a destination, essentially for its inherent or exhibited cultural value, historical significance, natural or artificial beauty, or amusement opportunities. Monuments, zoos, beaches, mountains, museums and art galleries, botanical gardens, and amusement parks, etc., are some examples. Destinations need to capitalize on the available resources in order to create an alluring amalgam of attractions. Some of the successful destinations develop authentic attractions using the cultural and natural features. Moreover, some also attempt to create modern artificial attractions. Even events of various kinds act as attractions for tourists. In fact, factors like authenticity, innovation, and degree of strangeness determine the competitiveness of attractions. Attractions are the reasons why tourists choose to visit a particular destination. They are difficult to define as they involve different perspectives. For example, sometimes, the purpose of attraction is not for attracting tourists. They are the single most important reason for leisure tourism to a destination (Cooper et al., 2005). They, in the backdrop of the natural and cultural resources available there, form the core of attractiveness of a destination. The degree of attractiveness is directly proportional to the lure, which is the most significant determinant of a destination's success that exerts a strong *pull* on a tourist to visit. Attractions are also shared by local people. They are usually single unit with a specific geographical area whereas a destination may be based on a series of attractions (Page, 2007). Pearce (1991) defines attraction as "a named site with a specific human or natural feature which is the focus of visitor and management attention".

The scope of attractions has been expanded dramatically and shopping opportunities, fairs and festivals are also part of attractions or even independent attractions. Attractions are perceived to allow access for entertainment, interest or education and finally have

Table 6.2: Basic classification of attractions

Natural Attractions	
Climate	Rivers
Beaches	Mountains
Landscapes	Forests
Spas	Wildlife
Lakes	Valleys, etc
Manmade attractions	
Artistic and cultural heritage	Entertainment
Historical buildings	Cinemas
Archeological sites	Night clubs
Museums	Zoos
Paintings/art forms	Racecourse
Art/music festivals	Theme parks
Monuments, etc.	Casinos, etc.
Sports facilities	Rides and transport
Ski stapes	Coaches
Tennis courts	Camel/elephant rides
Swimming pools	Railways
Water-based sports centres	Cruises
Polo centres	Houseboats
Adventure sports facilities	Shopping
	Duty-free shopping
	Handicrafts markets
	Hyper markets, etc.

to be open for public. Single attraction based destinations are also there. The attractions should influence tourists to visit and provide pleasurable experience. Tourists, as the consumers of the system, have to get satisfaction from their visit to attractions. Usually, the agencies that promote tourism provide appropriate level of facilities and services to meet and cater to the demands, needs and interests of the visitors. In a nutshell, it can be stated that visitor attractions have to offer both products and experience (Page, 2007). Attractions are categorized into:

- **Primary:** the chief reason why people chose to visit.
- **Secondary:** other attractions that influence the people to visit.
- **Tertiary:** attractions that visitors become aware of only at the destination (Kelly and Nankervis, 2009).

Table 6.3: Prentice's typology of tourism attractions

Types	Examples
Natural history attractions	Nature reserves, nature trails, aquatic life displays, rare breeds centres, wildlife parks, zoos, butterfly parks, waterfowl parks, geomorphological and geological sites, including caves, gorges, waterfalls, etc.
Science based attractions	Science museums, technology centres, "hands-on" science centres, "alternative" technology centres.
Attractions concerned with primary production	Agricultural attractions, farms, dairies, farming museums, vineyards, fishing, mining, water impounding reservoirs, etc.
Craft centres and craft workshops	Products and processes; including water and windmills, sculptors, potters, woodcarvers, hand-worked metals, glass makers, silk working, lace making, handloom weaving, and craft "villages".
Attractions concerned with manufacturing industry	Pottery and porcelain factories, breweries, cider factories, distilleries, economic history museums.
Transport attractions	Transport museums, tourist and preserved railways, canals, civil shipping, civil aviation, motor vehicles.
Sociocultural attractions	Prehistoric and historic sites and displays: like domestic houses, social history museums, costume museums, regalia exhibitions, furnishing museums, museums of childhood, toy museums.
Attractions associated with historic persons	Sites and areas associated with writers and painters
Performing arts attractions	Theatres, street-based performing arts, performing arts workshops, circuses.
Pleasure gardens	Ornamental gardens, period gardens, arboreta, model villages.
Theme parks	Nostalgia parks, "historic" adventure parks, fairytale parks for children (but excluding amusement parks, where the principal attractions are exciting rides and the like).
Galleries	Particularly art galleries.
Festivals and pageants	Historic fairs, festivals "recreating" past ages, countryside festivals of "rural" activities.
Field sports	Traditional field sports like fishing, hunting, shooting, and stalking.
State and ancestral homes	Palaces, country houses, manor houses.
Religious attractions	Cathedrals, churches, abbeys, priories, mosques, shrines, wells, springs.
Military attractions	Battlefields, military airfields, naval dockyards, prisoner of war camps, military museums.
Genocide monuments	Sites associated with the extermination of other races or other mass killings of populations.
Towns and townscapes	Mainly historic townscape, groups of buildings in an urban setting.
Villages and hamlets	Principally "rural" settlements, usually of pre-twentieth century architecture.
Countryside and treasured landscapes	National parks, other countryside amenity designations, "rural" landscapes which may not be officially designated but are enjoyed by visitors.
Seaside resorts and "seascapes"	Principally seaside towns of past eras and marine "landscapes".
Regions	Including places, counties, or other historical or geographical areas identified as distinctive by their residents or visitors

Attractions are also classified into natural and manmade along with a combination of both (Table 6.2). One of the most widely used classification is of Swarbrooke. He identified four main types, as follows:

- Features within the natural environment.
- Manmade buildings, structures and sites that were designed for a purpose other than attracting visitors, such as worship, but which now attract substantial number of visitors who use them as leisure amenities.
- Manmade buildings, structures and sites that are designed to attract visitors and are purpose-built to accommodate their needs, for example, theme parks.
- Special events (Swarbrooke, 2002).

Another extensive classification is done by Prentice, by categorizing attractions into 23 varieties. It is shown in Table 6.3

6.6 ACCESSIBILITY

Tourism is all about travel and the destination needs to be at a distance, much away from the place of origin of the tourist. *Accessibility* refers to 'how to reach' and the easiness in reaching a destination. A destination must be accessible if it is to facilitate visits by tourists. Most of the tourists will not be attracted to a destination unless it is relatively easy to reach. Efficient transportation system helps to reach the destination and also move about within the destination. An airport, railway station, bus stand, etc., near the destination increase accessibility. The distance from tourism markets, the availability of various modes of transport, frequency of transport, time taken for reaching, safety and security, and comfort of travel are factors associated with accessibility that contribute in making a destination successful. But in some rare cases like adventure tourism, inadequate accessibility may also be an attraction.

6.7 ACCOMMODATION

Like travel, stay is also fundamental to tourism. Destinations have to make sure that adequate stay facilities, commonly known as accommodation, are available for the visiting population. *Accommodation* itself is an industry, and referred to as 'hospitality', comprises a wide range of elements. Hotels, resorts, motels, bread and breakfast (B&B), lodges, and home stays constitute some of the common hospitality elements. Being a service sector, the quality of the services delivered influences the satisfaction level of tourists. Destinations should also ensure variety in the hospitality sector as per the needs of the tourists. Some tourists prefer up market hotels whereas some backpackers may prefer small scale non-serviced accommodation units. Accommodation is also considered a part of amenities.

6.8 AMENITIES

Amenities are those essential services which cater to the requirements of the tourists. In some cases, amenities are represented as infrastructure required for tourism. They are required for tourism, and include facilities such as food services, local transport, information centres and the necessary infrastructure to support tourism such as roads, public utility services, and parking facilities. In certain cases, amenities themselves act as attractions. For example, *Palace-on-Wheels*, is a world famous rail tour package in India, that passes through major destinations like Udaipur, Jaipur and Agra from Delhi. It is not part of 'accessiblity' as it can be used only by those who arrive at the boarding point, Delhi. The tourist using this rail package can visit many places, but the main attraction is the train itself. Another example is that a destination like France, which is famed for its regional food, encourage tourists whose motive in travelling may be largely to enjoy the food. Some of the amenities are in the public sector, whereas some others are private. In order to be more efficient, a high degree of cooperation is needed, particularly where tourist services may be seen to be competing with the needs of local residents. In certain other cases, if the level of amenities is more, it will take away the charm of the destination. For example, in wildlife tourism, there is a certain threshold limit in the case of amenities and if it is crossed, definitely the destination won't be able to attract many tourists henceforth.

6.9 ANCILLARY SERVICES

Tourism sector will not survive just with frontline businesses or other businesses/ agencies included in the amenities. *Ancillary services* refer to the auxiliary or supplementary services offered at the destination. While some are in the public sector, some others may be voluntary support bodies. There are some private organizations as well. Local organizations are the best examples which usually offer various services to the tourists. Some such organizations include:

- Destination marketing and promotion organizations
- Tourist statistics agencies
- Agencies that offer reservation and booking services
- Developmental agencies aimed at tourism
- Research organizations
- Agencies providing guidance to the local businesses.
- Guide services, etc.

6.10 ACTIVITIES

Of late, activities available for tourists in a destination are becoming increasingly relevant. Visiting tourists like to be more active, dynamic and take part in activities. These may be physical, for example, diving, swimming, and white water rafting, or they may be passive, for example, dolphin watch, sunbathing and relaxing on a beach. The current trends reveal that tourists prefer to have experiential tourism in which they would like to involve and enjoy the authentic experience. Successful destinations are now introducing possible activities along with the attractions carved out from natural and cultural resources. Majority of the activities are in the natural environment, yet artificial activities are also being arranged depending on the nature and type of destinations.

6.11 AWARENESS

In the globalised era filled with ICT, information is so powerful. Having all other elements like amenities, accessibility, etc., the destination is less significant if the awareness factor is missing. Information forms the core in awareness and it has to be disseminated efficiently and effectively. Awareness about the attractions should be there in the tourist market. Tourism industry service providers, developers and marketers of the destination should be aware of the tourism markets in detail. Destination image should be strong, and firmly implanted in the tourist's mind. Latest Information and Communication Technologies have to be effectively applied to use information as an operational and strategic weapon to beat the competition and bring about sustained success.

6.12 EVOLUTION AND GROWTH OF TOURISM IN A DESTINATION

Learning about the evolution of a tourist destination is interesting. In fact, a tourist destination may not be a tourist spot earlier and tourism might have been evolved with a humble beginning, in most of the destinations. "Visitor destinations evolve as the value of a particular destination's attractions or features are communicated and recognized...... To some extent, then, the evolution of a holiday destination reflects the degree of market acceptance" (Kelly and Nankervis, 2009). Many of the destinations had a natural evolution of tourism, instead of creating the site as a tourist destination in the beginning and then attracting tourists from far and wide. Usually, an attraction is identified by some explorers and that's the time when its tourist potential is identified. A destination is born when it has been discovered by some curious visitors who found something worth visiting. Once interest in the destination is generated, the word spreads, and more visitors flock there. The number of tourists increase slowly and that results in the shortage of basic facilities. Once the demand for such facilities arises, government at the local level may initiate steps to fulfil the basic needs such as parking space, toilets, refreshment centres and so on. Some basic accommodation facilities too emerge then. The state as well as national governments may catch the increasing popularity of the destination and make plans to develop tourism further over there. The destination thus enters into the tourism map and promotional measures may be introduced for attracting tourists. By that time other businesses may also come. Variety of industries will be established there, and the destination gets spatial expansion as well. Spatial expansion takes place in three ways:

- **Linear:** like along a road or a coastal area.
- **Star shaped:** extending outwards along two or more intersecting roads.
- **Radial:** by circular accretions around a core. (Kelly and Nankervis, 2009)

The linear growth is comprehended as a snowball that begins to gather momentum as it rolls down a hill. It explains that as tourism grows, the snowball rolls down a hill, and gains momentum. In the beginning, the public sector would have more control over tourism in the destination. Initially, it will be like a small snowball, without much vision about rapid growth. During this period tourists are also compromising and development is minimal. Local people show much affinity for tourism. Once the destination gains tourism momentum, many pressures are exerted by different stakeholders like industries, entrepreneurs, etc. By this time, the snowball increases in size and starts rolling down due to the increasing mass of tourism. The growing economic dependence on tourism in the destination adds further pressure. By this time, the snowball grows and gathers momentum, almost unstoppable and out of control. Intervention cannot resist the impact and antagonism from the local community. In the end, it will enlarge as mass tourism develops and control over it will be limited to public agencies (Page, 2007). All this will eventually make the destination less attractive to new tourists, with a lot of impact.

Another concept used to illustrate the growth and expansion of tourism is the *amoeba* concept. Tourism once introduced into a locality and is welcomed, it will act as a support mechanism to help stimulate economic activity. It may expand like an amoeba (Page, 2007). Tourism thus shows the characteristics to replicate itself, but then adapt and change to meet customer needs, and development takes place. Some ideas how tourist destinations develop over time are:

- Destinations develop and change over time.
- There are different types of visitors at different times.
- Visitor experience changes overtime.
- The involvement of locals in tourist destinations changes over time.
- New cycles involving new tourist destinations will happen (Christaller, 1963).

Table 6.4: Local tourism development: some conditions

- Tourists respect local, cultural and ethnic features and values.
- Opportunity for extensive local community involvement in the tourism industry through decisions made by the local government.
- Community-wide support for volunteer tourism programmes.
- Active participation in the direction of tourist development.
- Tourism is an economic mainstay, matching with other economic sectors, or as a desirable alternative to other industries.
- Themes and events that attract tourists are supported and developed by the local community.

Source: Cooke, 1982.

In the process of evolution, the 'unspoilt' nature of destination can be altered. Kelly and Nankervis (2009) opine two possibilities while tourism is developed in a destination. In their words, "in a process termed *visitor displacement*, those favouring only moderate levels of development and visitation will seek to substitute alternative destinations as development gains pace.... Recreational succession, relates to the changes in activities conducted at the destination (for example, from scuba diving to the less challenging snorkeling) as it becomes more developed". The point is that along with changes in the demand, supply can also be changed as tourism is developed in a destination. Moreover, changes are seen in local community involvement, attitude and behaviour of tourists. Instead of infrastructure, superstructure development gains momentum.

Various researches have pointed out that every destination has a life span and passes through various stages. Though there are some arguments against this view, the concept has been recognized widely. Butler (1980) had suggested a model (Fig. 6.1) representing the lifespan of a destination and is called **Tourism Area Life Cycle Concept (TALC).** He has pointed out that there are six or seven distinguishable stages in the lifecycle of a destination such as *exploration, involvement, development, consolidation, stagnation, decline* and *rejuvenation*. The concept illustrates that a destination will be an unidentified one in the very beginning and it would be explored by some enthusiasts. This will be the birth of a new destination and then onwards, the number of visitors would be on a gradual increase. After a certain period, the destination will get fame and the number of visitors will increase manifold due to some deliberate efforts by the developers/ authorities. The growth in arrival figures would reach a maximum at a certain period of time and then onwards, the destination may lose its charm to attract more tourists. Further, it may decline from that point of time. Maybe by some deliberate efforts, the destination can see rejuvenation in attracting more people to the destination. A brief on each stage is explained below.

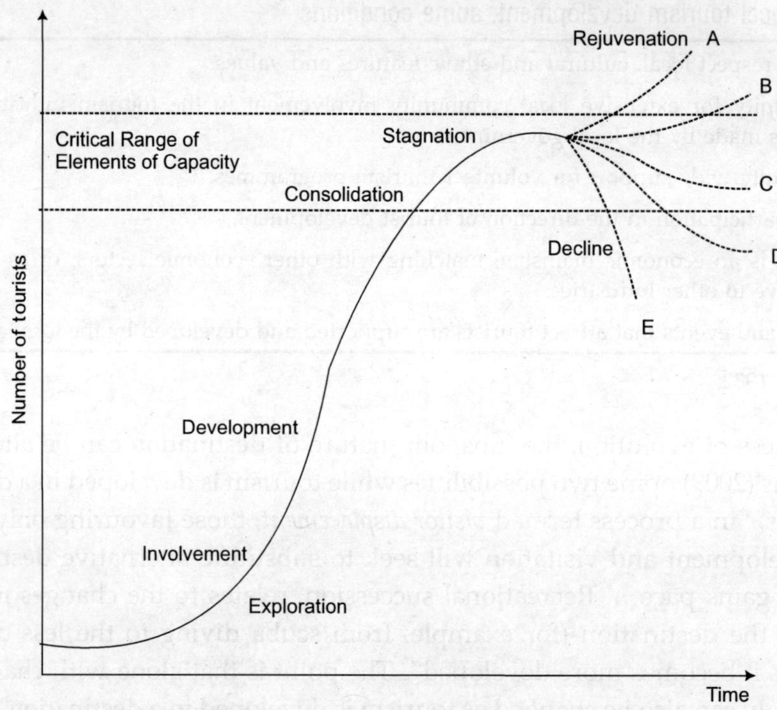

Source: Modified from Butler, 1980.

Figure 6.1 Tourism area life cycle (TALC): Stages.

6.12.1 Exploration

Here the resort/destination will be visited by a small volume of exploring type tourists who tend to shun institutionalized travel. At this stage, the destination may not have much accessibility and facilities. It is visited by a few adventurous tourists with individually planned itineraries and the visitation is irregular as well. Visitors may have interest in nature/culture and close interaction with local people. Moreover, this stage is featured by minimal effect on social, cultural and physical environments.

6.12.2 Involvement

At this stage, local initiatives will begin to provide facilities and services for the visitors. The destination will gradually begin to develop. Outsiders will start to arrive and the volume of tourist arrivals will get momentum. Provision of tourist facilities and some small-scale advertising may start taking place. The destination will see the start of tourist market and season, and the interaction stays high. Public sector will have more pressure to provide the necessary infrastructure and soon some changes in social life of locals may occur.

6.12.3 Development

By the development stage, large number of visitors are attracted and the control of tourism at the destination will pass out of the hands of locals. Government will start large-scale promotion and private enterprises will rush to begin establishments. The rate of tourist arrivals will be high. Extensive advertising and links to the generating region(s) can be generated. Loss of local control through increased foreign-owned facilities, and regional/national planning and provision of infrastructure may also happen as part of development.

6.12.4 Consolidation

In the later stages of the cycle, the rate of visiting population declines though the total number is still increasing. The resort, by now will be a full-fledged one. By this stage, growth rate declines and tourism would have become a major economic sector. Marketing efforts may be strengthened aiming to extend tourist season and market(s). Destination, by this time, may also witness some opposition due to increasing rate of negative impacts.

6.12.5 Stagnation

By the stagnation stage, peak tourist arrivals have now been reached and the destination is no longer fashionable. Tourist capacity reached/exceeded and reliance on repeat visitation and conventions can also be expected. The destinations will usually begin to show environmental, social and cultural problems at this stage. Surplus hotel capacity and changes in ownership is a common occurrence at this stage. Possibilities of new developments peripheral to the existing destination are also present.

6.12.6 Decline

By this stage, visitors show interest in newer resorts and negative impacts will be on the rise. The destination has a well-established image, but it is no longer in fashion. As tourist market is lost, and vacationers decline, more reliance may be on weekenders and day visitors.

6.12.7 Rejuvenation

Authorities of the destination, at this stage have to decide to rejuvenate/relaunch the destination by looking at new markets/product diversification. Satellite destinations can also be developed. It has been found that rejuvenation strategies are difficult to implement. Due to the efforts to have completely changed attractions and image, along with combined public and private sector efforts, a new tourist market may be found, often a special interest group.

6.13 DESTINATION ELEMENTS AND TOURIST FLOWS

The above discussed elements of destination have a high influence in tourist flows. As explained earlier, tourist destination is the most important sub-element of the tourism geographical element as per the Leiper's model of tourism system (Leiper, 1990). This area (destination) consists of different 'pull' factors as far as tourism is concerned. Apart from it, some of the industrial components of tourism are distributed in the destination. Each component, in one way or the other, is related to each of the elements of tourism destination.

Out of the fundamental elements of a destination, *attractions* are the most important category which have an appeal to the tourists. Much of the attractions of a destination are intangible in nature, and depend on the image which the potential tourist has of it. India will be seen by one group of travellers as exotic and appealing, while others will reject the destination because of the negative image due to many reasons or its alien culture. Different destinations will have different attractions and the appeal made by them and influence they exert will also be different. Anyhow, as stated earlier, attractions share the maximum contribution in the total 'pull' factors of a destination. The attractions are the major factors in creating customers'/tourists' view about the destination. Kerala has emerged as an important destination in India recently and the share played by attractions of Kerala in the scenario is very high. Kerala encompasses many destinations with diverse attractions. Natural beauty, cultural diversity, greenery, etc., are important components of Kerala's attractions and natural attractions like beaches, backwaters, etc., are really capable enough to influence anyone from the world. Such specialties play a big role in making a good image and positive outlook towards Kerala.

Accessibility is another important element of a tourism destination that influences tourists. If the accessibility is very high, it has been reported that, in some cases, it may cause crowding and congestion which may lead to loss of charm and ambience. It should be noted that the 'perception' of accessibility on the part of travellers is often as important as a destination's actual accessibility. For example, many people in Britain perceive Corfu as being more accessible than Cornwall, in terms of traveling time. Such perceptions will undoubtedly affect when tourists are planning their travel.

Amenities are the essential services catering to the requirements of tourists at a destination. Stay, local transport, shopping, etc., are vital components of tourism process. Amenities contribute to the image of a destination. Thus, it has a part in attracting and influencing tourists. The topless, double decker bus services in some cities of Europe, traditional food outlets in France, houseboat transportation in the backwaters of Kerala, etc., can be cited as examples. Apart from amenities, the ancillary services provided at the destination also influence in making decisions. Such services create more positive image among tourists and play an important role in tourist flows and tourists' views on destinations.

6.14 DESTINATION IMAGE

The images held by potential travellers are very important in the destination selection process. Most of the tourism products often compete via images (Pike 2008). Image is primarily a mix of beliefs, attitudes and impressions held by a person or group of people towards some phenomenon. Developing destination image is still in its primary stages as the existing conceptualization is 'vague'. Fakeye and Crompton (1991) pointed out that images are of paramount importance to destinations because they have the power to change and rearrange the tourists' impressions and perceptions of a destination and "give him or her a pre-taste of the destination". According to Pike (2008), destination image is a repertoire of brand associations held in the mind of the traveller. Simply, it is defined as "the sum of beliefs, ideas and impressions that a person has of a destination"

Table 6.5: Designing the visitor experience to add value

Identifying the visitor	Visitor survey research at the destination
Understanding the needs, wishes and choice behaviour of guests	Application of marketing segmentation techniques to target different groups of visitors to serve and identify those to customise the experience (e.g., families, individuals, senior groups).
Meeting the guest: encounter between buyer and seller	Customising and tailoring the experience to individuals.
The moment of truth: first impressions count	A visitor may form his/her initial satisfaction or irritation with a destination at the very outset on arrival when they are in a psychological state that can have heightened levels of stress, uncertainty and ambivalence.
The stages of an experience	The spirit of the place and location will have a clear impact on the type of experience which can be delivered. Hospitality of the staff will be an important determinant of the experience formed. The nature of the staff or technology employed will be critical and it will offer opportunities to delight the visitor, by building trust and a rapport with the visitor if the experience design engages them.
The enabling management structure	This involves the management processes employed to support the business and locale in developing the experience (e.g., in-house business processes such as accounting, marketing, leadership and management).
Quality management	This involves a corporate philosophy committed to total quality management and applies the necessary tools and techniques across the organization to develop quality experience and a profitable encounter.

Source: Developed from Haahti and Komppula (2006).

(Crompton, 1979). The image of a destination in the minds of a consumer may develop over time. Image created by the destination has to be distinctive, appealing, simple, and most importantly, believable and should be based on reality (Kotler & Gertner, 2004). MacKay and Fesenmaier (1997) argue that destination image formation is based on "a composite of individual inputs and marketer inputs" as well. Therefore, image formation has both a supply-side as well as a demand-side element. This denotes that the image being or attempted to be created and the received image are not always the same. The following classification can help in distinguishing the destination images:

- **Organic image:** This image is obtained by a tourist from various sources, which are not directly related to tourism, i.e., based on information assimilated from non-touristic such as mass media like television and newspaper; word of mouth, and educational background, etc.
- **Induced image:** This image is created through tourism communication and other tourism oriented sources of information. An attempt is made directly or indirectly by the concerned to create an image of a destination.
- **Experience image:** The tourist gains the image about a place from the actual experience during the trip. This is not a part of the attempt to create an image, rather this is generated as part of the real experience.

There is another classification through which destination image can influence decision-making.

- **Known image:** This is based on the knowledge about a destination. Tourist is completely aware of this. In fact, tourists consider this actively in making a choice.
- **Neutral image:** Tourists have a neutral feeling and have neither a positive nor negative opinion.
- **Negative image:** This image limits the tourist in selecting a particular destination. Tourists develop this negativeness according to their own beliefs, which may or may not be true.

Image creation in all possible ways is a prime task of the destinations and this is primarly vested with the national tourism organisations and destination management/ marketing organisations.

6.15 DESTINATION MARKETING ORGANISATION (DMO)

Destination marketing organization, also referred to as *destination management organization*, is an organization responsible for marketing of an identifiable destination. The cardinal rationale of the existence of DMOs is a means for enhancing destination competitiveness. Yet, this organization undertakes multiple responsibilities including planning, development, visitor management, ensuring sustainability measures, and the like.

According to Pike (2008), "a competitive destination is one that features profitable tourism businesses, an effective position, an attractive environment, satisfactory visitor experience, and supportive local residents". He also states that due to the multidimensional nature of destination competitiveness, it would be difficult in this competitive market for a destination to sustain, or even attain, competitiveness without an effective organization. A major element in attempting competitive advantage in the tourism markets is the development and implementation of effective strategies. In fact, ensuring quality tourist experiences is also an important role of a DMO. For the same, DMO has to be alert on quality aspects of the attractions, services and facilities offered. Major responsibilities of a DMO are:

- Market and promote the destination at various levels
- Enhance destination competitiveness
- Stimulate tourism businesses
- Plan, develop and diversify tourism
- Ensure quality tourism experience
- Establish an effective market position
- Maintain an attractive environment
- Ensure sustainable use of resources and sustainable development
- Diversify attractions and increase tourism activities.

Traditionally, DMOs are part of government mechanism. But recent trends show that public-private partnerships (PPP) are also seen in many countries. The benefits of cooperative public-private partnership in DMO or any authority mechanism are:

- Reduced antagonism through representation of all stakeholders.
- Avoidance of duplication through enhanced communication channels between various sectors in it.
- Combined areas of expertise (private sector efficiency and public sector holistic benefit seeking).
- Increased funding potential through the reduction in duplicated efforts as well as industry based taxes.
- The generation of a win-win situation through an increase in industry profitability and ensuring increase in government revenue. (Poetschke, 1997)

6.16 CONCLUSION

Destinations are specific areas where people would like to visit, stay and spend some time. Success of a destination depends on the quality and competitiveness of its basic elements such as attractions, accessibility and amenities. Though destinations are of different kinds, they share some common characteristics. They are amalgams, involve a range of elements like attractions, industrial components, ancillary services, basic amenities, etc. Seasonality, inseparability (tourism is produced where it is consumed), perishability and to a certain extent, intangibility are some other characteristics of tourist destinations. Attractions form the core of tourist destinations. They are fundamentally classified as natural and manmade. Accessibility is all about the transportation facilities to and inside a destination which makes it easy and comfortable for tourists to visit the place. Quality accessibility is vital for a destination to succeed. Amenities constitute the basic facilities that are required to cater to the requirements of a tourist while visiting a destination. Ancillary services, another component, consist of auxiliary or supplementary services offered at a destination by the local organizations.

It is argued that every destination passes through various stages in its lifespan. Butler (1980) had come up with a concept called Tourism Area Life Cycle (TALC), which describes that seven distinct stages can be identified in the lifespan of a destination. According to it, a destination will be identified by a small group of exploring type of tourists which will lead to the creation of small-scale facilities by the locals. Gradually, after realizing the potential of the destination, the authorities will identify it and start to develop and promote. These efforts will ultimately result in the increase of tourist arrivals to the place. The arrival growth trend will continue for a period. Later, after some years, visitor arrival growth will come down and gradually the destination may face stagnation in growth in visitor arrivals. Later it may lose charm to attract new tourists and may face decline in the inflow of tourists. Sooner or later, the destination may take efforts to rejuvenate its charm and to remain a destination that can attract more tourists.

Destinations have to remain competitive in the market. Creating a favourable destination image is crucial for it. Image exists in different ways and DMO plays an important role in creating a favourable image, along with sustainable management, marketing and promotion of the destination.

Key Terms

Tourist destination	Superstructure
Attraction	Natural attractions
Accessibility	Manmade attractions
Amenities	Intangibility
Ancillary services	Perishability
Tourism area life cycle	Inseparability
Tourist flows	Destination image
Destination amalgam	DMO
Infrastructure	

Review Questions

Short Answer Type Questions

1. Describe the concept and nature of tourist destination.
2. Explain common characteristics of tourist destinations.
3. Elucidate the role of attractions in tourism process.
4. Discuss in detail the classification of tourist attractions.
5. What are the components of a tourist destination?
6. Discuss the role of 'accessibility' in destination's success.
7. What amenities are required in a tourist destination?
8. Explain various ancillary services in association with tourist destination.
9. Discuss evolution, growth and development of a tourist destination.
10. Explain TALC. Discuss its stages.
11. Elucidate the role of each component of a destination in attracting tourists to visit.
12. What do you mean by destination image?
13. Classify destination images.
14. Discuss the role of DMOs.

Essay Type Questions

1. Discuss in detail the concept, characteristics and components of tourist destinations. While discussing, use suitable examples from the destinations near to your place.
2. Discuss the Tourism Area Life Cycle concept. What are the strategies that can be adopted by the developers and marketers in each stage of it to sustain/promote tourist influx to the destination?

7

TOURISM ORGANISATIONS

Learning Outcomes

After studying this chapter, you will be able to:

- understand the reasons why there are so many organizations in tourism sector at the national and international levels;
- understand the evolution of World Tourism Organization and its role and activities in promoting tourism equitably world over;
- Explain the involvement of IATA in order to promote safe, regular and economic air transport;
- understand the role and relevance of ICAO in promoting civil aviation across the world; and
- understand the importance and relevance of international organizations such as WTTC, UFTAA and PATA.

7.1 INTRODUCTION

Tourism, being a complex process, necessitates active involvement of a large number of organizations at various levels ranging from international to local for its effective and efficient functioning. These organizations have different roles to perform, such as to act as catalyst, facilitate planning and development, have effective coordination between different sectors, obtain financial and technical assistance, statistical support as well as for promotion. Tourism policy formulation, infrastructure development, protecting the rights of tourists and hosts, negotiations, technical and legal assistance, etc., are some other areas where these organizations are involved. The nature of these organizations varies on different bases. Some are quasi-government bodies, some are international associations, some others are professional bodies, etc. These organizations are either formed out of representations from governmental agencies or formed by the private agencies. The organizations directly and indirectly associated to tourism can be classified into two broad categories, such as:

- International organizations
- National organizations

7.2 INTERNATIONAL ORGANIZATIONS

These organizations operate at the international level and are further classified as global, regional and continental organizations. They can be further classified on different bases. The following is one type of subclassification of international organizations:

- **Intergovernmental bodies:** There constitute the organisations that are created by treaties entered into by sovereign states or nations. United Nations World Tourism Organisation (UNWTO) is a typical example of this.
- **Nongovernmental bodies:** Organisations consisting of individuals or organisations (rather than governments). World Travel and Tourism Council (WTTC) is such a professional body with operations spanning across the world.

International organizations can also be classified on the basis of the span of operation. The following are such two categories:

- **Global tourism organizations:** These organizations function at the world level, and are concerned with global tourism. Examples include both UNWTO and WTTC.
- **Regional tourism organizations:** The operation is limited to a specific region of the world. Pacific Asia Travel Association (PATA) is an example of a regional organization.

International organisations may also be classified depending on the nature of interest in tourism:

- **General organisations:** These organisations are concerned with all the aspects relating to tourism. United Nations World Tourism Organisation (UNWTO) is that kind of organisation which deals with almost all aspects of tourism happening across the world.
- **Specific organisations:** The focus of organisations belonging to this category will be only on a specific aspect of tourism. Tourism is a multidisciplinary subject and the possibility of such organisations is high. International Civil Aviation Organisation (ICAO) and International Air Transport Association (IATA) focus on civil aviation and commercial aviation areas of tourism.
- **Partial interest in tourism:** They are not tourism organisations, yet have partial interest in tourism with a certain amount of linkage with tourism. World Health Organisation (WHO), and UNESCO are examples.

There are a number of international tourism organizations functioning and have been formed with representation from both public and private sectors together as well as separately. A brief account on United Nations World Tourism Organization (UNWTO), International Civil Aviation Organization (ICAO), International Air Transport Association

(IATA), United Federation of Travel Agents Association (UFTAA), World Travel and Tourism Council (WTTC), and Pacific Asia Travel Association (PATA) are given below.

7.3 UNITED NATIONS WORLD TOURISM ORGANIZATION (UNWTO)

United Nations World Tourism Organization (UNWTO) is the most important intergovernmental organization to hold worldwide responsibilities, encompassing all tourism activities. This organization plays a major role in the development of international tourism.

7.3.1 Brief History

The WTO has its beginnings as the *International Congress of Official Tourist Traffic* set up in 1925 in Hague. It was renamed as the *International Union of Official Travel Organization* (IUOTO) after World War II and moved to Geneva. Around 109 national tourist organizations and 88 Associate Members from the public and private agencies were included in IUOTO. By 1960s, it became clear that there was a need for more effective tools to keep developments under review and to provide tourism with intergovernmental machinery especially equipped to deal with the movement of persons, tourism policies and tourist's aspects. In 1969, a movement was held in this direction and a resolution to the same effect was passed by the UN General Assembly, which recognized the decisive and central role the IUOTO should play in the field of world tourism in cooperation with the existing machinery within the UN. Following this resolution, the WTO's statutes were ratified in 1974 by the states whose official tourists organizations were members of IUOTO. Thus, IUOTO became World Tourism Organization (WTO) and its first general assembly was held in Madrid in 1975. The headquarters was set up in Madrid (Spain). In 1976, WTO became an executing agency of the United Nations Development Programme (UNDP) and in 2003, it became a specialized agency of the UN.

By 2015, its membership consisted of 157 countries, 6 Associate Members and over 480 Affiliate Members representing the private sector, educational institutions, tourism associations and local tourism authorities.

7.3.2 UNWTO's Mission

UNWTO is vested by the UN with a central and decisive role in promoting the development of responsible, sustainable and universally acceptable tourism, with the aim of contributing to economic development, international understanding, peace, prosperity and universal respect for, and observance of human rights and fundamental freedoms. In pursuing this aim, the organization pays particular attention to the interests of the developing countries in the field of tourism.

Table 7.1: UNWTO history: Key events

1925	International Congress of Official Tourist Traffic Associations formed. (Hague, Netherlands)
1934	International Union of Official Tourist Propaganda Organization (IUOTPO).
1947	IUOTPO converted to International Union of Official Travel Organization (IUOTO).
1969	Intergovernmental conference in Sofia, Bulgaria, and the UN General Assembly, call for creation of intergovernmental organization on tourism.
1970	(Sep. 27) IUOTO's extraordinary General Assembly adopts the statutes of WTO (Mexico).
1975	First General Assembly of the WTO was held in Madrid, Spain. (Robert Lonati, first Secretary General).
1976	WTO Secretariate moves from Geneva to Madrid.
1979	'World Tourism Day' created, to be celebrated on 27th September every year.
1980	WTO World Tourism Conference, Manila. (Manila declaration on world tourism).
1983	WTO general assembly held in New Delhi, India.
1996	Bali declaration of tourism, Indonesia.
2003	Transformation of the WTO into a UN specialized agency.

Source: www.unwto.org.

Acting as an umbrella organization for world tourism, UNWTO plays a catalytic role in promoting technology transfers and international cooperation, in stimulating and developing public-private sector partnership and in encouraging the implementation of the "Global Code of Ethics for Tourism," with a view to ensure that member countries, tourist destinations and businesses maximize the positive economic, social and cultural effects of tourism and fully reap its benefits, while, at the same time they minimize its negative social and environmental impacts.

Through tourism, UNWTO aims at stimulating economic growth, creating job, providing incentives for protecting the environment and cultural heritage, and promoting peace, prosperity and respect towards human rights.

7.3.3 Functioning of UNWTO

The UNWTO functions through the following five bodies:

- **General assembly:** This is the principal gathering of UNWTO and it meets every two years. Every four years it elects a Secretary General. This is composed of full members and associate members. The meeting approves budget and programme of work and debates topics of importance.
- **Executive council:** This is the governing board, responsible for ensuring that the organization carries out its works and adheres to its budget. It meets twice a year. It is composed of 27 members elected by the General Assembly. As host country, Spain has a permanent seat.
- **Regional commission:** UNWTO has six regional commissions – Africa, America, East Asia and the Pacific, Europe, the Middle East and South Asia. They meet at

least once a year and are composed of all the full members and associate members from that region.

- **Committees:** Separate committees on programme, budget and finance, statistics and macroeconomic analysis, marketing intelligence and promotion, sustainable development, education, tourism, etc., advice on management and programme content.
- **The secretariat:** The Secretariat is led by the Secretary General. It is located in Madrid. The officials are responsible for implementing UNWTO's programme of work and serving the needs of the members.
- **Membership:** UNWTO has three categories of membership:
  - (a) **Full members:** This category of membership is open to all sovereign states.
  - (b) **Associate membership:** This is open to all territories not responsible for their external relations. That means territories which are not sovereign states like Gibraltar.
  - (c) **Affiliate members:** This comprises a wide range of organizations and companies working directly in travel, tourism and related sectors. They may include airlines, other transport operators, hotels, restaurants, tour operators, travel agents, insurance companies, etc.

Apart from these categories of members, one permanent observer – *'The Vatican'* is also included in UNWTO.

7.3.4 Areas of Activities of UNWTO

UNWTO provides assistance in the following areas:

- Inventories of existing and potential tourism resources, national tourism development master plans, and formulation of policies, plans and programmes for development of domestic tourism.
- Institutional framework of national tourism administrative structures, tourism development corporation, legislation and regulation.
- Evaluation of the impact of tourism on the national economy and on the environment.
- Statistics, forecasting, statistical analysis, market research, market analysis, promotion, publicity and public relations.
- Training, feasibility studies for tourism and hotel schools, and management development.
- Planning and management of the aims of national, social and cultural value for tourism user.
- Area development, development of new tourism sites, development of particular tourism products.

- Tourist accommodation, planning, and operating assistance, and hotel classification systems.
- Source and methods of finance for tourism investments, pre-investment studies, feasibility studies of investment projects, cost-benefit analysis.
- Safety of tourists and tourist facilities.

Some important areas of activities, which UNWTO is engaged in, are listed below.

UNWTO is committed to ensuring ethics and social responsibility in tourism the world over. The following are the focus areas under *The Ethics & Social Responsibility Programme* of the UNWTO.

Global Code of Ethics for Tourism

- Promotes and disseminates the Global Code of Ethics for Tourism and monitors its implementation.
- Coordinates the activities of the World Committee on Tourism Ethics.
- Corporate social responsibility (CSR).
- Promotes the private sector commitment to the Global Code of Ethics for Tourism.

Accessible tourism for all

- Advocates for the accessibility of tourism facilities and services, to facilitate the travel of all persons, including those with disabilities, protection for children in tourism.
- Works to prevent all forms of exploitation of minors in tourism (sexual exploitation, child labour, trafficking of children, etc.).
- Coordinates the activities of the World Tourism Network on Child Protection.

Gender and Tourism

- Promotes gender equality and the empowerment of women in tourism.

Co-operation for development, share technical skills

The transfer of know-how to developing countries is one of UNWTO's fundamental tasks. Acting on requests from member states, UNWTO secures financing, location, world's leading experts and carries out a gamut of development projects. A joint programme with UNCTAD called *Sustainable Tourism-Eliminating Poverty* (STEP) has been organized by UNWTO, focusing on the twin subjects of sustainable tourism and poverty alleviation, in order to help developed and developing countries. STEP was launched at World Summit on Sustainable Development (WSSD) in Johannesburg (2002). The new initiative, **'Silk Road Programme'** is a collaborative initiative designed to enhance sustainable tourism development along the historic Silk Route. The programme attempts to maximize the benefits of tourism development for local Silk Route communities, while stimulating investment and promoting the conservation of the route's natural and cultural heritage. Moreover, it aims to have better co-operation between Silk Route countries and regions, along with providing a seamless and memorable Silk Route travel experience.

- **Regional activities:** Direct actions that strengthen and support the efforts of national tourism administration are carried out by UNWTO's regional representatives. Different activities are designed to help ensure the stature of national tourism administration within their own country, while at the same time building awareness of new developments in tourism, and improving technical and operational skills. In a special effort to help boost tourism to sub-Saharan Africa, UNWTO developed a specific programme of technical activities for the year 2003-04. Regional promotion programmes are also initiated in cooperation with UNESCO. Examples are the **'Silk Road Project'** (12000 km from Asia to Europe) and the **'Slave Route Project'** (launched in 1995).
- **Tourism and technology:** UNWTO works in the area of new Information Technology which aims to provide leadership in the field of IT and tourism, as well as helping to bridge the digital divide between the 'haves and have-nots' among UNWTO's membership. Researches are being undertaken in this area.
- **Education and training:** UNWTO Human Resource Development Department (UNWTO.HRD) works to add value to the tourism sector of UNWTO member states, improving their capacity building and providing direct support in tourism education, training and knowledge. The UNWTO-Themis foundation provides the administrative back-up to UNWTO.HRD, to develop and disseminate tourism education, training and knowledge products. UNWTO education council is made up of leading tourism education, training and research institutions worldwide.
- **Quality and ethics:** The programme on quality in tourism development focuses on the issues playing a major role in the perception and assurance of quality in tourism activities and experience tourism's social impact, safety, security, quality standards and regulatory trading framework. The Global Code of Ethics, adopted by UNWTO in 1999, and acknowledged by UN General Assembly in 2001, was set out as a ten-point blueprint for safeguarding the resources on which tourism depends and ensuring its economic benefits are equitably shared.
- **Sustainable development:** Ensuring the sustainable development and management of tourism, so that its benefits can be enjoyed for generations to come, is the philosophy behind the activities carried out by the sustainable tourism development section. Some projects are initiated, focusing on the same. *International Year of Ecotourism, 2002, World Summit on Sustainable Development*, etc., are examples of it. Sustainable Tourism-Eliminating Poverty (STEP) is an important initiative of UNWTO in this direction. Currently UNWTO is focusing on *10 YFP Sustainable Tourism Programme.* This 10-year Framework of Programmes on Sustainable Consumption and Production Patterns (10 YFP) is a global framework of action designed to enhance international cooperation to accelerate the shift towards sustainable consumption and production (SCP) in both developed and developing countries.

- **Statistics:** Proving the economic impact of tourism with solid facts and figures is the goal of UNWTO's statistics section and economic measurement of tourism. It helped to create the Tourism Satellite Account (TSA) and is now assisting governments to implement this system of measuring the demand and supply of tourism.
- **Market intelligence:** Assisting governments and tourism professionals in understanding the constantly changing tourism market is the aim of UNWTO's section on market intelligence and promotion. Identifying market trends, forecasting, analysing world's generating markets and conducting researches are just some of the activities carried out every year.
- **Communications:** Increasing awareness of the importance of tourism, promoting the UNWTO's work and objectives through effective communication in order to provide transparency of its activities; helping achieve the goals of all sectors; and keeping the involved communities informed about new projects, studies, seminar results and upcoming UNWTO activities, are the primary goals of UNWTO's press and communications sector.

  UNWTO has an extensive programme of publication and documentation activities to act as permanent source of information for its members and world community. Every year, it publishes a number of books and reports along with annual global and regional tourist statistics.

7.4 INTERNATIONAL AIR TRANSPORT ASSOCIATION (IATA)

International Air Transport Association (IATA) is a world association of scheduled airlines with which they coordinate their efforts to serve their passengers, share their experience and analyze their problems. It is a nongovernmental organization and membership consists of practically all the air carriers. IATA is a voluntary non-political industry association that serves as a forum for airlines to develop common programmes for the smooth running of the international air transport system. The principal function of IATA is to speed up the movement of persons from any point on the world air network to any other by a combination of routes on the basis of a single ticket bought at a uniform price in one currency. The same applies to the movement of goods and cargo. It's main headquarters are situated in Montreal, Canada (controlling American Continent) and in Geneva (covering Europe, the Middle East and Africa). One regional office is located in Singapore which controls operations in Asia and the Pacific.

7.4.1 Objectives

The rapid expansion of civil air services after the Second World War necessitated to have a controlling and co-ordinating authority in international air transport. IATA was founded in 1945 to help solve the problem. IATA has a successor, International Air

Traffic Association, which was set up in 1919 at Hague. As a nongovernmental organization, IATA draws its legal existence from a special act of the Canadian Parliament, given royal assent in December 1945. IATA was set up with the following aims:

- To promote safe, regular and economical air transport for the benefit of the people of the world, to foster air commerce and to study the problems connected therewith.
- To provide means for collaboration among air transport enterprises engaged directly or indirectly in international air transport service.
- To cooperate with *International Civil Aviation Organization* (ICAO) and other international organizations.

7.4.2 Organization

The activities of IATA are performed through different departments. IATA has a president and an executive committee comprising major airlines Chief Executive Officers. The IATA administration is headed by a Director General. Annual general meeting of IATA takes crucial decisions for the functioning of IATA. The six major departments of IATA are listed below with brief descriptions of activities.

- **Tariff department:** This provides a forum for tariff coordination discussion, acts as a central source of tariff information lists and verifies services of cargo and travel agents worldwide, coordinates training programmes for cargo and travel agents, acts as a forum for airlines to resolve scheduling problems, and helps represent the industry on air mail issues.
- **Legal department:** The major activities of this department are to give legal advice to members, distribute and publish information on legal or regulatory issues and formulate industry's legal positions vis-à-vis bodies like the ICAO and individual governments.
- **Technical department:** Many activities and functions are undertaken; some of the major ones are development standards to help maximize flight safety, advocating airline positions on operational needs, assembling safety statistics and organizing security and safety related seminars, etc.
- **Government and industry affairs department:** This section lobbies government and national organizations to promote and defend the interests of scheduled airlines, represents IATA on regional level, provides after-sales services to new members and analyzes various policies.
- **Industry automation and finance services department:** This department undertakes many functions like operating industry clearing house for handling financial affairs; maintain standard operating criteria and procedures to speed the flow of passengers, baggage and cargo; and assembling, analyzing and publishing comparative statistical data.
- **Public relations department:** This department represents and defends collective airline interests and positions vis-à-vis the media, consumer groups and the public

at large; maintains information flow to members; and serves as a channel for airlines of all sizes to benefit from each others' public relation experience and expertise.

7.4.3 IATA Services

The IATA provides some important services, such as:

- Global planning of international time-tables for airline services.
- Maintaining single formula for tickets and airway bills.
- Standardization of inter-company communication and reservation systems.
- International coordination of telecommunication networks and computer systems.
- Providing training for travel agents and freight agents, and undertaking various educational programmes.
- Regulating legal questions of general concern and develop security measures.
- Examining and solving the problems raised by tourism and the flow of passengers and goods at airports and to establish procedures and technical norms.

The priority areas for the services may change from time to time since issues in international air transport vary. The best example is IATA's focus on September 11 attacks and the aftermath. IATA wants the industry to return to full and rapid normal operating conditions after every crisis.

7.4.4 Current Priorities

- **NDC (New Distribution Capability):** This is an industry-supported programme launched by IATA for the development and market adoption of a new, XML-based data transmission standard, which can enhance the capability of communications between airlines and travel agents. Moreover, it will be open to any third party, intermediary, IT provider or non-IATA member, to implement and use, and claimed to facilitate a more efficient airline distribution system, thereby benefitting airlines, agents, GDSs, IT providers and travel start-ups.
- **ONE order:** This aims to modernize the order management process in the airline industry, and intends to replace the multiple and rigid booking, ticketing, delivery and accounting methods, using the data communications advances made possible by the implementation of the NDC.
- **IATA settlement systems (ISS):** IATA is on the process of implementing the new generation IATA Settlement Systems by which it aims to make a more efficient distribution and settlement of funds between travel agents/freight forwarders and airlines. It helps in **faster** improved cash flow management, **safer** increased protection of monies, **cheaper and easier** measures to lower the costs for participants and simplify processes, and provide more **relevant** and additional ways to do business with new payment methods and a choice of accreditation models. The existing *Billing and Settlement Plan* may be avoided when this becomes fully active.

7.5 INTERNATIONAL CIVIL AVIATION ORGANIZATION (ICAO)

International Civil Aviation Organization (ICAO) is a specialized agency of the United Nations, whose mandate is to ensure safe, efficient and orderly evolution and growth of international civil aviation. Their headquarters is located in Montreal, Canada, with seven regional offices throughout the world. From its beginning in 1944, it has grown to an organization with over 180 contracting states. Safe and orderly development of all aspects of international civil aeronautics is the ultimate aim of ICAO. It provides the forum whereby requirements and procedures in need of standardization may be introduced, studied and resolved.

7.5.1 Evolution and Objectives

For dealing with technical affairs and other important aspects of international civil aviation, a conference was organized in Chicago in 1944 (November 1 to December 7). The conference dealt with subjects of vital importance for international civil aviation such as:

- flying over territory of contracting states (air services, customs, rules of the air, spread of diseases, etc.);
- nationality of aircraft – facilitation (customs, accident, investigation, etc.);
- documents (recognition of certificates, licences, etc.);
- international standards and practices, including those for carriage of dangerous goods; and
- statistics, finance and technical assistance, etc.

Based on the discussions, a Provisional International Civil Aviation Organization (PICAO) started functioning from 6th June, 1945. International Civil Aviation Organization was founded in 1947 as a permanent body, as a specialized agency of the United Nations. ICAO is composed of states, generally members of the UN.

The aims and objectives are to develop the principles and techniques of international air navigation and foster the planning and development of international air transport, with a view to:

- ensure safe and orderly growth of international civil aviation worldwide;
- encourage the art of aircraft design and operation for peaceful purposes;
- encourage development of airways, airports and air navigation facilities;
- meet the needs of people for safe, regular, efficient and economical air transport;
- prevent economic waste caused by unreasonable competition;
- ensure that the rights of contracting states are fully respected, avoid discrimination between these states and ensure that every state has a fair opportunity to operate international airlines; and
- promote safety of flights and the development of all aspects of international civil aeronautics.

7.5.2 Organization

The organization of ICAO consists of *Assembly*, a *Council* and a *Secretariat*. The chief officers are President of the council and the Secretary General. The assembly, consisting of representatives from all contracting states, is the sovereign body of ICAO. It meets every three years. Assembly elects the council, the governing body for a three-year term. It is composed of members from 36 states who maintain their offices and conduct their business at the ICAO headquarters. *Air Navigation Commission* assists in technical matters; *Air Transport Commission* assists in economic matters; and *Committee on Unlawful Interference* in aviation security matters.

ICAO has been playing a vital role in the development of international transport over the years. Though, it is not directly concerned with tourism, indirectly, it too has a role in global tourism development.

7.6 WORLD TRAVEL AND TOURISM COUNCIL (WTTC)

The *World Travel and Tourism Council* (WTTC) is the forum for global business leaders comprising the presidents, chairs and the chief executive officers of 100 of the world's foremost companies. It is a body representing the private sector in all parts of the travel and tourism industry worldwide.

WTTC was established in 1990 with a view to play a key role in disseminating information about the economic impacts of tourism and to strengthen the tourism and travel industry along with efforts to transform the future challenges into opportunities. WTTC has set a *Blue Print for New Tourism* which provides a new strategic framework for ensuring that travel and tourism works for everyone in the future. It promotes travel and tourism as a partnership, delivering consistent results that match the needs of economies, local and regional authorities and local committees with those of business, based on:

- Governments recognising travel and tourism as a top priority.
- Business balancing economies with people, culture and environment.
- A shared pursuit of long-term growth and prosperity.

WTTC's mission is to raise awareness of the full economic impact of the world's largest generator of wealth and jobs – *Travel and Tourism*. WTTC realized that thorough and credible research is necessary for finding out benefits of tourism and to raise awareness of the same. Hence, WTTC has been working in the area of research and developing research methods for measuring tourism benefits. As part of it, WTTC developed *Tourism Satellite Accounting* (TSA) in partnership with Oxford Economic Forecasting (OEF), and undertakes research on an annual basis. Every year WTTC undertakes indepth TSA research studies on selected countries. The results will assist industries and economies in developing policies and in making decisions. Right now,

WTTC has 100 members who are key players in the world's most influential travel and tourism companies. The headquarters is located in London.

7.7 UNITED FEDERATION OF TRAVEL AGENTS ASSOCIATION (UFTAA)

United Federation of Travel Agents Association (UFTAA) is a world body representing travel agency and tourism industry. UFTAA effectively represents travel agents and tour operators' views on both inbound and outbound travel by continuous dialogue and consultation with other international organizations such as IATA, International Hotel and Restaurant Association (IH & RA), etc. UFTAA is an affiliate member of UNWTO and UN World Tourism Organization Business Council (UNWTOBC).

United Federation of Travel Agents Association emanates from the Universal Federation of Travel Agents Association created in Rome, Italy, on November 22nd, 1966. UFTAA started its operation as a confederation on 1st January, 2003. Now, it is a non-profit confederation of international scope, representing regional federations comprising some 100 national associations.

UFTAA's mission is to be an international forum where matters affecting the world travel industry are addressed, representing and defending the interests of incoming and outgoing tour operators, travel and tourism agencies before the governmental bodies, suppliers and other entities of international scope. It also aims at strengthening its members' image and enhance the world travel and tourism industry and a sustainable tourism.

Functions

To comply with its mission, UFTAA undertakes the following functions:

- To unite and consolidate the Federation of Travel Agents National Associations and to globally enhance the interests of their members.
- To represent travel agents' activities before various worldwide bodies, governmental authorities and suppliers.
- To work towards the adoption of measures that will ease travel for the consumer and to offer services to its member federations.
- To be an investigation and information centre supporting the members' federation's work and to offer information for technological development.
- To offer, as a voluntary mechanism, an arbitration service which assists in solving conflicts resulting from commercial relations for which amicable settlement cannot be reached.
- To organize a world congress of travel agents and other meetings necessary for the exchange and transfer of knowledge.

IATA conducts various travel agency training programmes in collaboration with UFTAA. The role UFTAA is playing in international travel and tourism industry is very important and it has contributed much to tourism development worldwide.

7.8 PACIFIC ASIA TRAVEL ASSOCIATION (PATA)

Pacific Asia Travel Association (PATA) is a non-profit organization set up with the objective of developing, promoting and facilitating travel to and within the Pacific area and the Asian region. By dedicating itself to the promotion of this tourism frontier, PATA's uniquely structured organization and its far-reaching efforts have helped many facets of tourism in the region. PATA has long been an advocate of balancing growth with responsible conversation measures, and its success till date has been extraordinary. It was founded in 1951 with 44 members. PATA's first conference was held in January 1952 in Honolulu. Headquarters were established in San Francisco, USA (1953). PATA's first Asian office was opened in Manila, Philippines in 1976. PATA's mission is to enhance the growth, value and quality of Pacific Asia travel and tourism for the benefit of its members.

Membership

PATA provides leadership to the collective efforts of 95 government, state and city tourism bodies, over 29 airlines and cruise lines, and hundreds of travel companies. In addition, thousands of travel professionals belong to more than 43 PATA chapters worldwide. PATA has nine categories of membership:

- Active government
- Associate government
- Active carrier
- Associate carrier
- Active industry
- Allied industry
- Affiliated allied
- Associate
- Sustaining

Functions

The major functions of PATA include:

- Organizing pacific travel conferences and workshops with the objectives of reviewing the progress, exchanging ideas and planning for future programmes.
- Initiate long-range marketing programmes which coordinate all the promotional functions of PATA for a maximum impact in the consumer market and also among sales agents.
- Organize research programmes to provide it with marketing information and to provide information to members for designing their own programmes.

PATA has been playing an important role in the tourism development in Pacific Asia region since the beginning. While international travel to Pacific Asia has increased three times in the last decade alone, PATA has provided a cohesive structure to help its members realize the economic prosperity from this growth.

7.9 CONCLUSION

Tourism is a complex process and its efficient functioning necessitates involvement of a number of organizations at various levels. These organizations perform different tasks that range from legal assistance to technological support. On the basis of area of operation, they are basically classified into two as international and national organizations. International organizations can be further classified into global, regional as well as continental. World Tourism Organization (UNWTO), a specialized agency of UN, is a global intergovernmental organization, to hold worldwide responsibilities, encompassing all tourism activities. The UNWTO plays a decisive role in promoting the development of responsible, sustainable and universally acceptable tourism across the world. Being a global body, it plays a catalytic role in promoting technology transfers, international cooperation, and developing public-private partnership in tourism. It functions through its different sections such as general assembly, executive council, regional commissions, functional committees and secretariat.

International Air Transport Association (IATA) is a global body of scheduled airlines, that aims to promote safe, regular and economical air transport; to provide means for collaboration among air transport enterprises; and to cooperate with global civil aviation organizations. International Civil Aviation Organization (ICAO), a specialized agency of UN, was formed as a permanent body in 1947. It being an intergovernmental agency, ultimately intends to develop principles and techniques of international air navigation and fosters planning and development of international air transport. World Travel and Tourism Council (WTTC) is a forum of global business leaders. United Federation of Travel Agents Association (UFTAA) is a global body representing travel agency business. Pacific Asia Travel Association (PATA) is a regional international organization set up with the objective to develop, promote and facilitate travel to and within the Pacific area and the Asia region.

Key Terms

Tourism organizations	UNWTO
International organizations	IATA
National organizations	ICAO
Civil aviation	WTTC
Air transport	UFTAA
	PATA

Review Questions

Short Answer Type Questions

1. Discuss the role and relevance of organizations in tourism.
2. Briefly narrate the history of UNWTO.
3. Discuss the functioning of UNWTO.
4. What are the different memberships of UNWTO?
5. What are the areas of activity of UNWTO?
6. Discuss how UNWTO is involved in the development and promotion of tourism in the world.
7. What are IATA services?
8. What are the objectives and activities of IATA?
9. Discuss the role and relevance of IATA in international air transportation.
10. Discuss how ICAO was formed.
11. What are the objectives of ICAO?
12. Discuss the role and relevance of ICAO in international air transportation.
13. Give a brief account of WTTC.
14. Expand UFTAA. What are the activities of UFTAA?
15. Give a brief account on PATA.

Essay Type Questions

1. Discuss the role and relevance of organizations in tourism.
2. Describe the history of organizations in air travel. Explain the role played by major organizations in the growth of air transportation.
3. Discuss the objectives and functioning of UNWTO. Explain the role played by it in promoting tourism in the world.

8 NATIONAL TOURISM ORGANISATIONS IN INDIA

Learning Objectives

After studying this chapter, you will be able to:

- understand the role of various tourism organizations at the national level in India;
- understand the importance and relevance of professional tourism organizations at the national level; and
- explain the role and activities of various national, regional and state governmental tourism agencies in developing and promoting tourism in the country.

8.1 INTRODUCTION

A number of tourism organisations function in public as well as private sectors in the destination countries world over. Role, functions and activities of those organisations vary. The organisations which are owned, funded and/or controlled by government directly or through dedicated authorities are called *public sector organisations*. In general, such organisations aim at developing and promoting tourism in a sustainable manner. Those organisations which are owned/funded/controlled by the commercial enterprises or the businesses are classified under the category of *private sector organisations*. Organizations at different levels can also be seen in a country. National organisations within tourism are at the following levels:

- **National organisations:** These are the organisations concerned with tourism at the country level. Examples include India Tourism Development Corporation (ITDC), Indian Association of Tour Operators (IATO), and Travel Agents Association of India (TAAI).
- **Regional organisations:** The organisations functioning at a specific region within a country. Examples include Tourist Guides Federation of South India (TGFSI).

- **State organisations:** These organisations function at the state level. Goa Tourism Development Corporation (GTDC), and Kerala Tourism Development Corporation (KTDC) are examples.
- **Local organisations:** Organisations concerned with tourism at the lower level, at a specific location within a country such as a city or town. For example, Agra Hotel and Restaurant Owner's Association (AHRA).

National organisations may also be classified depending on the nature of interest in tourism:

- **General organisations:** These organisations are concerned with all aspects relating to tourism. India Tourism Development Corporation (ITDC) is an organisation that deals with almost all aspects of tourism happening across the country.
- **Specific organisations:** These organisations focus on a specific aspect of tourism. Tourism is a multidisciplinary subject and the possibility of such organisations is high. Indian Association of Tour Operators (IATO) focuses on tour operation sector of tourism in the country.
- **Partial interest in tourism:** They are not tourism organisations, yet have partial stake in tourism with a certain amount of linkage with tourism. Confederation of Indian Industry (CII) is an example.

8.2 INDIA TOURISM DEVELOPMENT CORPORATION (ITDC)

During 1960s, on the basis of the recommendations of the Jha Committee Report on Tourism, Government of India set up three corporations under the department of tourism. The government later decided to merge these undertakings into a composite undertaking for the purpose of securing coordination in the policy and efficient and economic working of the three corporations. Thus, in 1966, by merging the three corporations, India Tourism Development Corporation (ITDC) was set up. It started functioning from October, 1966. It was established as an autonomous, public sector corporation, entrusted with the task of helping develop tourism infrastructure and promoting India as a tourist destination. ITDC provides a complete package of tourism services including accommodation, catering, travel-related services, event management, publicity, hotel consultancy, duty-free shops, in-house travel agency, entertainment and shopping.

The overall objectives and functions of ITDC can be summarized as follows:

- Construction and management of hotels, motels, restaurants, tourist bungalows, guest houses and beach resorts at various places for accommodating tourists.
- Provision of transport facilities to tourists.
- Arrangement of entertainment facilities to tourists by way of organizing cultural shows, music concerts, sound and light shows, etc.

- Provision of shopping facilities to tourists.
- Enhancing publicity services to assist India's promotion overseas as a tourist destination and projecting national importance of tourism at home.

The functions of ITDC are explained through the following points:

- **Owning and managing hotels and restaurants:** One of the primary activities which ITDC is engaged with is to provide hospitality services to the tourists. Earlier ITDC established a chain of hotels under the name, 'Ashoka' and owned and operated a number of hotels at many locations in the country. Some of them have been disowned as part of disinvestment policy and currently, it has a network of eight Ashok Group of Hotels, five Joint Venture Hotels and a Restaurant. In addition, it is also managing a hotel at Bharatpur, a restaurant at Kosi on behalf of the Department of Tourism, and also managing catering services at Western Court, Vigyan Bhawan and Hyderabad House, New Delhi. The hotels include Jammu Ashok, Jammu; The Ashok, New Delhi; The Janpath, New Delhi; Hotel Samrat, New Delhi; Kosi Tourist Complex, Kosi; Bharatpur Ashok, Bharatpur; Jaipur Ashok, Jaipur; Lakeview Ashok, Bhopal; Patliputra Ashok, Patna; Ranchi Ashok, Ranchi; Kalinga Ashok, Bhubaneswar; Brahmaputra Ashok, Gatongtok; Donyi Polo Ashok, Itanagar; Lalitha Mahal Palace Hotel, Mysore; and Pondicherry Ashok, Puducherry.
- **Duty-free shopping facilities and services:** Travellers require duty-free shopping services. Duty-free shop represents the retail outlet that are exempt from the payment of certain local or national taxes and duties, on the requirement that the goods sold will be sold to travellers who will take them out of the country. ITDC has been offering duty-free shopping services for a long time, almost 45 years. As tourist arrivals are seen in abundance through sea ports, especially as part of cruise tourism, ITDC expanded duty-free shopping services to seaports also. Presently, it owns Duty Free Shops at Goa International Airport, Coimbatore International Airport, and at sea posts in Chennai, Haldia, Kolkata and Goa seaports.
- **Travel and tour operations:** ITDC also arranges travel and tour operation services and a section has been set up called *Ashok Travels and Tours* (ATT), which is one of the largest travel and tour operators in India. Having a long history of offering hospitality and travel solutions, this group offers quality services and attractive packages for inbound and outbound tourists. It is also an IATA approved agency, and a member of national and international travel and tourism organizations, like, TAAI, IATO, JATA, ASTA and PATA. ITDC opened up branches of Ashok Travels and Tours in major cities in India, including Delhi, Mumbai, Chennai, Bangalore, Kolkata, Varanasi, Aurangabad, Hyderabad, Guwahati, Patna and Ranchi. Moreover, ITDC offers special assistance for medical tourists as part of promoting

medical tourism in the country. That includes 'meet and assist' services at airports; strong relationships with major hospitals; acts as a conduit of information between the client and the hospital/clinic and work with the client to determine the best facilities and staff to handle their particular medical needs; optional extensions that include the best guided regimens of Ayurveda, Yoga and meditation, which speed healing and bring the mind and body together as one; accommodations for family members near the hospital; and close association to coordinate explorations of India which can be facilitated as vacation for the patient and/or their travelling companion(s).

- **Consultancy and engineering services:** ITDC also undertakes consultancy and engineering services like market surveys, analysis of the marketing fields, identification of potential market segments, determination of the product profile, preparation of preliminary cost estimates and financial projections, architectural interior designing; engineering consultancy services in the field of civil, structure, plumbing, air conditioning and mechanical disciplines; and designing of industrial kitchens, including preparation of layouts and kitchen equipment. Its management consultancy and advisory services include providing assistance in project management, recruitment of personnel, and imparting in-house on-the-job-training of hotel staff. Moreover, it can also assist in group-marketing services through its network of *Ashok Reservation and Marketing Services* (ARMS) and it encompasses preparation of cost-benefit analysis and budgetary support; operation of hotels, business centres, convention halls, banqueting, etc.; and preparation of master plans for development of tourism. In the case of adventure tourism, it can assist in developing camping tourism and adventure tourism.
- **Advertising and marketing services:** Tourism promotion is a key area and it needs expertise and creativity. ITDC focuses on this area as well through *Ashok Creatives* which undertakes preparation of annual publicity plans; budget proposals; designing publicity material; advertising; production of films, audio visuals and sound and light shows; setting up of exhibitions from designing to fabrication on turnkey basis; designing and fabrication of tableaux; public relations, including media relations; print production of tourist literature; sales promotions, including organization of cultural and food festivals and participation in trade events in India and abroad; monitoring the impact of these efforts in terms of actual sales and increase in tourism business.
- **Catering services:** ITDC arranges catering services at Vigyan Bhawan, a major international conference venue and at Hyderabad House, the state guest house of India's prime minister.
- *Sound and light shows* at Purana Quila , New Delhi and at Red Fort, New Delhi.

- **Human resource development:** It is also engaged in human resource development activities suited for the hospitality and tourism sector.

Role of ITDC

ITDC has played an important role in Indian tourism development since its establishment. It acts as a catalyst in the growth of tourism in India. Developing tourism infrastructure and superstructure as well as marketing and promotion are the main areas which ITDC has been concentrating on. It has also helped in reviewing Indian art and culture. Since the beginning, ITDC has been helping the tourism industry in identifying and developing several new destinations. Development of Kovalam resort near Thiruvananthapuram is an example. The range of accommodation facilities offered by the ITDC is playing an important role in the tourism sector in India. Various schemes of ITDC like low-priced packages for senior citizens, students, etc., have gained much attention. One of ITDC's major contributions has been in offering national network of tourist transport services, cars and coaches with attractive packages. The duty-free shops in major international airports stimulate shopping tendencies of tourists.

In its role as a catalyst, ITDC picked up wide ranging expertise in technical and management consultancy. Tourism promotion and marketing that ITDC is concentrating heavily on helped Indian tourism to grow to a great extent. The publicity work also has an important role. The *three pronged business strategy* of ITDC, such as, to achieve market leadership in each market location and segment; accelerate the tempo of its activities; and maximize foreign exchange earnings, is really stimulating the growth and development of tourism in India.

8.3 DIRECTORATE GENERAL OF CIVIL AVIATION (DGCA)

Every country has separate authorities to streamline aviation activities and regulate them in order to ensure efficient and smooth functioning of air transport. For instance, the *Federal Aviation Administration* (FAA) is the authority in the US entrusted with that task. It is the national aviation authority of the United States, an agency of the United States Department of Transportation entrusted with the authority to regulate and oversee all aspects of American civil aviation. In India, the Directorate General of Civil Aviation (DGCA) is the regulatory body in the field of civil aviation responsible for regulation of air transport services and for enforcement of civil air regulations, air safety and airworthiness standards. It is the ultimate governmental regulatory body for civil aviation under the Ministry of Civil Aviation. A wide range of functions are entrusted upon DGCA which is headed by Director General. The following, according to DGCA, gives the glimpses of activities and its functions.

- Registration of civil aircraft
- Formulation of standards of airworthiness for civil aircraft registered in India and grant of certificates of airworthiness to such aircraft
- Licensing of pilots, aircraft maintenance engineers and flight engineers, and conducting examinations and checks for that purpose
- Licensing of air traffic controllers
- Certification of aerodromes and CNS/ATM facilities
- Maintaining a check on the proficiency of flight crew, and also of other operational personnel such as flight dispatchers and cabin crew
- Granting air operator's certificates to Indian carriers and regulation of air transport services operating to/from/within/over India by Indian and foreign operators, including clearance of scheduled and non-scheduled flights of such operators
- Conducting investigation into incidents and serious incidents involving aircraft up to 2250 kg all-up weight (AUW) and taking accident prevention measures including formulation of implementation of safety aviation management programmes
- Carrying out amendments to the Aircraft Act, the Aircraft Rules and the civil aviation requirements for complying with the amendments to ICAO annexes, and initiating proposals for amendment to any other Act or for passing a new Act in order to give effect to an international convention or amendment to an existing convention
- Coordination of ICAO matters with all agencies and sending replies to state letters, and taking all necessary actions arising out of the Universal Safety Oversight Audit Programme (USOAP) of ICAO
- Supervision of the institutes/clubs/schools engaged in flying training including simulator training, AME training or any other training related with aviation, with a view to ensuring a high quality of training
- Granting approval to aircraft maintenance, repair and manufacturing organizations and their continued oversight
- To act as a nodal agency for implementing Annex 9 provisions in India and for coordinating matters relating to facilitation at Indian airports including holding meetings of the National Facilitation Committee
- Rendering advice to the government on matters relating to air transport including bilateral air services agreements, on ICAO matters and generally on all technical matters relating to civil aviation, and to act as an overall regulatory and developmental body for civil aviation in the country

- Coordination at national level for flexi-use of air space by civil and military air traffic agencies and interaction with ICAO for provision of more air routes for civil use through Indian air space
- Keeping a check on aircraft noise and engine emissions in accordance with ICAO Annex 16 and collaborating with the environmental authorities in this matter, if required
- Promoting indigenous design and manufacture of aircraft and aircraft components by acting as a catalytic agent
- Approving training programmes of operators for carriage of dangerous goods, issuing authorizations for carriage of dangerous goods, etc.
- Safety oversight of all entities approved/certified/licensed under the Aircraft Rules, 1937.

8.3.1 Organization of DGCA

The organization is headed by Directorate General of Civil Aviation (DGCA), who is assisted by Joint Director General and Deputy Director General. Regional airworthiness offices also function under the directorate at 14 locations: Delhi, Mumbai, Chennai, Kolkata, Bangalore, Hyderabad, Trivandrum, Bhopal, Lucknow, Patna, Bhubaneswar, Kanpur, Guwahati and Patiala. In addition, there are five regional air safety offices at Delhi, Mumbai, Chennai, Kolkata and Hyderabad and a gliding centre at Pune. Moreover, a representative of research and development directorate is also deputed to National Aerospace Laboratories (NAL), Bangalore.

8.3.2 Services Offered

DGCA ensures the following services:

(a) *Permissions* provided to *air transport modes* in the following categories:
- Scheduled air transport services (passenger)
- Non-scheduled air transport services (passenger)
- Air transport services (cargo)
- Non-scheduled air transport services (charter operation)

(b) *Permissions* provided to *aircraft for airworthiness* in various categories, such as certificate of airworthiness of aircraft and its engines/propellers manufactured in India and also revalidate the certificate issued to an aircraft by foreign airworthiness authority. All aircraft registered in India should possess a current and valid certificate of airworthiness before it is flown, unless it is taken as a test flight.

(c) *Registration* of all civil aircraft and to grant certificates of registration in India.

(d) *Safety oversight airworthiness programme*: It is aimed to detect the weaknesses in the engineering activities of the operators, maintenance and other related organizations so that necessary corrective measures can be taken in time. This can enable the organisation to exercise airworthiness control to be maintained at or above the level required by the regulations.

(e) *Selection and licensing of key aviation personnel.*

(f) *Medical assessment*: The medical section of DGCA undertakes medical assessments required for the certification of licensed aviation personnel as per the international standards and recommended practices of ICAO.

(g) *Statistics preparation*: DGCA also monitors the trends in air transportation. Statistical division collects data pertaining to civil aviation from various sources such as Air India, Indian Airlines, Private Operators, Foreign Airlines and various airports managed by Airports Authority of India. The compiled data is published as "India Air Transport Statistics."

(h) *Licensing of airports*: Airports have to be licensed and the fee and other service charges collected are to be finalized. DGCA is also vested with this task. Licences are given for categories such as public use and private use (for use by the licensee and by individuals specifically authorized by the licensee).

(i) *Environment protection measures*: An aviation environment unit established in the R & D Directorate primarily deals with environment issues. Moreover, environment cells are functioning in airlines, airports, and air navigation service providers.

(j) *Surveillance, enforcement and safety activities*: The department concerned undertakes the preparation and monitoring of the annual surveillance programme, coordinating the monthly meetings to review the surveillance conducted by each directorate and maintains a database. Further, it coordinates the meetings of the Board for Aviation Safety (BFAS) to resolve Level I findings and maintains records of enforcement actions. The deficiencies identified during surveillance are categorized into Levels I and II, of which the first category is reviewed by the BFAS set up at the headquarters. The second category findings are also monitored and steps are taken accordingly.

(k) *International cooperation*: The *International Cooperation Group* (ICG) handles all the international programmes with international organizations on matters relating to policy, technical, and safety matters.

(l) *Vigilance functions*: A vigilance department functions in the DGCA which aims at initiating steps to curb corruption and malpractices in the department. It investigates complaints, monitors progress of actions recommended, studies and examines systems and procedures, identifies corruption prone areas and provides remedial measures, maintains surveillance on personnel posted and the like to maintain corruption-free environment.

The DGCA has been functioning with the vision: "*Endeavour to promote safe and efficient air transportation through regulation and proactive safety oversight system*", with necessary prudence over the last several years and it has been expanded since its inception so as to cope up with the increasing air transport sector in the country. In the future, increased intervention may be required.

8.4 AIRPORTS AUTHORITY OF INDIA (AAI)

In India, airports were set up as early as 1924. Construction of civil airports in India started in 1924 in Calcutta at Dum Dum, Allahabad at Bamrauli and in Bombay at Gilbert Hill. Since then, new airports in line with the economic development of various regions were developed. India, due to its vast size has a large number of airports and the number is on the increase significantly as the air transportation sector is witnessing enormous growth day by day. An official classification of airports in the country is shown as below.

- International airports
- Domestic airports
- Customs airports
- Civil enclaves at military airfields

The ultimate authority for making, maintaining, and managing civil aviation infrastructure in India is the *Airports Authority of India* (AAI) functioning under the Ministry of Civil Aviation. This authority was merged from two separate authorities that existed before for domestic and international air transport sectors. It was in 1972, the Government of India constituted the *International Airports Authority of India* (IAAI) to manage the indigenous international airports. The domestic airports and others were controlled by the *National Airports Authority* (NAA) that was constituted in 1986. These organizations were merged together by a legislative act of Parliament and was named Airports Authority of India (AAI). The merger brought into existence a single organization entrusted with the responsibility of creating, upgrading, maintaining and managing civil aviation infrastructure both on ground and air space in the country. Currently, this agency manages 125 airports, which include 18 international airports, 7 customs airports, 78 domestic airports and 26 civil enclaves at defence airfields. Moreover, this ensures air navigation services over 2.8 million square nautical miles of air space. According the the AAI, its main functions include:

- Design, development, operation and maintenance of international and domestic airports and civil enclaves.

- Control and management of the Indian airspace extending beyond the territorial limits of the country, as accepted by ICAO.
- Construction, modification and management of passenger terminals.
- Development and management of cargo terminals at International and domestic airports.
- Provision of passenger facilities and information system at passenger terminals at the airports.
- Expansion and strengthening of operation area, viz., runways, aprons, taxiway, etc.
- Provision of visual aids.
- Provision of communication and navigation aids, viz., ILS, DVOR, DME, RADAR, etc.

Airports Authority of India has its headquarters in New Delhi with regional headquarters in New Delhi (northern region), Guwahati (north-eastern region), Kolkata (eastern region), Mumbai (western region), and Chennai (southern region). Each regional office is headed by a regional executive director.

8.4.1 Functions of AAI

- **Arranging travel facilities:** Airports Authority of India is engaged with the construction, modification and management of passenger terminals; development and management of cargo terminals; development and maintenance of apron infrastructure including runways, parallel taxiways, etc. AAI also ensures the provision of communication, navigation and surveillance which includes provision of DVOR/DME, ILS, ATC radars, visual aids, etc. Airport planning has been an integral part of the AAI. Almost all departmental processes at airports are undertaken in-house, be it airport feasibility studies, design of passenger terminals, cargo terminals, aircraft hangars, aircraft parking stand with fuel hydrant systems, runways, taxiways, airport lighting systems, electric supply arrangements, runway and taxiway lighting, approach lighting systems, air conditioning arrangements, passenger information systems, baggage handling systems, car parking facilities, etc. The civil engineering department, consisting of civil and structural engineers, undertakes structural design of passenger and cargo terminals, aircraft hangars, runways and other pavements, technical buildings for installation of airport ground aids, etc., for AAI's in-house requirements and consultancy projects. To ensure timely completion of projects, without cost overrun, the department adopts its proven technique of deputing a project in-charge for each project undertaken, within the organization and on consultancy basis, with adequate delegated powers. The tasks of electrical engineering department include designing, planning and execution of various electrical and mechanical works comprising indoor lighting schemes, external lighting works, central air conditioning of terminal buildings, power supply schemes including standby power generating sets, firefighting and fire alarm systems, electromechanical equipment like elevators, escalators, travellators, passenger boarding bridges, elevated cargo transfer vehicle (ETV) and cargo storage and re-trivial system, etc., at various airports. In addition they are also responsible for planning, designing and execution of ground lighting works comprising runway lighting, taxiway lighting, approach lighting and other equipment connected with landing and navigation of the aircraft.

The engineering department is also responsible for constructing and maintaining the buildings/structures in which communication and other electronic equipment, used for landing and navigation of aircraft, are housed. Internationally approved standards in the electrical installations are adhered to keep abreast with the ever changing techniques and needs of the passengers and the airlines. Moreover, AAI arranges the provision of air traffic services, provision of passenger facilities and related amenities at its terminals. All such are undertaken with the purpose of ensuring safe and secure operations of aircraft, passenger and cargo in the country. In addition, future demand has to be always considered and keeping eye on the same many modification and extension programmes are undertaken at airports. A number of projects for extension and strengthening of runway, taxi track and aprons at different airports have been taken up. New flights with extra width is a challenge for existing airports and in order to meet this challenge, extension of runway to 7500 ft has been taken up to support operation of flights like Airbus-320/Boeing 737-800.

- **Air navigation services:** The technology related to air navigation is advancing day-by-day and it is of utmost importance to enhance the navigation services. In order to cope up with the advancements in air navigation infrastructure for seamless navigation across state and regional boundaries, AAI comes up with its plans for transition to satellite based communication, navigation, surveillance and air traffic management. It draws plans to upgrade ATM infrastructure in the country both in terms of conditional provision of automation systems and upgradation of technology which also involves shifting from ground-based navigation to satellite-based navigation. Recently, AAI entered into some cooperation agreements and memoranda of cooperation agreements with US Federal Aviation Administration, US Trade & Development Agency, European Union, Air Services Australia and the French Government Co-operative Projects and Studies initiated to gain from their experience. The ultimate objective is to expose the officials and professionals in AAI to latest technology, modern practices and procedures to improve the overall performance of airports and air navigation services. CNS is another important area that the AAI has to establish and maintain as per international standards. Planning, procurement and commissioning of all communication, navigation & surveillance (CNS) facililties and support systems for air navigation based on short-term and long-term requirements to synchronize the organisation's plan with ICAO's approved plans is managed by CNS planning department. Preparation of qualitative requirements and system specifications in coordination with all concerned agencies/organizations, preparation of estimates, invitation of tenders, tender evaluation of technical and commercial bids, placement of orders factory inspection of equipment and its subsequent installation and commissioning are the responsibilities discharged by the CNS planning department. Moreover, the AAI has to orient to the latest state-of-the-art equipment, as replacement of old equipment and also as new facilities to improve standards of safety of airports in the air. Adoption of new and improved procedures go hand-in-hand with induction of new equipment.

- **Ensuring safety and security:** New security threats may emerge at any time and the systems need to be updated accordingly. AAI has to be alert at every moment. The emerging security environments have brought into focus the need for strengthening security of vital installations. There was thus an urgent need to revamp the security at airports not only to thwart any misadventure, but to restore confidence of travelling public in the security of air travel as a whole, which was shaken after 9/11 tragedy in the US. With this in view, a number of steps were taken by the AAI which include the deployment of CISF for airport security, CCTV surveillance system at sensitive airports, latest and state-of-the-art X-ray baggage inspection systems, premier security, and surveillance systems.
- **Manpower development and training:** AAI has set up a number of training institutes across the country. The following are the key training centres managed by the AAI:
    - National Institute of Aviation Management and Research (NIAMAR) Society, Delhi
    - Civil Aviation Training College (CATC), Allahabad
    - Fire Training Centres at Delhi and Kolkata
- **ICT integration:** Information and communication technology is the lifeblood for efficient and smooth functioning of the aviation systems. In the environment of airports, it is essential to have operational and managerial efficiency, transparency and employee productivity. Adavanced technology tools and solutions are incorporated for it. In order to ensure the optimum utilization of ICT tools and solutions, AAI has initiated a range of programmes for its employees.

Table 8.1: Airports in India (public use)

1. Aizwal (Lengpui) Aerodrome, Aizwal, Mizoram
2. Cochin International Airport, Cochin, Kerala
3. Indira Gandhi International Airport, Delhi
4. Chhatrapati Shivaji International Airport, Mumbai, Maharashtra
5. Trivandrum International Airport, Thiruvananthapuram, Kerala
6. Netaji Subash Chandra Bose International Airport, Kolkata, West Bengal
7. Chennai International Airport, Chennai, Tamil Nadu
8. Jindal Vijaynagar Aerodrome, Vijaynagar, Karnataka
9. Sardar Vallabh Bhai Patel International Airport, Ahmedabad, Gujarat
10. Hyderabad International Airport, Begumpet, Hyderabad, Andhra Pradesh
11. Coimbatore Airport, Coimbatore, Tamil Nadu
12. Lucknow Airport, Lucknow, Uttar Pradesh
13. Jaipur Airport, Jaipur, Rajasthan
14. Lokpriya Gopinath Bordoloi International Airport, Guwahati, Assam
15. Lal Bahadur Shastri Airport, Varanasi, Uttar Pradesh
16. Amritsar International Airport, Amritsar, Punjab
17. Dr. Babasaheb Ambedkar International Airport, Nagpur, Maharashtra
18. Calicut Airport, Calicut, Kerala
19. Sonari Aerodrome, Jamshedpur, Jharkhand
20. Rajiv Gandhi International Airport, Shamshabad, Andhra Pradesh
21. Bangalore International Airport, Devenahalli, Karnataka
22. Mangalore Airport, Mangalore, Karnataka
23. Shri Guru Gobind Singh Ji Airport, Nanded, Maharashtra
24. Raja Bhoj Airport, Bhopal, Madhya Pradesh
25. Tiruchirappalli Airport, Tiruchirappalli, Tamil Nadu
26. Mysore Airport, Mysore, Karnataka
27. Vadodara Airport, Vadodara, Gujarat
28. Devi Ahilya Bai Holkar Airport, Indore, Madhya Pradesh
29. Maharana Pratap Airport, Udaipur, Rajasthan
30. Raipur Airport, Raipur, Chhattisgarh
31. Cooch Behar Airport, Cooch Behar, West Bengal
32. Biju Patnaik Airport, Bhubaneswar, Orissa
33. Aurangabad Airport, Aurangabad, Maharashtra

34. Madurai Airport, Madurai, Tamil Nadu
35. Dimapur Airport, Dimapur, Assam
36. Dibrugarh Airport, Dibrugarh, Assam
37. Khajuraho Airport, Khajuraho, Madhya Pradesh
38. Birsa Munda Airport, Ranchi, Jharkhand
39. Rajkot Airport, Rajkot, Gujarat
40. Imphal Airport, Imphal, Nagaland
41. Tirupati Airport, Tirupati, Andhra Pradesh
42. Tuticorin Airport, Tuticorin, Tamilnadu
43. Barapani Airport, Barapani, Shillong, Meghalaya
44. Jabalpur Airport, Jabalpur, Madhya Pradesh
45. Hubli Airport, Hubli, Karnataka
46. Lilabari Airport, Lilabari, Assam
47. Agartala Airport, Agartala, Tripura
48. Salem Airport, Salem, Tamilnadu
49. Jolly Grant Airport, Dehradun, Uttrakhand
50. Belgaum Airport, Belgaum, Karnataka
51. Rajahmundary Airport, Rajahmundary, Andhra Pradesh
52. Bhavnagar Airport, Bhavnagar, Gujarat
53. Kandla Airport, Kandla, Gujarat
54. Kangra Airport, Kangra, Himachal Pradesh
55. Pantnagar Airport, Pantnagar, Uttrakhand
56. Surat Airport, Surat, Gujarat
57. Gaya Airport, Gaya, Bihar
58. Pudducherry Airport, Pudducherry, Pudducherry
59. Shimla Airport, Shimla, Himachal Pradesh
60. Vijayawada Airport, Vijayawada, Andhra Pradesh
61. Kullu-Manali Airport, Bhunter, Himachal Pradesh
62. Ludhiana Airport, Ludhiana, Punjab
63. Porbandar Airport, Porbandar, Gujarat
64. Agatti Airport, Agatti, Lakshadweep
65. Juhu Airport, Juhu, Mumbai, Maharashtra
66. HAL Ozar Aerodrome, Nasik, Maharashtra

Source: DGCA (dgca.nic.in)

8.4.2 Training Institutes of AAI

- **Indian aviation academy:** Earlier in 1986, Institute of Airport Management was established in the vicinity of Indira Gandhi International Airport and the same was shifted to the present campus in 1988. It was renamed as *National Institute of Aviation Management and Research* (NIAMAR) in 1997 and functioned as such until 2010. *Indian Aviation Academy* was established on 22nd July 2010 under the ageis of NIAMAR. This institute is a joint training academy of Airports Authority of India (AAI), Directorate General of Civil Aviation (DGCA) and Bureau of Civil Aviation Security (BCAS). The major areas of training are on airport operations, airport engineering—construction, maintenance and project management, airport finance, human resource management, airport commercial and land management, aviation law, air cargo management, aviation security and aviation safety. Moreover, Indian Aviation Academy, under ICAO TRAIN AIR Programme of the International Civil Aviation Organisation (ICAO) offers standardized training packages (STPs) on *"Bird Hazard Control Management"* and *"Airport Pavement Maintenance"*. Also specialized training programmes are offered on 'Global Training Programmes on Aviation Security' and IATA training programmes and courses.
- **Civil aviation training college (CATC):** Civil Aviation Training College (CATC) located at Allahabad is an exclusive training institute in the area of air traffic management (ATM) and communication, navigation and surveillance (CNS) maintenance and operations. It is a modernized training establishment in terms of infrastructure, training facilities, laboratories and simulators. The courses are of different duration, ranging from 1 week to 50 weeks, depending on the course objectives and the course design. Both for CNS and ATM disciplines, the courses are grouped in three categories.
- **Fire training centres:** There are two fire training centres in India, one is in New Delhi and the other is situated in Kolkata.

8.5 ARCHAEOLOGICAL SURVEY OF INDIA (ASI)

Archaeological Survey of India (ASI) was established long back, in 1861, by the then rulers and has been involved in a variety of tasks including preserving monuments and sites, discovery and excavation of historical sites, and deciphering and describing thousands of important inscriptions. In 1861, Alexander Cunningham's memorandum to Lord Canning, which led to the conduct of a systematic survey of monuments in India, along with the appointment of the first archaeological surveyor. Ten years later, the ASI became a distinct department. The activities of the archaeological survey commenced since then and in 1921, it discovered the Indus Valley sites at Harappa (by Daya Ram Sahni) and at Mohenjodaro (by R.D. Banerji). Epigraphy, excavation, and setting up site museums were part of ASI activities from the beginning and the periodic

Table 8.2: UNESCO world heritage sites in India

Cultural
Agra Fort (1983)
Ajanta Caves (1983)
Buddhist Monuments at Sanchi (1989)
Champaner–Pavagadh Archaeological Park (2004)
Chhatrapati Shivaji Terminus (formerly Victoria Terminus) (2004)
Churches and Convents of Goa (1986)
Elephanta Caves (1987)
Ellora Caves (1983)
Fatehpur Sikri (1986)
Great Living Chola Temples (1987)
Group of Monuments at Hampi (1986)
Group of Monuments at Mahabalipuram (1984)
Group of Monuments at Pattadakal (1987)
Hill Forts of Rajasthan (2013)
Humayun's Tomb, Delhi (1993)
Khajuraho Group of Monuments (1986)
Mahabodhi Temple Complex at Bodh Gaya (2002)
Mountain Railways of India (1999)
Qutab Minar and its Monuments, Delhi (1993)
Rani-ki-Vav (the Queen's Stepwell) at Patan, Gujarat (2014)
Red Fort Complex (2007)
Rock Shelters of Bhimbetka (2003)
Sun Temple, Konârak (1984)
Taj Mahal, Agra (1983)
The Jantar Mantar, Jaipur (2010)
Natural
Great Himalayan National Park Conservation Area (2014)
Kaziranga National Park (1985)
Keoladeo National Park (1985)
Manas Wildlife Sanctuary (1985)
Nanda Devi and Valley of Flowers National Park (1988)
Sundarbans National Park (1987)
Western Ghats (2012)

Source: UNESCO, data accessed from http://whc.unesco.org/en/statesparties/IN/documents/

conservation of monuments and sites was taken up later, from the 1940s. The contribution it has made since its commencement has been immense.

Currently, the Archaeological Survey of India (ASI) is functioning under the Ministry of Culture. Its primary function is to undertake archaeological researches and protect the cultural heritage of the country. Its principal objectives revolve around maintenance of ancient monuments and archaeological sites and remains of national importance, and to regulate all archaeological activities in the country. These tasks are undertaken by:

- Dividing the entire country into 24 circles
- By allocating and utilising a large workforce of trained archaeologists, conservators, epigraphists, architects and scientists
- Conducting archaeological research projects through its circles, museums, excavation branches, prehistory branch, epigraphy branches, science branch, horticulture branch, building survey project, temple survey project and underwater archaeology wing.

8.5.1 Major Activities

- **Protection of monuments:** Protecting monuments is the prime duty of the ASI. Ancient monument is any structure, erection or monument, or any tumulus or place of internment, or any cave, rock-sculpture, inscription or monolith which is of historical, archaeological or artistic interest and which has been in existence for not less than 100 years.
- **Excavations:** ASI undertakes archaeological excavations at many locations. Other agencies are also involved in excavations. The database of excavations of around 2000 sites is available.
- **Conservation and preservation:** ASI undertakes archaeological researches and protection of the cultural heritage of the country. Maintenance of ancient monuments and archaeological sites and remains of national importance is, as stated before, a prime duty of the ASI. The activities are efficiently coordinated by dividing the nation into 24 circles. Both structural conservation and chemical preservation are undertaken.
- **Epigraphical studies:** Epigraphical studies are conducted at various locations in the country to deal with survey, documentation, estampaging of inscriptions and coins; and decipherment, research, study and publication of research.
- **Managing museums:** A fine collection of grand heritage of the country has its permanent settlements at various museums in the country. ASI has a separate museums branch which manages site museums. The monuments and sites under the ASI have vast quantities of antiquarian remains that were unearthed and collected at the archaeological sites across India by ASI. The first ASI site museum

was created in 1904 at Sarnath, Uttar Pradesh under the aegis of Sir John Marshall who was the first Director General of ASI. These were followed by site museums at Delhi Fort in 1909, Bijapur in 1912, Nalanda in 1917 and Sanchi in 1919. ASI has a number of period museums which showcase collections from the 17th-19th centuries or are conceptual museums such as the *Swatantrata Sangram Sangrahalaya* at Red Fort which deals with India's freedom struggle and the *Lucknow Residency Museum* showcasing the Mutiny of 1857.

- **Publications:** ASI produces a variety of publications, both annual and special with subject matters ranging from archaeological researches in excavations, explorations, conservation, architectural survey of temples and secular buildings besides epigraphy and numismatics. Apart from this, the survey brings out popular literature in the form of guidebooks, folders/brochures, portfolio and picture post-cards on centrally protected monuments and archaeological sites.
- **Institute of archaeology:** Established in the year 1985 in Delhi, by upgrading the School of Archaeology, this institute aims at imparting advanced training in multidisciplinary fields of archaeology, epigraphy, numismatics, museology, conservation, antiquarian law, etc. It conducts a postgraduate diploma in archaeology of two years' duration.
- **Central antiquity collection (CAC):** This is a centre for collecting the explored and excavated pottery and other antiquities of the Archaeological Survey of India (ASI). Formed in the 1910s, this centre mainly houses the explored antiquities from Sir Aurel Stein's Central Asian Expeditions (1906-1916). CAC was initially established in the main building of ASI at New Delhi, which was later shifted to Safdarjung Tomb complex in 1958 and then to the present location, i.e., Purana Quila in 1974.
- **Central archeological library:** This was established in the year 1902 in New Delhi and the collection of books at the library is around 1,00,000 which consists of books and journals. This library houses books and periodicals on various subjects, namely, History, Archaeology, Anthropology, Architecture, Art, Epigraphy, Numismatics, Indology, Literature, Geology, etc., along with many rare books, plates, original drawings, etc. Moreover, the ASI maintains library in each circle and branch to cater to its academic and technical requirements leading to research of primary nature.
- **Underwater archaeology wing:** It was established in the Archaeological Survey of India (ASI) in 2001 and it is actively engaged in conducting underwater archaeological studies in the Arabian Sea and Bay of Bengal.
- **Activities abroad:** Archeological activities are undertaken in regions such as Afghanistan, Indonesia, Egypt, Nepal, Cambodia, Bahrain, Maldives, Bhutan, Angola, Vietnam and Myanmar.

- **Horticulture:** ASI maintains gardens also along with major monuments. The maintenance of these ornamental gardens is a necessity, second in importance only to the maintenance of the monuments themselves, for without them the monuments are incomplete. In other cases, e.g., the Qutab and Lodhi monuments at Delhi, the gardens are primarily intended to provide a setting for the monuments and to make the surroundings attractive.

8.6 INDIAN RAILWAY CATERING AND TOURISM CORPORATION (IRCTC)

In order to promote tourism, Indian Railways has one more agency called *Indian Railway Catering and Tourism Corporation* (IRCTC). It, functioning under the Ministry of Railways, was incorporated on 27th September, 1999. It is operated as an extended arm of the Indian Railways to upgrade, professionalize and manage the catering and hospitality services at railway stations, on trains and other locations. Moreover, it aims to promote domestic and international tourism through development of budget hotels, special tour packages, information and commercial publicity and global reservation systems. A range of innovative services are introduced by IRCTC which include food plazas on railway premises, 'Rail Neer', 'Rail Tour Packages' and 'Internet Ticketing'. Further, it is managing onboard catering services in different trains such as Rajdhani / Shatabdi / Duronto and Mail / express trains. Static catering units are also run across the length and breadth of Indian railways and include refreshment rooms, AVMs, book stalls, milk stalls, ice cream stalls, etc. The corporation has its headquarters in New Delhi, which is headed by the Managing Director who is being assisted by three Directors: Director (Catering Services), Director (Tourism and Marketing) and Director (Finance) and nine Group General Managers. It has five zonal offices located at Delhi, Kolkata, Mumbai, Chennai and Secunderabad. South Zone Office is headed by Regional Director and all other Zonal Offices are headed by Group General Managers.

The major functions of IRCTC are decribed as follows.

8.6.1 Catering Services

Catering service is one of the prime functions of IRCTC. It includes onboard catering services in trains, at stations through stalls, food plazas/fast food units and automatic vending machines. The services are provided in trains that include nineteen Rajdhanis, thirteen Shatabdis, sixteen Jan Shatabdis, six Durontos, nine Garib Raths, two hundred and five mail/express trains and more than one hundred trains have train side vending facility. Moreover, it manages 53 food plazas, 13 fast food units and 1 quick service food kiosks, 677 automated vending machines, 2950 stalls, 3291 trolleys and *khomchas*, 698 book stalls, 249 milk stalls and 7918 static units spread across India. Moreover, it manages department's catering units as well. Currently, 518 stalls and 419 trolleys are under departmental operation. IRCTC owns two plants of 'Rail Neer', packaged drinking water; one situated at Nangloi (Delhi) and the other at Danapur (Bihar). One more plant is being set up at Palur, near Chennai.

8.6.2 Online Ticket Reservation Services

Indian Railways provide the services of *online ticket reservation services*, and IRCTC is entrusted with this task. The delivery of tickets is done either through the courier or a person can himself take the print for travelling after making online reservation. According to IRCTC, on an average more than 2,03,000 tickets are sold through IRCTC's website in a day. Indian Railways is benefited by saving on infrastructure like buildings, air conditioning, electricity, furniture, staff, etc.

8.6.3 Managing Call Centres

The concept of call centres has become a trend nowadays and customers get the freedom to obtain information at any point of time. On behalf of Indian Railways, IRCTC manages a *call centre* for passenger enquiry. A customer can dial 139 from anywhere in the country and get all information from related to train timing, PNR confirmation, train routes and other relevant information.

8.6.4 Quality Control and Complaint Redressal System

To maintain *quality of services* onboard trains, IRCTC has established control rooms at New Delhi, Mumbai, Kolkata, Chennai and Secunderabad. All the activities are coordinated from the central control room in New Delhi with efficient functioning and monitoring with all the five zonal offices. Moreover, a toll-free number has been launched for swift redressal of complaints and suggestions conveyed by passengers on phone. In order to facilitate another option of lodging complaint/suggestion by passengers, facility of receipt of complaint through SMS on a given number has been initiated and that will enable the travelling passengers to have easy access to the *complaints redressal system* without any charges.

8.6.5 Food Safety Audit

Food safety and hygiene audit is undertaken regularly keeping in view the importance of food safety and other related issues on static/mobile catering units.

8.6.6 Tourism Services

IRCTC has been undertaking a number of activities in order to improve the tourist influx into the country. The following are some major efforts:

- *Buddhist Circuit Special Train*
- *'Bharat Darshan' – Village on Wheels*
- *Rail Tour Packages*
- *Hill Charters*
- *Educational Tours*
- *Tourism Web Portal:* These contain essential details of destinations and attractions. Keeping this in mind, IRCTC manages *www.irctctourism.com,* which can meet all the information needs of a tourist. This site also offers online booking of tour packages, hotels and car rentals across the country.
- *Budget Hotel:* The plans in the pipeline to serve tourists with hospitality products include budget hotels to be set up near railway stations. Currently, four budget hotels are operational at New Delhi, Howrah, Puri and Ranchi.
- *Luxury Tourist Train:* The corporation has established a joint veture company called 'Royale India Train Tours Limited (RIRTL)' in association with Cox and Kings India Limited, a leading tour operator. It will run a Pan India Luxury Tourist Train, named *Maharajas' Express.*

8.7 TOURISM FINANCE CORPORATION OF INDIA (TFCI)

Tourism industry, in general, is a highly *capital-intensive sector*. Insufficient availability of fund has always been a barrier in its expansion and development. Considering this, Government of India established a financial institution, *Tourism Finance Corporation of India* (TFCI) in the year 1989. It was based on Yunus Committee set up in 1988, under the aegis of Planning Commission which recommended the need of a national financial institution for providing financial assistance to tourism sector in the country. In accordance with the above recommendation, IFCI Limited, other all-India financial institutions, investment institutions and nationalised banks promoted a public limited company under the name of *Tourism Finance Corporation of India Ltd* (TFCI). It was established as a public limited company under the Companies Act, 1956 on 27th January 1989 and became operational with effect from 1st February 1989. TFCI is primarily involved in the following activities:

- Financial services to the tourism industries, infrastructure, services and facilities.
- Advisory services which include high-quality research and consultancy services to the tourism industry in general, and to the investors in tourism industry, in particular.
- Guidelines to shareholders.

TFCI provides financial assistance to tourism industries for new projects, expansion of existing projects, diversification of services, and modernization of projects. It has been providing high quality research and consultancy services to the tourism and hospitality industry in general, and to the investors in those sectors, in particular. Its client base includes different central and state agencies by undertaking broad-based assignments to cover macro- and microlevel tourism related studies/exercises to facilitate identification, conceptualization, promotion/implementation of specific tourism related projects and for taking policy level decisions with respect to investment and infrastructure augmentation, etc. It also provides specific project related services to various clients and undertakes appraisal of individual projects for various state government agencies/individual clients.

Project related services include site evaluation studies, market potential assessment for tourism projects, techno-economic feasibility studies, loan/equity syndication services, financial restructuring of project proposals, review and appraisal, and the like.

Tourism related studies include tourism potential studies and identification of tourism circuits; preparing tourism development master plans for state/travel circuit/destination; tourist profiles and image rating studies; accommodation and other infrastructure assessment; studies for sustainable tourism development, environment impact assessment and determining carrying capacity of tourism activities in wildlife sanctuaries, national parks and other sensitive/critical areas; assessing need for and identifying specific policies and other promotional measures for tourism development in any state; and the similar.

Guidelines to shareholders include guidance in transfer of shares; change in the order of holders in the case of transportation sector; guidance and assistance for getting duplicate share certificate(s) in lieu of defaced/damaged share certificates.

8.8 TRAVEL AGENTS ASSOCIATION OF INDIA (TAAI)

Travel Agents Association of India (TAAI) is a leading trade association of the travel industry in India. It is a non-political and non-profit making body, formed with an aim to protect the interests of those engaged in the industry, to promote its orderly growth and development and to safeguard the rights of the travelling public. TAAI represents all that is professional, ethical and dynamic in our nation's travel related activity and has been recognized as the voice of the travel and tourism industry in India. The focus of its functioning is:

- It is conscious of the interest of the travelling public and maintains high ethical standards in the travel trade.
- It aims at the development of the travel and tourism industry in India by constantly improving the standard of service and professionalism in the industry so as to cater to the needs of the travellers and tourists from within India and overseas.

- It is engaged in promoting mutual cooperation among the different segments of the travel and tourism industry, among TAAI members, by contributing to the sound progress and growth of the industry as a whole.

It was formed in 1951 by a group of twelve leading travel agents at a situation when they felt the time had come to create an association to regulate the travel industry in India along organized lines and in accordance with sound business principles. It was established to protect the interests of those engaged in the industry, to promote its orderly growth and development and to safeguard the travelling public from exploitation by unscrupulous and unreliable operators. It commenced with just a membership of 12 and now approximately 2500 active, associate, allied, government and non-resident members. This association also aims to *promote, maintain* and *stimulate* the growth of travel and tourism in the country. Collecting, analysing and disseminating useful information on travel and tourism among members for their guidance is another task the association is engaged in. Since its commencement, it has always attempted to draw the attention of the controlling and regulatory authorities to the problems faced by the industry and discuss with them the means of survival and betterment of members.

Active members are IATA approved head offices of travel agents. Associate members are the branch offices of active members. Allied members consist of organizations engaged in allied businesses, i.e., various segments of travel and tourism industry such as excursion agents, tour operators, hoteliers, airlines, GSAs, CRSs, etc. Government members include central and state government departments and public sector tourism organizations. Overseas travel agents, tour operators and hotels come under the category of non-resident members. The members can enjoy networking opportunities with the TAAI membership via various formal and informal forums. Its main objective is to look after the interests of its members. It is manadatory to adhere to the *Code of Conduct* of the organization and abide by the Constitution of TAAI. The major activities of TAAI are to:

- function as a powerful platform for interaction of thoughts and experiences;
- help promote, maintain and stimulate the growth of travel and tourism in the industry;
- educate and equips the members to meet the challenges of tomorrow through conventions and seminars;
- draw the attention of the controlling and regulatory authorities in the country and discusses with them the problems of the industry and works for the survival and betterment of its members;
- maintain close contact with world bodies and represents matters affecting the travel and tourism industry of the country;
- gather useful information on travel and tourism and disseminates the same to its members for their guidance;

- help develop better understanding among the different segments of the travel industry and brings them into its fold by offering membership under different categories; and
- foster fraternity among its members.

It functions with a management committee with president and general secretary as leaders. Striving for a committed national membership, it is also committed to widening its area of influence by judiciously delegating authority and responsibility to regions, chapters and city committees.

8.9 INDIA ASSOCIATION OF TOUR OPERATORS (IATO)

India Association of Tour Operators (IATO) was established with an idea to promote international understanding and goodwill to the ultimate advantage, and it is a national body of the tourism industry. It is a non-profit, joint forum of tour operators for promoting and helping the development of tourism in India. Currently, it has over 1500 members covering all segments of tourism industry. Established in 1982, it has close connections and constant interaction with other tourism associations in US, Nepal and Indonesia, such as USTOA, NATO and ASITA, and has been increasing its international networking with professional bodies for better facilitation to international travellers visiting not only India but the entire region. In order to bring in better business environments for tourism industries in the country, it interacts closely with the government on all critical issues affecting the tourism industry in India with the highest priority to tourism facilitation. It has been made mandatory that the members of IATO have to maintain high-level standards of professional ethics and should offer personalized services to their clients. It has been the forum for the tourism industry for addressing crucial industry issues, at various levels. IATO also takes part in socially relevant issues, supports all major national causes, contributed by relief emergency operations in national crisis and calamities. The association function with a number of objectives such as to:

- promote national integration, welfare and goodwill.
- take all steps which may be necessary for promoting, encouraging and assisting in the development of tourism throughout the country and to take initiatives to secure the welfare of the tourism trade in all respects;
- communicate with chambers of commerce, other mercantile and public bodies in India, government departments or committees, International Air Transport Association and various foreign and local associations and corporations, companies and concerns, and promote measures in the interests of the travel trade and nominate members to act on them;
- encourage and promote friendly feelings among tour operators and travel agents on all subjects involving their common good and benefit;

- try to amicably settle the disputes of the members of this Association by referring the disputes for settlement to a sub-committee to be constituted for such purpose by the Executive Committee;
- protect the interests of the members of this Association from the malpractices of foreign tour operators;
- set up and maintain high ethical standards in the industry;
- undertake such welfare activities which the members cannot undertake individually;
- get affiliation with similar organisations in other countries;
- promote equal opportunities for all visitors to enjoy tourism and travel facilities without distinction of race, colour, creed or nationality;
- organise overseas promotional tours jointly with various airlines and government of India tourist offices abroad and other similar organisations;
- conduct aiding and assisting seminars, group discussions, course of studies, cultural meetings;
- institute awards for excellence in tourism related activities;
- assist students by scholarship to pursue higher education, study and research particularly in the field of development of tourism and international brotherhood, both in India and outside the country;
- institute chairs and fellowships in India;
- take initiatives and ensure that the problems affecting any of the services relating to tourism trade are sorted out through the mediation of the Association, failing which joint legal action to be taken for and on behalf of the members of the association for settling such problems;
- produce regular reports about the achievements of the members of the association and to do all such things as are incidental or conducive to the above objects; and
- print and publish information material for the benefit of its members;

Founded on 13th January 1982 with just seven members, it has now over 4000 members from different segments of the tourism industry like travel agents, hotels, airlines, government tourism departments/development corporations, educational institutions, transport operators and both national and international tour operators. There are four types of memberships in IATO such as active members, associate members, allied members, and honorary members. In addition to them, there are international members also.

Active members can be any firm or company having established place of business in India, and recognized by the Department of Tourism as tour operator/travel agent for a minimum period of two years. Certain financial standards are also fixed by the association for considering one firm as an active member. Any other office including overseas offices of an active or allied member shall be eligible for *associate membership* of the association. Though they are an important category of members, they do not have the right to vote in the proceedings of the association.

Allied member is the third category. Any firm or company, which is regularly engaged or associated with tourism and travel industry such as carrier companies, hoteliers, restaurants, excursion agents, transport contractors, forwarding and clearing agents, shipping companies, state tourist corporations/organizations, hotel marketing representatives/agencies, trade publications and any overseas firm/company/corporation/organization can become an allied member. They also do not have the permission to vote, but have the right to participate in the activities of the Association. The allied members will be represented on the Executive Committee by nomination of office bearers of various national trade associations who reciprocate membership to IATO executive members on their association. *Honorary members* can be anyone who is invited and who are Hall of Fame Awardees and distinguished society members and/or who have distinguished themselves by the services to the services of the tourism and travel industry in the national or international field. Any international firm or company which is engaged or associated with tourism and travel industry shall be eligible for membership as allied members of the Association and will be categorized as international members.

IATO has initiated 12 action committees to smoothen the effective and efficient coordination of activities and achieve the set objectives. Each committee has a *convener* assisted by the committee members. Executive committee is the cardinal body of IATO that takes the policy decisions of the Association. The committee will have minimum of 15 members and the maximum shall be 17. IATO has also established a number of agendas to be followed in short term as well as in long term.

8.10 TRAVEL AGENTS FEDERATION OF INDIA (TAFI)

Travel Agents Federation of India is a trade association aimed mainly at protecting the interests of those engaged in the travel industry, to promote its orderly growth and development, and to safeguard the travelling public from exploitation. Founded in 1986, this association tends to regulate the Indian travel business keeping close coordination with the set of strong business ethics and code of conduct. TAFI is a non-political, non-commercial and not-for-profit body, with eight specific categories for the members under which membership is available for IATA Accredited Travel Agents and Tour Operators, Branch Offices of IATA Travel Agents and Tour Operators, Airlines, Hotels, Car Coach rentals, Cruise Lines, Travel Service Intermediaries and so on. This basically attempts to safeguard the interests of the travelling public and maintains high ethical standards within the travel trade through better communications and awareness about regulations. Moreover, efforts are being taken to protect the interests of those engaged in the industry, to ensure its orderly growth and development, and to spread awareness and updated information on travel to efficiently cater to the needs of the travellers from within India and overseas.

From just eight members at the time of commencement, it has grown to accommodate 1400 members from all over India and it is itself a member of World Travel Agents Associations Alliance (WTAAA) and an affiliate member of the Southern African Tourism Services Association (SATSA). TAFI helps to bring together travel agents, tour operators, hoteliers, airlines, cruise companies and other travel industry related companies on a common platform and to help them on issues related to the travel industry. In addition, it integrates initiatives and proposals of all members and intervenes for them with relevant bodies through the different councils, committees and bodies formed in the organization. Moreover, it enhances the possibility to establish business relations with reliable companies and helps to avail additional benefits on an international scale or seek guidance wherever required.

Aims and objectives:

- to protect the interests of those engaged in the industry, to promote its orderly growth and development, to safeguard the travelling public from exploitation by unscrupulous and unreliable so-called travel agents;
- to safeguard the interests of the travelling public and to maintain high ethical standards within the travel trade through better communication and awareness about regulations;
- to augment the development of the travel industry in India by consistent improvement in the standard of services and inculcate professionalism;
- to spread greater awareness and updated information on travel to efficiently cater to the needs of the travellers within India and overseas;
- to promote mutual cooperation among members of TAFI and thereby ensure healthy growth of the travel industry;
- to represent the travel agent's trade before official bodies of government, airline bodies and other appropriate forums;
- to promote such schemes which would benefit the members of TAFI as well as provide mutually beneficial alternatives to the airline industry for better growth of travel;
- to safeguard the interests of the travel agents vis-a-viz service providers such as airlines, consulates, government authorities; and
- to ensure compliance of rules, regulations and guidelines sent by the consulates, government authorities, airlines, etc.

TAFI has got eight different types of memberships which is open to all persons who agree with the aims and objects of the association. Membership categories include: Chartered Members, Active Members, Allied Members, Associate Members, Affiliate

Members, Overseas Allied Members, Government Representatives, and Honorary Members. Members are claimed to have many benefits.

8.11 ASSOCIATION OF DOMESTIC TOUR OPERATORS OF INDIA (ADTOI)

Association of Domestic Tour Operators of India (ADTOI), a national body of domestic tour operators, was established with the purpose of consolidating the efforts of all those tour operators who are actively engaged in the promotion of domestic tourism. It was set up on 7th August 1996 with the strength of a few members and over the years of its existence, it has gathered around 400 members all over India. The association along with its members offers professional services to clients including accommodation providers, guides, railways, transporters and airlines.

The association makes attempts to promote and encourage environmental protection, cultural exchanges and national integration, and disseminate useful knowledge; and for that purpose, to organize, participate, manage, supervise or otherwise help in the promotion of educational or other kinds of activities and events. It disseminates knowledge for the development of domestic tourism in India, to prepare, draw up public plans, blueprints, surveys, schemes and reports concerning the status of the domestic tourism industry. Moreover, it establishes channels of communication and liaison with the Department of Tourism, Government of India, State, and other public and private bodies and take all necessary steps to promote and develop domestic tourism. Formulating a uniform code of conduct to govern the procedures of booking, confirmation, payment, refund, cancellation, no-shows, changes, postponement, preponement, retention charges, commissions and discounts has always been a priority of the association. It attempts to gain benefits by being affiliated with other societies or associations of tour operators in India as well as abroad, and takes efforts to set up and maintain high ethical standards in the tourism industry. It prepares and publishes periodicals or reports relating to the activities of the society and make efforts to assist monetarily in the case of necessity as well. Its membership includes active, allied and honorary members.

8.12 ASSOCIATION OF TOURISM TRADE ORGANISATIONS INDIA (ATTOI)

Association of Tourism Trade Organisations India is a non-governmental, non-profitable, apolitical organization, committed to promote tourism in various sectors and also to generate interest for a healthy business relationship and harmony among parties in the trade. It was established in 2003 with an idea to create a platform for all tourism service providers to build business relationships among members and explore avenues as community in harnessing resources outside the normal gambit of individual resources. It is claimed as the first tourism industry association to incorporate into its business charter a commitment to *Responsible Travel and Sustainable Tourism.* It is functioning with the ultimate objective to generate awareness within India and overseas about the potential of tourism in India. Moreover, it makes efforts towards promoting ecotourism, responsible tourism, environment conservation and the ethical way of doing business.

The executive committee, elected by the active members manages the association and its activities. The executive committee comprises known personalities of the trade with work experience of more than a decade. Protecting the natural and cultural environment and responsible travel are its key concerns. It is an association of individuals and independent companies, each with its own distinctive style and field of operation. As such, each of these individuals and independent companies has its own ways and means of fulfilling their responsibilities by publicizing good practice to encourage and spread *responsible tourism*. The association was set up in order to act as a representative of the tourism service providers by creating a platform for all tourism service providers to build business relationships among its members. ATTOI encourages memberships in order to expand and strengthen the activities of the association. Any individual above 21 years of age can become a member, provided he/she can subscribe themselves to the aims, objectives and rules of the society. Organisations can also become members. The members get advantages such as guidance towards getting statutory approval from concerned departments; getting opportunities to participate in travel marts both inside and outside India, assistance in finding vacancies arising in the tourism industry as well as in finding suitable candidates in the tourism industry; help in exchanging ideas to promote tourism business and the permission to use its logo for business related purposes.

8.13 ADVENTURE TOUR OPERATORS' ASSOCIATION OF INDIA (ATOAI)

Adventure Tour Operators' Association of India (ATOAI) has been founded to promote adventure tourism in India and to create awareness overseas about its potential in India. It was founded in 1994 by joining together a few operators and now, after 20 years, it is a national body comprising over 200 members across the country and abroad actively promoting adventure and ecotourism in India. With her natural topography of towering mountains, steep cliffs and dizzying heights on one hand and swiftly flowing currents, cascading rapids and fierce swells on the other, India is a natural paradise for the discerning traveller who enjoys adrenalin high activities, and ATOI works on a mission to promote adventure tourism in those incredible natural wonders. The members are claimed to strictly follow environmental practices, promote employment of the local community and promote social responsibility. Its mission is to facilitate the delivery of responsible and sustainable adventure travel experience; fostering growth and partnerships among the members. The association is involved in a wide variety of activities like camel safari/jeep safari, camping in India, cycling; horse safari, hot air ballooning, mountain biking, mountaineering, paragliding, rafting, trekking, scuba diving, and youth adventure programmes. Moreover, it undertakes Adventure First Responder and Safety Workshop; Youth Cross Cultural Mountain Conservation Meet; seminars; presentation on India Adventure Tourism products at international trade fairs; adventure tourism roadshows in foreign countries; adventure guide training programmes; and liasoning with the government departments.

8.14 INDIAN MEDICAL TRAVEL ASSOCIATION (IMTA)

Indian Medical Travel Association (IMTA) acts as a professional and expert body representing all stakeholders in the medical tourism industry. It consists of hospitals, healthcare providers (both modern medicine and traditional Indian medicine), travel and medical tourism industry providers and functions with the mission: "To empower all the stakeholders in the medical travel industry and work together to make India the leading global healthcare destination."

There are a number of aims of this association which mainly include making India the leading global healthcare destination and providing a forum for communication on a regular basis for interacting on various aspects associated with the industry. It acts as a voice for the medical tourism industry on various issues and to raise awareness on medical tourism potentials of the country across the world and educates its members on the latest technologies and techniques related to the industry in order to remain competitive.

8.15 FEDERATION OF INDIAN CHAMBERS OF COMMERCE AND INDUSTRY (FICCI)

FICCI is considered the largest and oldest apex business organisation in India. It, being established in 1927, FICCI's evolution is closely connected to the freedom struggle of the country as well as latest emergence of the country as the world's leading economy. Simply, it is an association of business organizations in the country with substantial impact on policy making and other important aspects related to businesses in India. A non-government, non-profit organisation, FICCI is the voice of India's business and industry. It has been playing a lead role in policy debates that are at the forefront of social, economic and political change. With a nationwide membership of over 2000 corporates and over 500 chambers of commerce and business associations, FICCI espouses the shared vision of Indian businesses and speaks directly and indirectly for over 2,50,000 business units. The federation is active in 38 sectors of the economy and its viewpoint and opinion on policy issues is sought out by think tanks, policy makers and the academia alike. Moreover, it has joint business councils with 79 countries across the world.

The activities are mainly focussed on a range of areas such as working closely with the government on policy issues, enhancing efficiency, competitiveness and expanding business opportunities for industry through certain specialized services and global linkages. The following are the prominent services of the federation:

- Arbitral services on behalf of the industries whenever disputes arises.
- ATA Carnet (a universally acepted customs document) documentation service for the exporting and importing sector.
- B2B Solutions through Business Information Services Network (BISNET).
- Customer care services through FICCI Alliance for Consumer Care (FACC) to enhance consumer care practices and facilitate stakeholder interactions.
- Exclusive association for food sector, i.e., Confederation of Indian Food Trade and Industry (CIFTI).
- Corporate social responsibility services (CSRs).
- Economic affairs and research services.
- FICCI Ladies Organization (FLO) to promote entrepreneurship and professional excellence in women and to enhance their skills.
- Indian Council of Arbitration (ICA) services.
- FICCI quality forum services.
- Resource conservation and management (RCM) services.
- Technology commercialization, jointly with the Lockheed Martin Corporation and the IC2 Institute at the University of Texas, Austin.
- Web initiatives through its own division, BISNET.
- FICCI – Entertainment Division serves as a crucial link between the media and the entertainment industry, Information and Broadcasting Ministry and global interests.

8.16 CONFEDERATION OF INDIAN INDUSTRY (CII)

The *Confederation of Indian Industry* (CII) is a non-government, non-profit, industry-led and industry-managed organization, working with the aim to sustain an environment conducive to the development of India, partnering industry, government, and civil society, through advisory and consultative processes. It was established in 1895, and the history is all about the story of the transformation of a miniscule association, representing a small segment of industry, to the premier business association of modern India. Currently, this confederation has more than 7200 members, from private as well as public sectors, including SMEs and MNCs, and an indirect membership of over 1,00,000 enterprises from around 242 national and regional sectoral industry bodies. The functioning of CII is primarily oriented over four prongs of key initiatives/ information, global integration, commitment to society and competitiveness of industry. Enabling members to become more productive and efficient so as to match global benchmarks and compete globally has always been a crucial aim of the confederation by providing a wide range services to its members, from building a better climate for doing business to international networking and creating robust platforms for business interaction.

Moreover, CII rigorously interacts with policy makers, including parliamentarians, ministers and officials to represent industry opinion on emerging trends and help shape policies. While services are provided through its own centres of excellence that focus on various aspects such as quality, energy management, sustainable development, logistics, small business competitiveness, etc. Its different departments deal with technology and innovation, IPR (Intellectual Property Rights), WTO-related issues, skill development and a host of other areas. There are many other services offered by the CII, of which the major ones are discussed below. The ultimate objective of the CII is to develop Indian industry and to ensure that government and society as a whole, understand the needs of industry and its contribution to the nation's well-being. Having 64 offices, including 9 centres of excellence, in India, and 7 overseas offices in Australia, China, Egypt, France, Singapore, UK, and USA, as well as institutional partnerships with 312 counterpart organizations in 106 countries, CII serves as a reference point for Indian industry and the international business community. The following are the aims of the confederation:

- To identify and strengthen industry's role in the economic development of the country.
- To act as a catalyst in bringing about the growth and development of Indian industry.
- To reinforce industry's commitment to society.
- To provide up-to-date information and data to industry and government.
- To create awareness and support industry's efforts on quality, environment, energy management, and consumer protection.
- To identify and address the special needs of the small sector to make it more competitive.
- To promote cooperation with counterpart organisations.
- To work towards globalisation of Indian industry and integration into the world economy.

8.17 INDIA CONVENTION PROMOTION BUREAU (ICPB)

Business tourism is one kind of tourism which all governments like to promote. MICE (Meetings, Incentive, Conventions and Exhibitions) business, the largest component of business tourism is a large revenue generator for many economies world over. Business tourism is usually high quality, high yield category of tourism and complementary to leisure tourism as well. Moreover, it has been reported that approximately 40% of business travellers return with their families or colleagues as leisure visitors later.

Business tourism, in general, involves the following elements:

- Professional congress organizers
- Convention and trade fair centre
- Hotels, resorts, and other accommodation sectors
- Food and beverage sector
- Airlines and surface transport
- Travel agencies
- Recreation activities
- Specialist suppliers: projection and audio systems, translation and simultaneous interpretation, lighting, catering, signposting, accreditations, auxiliary staff, training institutes, etc.
- Freight/customs/logistics agencies
- Handicraft and souvenir companies
- Security and cleaning companies
- Design and printing companies, etc.

The western countries had the hegemony of MICE sector for a long time and still, US is the top spot for the highest number of meetings as a single country destination. The scenario is changing as Asian countries are now also getting adequate number of events from across the world. The steady shift in conference/convention venues can be attributed to the emergence of several strong Asian economies, e.g., India, China apart from Korea and Japan can be a major reason for the situation. Currently, there are top venues in Asia, including, Singapore, Hong Kong and Bangkok and many other cities. India realized the potential of business tourism rather late and since then, massive promotional and development efforts have taken place.

ICPB is the apex body in India functioning mainly with the objective of promoting India as a prominent business tourism destination. It is a management oriented organization which draws its membership from the length and breadth of the hospitality industry as well as other private and government organizations involved directly and indirectly in MICE tourism. This has been functioning under the direction of the Ministry of Tourism, Government of India. This organization has been providing free information and infrastructural assistance to its members in organizing and hosting many successful international conferences and conventions, and taking all efforts to have MICE business from across the world. Besides, it facilitates and supports event planners and other related organizations during the bidding process for international conferences. The following are the aims and objectives of ICPB:

- To promote India as a competent and credible venue/destination for meetings, incentives, conferences and exhibitions (MICEs).

- To undertake a continuing programme of creating better awareness of the role and benefits of MICE in the context of national objectives.
- To collect, both from primary and secondary sources, relevant information that could be used to develop a data bank and to disseminate such information to the membership.
- To undertake research for development of India's MICE industry.
- To undertake a continuing programme of advertising and other publicity, using various media aimed at motivating national associations/organizations to bid for conventions/events, etc.
- To encourage the growth of professionalism in the MICE segments with particular regard to the solicitation and servicing of MICE and evolve an industry code of ethics.
- To provide necessary guidance and feedback to the central government and advise the state governments in the development of infrastructure and facilities for MICE industry segments.
- To disseminate knowledge to MICE industry personnel through educational programmes in association with leading business schools in India and abroad and also to develop modules on convention management with educational institutions.
- To conduct seminars, group discussions, courses of study and exchange of visits with Indian associations/organizations and relevant world associations/organizations.
- To seek affiliations with world bodies having similar aims and objectives.
- To perform or get done other lawful activities that are incidental or conducive to the attainment of the above aims and objectives.
- To promote interests of members at national/international forums.

8.17.1 Membership

ICPB also has different types of membership. Its membership is open to all the segments of conference and conference related industries registered and approved by the Ministry of Tourism, Government of India wherever applicable. There are four categories of membership: active, observer, allied and patrons. *Active members* comprise the corporate entities located in India that are directly concerned with India's MICE industry. *Observer membership* is given to those organizations do business towards the growth of MICE traffic. Subcategories of this include tour operators and travel agents. *Allied members* have to be any organization located in India, which is directly or indirectly involved with MICE industry other than those given under active category and patrons. State/union territory tourism development corporations, airport authorities, chambers of commerce and industry, air cargo agents, etc., can become members in this category.

Patrons include honorarily awarded member associations based in India, who are preferably concerned with the development of MICE industry and also to individuals whose association benefits ICPB.

Some of the major activities of ICPB include:

- **Market development assistance (MDA) scheme:** Active members can bid for international conventions and conferences to bring them, to be held in India and under this scheme financial assistance would be given to those on winning the bid.
- **Ministry support for international conferences:** This scheme is envisaged to attract foreign organizations who can bring in more than 200 foreign delegates which will enable those organizations to avail special incentives in the form of:
  - Complementary cultural programme
  - Cocktail reception or dinner
  - Gifts to all delegates
  - Cultural evening at one of the monuments
- **International trade shows:** Trade shows such as IMEX, EIBTM, IT&CM and AIME may be jointly promoted under the banner of ICPB and overseas India tourist offices. This will help to have better and focussed stands, better collateral interaction with media and more focussed planning. ICPB can coordinate and assist India tourist offices with space design, pre- and post-marketing and onsite management.
- **Roadshows:** ICPB becomes instrumental in coordinating roadshows and similar promotional efforts abroad. Every year, a minimum three roadshows in Europe, UK and USA are organized. Tourist offices become facilitators in this process.

  Roadshows are also conducted in India in important places and major cities which have more number of institutions and associations like Delhi, Mumbai, Bangalore, Chennai, Kolkata, Chandigarh, and Hyderabad. This aims at targeting the potential conference organizer in educating them about the benefits of organising international conferences financially as well as gaining on knowledge economy.
- **Overseas marketing:** This responsibility is undertaken by organizing India Evenings in trade roadshows; by organizing FAM trips to India for foreign conference planners and buyers; by having a PR agency exclusively for MICE, who could do all related media – publicity activities for all types of events abroad and like that.
- **Advertising:** Advertisements are given in general and professional journals, i.e., scientific, medical, law, engineering to educate and bring about awareness to the domestic buyer fraternity, both in India and abroad.

- **Research and development:** Research and studies are undertaken by ICPB, on areas such as economic impact of holding international conferences in the cities, to evolve a system of collection and compilation of statistics on MICE in India, to study for creation of comprehensive database for making India a MICE destination, and the similar.
- **Training and development activities:** To enhance professional capabilities and building confidence in organizers in organizing conferences more effectively, training and development activities are undertaken. Members can gain knowledge and expertise so that they could share, educate and execute successfully.

8.18 RAJASTHAN TOURISM DEVELOPMENT CORPORATION (RTDC)

Rajasthan is one of the leading tourist destinations in India. The state is featured with plethora of resources, both natural as well as manmade. The culture and heritage related attractions form the core of tourism here. Tourism development and management in the state depends much on Rajasthan Tourism Development Corporation, a public sector agency. It functions as a company, fully owned by the government, registered under the Companies Act, 1956 with its headquarters at Jaipur. RTDC acts as a catalyst to establish, develop and execute projects and schemes that accelerate tourism in the state. Moreover, RTDC acts as a major service provider by owning and operating tourism companies. Unlike other state tourism development corporations in the country, RTDC is well known as a service provider by running quality accommodation units, professional package tours and many other tourism businesses. For instance it manages a number of restaurants, cafeterias, hotels, motels, bars, boating and transport. To enhance the experience of tourists, it also organizes package tours, fairs, festivals, and entertainment, shopping and transport services. Marketing and promotion is another crucial of RTDC. Through its well established marketing network in India and abroad, it plays a vital role in promoting tourism markets at domestic and international level.

Provision of travel arrangements is another major task undertaken by RTDC. It offers package tours, arranges daily trips using buses, cars, etc. Moreover, the luxury tourist trains run by RTDC, in collaboration with Indian Railways is world class and constitute some of the unique tourist attractions of the country. In collaboration with Indian Railways, luxury tourist trains run successfully to give travellers a royal experience while enjoying the nuances of cultural and natural tourist attractions in Rajasthan. There are two luxury tourist trains managed by RTDC, *Palace on Wheels* and *Royal Rajasthan on Wheels*. Moreover, ITDC manages a well-developed network of product distribution including its own booking offices and other agents. RTDC is well known for the accommodation services and grand hospitality. It owns and manages a number of accommodation centres which include hotels, motels, resorts and other lodging facilities.

8.19 DELHI TOURISM AND TRANSPORTATION DEVELOPMENT CORPORATION (DTTDC)

Delhi is the hub of tourism activities in India. Though Kolkata is the cultural capital of the country, Delhi is also equally significant in terms of cultural features, particularly remains of the grand history and culture of India. In addition to the magnificent cultural tourist attractions, Delhi also has a number of natural attractions. It is one among the Golden Triangle where tourists visit maximum in the country. India's *golden triangle* comprises the three most visited cities in the country, Delhi, Agra and Jaipur, which are all connected to each other by good road and rail links. Moreover, it being the capital city of the country, Delhi has numerous political attractions as well. Being the most significant city in the country in terms of tourism, Delhi plays a crucial role in attracting tourists to the country. This hints at the importance of an agency that has to plan, develop, manage and market the destination. The government agency that looks after most of such tasks is *Delhi Tourism and Transportation Development Corporation*, an undertaking of the Government of National Capital Territory of Delhi. It is established with the view to the overall development and promotion of Delhi as a tourist destination for domestic and international tourists visiting India. It was incorporated in 1975 for promoting tourism and in 1989, it was expanded by combining transport infrastructure development as well. The activities of the corporation are mainly categorized under the following sections:

- Tourism division or developing tourist attractions and destinations.
- Travel division which takes care of the travel requirements of tourists who wish to visit.
- Transport department handles transport and travel related services for events and other travel purposes.
- Catering division offers food services.
- Education and training institute that conducts tourism courses and training programmes.
- Engineering and construction wing which looks after the infrastructure development aspects.

8.20 GOA TOURISM DEVELOPMENT CORPORATION (GTDC)

Goa is an amazing tourist destination that attracts tourists from across the world. Pristine beaches being the core of attraction in Goa as an international tourism destination, yet it is also branded as a land of amazing contrasts with highest number of such resources packed in the smallest geographical area of 3700-odd square kilometres. The contrasts vary from 30,000-year-old human settlements to 300-year-old Portuguese houses, from the quietest beaches to the busiest flea markets, from the most honest-to-goodness local cuisine to the most authentic international flavours, from the local Shigmo festival to the Rio-inspired Carnival, from some of the oldest churches to some of the oldest temples in India, and so on. The destination is developed and marketed by the Department of Tourism, Government of Goa. *Goa Tourism Development Corporation* acts as a facilitator in the process of destination management and promotion. It was established way back in 1982 for the sole purpose of running commercial activities, including managing accommodation units, arranging sightseeing tours and cruises for the benefit of tourists who like to visit Goa. The corporation was established as a public limited company. It has been making efforts to ensure that every visitor to Goa has access to accommodation at prime locations at reasonable prices. In addition, it facilitates tourists in exploring Goa through our well designed tours. It also organizes cruise trips. Major functions of GTDC are:

- Hospitality activities: manage accommodation units.
- Organize sightseeing trips.
- Provide authentic and quality experience to the tourists.
- Organize package tours.
- Arrange tour guide services.
- Arrange local cruise trips.
- Undertake bookings/reservations of its hotels and other facilities like tours, cruises, transport, etc.

8.21 UTTARAKHAND TOURISM DEVELOPMENT BOARD (UTDB)

Uttarakhand Tourism Development Board, one of the youngest of that kind in the country, has been functioning well in order to promote tourism potential of the state domestically and internationally. Uttarakhand is the home of Himalayas and is a beautiful region that allures everyone from everywhere. It is rich with natural resources. An important centre of Hindu religion and culture, Uttarakhand is called the *Land of the Gods* (*Dev Bhoomi*) because it is home to countless holy spots and shrines. Ganga and Yamuna, the two most revered rivers of India, originate from the Himalayan glaciers in Uttarakhand. Vast majority of the state is mountanous and seventy per cent of the area is under forest-cover with some of the best national parks and bird sanctuaries which number to twelve with an area of 13.8 per cent of the total area of the state. There are a number of world heritage sites including the Valley of the Flowers, the Nanda Devi Biosphere and the Corbett National Park. Moreover, the place is suitable for adventure sports as well, like skiing and water sports. It offers a multitude of trekking possibilities—from mountaineering to trekking on high altitudes or hiking on unusual routes. It has been world famous as a seat of Yoga and one of its ancient cities on the banks of river Ganges, *Rishikesh* is popularly known as the *'Yoga Capital of the World'*, jostling with backpackers and pilgrims seeking spiritual enlightenment. White-water rafting is also quite popular.

The government, soon after the formation of the state, decided to develop and promote tourism and set up UTDB for that purpose exclusively. Currently, it is the highest body to advise government on all matters relating to tourism in the state. The statutory board is chaired by the Tourism Minister, Govt. of Uttarakhand and Chief Secretary of Uttarakhand as its vice chairman.

Apart from the statutory and political roles, the Board also encourages commercial activities in coordination with Kumaon Mandal Vikas Nigam (KMVN) and Garhwal Mandal Vikas Nigam (GMVN). The principal activities include offering hospitality services and tour packages. GMVN, a enterprise of Government of Uttaranchal was formed on 31st March 1976. Presently, with a share of over Rs. 10 crore and a dedicated workforce of over 1200 employees, it has more than 75 guest houses and tourist bungalows all over Garhwal. KMVN is another one of the same kind for Kumaon region. As part of the hospitality services, in order to ensure comfortable stay, it conducts and promotes various activities. It offers a wide range of services and facilities. KMVN manages a number of rest houses and other budget class accommodation units across the state. GMVN organizes a number of package tours along with managing quality accommodation establishments. Its pilgrimage tourism packages include Char Dham Package, Do Dham Package and Ek Dham Package.

8.22 KERALA TOURISM DEVELOPMENT CORPORATION (KTDC)

Kerala is one of the most fascinating tourist destinations in the country with lush greenery and natural beauty. The varied and unique geographical features of the state has already gained international attention and its tourism sector has been growing at a tremendous pace over the last three decades. Tourism in the state is regulated, marketed and promoted by the state department of tourism with a separate directorate called *directorate of tourism*. The present Department of Tourism (DOT) had its beginning in the State Guest Department of the erstwhile Travancore state and hospitality organization of the Cochin state, before independence. There are some other key establishments functioning under the department which facilitate the growth and development of tourism in the state such as:

- Kerala Tourism Development Corporation (KTDC)
- Tourists Resorts (Kerala) Ltd. (TRKL)
- Bekal Resort Tourism Corporation
- The District Tourism Promotion Council

- Kerala Institute of Travel and Tourism Studies (KITTS)
- Kerala Institute of Hospitality Management Studies (KIHMS)

KTDC is a public sector tourism corporation with headquarters at Thiruvananthapuram. It has been engaged with a number of activities and the emphasis of those is mainly on hospitality management and tour operation. Accommodation units of different levels are owned and managed by the corporation. The properties range from premium to budget and are built and managed in such a way so as to offer unique holiday experience with unique ambience due to the locational advantages. The following are the major functions of KTDC:

- Identify new tourist destinations and develop tourism infrastructure.
- Build and manage different types of accommodation units.
- Manage wayside tourist facilities.
- Provide food and beverage services to the travellers.
- Arrange venues for holding events at various levels.
- Conduct package tours and excursions.

Providing banquets and venues for events is another major task being undertaken by the corporation. In addition to meeting and conference halls provided inside the hotels and resorts, KTDC also makes available venues for holding international conventions and conferences.

KTDC also offers well-designed inbound package tours, formulated as budget holiday packages under the brand *Discover Kerala*, a novel initiative to encourage the new generation and for families to explore the beauty and culture of the state.

8.23 HIMACHAL PRADESH TOURISM DEVELOPMENT CORPORATION (HPTDC)

Himachal Pradesh is one of the most popular tourist destinations in the country. In the early years, it was restricted only to *pilgrim tourism*. Tourism scope expanded once the British established a chain of hill stations in the state. It got intensified when the then rulers declared Shimla *The Summer Capital of India*, in 1864. The trend continued and since independence, increased investment in the infrastructure sector led to the opening up of tourism industry in the state. The growth culminated in the 1980s and 1990s as the state became very popular among both domestic and international travellers.

The tourism potential of the state is developed and promoted by the Department of Tourism and Civil Aviation and while traditionally Himachal was known as a summer destination, it has taken special efforts to break the seasonality factor and has developed diversified tourism products to attract tourists in other seasons too. The efforts paid off and it has now become *A Destination for All Seasons and All Reasons*. Himachal Pradesh

Tourism Corporation was been established with the intention to stimulate influx of tourists into the state and to undertake commercial activities with the scope of promoting sustainable tourism. As part of it, HPTDC is involved in a variety of activities which include hospitality services, organizing package tours and reservation and booking facilities. In order to smoothen the tourism activities in the state, the corporation has divided the state into four circuits, which pass through different terrains that can give the tourists the feel as if they are trekking through ages at different times. The following are some of the major activities HPTDC:

- Undertake package tours and sightseeing trips.
- Provision of hospitality services.
- Ensure meeting and conference facilities to promote business tourism.
- Promote adventure tourism.
- Arrange transport services.
- Provision of accurate and authentic information on tourism in the state.
- Arrange reservation and booking facilities in tourism services both online and offline.
- Miscellaneous services.

The services offered are:

- Circuit tour arrangements.
- Hospitality services.
- Business tourism services.
- Adventure tourism promotion.
- Transport services.
- Online reservation services.
- Special offers.

8.24 CONCLUSION

Indian tourism is blessed to have a number of national, regional and state level tourism organizations that facilititate the growth of tourism in the country. These organizations facilitate sharing of relevant knowledge, technology transfers, cooperation, developing public-private partnership in tourism and the like. Each and every organization is playing significant role in sustainable and ethical tourism development. State tourism organizations are also playing vital role in tourism in their respective states.

Key Terms

National organisations	ADTOI
State organisations	ATTOI
Professional bodies	ATOAI
General organisations	IMTA
Specific organisations	FICCI
ITDC	CII
DGCA	ICPB
AAI	RTDC
ASI	DTTDC
IRCTC	GTDC
TFCI	UTDB
TAAI	KTDC
IATO	HPTDC
TAFI	

Review Questions

Short Answer Type Questions

1. Discuss the classification of national organizations in tourism.
2. Briefly narrate the history of ITDC.
3. Discuss the functioning of ITDC.
4. What are the areas of activity of ITDC?
5. Discuss how ITDC is involved in the development and promotion of tourism in India.
6. Give a brief account on DGCA.
7. What are the objectives and activities of AAI?
8. Discuss the role and relevance of AAI in aviation.
9. What are AAI services?
10. Write a short note on ASI.
11. What are the objectives and activities of TFCI?
12. Discuss the role and relevance of TAAI and IATO.
13. Give brief accounts on CII and FICCI.
14. Expand ICPB. List its activities.
15. Write short notes on any three state tourism organisations.

Essay Type Questions

1. Discuss the role and relevance of organizations in tourism in India.
2. Describe the history of organizations in aviation in India. Explain the role played by major organizations in the growth of air transportation in the country.

9 TOURISM PLANNING

Learning Outcomes

After studying this chapter, you will be able to:

- understand the concept of planning in general;
- comprehend the importance of planning in tourism;
- identify tourism planning at different levels;
- recognize different tourism planning approaches;
- explain tourism planning process; and
- understand the nuances tourism policy.

9.1 INTRODUCTION

Planning is fundamental in all organized functions. It is performed in all kinds of organizations by all managers at all levels of hierarchy, and hence, it is featured with universality. *Planning* is a process that we, as individuals, carry out everyday and is also an important business function. It is basically considered conscious determination of a future course of action to achieve the desired result (Aggarwal, 1993). Being a process starting with setting of objectives, planning determines the means by which those objectives can be achieved. The plan thus formed is considered a future picture and offers a framework for future activities. As far as a business organization is concerned, achievement of objectives depends on the efficiency in utilizing various resources, like human, financial and material. It is in this context, the applicability of planning becomes relevant in all managerial contexts. Proper and effective planning results in optimization of resource utilization. An efficient plan would give answers to the most vital questions concerning an organization—what to do, when to do it, where to do, how to do, who will do the various activities, and how the results are to be evaluated. Moreover, it implies making choices, committing resources and a time horizon, along with selecting missions, objectives and actions to achieve them. Here, decision making is relevant, which pertains to choosing the future course of action among the alternatives.

Plans are of different types. On the basis of duration of future courses of action, plans are classified into two, as *long term* and *short term*. Departmental plans are another type, which are set by various departments on the basis of their functions. Strategic and operational plans constitute another classification, based on the nature of plans. Strategic plans are more future oriented whereas operational plans are activity oriented. Large organizations may have some other categories of plans. Planning is not possible without required information and hence accuracy, relevance and quality of information available to the planners matters in making efficient plans. Planning for tourism development need not be radically or fundamentally different from planning in any other business context. Some variations may occur, however, in the basic planning model, and it is the nature of these variations which would distinguish tourism planning from other forms of planning. Tourism destination planning also differs from other forms of business planning, wherein usually a large number of interest groups are involved, and balancing such a diverse range of interests requires specific planning (as well as interpersonal) skills.

9.2 PLANNING IN TOURISM

As tourism is a major economic activity with wide social, cultural and environmental ramifications, careful planning is essential. Tourism development planning is done at different levels, particularly international, national and regional/local levels. *Sustainable tourism development* is a strategy proposed world over to minimize the impacts and to develop tourism. Sustainability principles are usually applied at all levels of planning. (The concept and nature of sustainable tourism is discussed later in this book.) The increasing recognition by government and industry of the nexus between tourism and sustainability demands for a more socially responsive and environmentally sensitive tourism sector. The design, planning and management of tourism environments require serious approach and a sustainable tourism industry necessitates a commitment towards sustainable development principles by representatives of all the stakeholders involved in the planning process. Major organizations involved in tourism like World Tourism Organization, European Union, etc., undertake planning in a limited manner and these form the base for national agencies while they develop plans for tourism development in their respective countries. Tourism planning tends to be an amalgam of economic, social, cultural, political, and environmental considerations that reflect the diversity of factors that influence tourism development (Hall and Page, 2006). Tourism planning encompasses many disciplines and fields, including politics, policy studies, public administration, organizational studies, sociology, economics, geography, history, law and psychology. Tourism planning and policy, like town planning, can be likened to a

Table 9.1: Stages in the evolution of tourism development planning

1. Unplanned tourism development era:
At this stage tourism planning is 'uncommon, unpopular and an unwanted idea', and therefore tourism emerges as an unplanned activity.
2. Beginning of partly supply-oriented tourism planning stage:
The construction of basic infrastructure, such as hotels, restaurants, transportation, etc. will take place in this stage.
3. Entirely supply-oriented tourism planning stage:
Planning is directed towards the creation of facilities that satisfy increased tourism demand, though it ignores most resulting problems.
4. Market or demand-oriented tourism development planning stage:
At this stage, focus of tourism planning is mainly on greater number of tourists and how to satisfy them.
5. Contemporary planning approach stage:
Once there is an increase in the number of tourist arrivals, along with the 'careless and myopic tourism development planning approaches', environmental, socio-cultural and economic problems arise, and that attracts the attention of developers and planners.

Source: Tosun & Jenkins, 1998.

magpie profession, picking relevance from a variety of disciplines. Planning for tourism occurs in a number of:

- forms like development, infrastructure, land and resource use, promotion and marketing, etc.;
- structures, like different government, quasi-government, NGOs;
- scales of governance: international, transnational, national, regional, local, and site;
- spatial scales: international, supranational, national, regional, local, and site; and
- temporal (time scale, like for measuring change, development, implementation, evaluation and satisfactory fulfilment of planning objectives) (Hall, 2008).

9.3 SIGNIFICANCE OF PLANNING IN TOURISM

Contemporary tourism planning is very much oriented towards the notion of sustainable tourism development. The inevitability of integrated tourism planning arises out of the need to balance the interests of different interest groups within a nation, as well as the needs of the nation as a whole. According to Gunn (1994), the focus of planning is mainly to generate income and employment, and ensure resource conservation and traveller satisfaction. Specifically, through planning under- or low-developed destinations can receive guidelines for further tourism development. The development of a structured tourism plan recognises the long-term benefits (economic, social and cultural) to be gained from tourism, while at the same time addressing the potential that tourism development may degrade both human and natural resources. According to UNWTO, for already developed countries, planning can be used as a means *"to revitalize the tourism sector and maintain its future viability"* (WTO, 1994). Ideal planning should be integrative, which seeks to combine environmental, social and economic planning goals along with satisfying a range of stakeholders' aspirations (Cooper and Hall, 2008). Properly planned and managed tourism development can provide host communities with benefits that far outweigh any associated disadvantages. According to Gunn (1979), destination planning is important due to the following reasons:

- Planning can avert negative impacts; though for planning to be effective, all 'actors' must be involved, not just professional planners.
- Tourism is more symbiotic with conservation and recreation, not conflicting with irreconcilably incompatible objectives or effects.
- Planning should by pluralistic, involving social, economic and physical dimensions.
- Planning is political and as such, there is a vital need to take into account social objectives and balance these with other aspirations.
- It must have a regional planning perspective as many problems arise at the interface with areas; thus a broader planning horizon is essential.

According to Inskeep (1991), following are the reasons for tourism planning:

- Modern tourism is still a relatively new type of activity in many areas, and some governments and private sectors have little or no experience in how to properly develop it. A tourism plan and development programme can provide guidelines for developing this sector.
- Tourism is a complicated, multi-sectoral, and fragmented activity, involving other sectors such as agriculture, fisheries and manufacturing, historic, park and recreational features, various facilities and services, transportation and other infrastructure. Planning ensures that all these elements are developed in an integrated manner.
- Much of tourism is essentially selling a product of an experience comprised of visitor use of certain facilities and services.
- Tourism brings various direct and indirect economic benefits, and generates various sociocultural benefits.
- Planning is necessary to determine the optimal type and level of tourism that will not have negative impacts.
- Planning can be used to revitalise the existing outdated or badly developed tourism areas.

- Planning enables education and training.
- Planning provides a rational basis for development, staging, and project programming, which are important for both public and private sectors utilised in their investment planning.

Other important factors include:

- Proper planning ensures the achievement of cultural and environmental conservation and preservation objectives.
- Quality of visitor experience can be ensured through proper planning.
- Tourism demand and supply can be managed without worries and consequences.
- Optimization and equitable distribution of economic, social, cultural and environmental benefits.
- Community integration: an important goal of tourism planning is to integrate all tourism development into the social and economic life of a community.
- Tourism is a multi-sectoral social activity and an intricate process, and hence planning is inevitable in ensuring due consideration of every viewpoint and in having smooth coordination among all elements.

Tourism planning encounters many limitations and resistances. In fact in some localities and societies, tourism development can face more constraints. It can have social, cultural and political dimensions. In some other situations, there can be more environmental concerns. At the national level, planning may not face many obstacles as it is highlighted economic imminency. But when it comes to the destination or local level, possibilities of issues can be more. Some of the limitations pointed out by Blank (1989) are:

- Lack of comparative advantage (location, quality of potential).
- Carrying capacity limitations.
- Myopic view of tourism.
- Fear of tourism-erosive characteristics.
- Lack of community's acceptance to change or preference for status quo.
- Power structure's preference for other development.
- Environmentalist resistance to any development.
- Narrow and inflexible policies on public lands.

Lack of planning can result in chaos in tourism development and some of the following consequences are common:

- Lack of direction and guidance for development.
- Unsustainable use of resources.
- Wastage of vital natural resources.

Table 9.2: Benefits of national and regional tourism planning: UNWTO

• Establishing the overall tourism development objectives and policies, namely, what is tourism aiming to accomplish and how these aims can be achieved.
• Developing tourism so that its natural and cultural resources are indefinitely maintained and conserved for future, as well as present use.
• Integrating tourism into the overall development policies and patterns of the country or region, and establishing those linkages between tourism and other economic sectors.
• Providing a rational basis for decision making by both public and private sectors on tourism development.
• Enabling coordinated development of all the elements of tourism sector. This includes interrelating tourist attractions, activities, facilities and services and the various and increasingly fragmented tourist markets.
• Optimizing and balancing the economic, environmental and social benefits of tourism, with equitable distribution of these benefits to the society, while minimizing the possible problems of tourism.
• Providing a physical structure which guides the location, types and extent of tourism development of attractions, facilities, services and infrastructure.
• Establishing the guidelines and standards for preparing detailed plans of specific tourism development areas that are consistent with, and reinforce, one another, and for the appropriate design of tourist facilities.
• Laying the foundation for effective implementation of the tourism development policy, and planning and continuous management of the tourism sector by providing the necessary organisational and other institutional frameworks.
• Providing the framework for effective coordination of public and private sector efforts and investment in developing tourism.
• Offering a baseline for continuous monitoring of the progress of tourism development and keeping it on track.

Source: WTO, 1994.

- Lack of coordination among diverse sectors.
- Possibility of resistance and conflicts.
- Generation of impacts of all kinds.
- Poor involvement of local community.

9.4 PLANNING LEVELS IN TOURISM

Planning and development for tourism can be considered at both geographical level as well as business level. Also tourism planning, pertaining to destinations, can be classified at international, national, regional and sub-regional levels.

9.4.1 Geographical Level Planning (Destination Planning)

Tourism has a spatial aspect, which is fundamental in the tourism system. Every place on the earth has its own peculiar characteristics, both as result of natural physical forces and acts of man.

As we discussed in the concept of tourism system, there are three geographical areas: tourism generating region, transit route region and tourist destination region. The third region, the destination region, shows the necessity for being planned for developing and managing tourism since the real tourist phenomenon takes place in that region through the tourist's visit. The size of this region varies: it can be a small area with tourist visits, or a state, country and even a continent. Hence, the concept of planning can vary from the macro (region, nation, continent, etc.) to the micro (destinations and sites) levels. Gunn (1979) was one of the first experts to define tourism planning as a tool for destination area development, and to view it as a means for assessing the needs of a tourist receiving destination. The horizons of tourism planning from the destination point of view have been expanded and it encompasses a range of complicated aspects as well. This kind of planning is often referred to as *destination planning*. The following, according to the UNESCAP, are different planning levels at geographic/territorial bases:

- The *individual site*: Examples include a beach, a heritage site, a park or a theme park.
- The *destination*: In some cases, the site and the destination may be the same, but usually it refers to the larger geographical setting where the site is situated.
- A *region within a country*: This can be a geographic or political boundary or it can be based on tourism attraction factors.
- The *nation*: Especially true in the case of smaller island countries.
- *Several countries*: A good example can be a theme-related destination involving several countries. (UNESCAP, 1996)

Geographical level tourism planning can also be classified from different aspects of space. They are:

- International level planning
- National level planning
- Regional planning
- Sub-regional planning
- Local/site level planning
- **International level tourism planning:** This happens at a wider scale spanning over a number of countries, with a broader outlook. Specificity may be ignored, yet the commonness of a region at the international level or at a much wider level can be considered. According to Mill (1990), tourism planning is important to be begun from an international level as it helps to promote the tourism industry as well as highlight any social, economic and environmental issues that may prove to be hazardous. The focus of such planning can be on the preservation and

conservation of nature and the natural recourses in order to ensure sustainability. Moreover, the cultural features and social aspects too have a considerable significance in the international tourism plans. The other essential aspects include the provision of transportation services and ensuring accessibility as much as possible. International understanding and cooperation among the countries involved on various aspects of tourism can also be a matter of concern. The pattern of tourist movement and the flow of tourists among countries and destinations is also considered. Smoothening of tourist flow and elimination of travel barriers is an important aspect here. Complementary development of major attractions, features and facilities in nearby countries too have adequate significance in the international tourism plans. Another important aspect of concern is *marketing and promotion*. Mutual cooperation in marketing is important. Multi-country marketing strategies and promotion programmes are formulated and specified in such type of plans. In fact, a number of organizations are responsible for making such type of plans. Some of them include United Nations World Tourism Organization (UNWTO), World Travel and Tourism Council (WTTC), Pacific Asia Travel Association (PATA), etc.

- **National level planning:** Countries with tourism activities usually make tourism plans at the national level. This forms the base for rest of the plans of the country. These plans are called *national tourism plans* and that can be the basis for the 'national action plan'. National tourism policy can establish the overall tourism development objectives and policies for the country in a stipulated period of time. According to Baud-Bovy (1982), tourism development plan has to be integrated into the nation's socioeconomic and political policies, natural and manmade environment, sociocultural traditions, many related sectors of the economy and its financial schemes, and into the international tourism market. Moreover, resources allocation, their sustainable use for tourism and maintenance from a sustainable development perspective can be ensured with the help of national plan. Tourism is always part of the overall developmental objectives of a country and preparing a national plan can help in integrating tourism into the overall development policies and patterns of the country, with proper link with economic sectors. This national plan certainly specifies the direction in which the host population wishes to see tourism develop, as well as the specific objectives of that development, along with the provision of a rational basis for decision making by both the public and private sectors involved in tourism development in the country Tourism is a highly fragmented industry that needs closer and intimate interaction. A national plan can facilitate the coordinated development of all the elements of the tourism sector. Certainly a national plan will focus on the economic aspects, particularly in increasing revenue, employment opportunities and to have increased role in 'balance of payments', along with other social and cultural considerations have to be taken care of.

Proper and scientific plan can ensure balanced and equitable development perspectives with equitable distribution of the socioeconomic benefits to the society, while minimizing possible problems of tourism. The plan will contain the overall tourism policy and physical structure and pave the way for establishing the guidelines and standards for preparing detailed plans of specific tourism development areas. Moreover, this plan can be the baseline for the continuous monitoring of the progress of tourism development and keeping it on track. Other elements of the plan can be accommodation and other facilities and services required, major tourist routes and circuits and inter-regional connections; the tourism organizational structures, legislation and investment policies; overall environmental impact assessment reports and essential social, cultural and environmental considerations to be taken care of; and the measures and techniques of implementation of the plans, and staging of development and short-term development strategies and project planning. Marketing and promotion is always an essential part of national tourism plans.

At the national level, tourism plans encapsulate plans for a country as a whole with broader, yet specific objectives. Based on them, plans are developed at the regional levels as well as at local levels. These plans should be focused and specific. Planning at all the levels requires large amount of data and information. A list of information requirements is given in Table 9.3. Since tourism is a multidisciplinary subject, planning should involve experts from all interdisciplinary areas like management, geography, environment, sociology, economics, etc. Environmental impact assessment is also incorporated with planning of a tourism destination.

- **Regional level:** Tourism planning can be done at the regional level also. Similar to national level, this should also cover accessibility aspects, resources and attractions, location considerations, infrastructure and superstructure assessment, capacity building requirements, marketing elements, legislation, regulations, and investment policies; and implementation techniques including staging of development, and regional zoning regulation. Unlike national planning, this will be more specific, yet, will be based on the national level objectives as well along with the specific consideration of regional environments.
- **Sub-regional level:** Planning can be done at sub-regional level also. In the context of India, state level tourism planning has more relevance. Even lower level plans can be seen for the development of destinations. Each destination needs specific and scientifically constructed plans for the development of tourism over there.

9.4.2 Business Level Planning

In contrast to the above, business level planning is constrained to the projects associated with businesses. For instance it can be development of individual tourism projects, such as the construction of a hotel or theme park. This also needs to have utmost planning

Table. 9.3: Public and private tourism planning and development decisions: information required

• Tourism projects inventory	• Quality of tourism/recreation experience
• Municipal financial impacts	• Baseline information summary
• Transportation analysis	• Municipal operative workshops
• Service and utility needs	• Annexation proposals
• Private sector EIAs and NRCB	• Employee housing issues
• Tourism market demand study	• Rock industry study
• Visual impact assessment	• Recreation trails study
• Assessment of natural areas	• Updates of general municipal plans
• Needs of expanded public services	• Utilization study
• Water quality evaluation	• Sustainable wildlife study
• Analysis of environmental issues	
• Environmentally significant areas	

Source: Wight (1992).

efforts to minimize the contribution of impacts and to function effectively, without much wastage of resources and capabilities.

9.5 APPROACHES TO TOURISM PLANNING

Different approaches towards tourism planning can be seen in the literature. Boosterism, an economic and industry-oriented approach, a physical/spatial approach, a community oriented approach, and sustainable tourism approach are the common planning approaches seen at destination level (Getz, 1987). A brief description of some of the prominent approaches is given below.

- **Boosterism:** This is a planning approach evolved from the perspective of tourism development that tourism is inherently 'good' and will provide benefit to the destination immensely. It further attempts to state that benefits are more significant, and costs and consequences are insignificant when such benefits are generated. Basically, *boosterism* views tourism as beneficial for a destination and its inhabitants; environmental objects are promoted as assets in order to stimulate market interest and increase economic benefits, and barriers to development are reduced (Hall, 1991). According to C.M. Hall (2008), boosterism is a "simplistic attitude that tourism development is inherently good and of automatic benefits to the host. Under this approach little consideration is given to the potential negative impacts of tourism, and instead cultural and natural resources are regarded as objects to be exploited for the sake of tourism development". Tourism results in a wide variety of benefits ranging from income and employment generation to regional development and uplifting of well-being of the host population. The focus of tourism planning, as per this concept is the highlighting of socioeconomic benefits. Here, the missing links are the aspects of sustainability, equitable distribution of economic benefits, local community involvement and the like. Getz (1987) pointed out that this approach does not provide a sustainable solution to development and is practised only by "politicians who philosophically or pragmatically believe that economic growth is to be always promoted, and by others who will gain financially by tourism". This concept was prevalent for a long period after the Second World War, but the emergence of irrevocable impacts of haphazard development led to different thoughts on tourism planning.

- **Physical/spatial approach:** In this approach, *land use* is the base of tourism development, by managing spatial strategies. The land and the physical space are considered from an ecological point of view. Hence, development needs to based on spatial patterns, capacities or thresholds in such a way that development may not result in consequences on the physical environment. Such kind of planning may involve pre-feasibility and feasibility studies, resource appraisal and allocation evaluation of environmental and socio-cultural influences, and zone planning. Other relevant measures like carrying capacities of different kinds are also essential in this type of planning approach. "Planning with a spatial, or geographical component in which the general objective is to provide a spatial structure of activities (or land use) in someway is better than the pattern existing without planning" (Hall, 1992). The tools used in planning may include zoning regulations, architectural landscaping and engineering design standards as well. Ultimately, this planning also aims at minimizing the impacts.
- **Community:** As per the latest trends, *community involvement* in tourism is inevitable in the process of tourism development. In fact, all the new forms of tourism like sustainable tourism, ecotourism, responsible tourism, geo tourism, etc. demand greater degree of local community participation. Moreover, those stipulate equitable distribution of economic benefits among all sections of the society and stakeholders, in general. Planning and development approach focusing on involvement is the base of community led tourism planning at various levels nationally and even internationally. Local community participation can begin from the stage of idea generation and can go along with the management of tourist destinations. The opinion of local people needs to be seriously taken care of while developing tourism in a positive way. This can contribute to generate a responsible local community in a destination, which can help in minimizing the impacts of tourism to a large extent. In effect, community involved tourism can ensure increased employment opportunities available to the locals as more community is involved in the process, while it also contributes positively to the improvement in household income and general quality of life, though the extent of contribution varies from one aspect to another. Moreover, conservation and preservation of natural and cultural heritage and its various forms can be more effective with the participation of local community.

Table 9.4: Elements of planning guidance

Attraction development	Community infrastructures
Hospitality services	Financing of development
Activities	Resource quality and management
Promotion/advertising	Agency responsibility and coordination
Transportation systems	Special market thrusts
Community ambience and aesthetics	Seasonality
Local information, direction, and interpretive system	Residents' living quality

Source: Adapted from Blank, 1989.

- **Sustainable approach:** Increased tensions due to the negative impacts of tourism and the world level concerns about tourism problems led to many discussions and summits and they realized the importance of implementing *sustainable development principles* in the tourism sector. Apart from that, the UN agencies concerned with development the and sustainability wanted the tourism sector also to adopt the sustainability principles. That formed the base for sustainable planning and development the approach world over. It is an integrated and comprehensive approach towards planning and development of tourism in destinations so that the impacts can be minimized while increasing benefits equitably. Every form of sustainable aspect such as social, cultural, economic and environmental is considered in the form of planning and hence the impacts can be ameliorated significantly.
- **Strategic tourism planning:** It is also considered a significant component of sustainable planning approach. *Strategic planning* is "long-term, visionary, goal-oriented, action-oriented, dynamic, flexible and adaptable, and ensures that formulation and implementation of the strategic plan are not separate, but closely linked through constant monitoring, environmental scanning, evaluation and adjustment; and is not a linear process." (UNEP/PAP/RAC, 2009). It is "proactive, responsive to community needs, perceiving planning and implementation as part of a single process, and ongoing (Hall, 2008). Here, the strategy is all about the measures to ensure conservation of tourism resources' values; enhancing experiences of tourists who interact with those resources; and maximizing the economic, social and environmental returns to the stakeholders in the host community (Hall and McArthur, 1998).

Other approaches to tourism planning include:

- **Interactive planning:** It proposes to have planning with maximum interaction with the local community as they have more experience, opinions and constructive recommendations about tourism in their vicinity, and it aims at top-down, together with bottom-up input, for the better implementation of plans (Gunn, 1994). Increased interactive involvement with local community is the essence of this type of planning.

- **Integrated planning:** It denotes a comprehensive and integrated approach which recognizes that all development sectors and supporting facilities and services are interrelated with each other and with the natural environment and society of the area (UNEP/PAP/RAC, 2009). This is a more comprehensive planning approach than most of the others.
- **Collaborative tourism planning:** This is similar to the above, and proposes to have greater collaboration with all stakeholders, particularly the local community in order to bring in sustainability and maximum benefits for the people.
- **Cooperative and participatory planning:** Timothy (1998) suggests that for this type of planning, better decisions can be reached by means of a participative process so that the superior benefits for long-term survival of tourism is increasingly possible.
- **Market oriented planning:** This is planning and development with a focus of creating facilities, services and attraction to satisfy the needs and wants of tourists.
- **Supply-led planning:** This approach views that only those types of attractions, facilities, and services that the destination believes can best be integrated with minimum impacts into the local development patterns and society are provided, and marketing is done to attract only those tourists who find this product of interest to them (Inskeep, 1991).
- **Economic tradition/tourism as an industry:** This approach considers tourism as a measure of economic growth, and restructuring, employment generation and regional development by providing financial incentives, research, marketing and promotional support (Hall, 2008).
- **Systems Approach:** This considers tourism as a system. It considers the inputs and outputs of the system while treating it as a mixture of demand and supply elements. Laws (1997) identifies inputs, like the supply of facilities and demand associated with tourism; and outputs like tourist satisfaction, and various related environments and external factors conditioning the system.

9.6 TOURISM PLANNING PROCESS

Tourism planning is site specific, with many considerations pertaining to an area. Many aspects come into play while planning for developing tourism in a region, and those may not be same for other regions. Planning can vary from place to place as well. Yet, some commonness can be found out and a general process can be formulated. In fact, there are a number of planning process models suggested in tourism literature. Planning process suggested by Anderson (1995) consists of the following stages:

- Identify issues and options.
- State goals, objectives and priorities.
- Collect and interpret data.
- Prepare plans.
- Draft programmes for implementing the plans.
- Evaluate the potential impacts of plans and implementing programmes.
- Review and adopt plans.
- Review and adopt plan implementing programmes.
- Administer implementing programmes, and monitor their impacts.

Cooper et al., have propounded a nine stage process. It gives importance to research as well. Policy making and plan creation are based on the findings of the analysis of the data collected. The stages in planning process are:

- Recognition of the need for tourism planning/strategy.
- Setting the objectives/goals for a specific planning strategy.
- Survey of existing data.
- Implementation of new surveys.
- Analysis of secondary and primary data.
- Initial policy and plan creation.
- Recommendation of the plan.
- Implementation of the plan.
- Monitoring, evaluation and reformulation (Cooper et al., 2000).

After going through the above and some other models, the following stages are suggested for tourism planning in general.

- Need recognition
- Establishment of objectives
- Research
- Situational analysis and inventory
- Market analysis
- Drafting policy and plan formulation
- Plan finalization and recommendations
- Implementation of the plan
- Evaluation and monitoring

Table 9.5: Planning process models

Model by Weaver and Koth et al.	Model by Goeldner and Ritchie
Planning Process Stages by Weaver (1991) • Describe the social, political, physical, and economic development. • Forecast or project trends for future development. • Set goals and objectives. • Study alternative plans of action to reach goals and objectives. • Select preferred alternative(s) to serve as a guide for recommending action strategies. • Develop an implementation strategy. • Implement the plan. • Evaluate the plan. Planning process stages by Koth et al. (1991) • Getting organized. • Identifying community values. • Attraction inventory. • Attraction assessment. • Attraction packaging. • Organizational funding strategies. • Business inventory. • Marketing situational analysis. • Identifying a community tourism product. • Identifying target markets. • Setting market objectives. • Selecting promotional strategies. • (Optional) Tourism business retention and expansion. • (Optional) Community appearance. • Evaluation	*Stage 1: Define the system* Specify the scale, size, market, character and purpose. Formulate objectives. In doing so, ensure that the definitions for policy formulation and destination planning are consistent. *Stage 2: Gather necessary data* Fact finding or research provides basic data that is essential to developing plans. Again, much of the data used for policy formulation may be helpful for planning process. However, additional and detailed data will be required for the planning process. *Stage 3: Analyze and interpret data* Interpret the fragmented information to get meaning to the gathered information. In doing so, it is useful to relate data to the specific facilities, events, activities and programmes that impact the factors that determine/ influence destination success. *Stage 4: Create preliminary plan* Alternatives are considered and alternate physical solutions are drawn up and tested. The plan should clearly state the detailed nature of the facilities, events, activities and programmes that will deliver the unique, high quality destination experience that will enhance the competitiveness of the destination with strategic market segments. *Stage 5: Approve the plan* The parties involved have to look at plans, drawings, cost estimates, etc. It is critical to ensure that where approval is required, no relevant stakeholders are overlooked. *Stage 6: Create the final plan* This phase involves a definition of land use, plans for infrastructure, architectural standards, market analysis, etc. At this stage, the level of details becomes increasingly rigorous and is directly related to the specific geography, legislation, financing and timing of the "real world". *Stage 7: Implement the plan* Implementation means carrying out the plan to create operational tourism development. This stage allocates responsibility for development actions to specific individuals and organizations, defines the exact timing of these actions and establishes contingencies for unexpected occurrences. Also, this stage monitors, follows up and evaluates (Goeldner & Ritchie, 2006).

9.6.1 Need Recognition

Prior to the commencement of planning, the need for developing tourism in a place has to be clear. There can be many areas with tourism potential, yet developing tourism should be based on need identification with due regard given to social, economical, and environmental aspects. Once tourism is developed, the area cannot be brought back to previous situations, and it is more crucial in the case of fragile geographical areas. This recognition should have consensus from all the stakeholders, particularly from the local community since they are the people who have to suffer the cost as well as enjoy the benefits. A tourism *development need* identified by the authorities should follow the recognition and consensus of the same by other stakeholders as well. Every stakeholder should feel the need of developing tourism, along with a consensus that it is a desirable development option over there.

9.6.2 Specify the Objectives

Planning may not be possible without specifying objectives. In fact, even planning is a mechanism proposing the manner in which the pre-set objectives can be achieved after a stipulated period of time. A tourism development plan should have a clear understanding of the objectives that are to be achieved by the development of tourism. Countries go for tourism development with a clear economic agenda. *Objectives* may involve job creation, economic diversification, foreign currency earnings, redistribution of economic benefits, elimination of poverty, creation of income generating opportunities, inflow of investments, accelerator effect, and the like. The social objectives may include enhancing the well being and lifestyle of the society, regional development, and the like. Culturally, the authorities or planners may aim at conserving and preserving the cultural features and heritage remains. Similar objectives can be set for environmental aspects as well.

Table 9.6 National tourism planning objectives

- *Political,* such as enhancing national prestige and gaining international exposure.
- *Socio-cultural,* the encouragement of activities that have the potential for the advancement of social and cultural values and resources of the area, its traditions and lifestyles.
- *Environmental,* e.g., control of pollution.
- *Economic,* such as increasing employment and real incomes.

Source: Sharpley and Sharpley (1997)

9.6.3 Research

This stage primarily focuses on *data collection* from both the existing sources as well as from the field directly. Once the existing data search or the secondary data search is completed, a new survey can be employed to generate necessary information for planning for the future. Plenty of areas have to be examined as part of it. The existing resources in the area and their tourism potential constitute an important aspect to be enquired into. The fragility and sensitivity of resources along with the possible consequences need to be investigated. Land availability and the possible land use patterns have to be elucidated. Other information such as tourism characteristics, travel patterns, tourism attractions and their status, economic possibilities, socio-cultural characteristics, investment possibilities, public and private sector organizations, infrastructure and superstructure needs, capacity development, environmental indicators, and the similar can also be researched upon. Necessity of rules, regulations and guidelines also need to be looked into.

9.6.4 Situational Analysis and Inventory

In this stage, based on the data and information made available from the research step, *asset evaluation* has to be done by examining the existing and potential stock assets. Undertaking *environmental impact assessment* (EIA) is good to proceed further. It can comprehend the possible impacts of development on various spheres, particularly on nature. The social and cultural consequences along with visual pollution possibilities also need to be assessed. By this stage, the inventory of resources along with the existing flora and fauna need to be finalized. Analysis of transportation needs, service and utility needs, public services needs, scope of quality tourism experience that can be provided, and the like need to be undertaken. A SWOT analysis would be ideal to get a clear picture to proceed further.

9.6.5 Market Analysis

Tourist is the ultimate consumer, and getting an idea about the possible nature of the demand and the market would be ideal prior to making the plan. By this time, it has to be clear which market segments have to be pursued. Their interests and needs will provide ample information about the components of tourism product to be offered over there. Moreover, marketing strategies that can be used to pursue the target market, the prices to be charged, etc., can be made clear to proceed further. An examination of various aspects with regard to the competitors can also be of use for further activities.

9.6.6 Policy Drafting and Plan Formulation

The above steps shall provide the necessary data and information for making the policy and the plan. The objectives have to be initially finalized, after which the policy and plan formulation need to be done with the intention to achieve those set objectives. Alternatives are considered and alternate physical solutions are drawn up and tested. The policy should be able to clearly state the direction of development and the plan has to comprehend the ways to achieve those objectives using the set policy. The plan should define the detailed nature of facilities, events, activities and programmes that will deliver unique and quality destination experience that can enhance competitiveness of the destination with strategic market segments.

9.6.7 Plan Finalization and Recommendations

The draft plan has to be reviewed by representatives of all the stakeholders concerned. Once the suggestions are gathered, analyze them and consider the ones required for modification of the plan. Once the policy is made, the plan can be finalized taking into account all the aspects and views, along with the recommendations. The preferred plan that has been selected, having now been completed in detail, is submitted to the authorities by the planning team.

9.6.8 Implementation of the Plan

At this stage, the plan will be implemented along with necessary recommendations and precautions to be taken. Some bottlenecks may exist once the implementation process begins. If there is lack of understanding and community involvement, there can be resistances against the implementation of tourism development plans and strategies. Some of the common resistances as suggested by Go et al. (1992) are:

- Tourism involves such a diversity of actors and hence, clear mandates for development start lacking.
- Local jurisdictions seek a quick fix and fail to provide financial and human resources to perform the job.
- Lack of local guidance and will.
- Mandates are not clear or in conflict.
- Lack of monitoring system to measure success.

Hence, it is crucial to ensure the need, community involvement, stakeholders participation and to generate consensus along with taking care of social, cultural and environmental factors during the planning stage and prior to the implementation of the plan.

9.6.9 Evaluation and Monitoring

Vigilant monitoring of the plan's implementation is inevitable. At every regular interval of the plan implementation, evaluation of the progress will be done. If any deviation from the set plan path is observed, necessary reformulation of the plan can be done according to the situation.

9.7 TOURISM POLICY

Tourism policy is an essential tool for developing and promoting tourism in a country. According to Goeldner & Ritchie (2006), tourism policy can be defined as "a set of regulations, rules, guidelines, directives, and development/promotion objectives and strategies that provide a framework within which the collective and individual decisions directly affecting long-term tourism development and the daily activities within a destination are taken". Tourism policy is all about what government chooses to do or not to do with respect to tourism (Hall, 1994), i.e., what governments decided to do or not to do (Dye, 1992). Policy emanates from political stimulus, cultural and value systems, institutional frameworks, the distribution of power and decision making process (Simon, 1997). According to UNWTO, tourism policy is directed to guide all tourism development, operations and management so as to meet the government's immediate and long-term objectives for tourism. The policy, based on the principles of sustainability, is in line with international best practices to ensure the competitiveness of the national tourism industry within a regional and global scenario". A tourism policy provides the direction or course of action that a particular country, region, locality or an individual destination plans to take when developing or promoting tourism. The key principle for any tourism policy is that it should ensure that the nation (region or locality) would benefit to the maximum extent possible from the economic and social contributions of tourism. The ultimate objective of a tourism policy is to improve the progress of the nation (region or locality) and the lives of its citizens (Biederman, 2007). Policy making is a complex process and involves a series of stages. It needs considerations of various external and internal environments. Consensus from all the stakeholders also needs to be obtained and their suggestions and recommendations are to be evaluated in order to be considered during policy making. The following are the stages involved in policy making in general, as suggested by UNWTO:

- **Phase 1:** *Preparation of an Issues Paper*: This stage consists of a detailed review and assessment of the current tourism scenario in the country, based on review of the existing tourism policies, strategies and plans, and is finalized after exhaustive discussions with all stakeholders. This can also include policy constraints and challenges, along with opportunities and benchmarks for the future growth of the industry. Focus areas include:
  - policy and strategy;
  - institutional strengthening;
  - legislation and regulation;
  - product development and diversification;
  - marketing and promotion;
  - economic impact of tourism and tourism investment;
  - tourism infrastructure and superstructure;
  - human resource development; and
  - socio-cultural and environmental impacts of tourism.
- **Phase 2:** *Dissemination of Issues Paper Among Various Stakeholders:* A series of regional workshops can be organized with the intention to disseminate the Issues Paper to

regional public and private tourism stakeholders. This will help to ensure that existing and future needs of the tourism industry are well identified.

- **Phase 3:** *Formulation of a draft tourism policy.*
- **Phase 4:** *Organization of a national forum* to receive feedback from stakeholders on the draft tourism policy.
- **Phase 5:** *Finalization of the tourism policy* based on consultative feedback.
- **Phase 6:** *Formulation of an action plan* to implement the policy recommendations. (UNWTO/tourism policy).

A tourism policy will be shaped according to a particular region's characteristics, along with national and international policy considerations and recommendations. A region will have many aspects to consider based on the prevailing economic, social, cultural and environmental conditions. Local community involvement is also crucial in this process.

9.8 CONCLUSION

Planning and policy making are two crucial responsibilities vested with the authorities of a destination. Improper planning and an inappropriate policy can be destructive in any situation and can lead to increased impacts and issues. Tourism, being a multi-sectoral and multifaceted phenomenon, careful and scientific approach is inevitable, with utmost local community involvement. The design, planning and management of tourism environments require serious approach and a sustainable tourism industry necessitates a commitment towards sustainable development principles by representatives of all the stakeholders involved in the planning process.

Key Terms

Planning	Local/site level planning
Tourism planning	Boosterism
Sustainability	Physical/spatial approach
Geographical planning	Community approach
Destination planning	Sustainable approach
Business level planning	Integrated approach
International level	Strategic planning
National level planning	Planning process
Regional planning	Tourism policy
Sub-regional planning	

Review Questions

Short Answer Type Questions

1. What do you mean by planning?
2. Discuss why planning is important in tourism.
3. What are the limitations of tourism planning?
4. Distinguish between geographical planning and business level planning in tourism.
5. What are different territorial planning types in tourism?
6. Write short notes on international and national tourism planning.
7. Discuss 'Boosterism' planning approach in tourism.
8. Write the stages in tourism planning process.
9. Discuss the tourism policy.

Essay Type Questions

1. Explain tourism planning process.
2. Discuss in detail various tourism planning approaches.
3. Write an essay on tourism planning and its significance.

10

BENEFITS OF TOURISM

Learning Outcomes

After studying this chapter, you will be able to:

- explain the economic significance of tourism;
- elucidate the mode of tourist expenditure pattern;
- understand the economic benefits of tourism;
- explain the multiplier effect due to tourism;
- comprehend the social benefits of tourism;
- appreciate the cultural benefits; and
- understand how tourism benefits the environment.

10.1 INTRODUCTION

Tourism, of late, is an inevitable development priority of countries. Countries regard tourism as an engine of economic growth. Economic benefits of properly planned tourism development reach everyone virtually in the region, in one way or the other. As discussed in the previous chapter, tourism planning is an important activity that needs utmost care and consideration of each and every aspect. The economic benefits are certainly an important consideration in state, regional and community planning and economic development. Properly planned tourism development can reap increased equitable economic contribution. There are a number of substantiating facts why tourism is given much significance in the developmental priorities of countries and regions. The data proves that tourism is one of the largest industries in the world and a rapid growing economic sector. The employment generation potential of tourism is remarkable. The following summary of the WTTC Annual Economic Impact Update reveals the economic significance of tourism in the world:

"In 2015, travel and tourism in total contributed US$ 7.2 trillion to world GDP, representing 9.8% of global GDP. The sector supported 284 million jobs, or 1 in 11 jobs in the world. Travel and tourism grew by 3.1% in 2015 - the 6th consecutive year of positive growth for the sector. The sector's contribution to GDP is forecast to grow by 3.3% in 2016. Travel and tourism will outperform the global economy throughout the next decade, growing by an expected 4% on average annually over the next ten years" (WTTC, 2016).

Moreover, UNWTO regularly updates the volume and value statistics of international and country-wise tourism. It specifies the amount generated from tourism as tourism receipts from international tourism. As per the latest figures, international tourism receipts in destinations around the world grew by 3.6% in 2015, recording a faster rate than world merchandise trade. Tourism's share in world's exports is around 7%, and of the services exports, it had a share of 30% in 2015, and the total export value from international tourism amounted to US$ 1.4 trillion. Income generated due to the expenditure made by international tourists on accommodation, food and drink, entertainment, shopping and other services and goods reached an estimated US$ 1,232 billion. 1.18 billion tourists made international visits in 2015. In terms of global exports, tourism ranks third after fuels and chemicals and ahead of food and automotive products. In many developing countries, tourism ranks as the first export sector (UNWTO, 2016). Benefits of tourism need not be confined to economic aspects alone. The local community is benefited by tourism socially as well. There are benefits that can also be associated with the culture of a destination. Even environment, that is more vulnerable to tourism development is benefited greatly from properly planned tourism development. A range of benefits, thus, can be associated with tourism development in destinations. The benefits of tourism have been discussed in this chapter.

10.2 ECONOMIC BENEFITS OF TOURISM

Tourism is one of the most significant economic sectors. The benefits it can provide to a tourist destination are of various kinds. In fact, the benefits are enjoyed by all sections of the society, from individuals to industries and even the government. Tourism contributes directly, indirectly and with induced effects, and penetrates deep into the local economy where the destination is located. According to Lickorish (1994), tourism in general contributes foreign currency and government revenue, generates employment in large numbers, and contributes significantly to regional development. The government is benefited in a number of ways which will be further diverted into other developmental and welfare activities. All such economic benefits are a result of the expenditure made by the tourists. Tourists contribute to sales, profits, jobs, tax revenues, and income in an area. The direct contribution is in the primary tourism sectors such as lodging, restaurants, transportation, amusements, and retail trade. This penetrates further into the economy by generating different rounds of expenditures. Thus, through secondary effects, tourism affects most of the sectors of the economy. Let us examine the nature and nuances of visitor expenditure first before going into the details of the economic benefits.

10.2.1 Visitor/Tourist Expenditure

Tourist expenditure or visitor expenditure is directly associated with tourism consumption. A *tourist* is the ultimate customer or consumer in the tourism system. Tourists spend money for consuming various products and services. Tourism consumption, in general, conforms to the concept of "final consumption" in the system of national accounts, regardless of the type of consumer. This relates to the phenomenon called *tourist expenditure*. WTO defines tourist expenditure as "the total consumption expenditure made by a visitor or on behalf of a visitor for and during his/her trip and stay at destination" (WTO, 1994). Tourists spend money to use facilities like accommodation, food and beverage, transport, communications, entertainment services, goods from retail outlets and others. *Visitor expenditure*, another term used in this concept, refers to "the amount paid for the acquisition of consumption goods and services, as well as valuables, for own use or to give away, for and during tourism trips. It includes expenditures by visitors themselves, as well as expenses that are paid for or reimbursed by others" (UN & UNWTO, 2008). Tourists give rise to many expenditure types as they face a large variety of needs throughout their journey, i.e., the needs are of different kinds and are seen in different phases of the journey. For a country, the expenditure made by an international tourist is a receipt for the destination country. On the other hand, it is an expenditure in the tourist generating country. Common tourism expenditure classification includes:

- Package travel, package holidays and package tours
- Accommodation
- Food and drink
- Local transport
- International transport
- Recreation, culture and sporting activities
- Shopping
- Others

Certainly tourists make expenditures not only in the destination, but it spans from the origin place, throughout the travelling region until he/she returns home. The nature of expenditure made by tourists at origin place can be to satisfy a different kind of need. While at the destination, it can be for some other need. Hence, tourism expenditure can also be classified according to the location of the tourists as part of their journey. WTO further states that the various components making up tourist expenditure can be divided into three categories, such as:

- Expenses made during *preparation of the trip*: this constitutes the advance outlays necessary for preparation and undertaking the trip.

- Expenses made *during the trip*: This comprises the expenses arising while travelling and at the places visited.
- Expenses made *after the trip*: Travel related outlays made in the country of origin when returning from a trip.

This reiterates that tourist expenditure occurs at different phases of the journey and hence, economic benefits also occur at different locations. Yet, while we discuss the economic contribution, it is mainly linked to a destination. In the destination, apart from the direct expenditure made by the tourists on front line establishments, a part of the money will go out of the local economy for providing various services and goods. Expenditure is made in a variety of areas and the major categories include travel, accommodation, food and drinks, recreation and related activities, sightseeing, and shopping. For example, when a tourist is visiting India, and staying in a deluxe hotel, asks for Russian-made Vodka, then the hotel will have to supply the same. Here, the money spent for the same goes out of the local/national economy. At the time of economic impact measurement, this 'leakage' of money is referred to as *import*. In tourism, the amount of leakage has to be taken into account seriously. In developing and undeveloped countries, the leakage is high, particularly.

Table 10.1 Tourism expenditure types

There are various types of tourism expenditure other than monetary expenditure on consumption goods and services paid directly by visitors.

- Monetary expenditure on consumption of goods and services *paid directly by the employer* for employees on business travel.
- Monetary expenditure by the visitor *refunded by a third party*, either employers, other households or the social insurance scheme.
- Monetary payments *made by visitors for the individual services* provided and subsidized by Government and non-profit institutions serving households in the areas of education, health, museums, performing arts, etc.
- *Out-of-pocket payments* for services provided to employees and their families on tourism trips financed principally by employers, such as subsidized transport, accommodation, stays in holiday residences of employers or other services.
- *Supplementary payments* made by visitors to attend sports or any other cultural events on the invitation of, and principally paid for by, producers.

Source: UN & UNWTO, 2008.

10.2.2 Invisible Export

International tourists generally buy services from another country and therefore pay for *invisibles*. When a tourist from the UK comes to India, there is an invisible payment of the UK's balance, while India's balance gets an invisible receipt. Tourist expenditure is as 'real' as any other form of consumption and international tourist expenditure can be seen as an invisible export from the host country. Usually, countries try to maximize their travel receipts through promotional and marketing strategies. A tourist spends money on various heads. Accommodation, shopping, travel, entertainment, etc., are the major areas where tourist spends money. International tourist has to exchange currency into the regional currency before making any purchases. Tourist can purchase goods and services from the host country by paying accepted international currencies also. Thus, the consumption of tourism products will generate activity which can be compared to export, even though most of the tourism products are intangible in nature.

In the case of domestic tourism, tourism expenditure is considered an 'export' between the local regions, and perhaps an import substitute for the national economy. Domestic tourism encourages redistribution of income of the country.

10.2.3 Role in the 'Balance of Payments' of a Country

Internationally, tourism is a leading economic sector which generates income and consequently affects the balance of payments positively. For a country with significant amount of inbound tourism, it may have a major influence on a country's *balance of payments*. As tourism is treated an exporting sector that can help improve the balance of payments, international tourism represents consumption of goods and services outside the source country of tourists. A country's balance of payments reflects its transactions with the rest of the world, an important part of its system of national and macro-accounting. It is a statement that summarizes an economy's transactions with the rest of the world for a specified time period. A country's balance of payments is important for the maintenance of the value of its currency in foreign exchange. Continuous balance of payment deficits for a country normally lead to an imbalance between the international supply of the country's currency and the international demand for it, in the direction of an excess supply. It may lead to the country's *currency weakness*. The activity of export of tourism sector focusses on selling of goods and services on the part of the citizens of the host country to the international tourists (Samuelson, 1972).

10.2.4 Government Revenue

Tourism activity is used by certain economies as an important resource for generating *government revenue*. Tourism generates tax income, some of which is directly applied and some computed indirectly. Most of the taxes come in the form of sales tax on various items the tourist purchases, like cigarette, liquor, accommodation facilities, etc. Tourists also pay taxes indirectly by the consumption of various imported items. Moreover, the government is involved in tourism commercially as well. Government provides various services for tourists in the possible ways. Some of them which have commercial orientation bring revenue in the form of profits and service charges. Some tourist attractions are also managed by the government or its agencies. For example, museums, palaces, monuments, etc. In such cases, government generates income as entry fee. When we consider the direct, indirect and induced effects of the expenditure by a tourist, it can be inferred that he is paying taxes to government in different ways.

10.2.5 Employment Generation

Tourism, in common with most personal service industries, is *labour intensive*. For developing and developed countries with high unemployment rates, tourism is considered an attractive alternative. Tourism involves a wide variety of industrial sectors, and this makes it particularly difficult to derive estimates concerning the number of employees associated with tourism. Currently, tourism is the largest employment generating economic sector in the world. As per WTTC (2016), travel and tourism directly generated 107,833,000 jobs (3.6% of total employment in 2015). This figure may rise by 1.9% in 2016 and rise by 2.1% pa (135,884,000 jobs, i.e., 4.0% of total employment) in 2026. In addition to this, tourism has a diverse range of linkages between tourism sectors and other sectors of the economy. Thus, employment generation happens not only in tourism industry, but even in all allied and other sectors with direct or indirect linkages with tourism activities. This is shown as employment generation directly and indirectly. In the same report of WTTC, it is estimated that the total contribution of travel and tourism to employment, including jobs indirectly supported by the industry, was 9.5% of total employment (283,578,000 jobs), which is expected to rise by 2.2% in 2016 (289,756,000 jobs) and rise by 2.5% pa (370,204,000 jobs) in 2026.

Tourism products mainly consist of service products and they usually tend to generate more employment opportunities. The concept of *multipliers* has the same impact in employment generation as well. Tourists staying at a destination results in creation of jobs directly in the industry. Apart from this, due to the effect of tourist's stay, many other sectors indirectly related to tourism are impacted to create more job opportunities. Direct employment generation includes employment in travel agencies, as tour operators, transport undertakings, accommodation establishments and enterprises engaged in marketing destinations. Indirectly tourism will cause employment generation in other sectors like financial institutions, organizations that supply raw materials to the tourism organizations, etc. But still there are a variety of criticisms in this area in comparison with other industries, such as tourism employment potential is seasonal, most of the jobs generated are only inferior employment, share of local population is often too small to fill the vacancies, etc. There may be counter-arguments but those that cannot be discussed as these are beyond the scope of this book.

10.2.6 Investment and 'Accelerator Effect'

The development and growth of tourism in an area will attract more private and public investments. The private and public sectors may be induced to invest even more in that area and this is what economists call *accelerator effect*. It primarily denotes that tourism

DIRECT CONTRIBUTION

COMMODITIES

- Accommodation
- Transportation
- Entertainment
- Attractions

INDUSTRIES

- Accommodation Services
- Food and Beverage Services
- Retail Trade
- Transportation Services
- Cultural Sports and Recreational Services

SOURCES OF SPENDING

- Residents: Domestic Travel and Tourism Spending
- Businesses: Domestic Travel and Tourism Spending
- Visitor Exports
- Individuals Government: Travel and Tourism Spending

INDIRECT TRAVEL and TOURISM CONTRIBUTION

- Travel and Tourism Investment Spending
- Government Collective Travel and Tourism Spending
- Impacts of Purchases from Suppliers

INDUCED CONTRIBUTION (Spending by Direct and Indirect Employees)

- Food and Beverage
- Recreation
- Clothing
- Housing
- Household Goods

TOTAL TRAVEL and TOURISM CONTRIBUTION

- To GDP
- To Employment

Source: Modified from WTTC, 2016.

Figure 10.1: Economic contribution of travel and tourism

investment encourages further investment in the same area. Growth in tourism will see a surge in capital spending by businesses when an economy is growing quite strongly. Expansion of tourism activities leads to the requirement of further activities and further investment and expansion. Thus, if tourism in an area booms and the value of TIM (tourism income multiplier) is high, more investments in both tourism and allied industries can be expected. Tourism investment also results in subsequent investments in supporting sectors, allied sectors and even indirect sectors. Superstructure development is an important aspect in relation to a destination at this juncture. Travel and tourism investment in 2015 across the world was USD 774.6 bn, or 4.3% of total investment. It should rise by 4.7% in 2016, and rise by 4.5% pa over the next ten years to USD 1,254.2 bn in 2026 (WTTC, 2016).

10.2.7 Income Generation

Income is generated in the local community directly, indirectly and in induced forms. Income is created in different forms, in general it accrues from wages and salaries, interest, rent and profits. Since tourism industry consists majorly of service products, the greatest proportion is likely to be in wages and salaries as far as income generation is considered. And hence, the level of income generation from tourism is closely bound with the level of employment. Here, wage levels also have much importance. If it is high, income level will also be high. Income is also generated from interest and rent. Rent potentials vary in tourism, ranging from parking space to a large hotel building with a local owner, but rented out to an international chain of hotels. The sum of all incomes in an economy is called *national income* while the significance of tourism in a country's economy can be identified by its contribution on the proportion of national income.

10.3 ECONOMIC GROWTH AND DIVERSIFICATION

Tourism contributes to the economic growth of a country, regionally and locally. All the above discussed factors in one way or the other lead to economic growth of a country. According to World Travel and Tourism Council, tourism stimulates economic growth by generating income, employment, investment and exports. But it also generates valuable spin-off benefits, including preservation of cultural heritage, improved infrastructure and local community facilities (WTTC, 2013). Moreover, tourism of late, is considered the most suitable option for economic diversification. The oil price crisis that took place in the GCC region is an example. Due to a sharp decline in oil prices, the oil dependent economies in the GCC started facing economic stringency and that led them to promote tourism as an option for tourism development. The following report of CNBC reveals the significance of tourism in a declining economy:

"The revenue that Saudi Arabia generates from oil could be overtaken by tourism one day, according to tourism industry experts and economists. Speaking on the rapid growth of tourism to the country at an event organized by the Saudi state, economists and experts said that tourism and national heritage are the sectors most likely to become pillars for Saudi Arabia's future economy- one that is currently predicated on oil exports." (CNBC, 1/10/2015). Tourism itself is a sector with diverse businesses and industries and moreover, it causes investments in other sectors.

10.4 LOCAL ENTREPRENEURSHIP DEVELOPMENT

Tourism, across the world is dominated by small and medium enterprises, though large-scale businesses have a significant market share. Many tourism businesses comply with 'standard' definitions of small businesses because they are small in terms of both number of employees (usually less than 20) and market share. Investment for large-scale businesses from multinational companies is there in most of the destinations, yet, there are large number of small and medium tourism enterprises (SMTEs) and other supporting businesses that are run by the local entrepreneurs. *Bed & Breakfast* (B&B), a small lodging establishment that offers overnight accommodation and breakfast, is an ideal example for this. In European tourism, B&Bs have significant role. These establishments are privately owned small-scale businesses, which give entrepreneurial opportunities to local people. Tourism, unlike many other large-scale economic sectors, offers ample scope for local entrepreneurship.

10.5 REDISTRIBUTION OF WEALTH

Tourism helps in the *redistribution of wealth.* This is particularly relevant for domestic tourism as it facilitates the redistribution of wealth from urban regions to peripheral regions and rural areas. It helps to distribute demand and supply to different regions of a country, some of which have not otherwise been developed industrially. Within each country, domestic tourism contributes to an improved balance of the national economy through a redistribution of the national income. *Redistribution* refers to the transfer of income/wealth from that section of the society or individual in which the same is accrued to the other sections. Due to domestic tourism, the rich with significant income travel to many locations and spend money for consuming various travel and tourism products. Through this process, the money is passed to the not so rich.

10.6 DIRECT, INDIRECT AND INDUCED BENEFITS

Economic benefits created by tourism is measured in three ways such as direct, indirect and induced. The money spent by a tourist will generate additional demand in the economy. This concept is explained in multiplier analysis later. The full assessment of economic benefit must take into account all the aspects including the direct, indirect and induced benefits. The total economic impact of tourism takes into account the direct, indirect, and induced effects within a region. These are indicated as gross output or sales, income, employment, or the value added. In fact, assessing economic impact has other dimensions as well, like the need for considering the *leakage* and *displacement effect* and *opportunity costs*. Economic benefits are generated not only in the tourism sector itself, but it passes to other sectors also. When we come to direct level benefits, it shows the benefits coming to the tourism establishment that are directly connected to tourism and offer tourism services, i.e., in frontline tourism establishments like hotels and resorts. They are also viewed as *production changes* associated with the immediate effects of changes in visitor expenditures. In some cases, it is also referred to as the money *directly spent* by the tourists. More tourists visiting a destination cause increased spending and increased production and consequent sales. For instance, an increase in the number of tourists staying there would directly lead to increased sales in the hotel sector. Furthermore, this addition in revenue would directly lead to additional associated changes in hotel payments for wages and salaries, taxes, and supplies and services. Technically speaking, it is the value of tourist expenditure, less the value of imports necessary to supply those 'frontline' goods and services. Here, the factor of 'leakage', which is the amount leaked out of the local economy for importing goods and services come into play. Hence, in general, the direct impact is likely to be less than the value of tourist expenditure. Direct impact depends on the capability of the local economy to provide for tourist's demands from its own production sectors. The direct effect is more when the leakage is less.

The establishments which directly receive tourist expenditure also need to purchase goods and services from other sectors within the local economy. For example, restaurants will have to purchase raw food materials from retail shops available there. The suppliers to those frontline establishments will need to purchase goods and services from other establishments and the process continues.

The generation of economic activity brought about by these subsequent rounds of expenditure is known as the *indirect effect*. It is also viewed as the production changes resulting from various rounds of re-spending by the tourism frontline establishments' receipts in other backward-linked industries. It means the income generated will be passed on to the suppliers and other service providers of the frontline tourism establishments. Corresponding changes will be visible in other economic parameters like production, sales and employment as well. This creates secondary rounds of tourist expenditure. Businesses supplying products and services to the direct tourism businesses also create further expenditures from the local economy and thus the tourism industry gets linked with varying degrees to many other economic sectors in the region.

During the course of direct and indirect rounds of expenditure, income will be accrued to local residents in the form of wages, salaries, rent, interest and distributed profits. This addition of income to the local income will, in part, be re-spent in the local economy on goods and services, and this will generate further rounds of economic activity. There will be changes in economic activity resulting from household spending of income earned directly or indirectly as a result of tourism spending. This phenomenon is referred to as *induced effect*. For example, a hotel employee will be getting salary and a part of that will be spent on various household requirements, and that creates another economic impact in the economy.

10.7 MULTIPLIER EFFECT

Multipliers are known as means for estimating how much extra income is produced in an economy as a result of the initial spending or injection of cash. This concept was conceptualized during the nineteenth century and became established as a theory as part of the works of John Maynard Keynes in 1930. Richard Kahn's works on the same area in 1930s too contributed to it. Concept of multiplier is based upon the recognition that sales for one firm requires purchases from other firms within the local economy. To put it simply, the definition given by Dictionary.com seems relevant. According to it, *multiplier effect* is "an effect in economics in which an increase in spending produces an increase in national income and consumption greater than the initial amount spent. For example, if a corporation builds a factory, it will employ construction workers and their suppliers as well as those who work in the factory. Indirectly, the new factory will stimulate employment in laundries, restaurants, and service industries in the factory's vicinity." This shows that the industrial sectors of an economy are interdependent. This kind of analysis would apply in the case of tourism, since tourism brings expenditure into an area from outside. Revenue from international tourists is like exports for the local economies. Changes in the level of activity in one industry/sector lead to changes in the level of activity in other industries/sectors. The multiplier idea is that the initial expenditure of a sum of money is just the start of a process, not the end. The money entering into an economy circulates within it and is spent again and again until it disappears from the local economy. That means, it could create a *'ripple effect'*, also called multiplier effect throughout the economy. The firms in the sector/industry, purchase not only the primary inputs such as labour, imports, etc., but also intermediate goods and services produced by other establishments within the local economy.

In the case of tourism, this concept has more relevance. This represents the economic impacts brought about by a change in the level or pattern of tourist expenditure. Tourist expenditure has a *cascading effect* throughout the economy. According to Horváth and Frechtling (1999), multiplier effect of tourist expenditures embodies "the total sales, output or other measure of economic benefits generated once the initial visitor spending has worked its way through the economy under study through inter-industry transactions (the *indirect impact*) and through employee consumption expenditures (the *induced impact*)". Because firms in the local economy are dependent upon other firms for their supplies, any change in tourist expenditure will bring about a change in the economy's level of production, household income, employment, government revenue and foreign exchange flows. Tourist multiplier measures such changes. Ultimately, the multiplier quantifies the impact of extra expenditure made by tourists into an economy.

Tourist is spending money in frontline establishments (e.g., hotels, airlines, etc.), which provide the tourist with their goods and services. Keynes referred to this entry of money, through international tourist expenditure, as *injection* of money for the economy. The money received by the organizations will be re-spent. A portion of the money will leak out directly from the economy in the form of 'imports', which represent the expenditure flowing overseas. For example, a hotel is purchasing foreign-made liquor to supply to the tourist, then the money paid for the same will leak out of the economy. These imports may be in the form of food and beverage also, when the tourist eats foods that are not provided locally. Here the value of tourist expenditure that actually circulates in the local economy is immediately reduced. The remaining sum of money will be used to purchase locally produced goods and services, labour and entrepreneurial skills and to meet government taxes, licences and fees. From local businesses also, the money is spent again. Some part of it again leaks out of the local economy in the form of imports. Some part of it will go to the government. A good share of the money is again passed to local business. Thus, the indirect impact arises. This process will continue. The magnitude of secondary effects depends on the propensity of businesses and households in the region to purchase goods and services from local suppliers. During each round of expenditure, some portion of money is accrued as various forms of income. Some of the money will be saved by either households or businesses. This is also a form of leakage. If the money is spent again, leakage happens and some part goes to the government. This spending of income accrued as a result of the initial tourist expenditure will generate further rounds of economic activity and is referred to as induced effect. Keynes argues further that 'greater the volume of leakage, lesser the multiplier effect and economic growth is possible when 'injections' are greater than leakages. It is also illustrated as: "the size of the multiplier effect will depend upon the amount of original injection under examination and the leakages from the economy" (Tribe, 2008). Value of multipliers will be high when leakage is low and impact of expenditure on the income is high. Measurement of economic impact of tourism has to take into account the flow of money through various sectors of the economy and the corresponding generation of different rounds of expenditures, which include direct, indirect, and induced effects.

10.7.1 Types of Multipliers

In order to translate tourist expenditure data into economic impact information, the appropriate multiplier values have to be calculated. "Tourism multipliers embody the total increase in output, labour earnings and employment through inter-industry linkages in a region as a result of tourism expenditures"(Douglas et al., 1999). There will be some value by which the initial change in tourist expenditure must be multiplied to estimate the total change in output. This change is referred to as *output multiplier*. It has been comprehended as a "numerical value which is useful to estimate and measure the additional increase of economic scale such as the output, the income and the employment of the area concerned, through effect on the spread of the increase (initial expenditure) of this expenditure due to the increase in the total tourist expenditure of the sightseer in a certain area" (Hojo, 2002). Similarly, there will be a value that, when multiplied by the change in tourist expenditure, will estimate the total change in household income. According to Brian H. Archer (1977), there are five tourist multipliers such as *income* multiplier, *sales* (transactions) multiplier, *output* multiplier, *employment* multiplier, and *input-output* multiplier. Some of the major multipliers are given in brief below.

- **Income multiplier:** This is the most common type of Keynesian multiplier (Wanhill, 1994) and it measures the net changes in new economic activity as an initial unit of expenditure cycles through the economy. It denotes the amount of additional income (wages, salaries, rent, interest, distributed profit, etc.) created in an economy on account of an increase in tourist expenditure.

- **Output multiplier:** This shows the amount of additional output generated in the economy as a result of an increase in tourist expenditure.
- **Employment multiplier:** A measure of either the total amount of employment generated by increased tourist expenditure or the ratio of total employment generated by this same expenditure to direct employment alone (i.e., employment generated during the first round in the directly related tourism sectors).
- **Sales (transactions) multiplier:** This measures the extra business turnover created directly and indirectly as a result of extra expenditure by tourists.
- **Government revenue multiplier:** It denotes either the gross increase or net increase in government revenue; public revenue in all forms and from all sources; as a result of increase in tourist expenditure.

10.8 MEASURING ECONOMIC IMPACTS

Measuring economic impacts is not an easy task. The economic benefits of tourism are of different types and many levels and dimensions are involved in it. Some of the most commonly used measures are described here.

10.8.1 Tourism Satellite Account (TSA)

TSA, of late, is the most common method used to estimate the economic benefits of tourism at the national level. It is a standard framework for organizing statistical data on tourism. It eventually provides the structure and size of tourism in a country, from an economic perspective. It is a set of accounts that can be used to determine the size or significance of tourism within an economy. Akin to input-output models, it also provides means whereby tourism can be viewed in parallel with other industries and across international boundaries. It was initiated by the UNWTO since 1995 (UNWTO, 2011). In fact, countries faced the difficulty of estimating value statistics and that led to the concerted efforts to address the shortcomings in quantifying the potential value of tourism in national economics. According to Tribe (2008), "TSAs are generally prepared using tourism surveys to impute tourism values to broader economic activities. Typically, TSAs are compiled using combination of visitor expenditure data from surveys conducted in tourists and industry data from national economic accounts". In fact, the base of it is a UN framework of a System of National Accounts for countries from which estimates are derived using the economic data associated with a specific economy. According to the UN and UNWTO, the need for establishment of TSA are:

- as an instrument that recognized that tourism cuts across many products and productive activities, facilitating a deeper understanding of tourism's linkages to other economic areas;

- as a structural link to the System of National Accounts, the balance of payments and the statistics of international trade in services, and as a consequence, to other macroeconomic frameworks;
- as a structural link to National Accounts aggregates and their general estimation approach, from which to derive credibility and legitimacy for tourism statistics data and development programmes;
- as a methodology and framework for a comprehensive reconciliation of tourism data related mainly to supply by tourism industries and other industries and demand by visitors and other types of associated variables, in particular, those related to the characterization of visitors, tourism trips and employment in the tourism industries;
- as the unique framework to properly compile tourism gross domestic product (GDP) regarded as the basic macro aggregate to characterize the size of tourism, among other aggregates; and
- as a reference and milestone for future statistical developments and economic research on tourism (UN & UNWTO, 2008).

In fact, TSA has been developed to provide clear data on the impact of tourism and associated employment; and will help in designing economic policies related to tourism development. It also provides data on tourism's impact on nation's balance of payments and tourism human resources characteristics. UN and UNWTO (2008) illustrate TSA in the following way.

It is a conceptual framework for understanding tourism from a macroeconomic perspective, with a focus on the description and measurement of tourism in its different forms, such as *inbound, domestic* and *outbound*. The relationship between consumption by visitors and the supply of goods and services in the economy, principally those from the tourism industries, are highlighted. Tourism GDP can be estimated; the direct contribution of tourism to the economy can be established and the complex and elaborated schemes building on the intrinsic relationship of the TSA with the System of National Accounts and the balance of payments can be developed using this framework. It includes a set of 10 interrelated tables in the following manner:

Tables 1 to 4: Different categories of consumption by visitors associated with different forms of tourism.

Tables 5 and 6: Production by tourism industries and other industries of tourism characteristic products, tourism connected products and other products and allows the calculation of tourism GDP.

Table 7: Employment in tourism industries.

Table 8: Tourism's gross fixed capital formation.

Table 9: Government administrative expenditures associated with the support and control of tourism.

Table 10: Some important non-monetary indicators to support the analyses of the above economic data.

It is claimed that TSA can measure the following:

- Contribution of tourism in the gross domestic product (GDP).
- Ranking of tourism according to other economic sectors.
- Estimation of tourism employment in an economy.
- The amount of tourism investment.
- Tax revenues generated by tourism industries.
- Tourism consumption.
- Impact of tourism on national balance of payments.
- Characteristics of tourism human resources.

World Travel and Tourism Council (WTTC), a global tourism professional body, also initiates TSA at national and international levels. It, in association with Oxford Economics, attempts TSA at country-level, consistent with UN framework and utmost efforts are undertaken to have complete TSAs in most of the countries.

10.8.2 Economic Analysis

Variety of economic analyses can be undertaken to find out the economic contribution of tourism. Some of them are:

- **Economic impact analysis:** Provides the contribution of tourism activity to the economy of the region.
- **Fiscal impact analysis:** It denotes how government revenues from tourism activity, taxes, direct fees, and other sources, cover the added costs for infrastructure and government services.
- **Financial analysis:** Potential of profit from tourism developmental activity/project.
- **Demand analysis:** Shows how the number or types of tourists to an area change due to changes in prices, promotion, competition, quality and quantity of facilities, or other demand shifters.
- **Cost-Benefit analysis:** Cost-benefit analysis is a technique designed to estimate and compare all the costs and benefits of a project in money terms. It provides clue on which alternative policy will generate the highest net benefit to society over time.
- **Feasibility study:** Denotes how a tourism project or policy is to be undertaken.

Measuring Methods

Some of the commonly used methods of analyzing economic impacts are introduced below.

(a) Survey Method

Survey method is the most common method used for measuring economic impacts of tourism. A survey can be undertaken on a sample, preferably, using a questionnaire. The sample can include respondents chosen from the consumers—tourists, organizers and operators of the travel businesses, and representatives of other stakeholders in tourism. Characteristics statistics can be measured easily using this method along with the value and volume statistics. *Modeling* can also be done on the basis of data collected from the survey method. Data from other sources are also used. (Kumar et al., 2015). Evaluating method is also used widely to estimate the economic benefits and impacts.

(b) Multiplier Analysis

Multiplier analysis is undertaken using different techniques to estimate multiplier values and the following are some of the commonly used methods.

- **Base theory model:** It suggests that the export sector is the most important factor for determining a region's economic health. As per this model, there is a relationship between the export sectors and the local sectors of an economy so that the changes in the level of tourist expenditure lead to predictable and measurable changes in the level of activity in local sector. The model distinguishes between the region's export sector (which sells its output to other regions) and its domestic sector.
- **Keynesian multiplier model:** These are used to measure the income generated in an economy by an additional unit of tourist expenditure. It is based on identifying streams of income and employment which are generated in "rounds", which diminish in geometric progression because of leakages at each round.
- **Input-output model:** This model describes the flow of money between sectors within a region's economy and it shows how those tourism economic effects work through an economy, based on the specific supply and demand interactions between different industries or sectors. By this, it analyses the economy into its sectors and expresses a relationship of these sectors in matrix form, based on the results of research into the effects of tourist expenditure. This enables to identify and quantify the backward and forward linkages emerging from the flows of transactions taking place amongst the different sectors of the economy over a specific period of time.

(c) Expert Opinion Method/Delphi Study

An expert opinion survey or a Delphi study can be useful when primary data collection is difficult or cost-prohibitive. Care is needed in choosing the experts as respondents to avoid misleading information.

(d) Referenda Method

This is used more for measuring impacts and the costs associated with tourism development. An important direct cost issue, such as substantially increasing the state tourism marketing programme, budget is placed before the public in the format of a referendum. If the referendum fails or succeeds, then some insight into the willingness to pay by the residents is reflected in that decision.

Forecasting is also done in tourism. Application areas of forecasting get diversified from tourism demand to other areas as well. Tourism demand, expenditure and receipts, supply requirements, etc., are forecasted commonly in the parlance of tourism.

10.9 SOCIAL SIGNIFICANCE OF TOURISM

Tourism is a social activity as well. Different groups of people are linked to tourism, directly or indirectly. All those groups may enjoy the benefits of tourism. On the other hand, there are a range of social consequences also which are discussed in the next chapter. Indeed, social significance of tourism is intricately linked to its economic advantages, yet the social benefits of tourism can be distinguished as follows:

- **Better set of amenities and facilities:** Increase in infrastructure is a prerequisite for tourism development. Infrastructure is shared by both tourists and locals. The introduction of community facilities and services, primarily to cater to the tourists, are also of benefit to locals. Tourism supports the creation of community facilities and services that otherwise might not have been developed. A well established destination will have almost all the facilities required for a town. Thus, tourism can stimulate new and expanded community facilities and infrastructure initiatives, such as the improvement of retail, restaurant and entertainment options, transport services, education and sporting facilities.
- **Local/regional development:** As tourism progresses in a region, all facilities and services will be made available. The accessibility of the destination will be improved remarkably. Basic infrastructure of the region or the destination will be enhanced manifold. Along with tourism, other businesses, facilities and services that are directly or indirectly linked to tourism will also emerge. Eventually, the place or region will acquire the characteristics of a town or a city in general. Many destination locations across the world are examples that have turned into developed regions primarily due to tourism.

- **Increase in quality of life:** As the location develops and facilities and services improve, local people will have increased options for employment, and income. Side by side, basic requirements like education and health facilities also get enhanced. Education and community empowerment is a usual result of regional development as a result of tourism. Benefits can include upgraded infrastructure, health and transport improvements, new sports and recreational facilities, restaurants, and public spaces as well as an influx of better quality commodities and food. The vitality of communities increases in different ways. For instance, the events and festivals of which local residents have been the primary participants and spectators are often rejuvenated and developed in response to tourist interest. The jobs created by tourism can act as a vital incentive to reduce emigration from rural areas. These enhance the quality of life for the community, which may otherwise not warrant the improvement based on the residential population alone.
- **Revitalization of poor or non-industrialized regions:** Tourism, in many a cases, is a tool for development in poorer regions with limited resources for industrial development. Yet, those with rich natural and cultural heritage have ample options for developing tourism. This will certainly give a ray of hope for such regions. Tourism is increasingly being utilized by developing and emerging economies as a way to jumpstart and consolidate economic progress and inclusive development. Same is the case with some of the undeveloped regions also. Some of the African countries have gained economic significance through tourism.
- **International and intra-regional understanding:** "In a global environment marked by rising intolerance and cross-cultural tensions, often exacerbated by the economic divide between nations, tourism can foster spiritual and cultural respect among and between people, while creating economic opportunities to benefit disadvantaged populations," United Nations Secretary-General, Ban Ki-moon said in a message at the International Conference on Tourism, Religions and the Dialogue of Cultures held in 2007 in Cordoba, Spain. It is true that tourism has a power to create an understanding among different cultures. Tourism helps in respecting other cultures and enables to create peace. Moreover, tourism won't be successful where peace is not there. Within a country also, tourist movement between different regions helps to understand others and develop a sort of understanding between different cultures.
- **A tool for promoting peace:** At times, tourism is also viewed as a tool for peace. For instance, United Nations Environment Programme (UNEP) considers tourism as a force for peace. UNEP illustrates it in the following way:

  "Travelling brings people into contact with each other and, as tourism has an educational element, it can foster understanding between people and cultures and provide cultural exchanges between hosts and guests. Because of this, there are increased chances for people to develop mutual sympathy and understanding and reduce their prejudices. For example, jobs provided by tourism in Belfast, Northern Ireland, are expected to help demobilize paramilitary groups as the peace process is put in place. In the end, sympathy and understanding can lead to a decrease of tension in the world and thus contribute to peace" (www.unep.org).

- **A broadened community outlook:** Tourism causes demonstration effect (discussed in detail in the next chapter) through which local people on a destination are exposed to the nuances of different cultures. It provides opportunities for residents to interact with other people, lifestyles and cultures. Moreover, tourism helps in learning about different cultures and in developing a sort of understanding. This can encourage communities to widen their outlook and embrace new ideas.
- **Self-esteem and community pride:** Local community develops greater pride and ownership while attracting tourists to their place and in showcasing their culture and related features. The community takes stock of its assets and distinctive characteristics, and increases awareness and interest in their own cultural remains and natural features. This increase in pride enhances community celebrations or revival of cultural activities. Tourism also helps in enhancing local awareness of the financial value of natural and cultural sites and can stimulate a feeling of pride in local and national heritage. While tourists from different parts of the world visit and appreciate their cultural and natural varieties, it can considerably boost a community's collective ego.
- **Decentralization:** Indeed tourism development can take place in urban as well as rural areas. While other developments are limited to urban areas, tourism has the potential otherwise as well. Moreover, every kind of population has an opportunity from tourism for employment and income options, which can ensure the socio-economic benefits of tourism to all social strata of a community. Local people can also increase their influence on tourism development, as well as improve their job and earning prospects, through tourism-related professional training and development of business and organizational skills. Furthermore, modern tourism development principles ensure local community participation in tourism and properly planned development of tourism.
- **Poverty alleviation:** Many countries with least developmental options and poverty could utilize tourism as a tool for economic growth. Poverty alleviation is one of the objectives of tourism world over wherever it is necessary. UNWTO takes up the pivotal role in propagating tourism's potential in alleviating poverty and utilize it to eradicate poverty, be it anywhere. The reasons and features of tourism in association with poverty alleviation as per UNWTO is given in Table 10.2.

10.10 POSITIVE CULTURAL IMPACTS OF TOURISM

Tourism is a force in protecting cultural features. It can help to protect real cultural bases (Urry, 1990). World over, tourism is the prime reason for protecting the cultural remains, in revitalizing the indigenous cultural features and in preserving the heritage and monuments. Some of the major cultural benefits are briefed below.

- **Preservation and restoration of art and art forms:** All over the world, due to the urge to experience post-modern lifestyle, people are forgetting the past and sidelining traditional things. Traditional arts and crafts are dying out, and generations of people with particular skills are replaced by generations that do not learn these skills because these are thought to have become irrelevant to their modern way of life. Cultural features are always an important category of

Table 10.2 Role of tourism in poverty alleviation

The Special Position on Tourism in Poverty Alleviation: UNWTO

- The size and growth of the sector

Tourism acts as an 'engine for development' through foreign exchange earnings and the creation of direct and indirect employment.

- The relative importance of tourism in developing countries.

In many countries, tourism is the most viable and sustainable economic development option, and also a fast earner of foreign currency. Due to multiplier effect, the benefits of tourism penetrate down to all sections of the economy and hence it can directly benefit the poorer groups through employment of local people in tourism enterprises, goods and services provided to tourists, or the running of small and community based enterprises, etc.

- The character to tourism

Some features of tourism make it particularly relevant to low-income countries and to poor communities within them. Its response to particular assets: Some of the features of developing countries, such as warm climate, rich cultural heritage, inspiring landscapes and abundant biodiversity can be utilized positively in the ambit of tourism. This can be made use through tourism development.

- Its accessibility to the poor.

  The following reasons help tourism to be more accessible for the poor.

  - Labour-intensive sector
  - Domination of small and micro-enterprises.
  - Many activities are suited to women, young people and disadvantaged groups such as ethnic minority populations.
  - Some of the jobs are easily accessible as there are plenty of semi-skilled or non-skilled job options in tourism.
  - Some may also be part time and used to supplement income from other activities.
  - Its connectivity.

Tourism is directly and indirectly linked to so many other sectors. Hence, the benefit goes to a large number of sectors. Many intangible benefits also emanate as part of tourism like increased awareness of cultural, environmental, and economic issues and values, mutual benefits of tourists and host community from improved local investment in infrasturcture.

Source: Adapted from UNWTO/STEP.

attractions for tourism. Hence, restoring and preserving become essential for tourism. Tourism created a great demand for souvenirs. Apart from this, the indigenous art and craft forms will add value to the attractions of a destination. The preservation and transmission of cultural and historical traditions can contribute to the conservation and sustainable management of natural resources, the protection of local heritage, and a renaissance of indigenous cultures, cultural arts and crafts. In certain areas, some traditional craft forms are still surviving only because of tourism. Dance, music and others are also modified and preserved for tourism purposes. In Kerala, *Kathakali* (an endangered traditional classical performing art form) is widely performed as part of tourism activity. Thus, tourism contributes a share in restoring and preserving the traditional cultural and art forms. If tourists appreciate the cultural heritage of a destination, it can stimulate the host's pride in their heritage and foster local crafts, traditions and customs. Traditional customs and crafts can be sustained by tourist interest and purchase of local goods.

- **Preservation and maintenance of monuments, historical sites, etc:** As mentioned earlier, traditional remains are an important component of attractions in cultural tourism. In Indian tourism, a large number of historical buildings, monuments, and sites play an important role. The Taj Mahal, the grand forts of Rajasthan, the Buddhist centres, etc., are the best examples. Tourism play a vital role in preserving and maintaining the same. This is a significant positive cultural impact of tourism and this conveys the grand cultural heritage of the nation.
- **Cultural exchange:** Through demonstration effect as well as learning and understanding, tourism contributes in cultural exchange. This is more relevant for cultural tourism, when it is promoted adhering to the sustainable development principles. UNEP describes this in the following way:

  "Tourism is one of the foremost drivers of cultural exchange, providing a personal experience, not only of that which has survived from the past, but of the contemporary life and society of others. Tourists are not only bringing their suitcases to destinations they visit; but are also bringing their lifestyles, habits and customs. At the same time tourists are willing to discover a different culture, a specific lifestyle, to enjoy local food, see other aspects of daily life, even living in local homes to experience "exotic" customs (www.unep.org).

10.11 ENVIRONMENTAL BENEFITS OF TOURISM

Tourism is often criticized for negative impacts on environment. Yet, tourism contributes positively to nature in certain cases. When tourism and environment exist together in harmony, tourism can benefit the environment in certain ways. Following are the positive environmental benefits, according to Mason (1995):

- Stimulate measures to protect the environment and/or landscape.
- Help to promote the establishment of natural parks, wildlife reserves, etc.
- Raise money to protect, maintain and preserve the natural and cultural heritage.
- Help preservation of historical buildings/monuments.

Most of the benefits in this category fall into any one of the two types of benefits to environment such as conservation/preservation and creation of new naturally protected areas (Cooper et al., 1993).

- **Creation of national and wildlife parks:** Tourism in protected environment is a trend in some locations. In order to attract tourists, some of the unprotected lands with variety of flora and fauna are being earmarked and protected. Due to the attractiveness, pristine sites and natural areas are identified as valuable and the need to keep such attractions alive can lead to the creation of national parks and wildlife parks. Some of the African countries encourage tourism in protected natural attractions.
- **Protection and preservation:** Green movement and wave of sustainable development is prevalent in tourism. Tourism in natural areas demands protection, preservation and maintenance. Littering has been restricted in many of the well preserved natural destinations. Tourism can significantly contribute to the environmental protection if it is developed and managed applying scientific and sustainable rules and principles. The positive effect on wildlife preservation and protection efforts is seen strongly in many regions, like Africa, South America, Asia, Australia, and South Pacific. Protection of rare and extinct species is now being taken care of. Many examples demonstrate how tourism can benefit the environment by saving what otherwise might have been lost completely. But mass tourism and improper planning may lead to other impacts on environment which are multifarious, far-reaching and often irreparable. A number of countries have established wildlife reserves and enacted strict laws protecting the animals that draw nature-loving tourists (www.unep.org).
- **Maintenance and regeneration of forests:** The revenue created from tourism as entry fee, etc., is used for the maintenance and protection of natural areas. Both the built and natural environment benefit from upgrading and regeneration when a tourist opportunity is uncovered by local and national governments. Reforestation is being done in some locations where ecotourism is developed in its true sense. As per the modern tourism development agenda, effective and efficient environment management measures are part of it. Ensuring proper planning, Environmental Impact Assessment (EIA), environmental audit and management mechanisms, etc., help in maintaining the environment in a positive way for a longer period of time.

- ***Enhancing environmental awareness:*** Many agencies involved in tourism and other sectors provide information and education for tourists to increase their environmental awareness. Local people have also gained increased awareness on environmental value of places. Moreover, seeing the natural wonders and exotic and unique species, tourists could generate a sense of appreciation and respect for nature and evolve the sense of preserving them. One of the objectives of ecotourism in fact, is increasing awareness about nature and its protection.

10.12 CONCLUSION

This chapter discussed in detail the economic, social, cultural and environmental benefits of tourism. Undeniably, tourism is beneficial in a number of ways. This is the prime reason why tourism is being developed aggressively by countries and regions across the world. Tourism is now in the forefront of developmental priorities of countries. The existing trends point to further growth and development potentials of tourism for decades to come.

Key Terms

Economic benefits	Indirect benefit
Visitor/tourist expenditure	Induced benefit
Invisible export	Multiplier effect
Balance of payments	Tourism Satellite Account (TAS)
Government revenue	Economic analysis
Employment generation	Multiplier analysis
Accelerator effect	Social benefits
Income generation	Poverty alleviation
Employment generation	Cultural benefits
Redistribution of wealth	Environmental benefits
Direct benefit	

Review Questions

Short Answer Type Questions

1. Write in brief about visitor/tourist expenditure.
2. Describe the manner through which tourist spends money in a destination.
3. Discuss how tourism can be considered an export.
4. Write the significance of tourism in the balance of payments of a country.

5. What are the opportunities for government revenue from tourism?
6. Discuss the potentials of tourism in employment generation.
7. Elucidate how tourism can enhance investment potential of a region.
8. Discuss the role of tourism in economic diversification.
9. Write how tourism is useful for employment generation.
10. Comprehend the potential of tourism in redistribution of wealth.
11. Distinguish between direct, indirect and induced economic effects.
12. Explain multiplier effect in tourism.
13. Write short notes on different tourism multipliers.
14. Give a brief account on Tourism Satellite Account (TSA).
15. Elucidate multiplier analysis.
16. Write a short note on social benefits of tourism.
17. Write how tourism contributes in poverty alleviation.
18. What are the cultural benefits of tourism?
19. Discuss how tourism benefits environment conservation.

Essay Type Questions

1. Explain economic benefits of tourism.
2. Write an essay on multiplier effect in tourism.
3. Describe the sociocultural benefits of tourism.

11

IMPACTS OF TOURISM

Learning Outcomes

After studying this chapter, you will be able to:

- comprehend the economic consequences of tourism;
- explain opportunity cost, inflation, and migration of labour due to tourism;
- describe social issues due to tourism;
- elucidate Doxey's Irridex of tourist irritation;
- explain cultural implications; and
- comprehend various impacts on nature and ecosystem as a result of tourism development.

11.1 INTRODUCTION

Once upon a time, tourism was promoted with the hash tag '*smokeless industry*' (Holden, 2000). Within a few decades, this propaganda reversed and started highlighting tourism as an industry causing irreversible damages on various spheres of life on the earth. The second half of the last century has seen tremendous developments in tourism sector and soon, it started showing consequences of various kinds in varying degrees. As discussed in the previous chapter, contribution of tourism towards economic and regional development was quite significant. But the social, cultural and environmental consequences of tourism became a matter of concern within two decades. The 1970s saw impacts of tourism development on environment, society, and culture. There were local environmental mobilizations against tourism activities in Greece, Spain, and Portugal from the early 1970s as well. Due to the increasing concerns of impacts and sustainability issues, 1990s saw the emergence of a number of newer ideologies and environment-friendly tourism concepts. Those were complimented by favourable policy efforts, planning guidelines, statements of good practices, collaborations, codes of conduct for tourists and the like. It is natural for people belonging to different cultures, lifestyles or social settings to interact and leave an impact on each other. This prevails at a massive scale in tourism. Tourists generally may try to explore the social life at destinations; whereas the local community may attempt to imitate the lifestyle of tourists. Friendships, learning from each other, better understanding among people, etc., are considered positive impacts of tourism. At the same time, there are impacts which have been termed negative. Sometimes, *visitor* is referred to as an agent of change in destinations due to the impacts created directly or indirectly by their actions (Page, 2007).

Though tourism is economically *very* significant for a place, it also causes some economic consequences, say, for instance, *inflation*. Tourism generates a range of issues in society and culture as well. Many examples can be cited worldwide for the negative impacts of tourism in the social and cultural spheres of human life. Adopting pseudo behaviours, involving in drug and mafia activities, inspiring prostitution tendency, loss of local and traditional culture, etc., are considered the major menaces caused due to tourism. Commercialization of art and art forms is another one which can be added to the negative impacts of tourism. But, on the contrary, the preservation and maintenance of culture and cultural features are highlighted as significant positive impacts of tourism. Apart from the impacts in economy, society and culture of the host population, environment and ecology is another important area where tourism causes varied impacts. Different kinds of tourism activities affect the natural and built environment. There is a complex relationship between tourism and the environment. Environmental impacts are inherently multidimensional and these may be irreversible. In other words, tourism tends to destroy tourism itself.

Impacts of tourism to some extent vary according to the type of visitors attracted to an area and their activities while they are at the destination. A range of other factors also influence the nature and quantum of tourism impacts. The impact of tourism on any destination will be determined by a wide variety of factors, some of them are:

- Location: rural/urban, coastal/inland, developed/developing country.
- Scale: how many tourists are involved, etc.
- Tourists: type, origin, etc.
- Type of activities: passive or active, are they consumptive resources, high/low level of interaction with local population.
- Infrastructure (road, sewage system)
- Duration of the establishment of tourism.
- Season: time, duration (Davidson, 1996; Mason, 2008)

Apart from this, the interests of various stakeholders in preserving and maintaining local environment and culture constitute an important determinant in generating impacts. The political factors, including policies also have the capacity to influence impacts of tourism. Tourism is functioning in different environments and these environments play a role in determining impacts. The greater the economic and social diversity of the destination, the more facilities it has for visitors, and more easily will it accommodate additional tourists. In practice, it has been reported that the destination area's landforms and ecology, its economic and social structure and political organization determine the form and structure within which tourist activity produces specific local results. The carrying capacity of a destination has an important role in determining the impact of tourism. A variety of factors determine the carrying capacity like social structure, culture, environment, political structure, tourist activities, tourist characteristics, etc. Such factors are classified as either *local* factors and *alien* factors. The local and alien factors, manipulated by planning and management of tourism development, will result in impacts on the social structure, culture, environment and economic structure.

Given the interaction of the local and alien factors within the host environment, the planning and management process should aim to secure the maximum positive benefits while incurring minimum costs. Laws (1995) has come up with a *systems model* (destination system model) which suggests that introducing or expanding tourism in any region/area results in multifarious changes. Care has to be taken to control the factors leading to negative impacts and to enhance positive benefits. The following description will give an idea about the various identified/reported positive and negative impacts of tourism.

11.2 ECONOMIC IMPACTS

Benefits or the positive impacts of tourism have already been discussed in the previous chapter. Despite the fact that tourism is considered more for its economic significance, there are some consequences as well. Some of the commonly discussed economic impacts of tourism are:

- Inflation
- Migration of labour
- Overdependence on tourism
- Opportunity cost
- Seasonal character of jobs
- Friction at different job levels
- Economic inequality
- Leakage of economic benefits

11.2.1 Inflation

Tourism is a major determinant of inflation in geographical regions where mass tourism is established. *Inflation* is the steady rise in prices of various goods and services, as measured by some broad index (such as CPI) over months or years. Inflation relates to the increase in prices of land, houses and even food that can occur as a result of tourism. Prices for these commodities can increase when tourists place extra demands on local services at a tourism destination. This leads to decline of the value or worth of money as well. Increasing demand for basic services and goods by tourists often causes price hikes that negatively affect local residents whose income does not increase proportionately. Tourism can sometimes inflate the cost of housing and retail prices in the area, frequently on a seasonal basis. Inflation related to tourism is mainly associated with the steady temporary hike in prices of land, houses and other accommodation units, and food. Tourists constitute a group of consumers from outside the economy and who stay at any destination for a limited period of time. Tourists bring additional financial resources into the economy, and if the supply of goods and services cannot adapt according to the increasing demand, the general price levels tend to increase. Their knowledge about the prices and bargaining capacity has a limitation. Moreover, in peak seasons the demand for various tourism products and services will be maximum. These circumstances lead to inflation which the local community also has to bear. It is also seen widely that the same product has different price levels in a tourism destination and in a non-tourist area. Outbound tourism, at times, may cause deflation as well.

11.2.2 Migration of Labour

When tourism development occurs in rural areas, possibilities arise for *migration of labour* towards the tourism sector. In such areas, primary sectors of production like agriculture, fishing, etc., would have been the major source of employment before the arrival of tourism. But the introduction of tourism will generate employment opportunities there, and usually a share of the population employed in primary sector may move to tourism sector for employment since it may provide jobs with better salaries, etc. In tourism sector, they may be employed in non-skilled categories, but, they might had been skilled employees in the former sector. This will affect labour in primary sector, which may suffer from lack of enough skilled labour. This will raise the cost of labour and ultimately, production cost. This scenario may occur in urban tourism also where labour units may be migrated from rural areas. The migrated labour units are likely to experience additional infrastructure pressure for health, education and other public services.

11.2.3 Overdependence on Tourism

If a country becomes overdependent on tourism, a decrease in tourism revenue can be devastating. Tourism becomes the main economic sector in some of the tourist destinations the dependence on it reaches the maximum level when destinations get established for mass tourism. *Overdependence on tourism* can occur, for example, in small states where tourism is seen by the government as the best method of development. Over time, emphasis on tourism becomes such that there is virtually no other approach to development. As a result, the country becomes dependent on tourism revenue to the extent that any change in demand is likely to lead to a major economic crisis.

Tourism related industries flourish and thus, tourism becomes the main income and employment source. The tourism industry is extremely vulnerable to economic, social, and political changes in either the generating or host countries. A major incident can dampen tourism substantially. For instance, in Bali, Indonesia, when terrorist attacks happened, the whole economy had a catastrophic effect and it took some years to recover from it. Let us see the illustration given by UNEP.

"In the Gambia, for instance, 30% of the workforce depends directly or indirectly on tourism. In small island developing states, percentages can range from 83% in the Maldives to 21% in the Seychelles and 34% in Jamaica, according to the WTO. Over-reliance on tourism, especially mass tourism, carries significant risks to tourism-dependent economies. Economic recession and the impacts of natural disasters such as tropical storms and cyclones as well as changing tourism patterns can have a devastating effect on the local tourism sector" (www.unep.org).

11.2.4 Opportunity Cost

Tourism development can cost the local government and local taxpayers a great deal of money since tourism development necessitates immense investment in creating infrastructure and superstructure. *Opportunity cost* refers to the cost of engaging in tourism compared to another economic activity. The opportunity cost of given economic resources is the foregone benefit from the next best alternative use of those resources, i.e., the sacrifice or loss of alternative use of a given resource is termed "opportunity cost". It refers to the cost of engaging in tourism rather than another form of economic activity. For example, in a coastal area, with a predominantly rural hinterland, this could be the costs of investing in tourism instead of arable farming, market gardening or fishing. Public resources spent on subsidized infrastructure or tax breaks may reduce government investment in other critical areas such as education and health. The use of capital resource (in developing and developed countries, it is often scarce) in the development of tourism related establishments precludes their use for other forms of economic development. The opportunity cost of resources, especially land, is also relevant to be considered in the parlance of tourism as many of the tourism activities consume resources in large quantity. Hence, opportunity cost has to be considered in measuring tourism economic impact.

11.2.5 Seasonal Character of Jobs

Seasonality is a feature of tourism. *Seasonal fluctuation* in tourist arrivals and the changes in demand will severely impact the supply. The seasonal character of the tourism industry creates economic problems for destinations that heavily depend on it. Some of the industries face much difficulty to maintain the human resource during off seasons. Human resource requirement in peak season is often the maximum. Due to this reason, to some extent, some of the industries provide jobs more on contract basis. Moreover, low paid jobs are also a common feature in some of the tourism related industries.

11.2.6 Job Level Friction

As stated above, a good share of employment in tourism is in the low paid category. In developing or undeveloped regions, local community may be able to acquire jobs in the lower strata of the job hierarchy. In such cases, many of the jobs occupied by local people in the tourist industry are at a lower level, such as housemaids, waiters, gardeners and other practical work, while higher-paying and more prestigious managerial jobs go to foreigners or "urbanized" nationals. A range of reasons includes lack of adequate training, qualifications, awareness, etc. Such a situation may lead to friction and irritation among the local community. Moreover, it widens the gap between the tourism sector and the community.

11.2.7 Economic Inequality

Most of the tourists have varied buying behaviour. They, with different consumption patterns and lifestyles, come for pleasure, spending large amounts of money. Locals, on the other hand, feel the difference in economic standards and there is likely to be a growing distinction between the 'haves' and 'have-nots', which may increase social and, at times, ethnic tensions.

11.2.8 Leakage of Economic Benefits

Though the tourism sector utilizes the local resources, the possibility of *economic 'leakage'* from the local economy is very high when the destination supply is dominated by large scale operators and *'enclave tourism'*. In order to get maximum benefit, destinations have to ensure maximum local entrepreneurship and SMEs from the locality.

11.3 SOCIAL CONSEQUENCES

Tourism, as an economic activity, brings many opportunities for employment and income generation. More people in the locality get employment and opportunities for starting enterprises also increases. This leads to the generation of increased income in the society which ultimately leads to having better living conditions and lifestyles. The development of infrastructure for tourism gives enough facilities for the local people also. Regional development is sometimes a result of tourism (e.g., Khajuraho) and by it, the primary conditions necessary for living for a population emerge like education facilities, health facilities, etc. Altogether, the social benefits of tourism cannot be neglected and especially in undeveloped countries, tourism has been promoted as a means for poverty alleviation and regional development. At the same time, tourism's social consequences are well debated world over. A range of issues have been identified. In fact, the nature and the extent of social consequences depend on certain reasons, in general. The following are the dimensions that are identified by UNWTO, 2011 in that regard:

- The type and number of visitors to the community. A general rule of thumb is that greater the number of visitors, higher is the impact, although this is not necessarily always the case as it depends on how visitors integrate with the local community.
- The importance of tourism to the community, especially the level of dependence on this activity.
- The size, scale and pace of development, as a fast growing tourism sector will bring with it considerable levels of change for the community.
- Sociocultural differences between the tourist and host populations.

Added to these factors are:

- The nature of the host-guest contact.
- Community attitudes towards tourism which will be affected by the type of interactions that occur between visitors.
- Residents and the community's levels of tolerance towards tourism.

Major social impacts are:

- Demonstration effect.
- Changing attitudes of host population.
  - Change in hospitality.
  - Pseudo behaviour.
  - Removal of charity.
- Increasing social menaces.
- Displacement of local community.
- Irritation within local community due to tourist behaviour.
- Overcrowding.
- Tourist intrusiveness and intensive interaction.

Demonstration Effect

The likelihood of the host community in a tourist destination being exposed to the nuances of diverse cultures from different parts of the world is high when tourism gets established there. This has both positive as well as negative aspects. On one hand, it helps in learning about other cultures and in cultural exchange. On the other hand, the vulnerability of the local community gets lured by the extravaganza exhibited by the tourists and the possibility of being influenced by it is high. The phenomenon which causes the occurrence of indigenous and rural communities and cultures adopting foreign style and behaviour that they are exposed to due to regular tourist visits is referred to as *demonstration effect*. This attracts local people to the material possession of tourists and they aspire for those. Local people may emulate a leisured and apparently richer lifestyle that is unrealistic and unaffordable. In the long run, it can lead to behavioural changes in the resident population (Williams, 1998). According to Burns (1999), the demonstration effect refers to the process by which traditional societies, especially those which are particularly susceptible to outside influence such as youth, will voluntarily seek to adopt certain behaviours (and accumulate material goods). That possession will lead to achievement of the leisured, hedonistic lifestyle demonstrated by the tourists. This is particularly relevant in undeveloped and developing societies, specifically in traditional societies.

Murphy (1985) is of the opinion that tourists generally possess greater financial and leisure time affluence than many locals, and their holiday experiences are based frequently upon conspicuous consumption. This primarily involves the tendency of the host population emulating their behaviour, especially their consumption practices. It also can lead to residents' jealously, resentment, and even hatred towards tourists, when locals see they are unable to be as wealthy as tourists and have the same standard of living (Reisinger, 2009). Young people are particularly susceptible to the demonstration effect. Tourism may then be blamed for societal divisions between the young and older members. The demonstration effect may also encourage the more able younger members of a society to migrate from rural areas in search of the 'demonstrated' lifestyle in urban areas or even overseas.

Changing attitudes of host population

Mass tourism can bring different changes in the attitudes of a self-contained, small community with simple, basic lifestyle, living in remote locations. Usually, attitudes and others shall change in a very slow manner. This can be positive also, but generally it has resulted in some negative impacts. Some areas of attitudinal and behavioural changes due to tourism are as follows:

- **Change in hospitality:** Even peace-loving, nature-friendly host population can react with hostility towards tourists who constantly clash with traditions and customs of the country they are visiting. In religious aspects, this dominates and in some places continuous tourist-host conflicts and clashes have been reported.
- **Imitation:** Another possible response of the host population to tourists is that of imitation. This is discussed above under demonstration effect.

- **Pseudo behaviour:** In the context of commercialization and in retail businesses, the host community involved will only be concentrating on selling and getting profits. Pleasing the tourists and convincing them to buy as many products will be the main concern. This situation may lead the host population to have pseudo behaviour throughout their approach in tourism activities.
- **Removal of charity:** The relationship between the host population and the tourists becomes a commercial one, with tourism becoming a business. As a result, the custom of giving charity (prevails in some cultures) to visitors either disappears completely, or the host population takes steps to defend themselves from going bankrupt through their own generosity.

Increasing social menaces

In many areas, tourism encourages numerous antisocial activities knowingly or unknowingly. From the sustainable point of view, such situations are big issues and should be controlled. Prostitution is one such area on which discussions have been going on worldwide. The presence of large member of tourists carrying relatively large sums of money and valuables with them provides a source of illegal activities including drugs trafficking, robbery and violence. There have been rampant complaints that tourism opens the gates for both male and female prostitution. Child abuse is another threatening area in relation to social impacts of tourism. International tourists are sometimes obvious victims of crime where they are clearly identifiable by language or colour and can be expected to be carrying significant sums of money with them.

Displacement of local community

Tourism development directly or indirectly may cause displacing local community from their habitats. At times, it happens forcibly and in a quick succession of time. Gradual displacement as tourism industries expand is very common. Tourism Concern, a global voluntary organization, illustrates it in the following manner.

"Tourism development has caused many communities to be forcibly displaced. Indigenous groups, people living in informal settlements, or who lack official title deeds to their lands are particularly vulnerable to displacement or loss of access to lands and waters essential for their livelihoods. This often happens with little or no warning, compensation or alternative provision. Governments and private companies have forced many tribal people from their ancestral lands to make way for national parks and *ecotourism*. Fishing communities are removed from their coastal villages and blocked from accessing the sea as hotels are built and beaches are privatised, destroying livelihoods and traditional ways of life. Informal settlements are bulldozed under beautification projects to encourage international sporting events. The arrival of mass tourism can seriously disrupt thriving local communities; small businesses are forced to compete with well-established multinational companies; land prices and the basic cost of living commonly escalate, and competition over scarce natural resources, such as water, can intensify, with wealthy tourism developers usually winning over the basic needs of local people"(www.tourismconcern.org.uk).

The following is a case of local people migration due to increase in tourism.

"Cape May County's year-round population continues to shrink even as its tourism industry posts record numbers. The county lost 2.5 per cent of its population over the past five years, down to 94,727 in 2015, according to U.S. Census figures. Economists and county officials say the high price of homes in the area combined with comparatively fewer year-round jobs is keeping newcomers out and prompting recent graduates to look elsewhere for work." (Miller, 2016)

Irritation due to Tourist Behaviour

Tourists, out of ignorance or carelessness, often fail to respect local customs and moral values. When they do so, they unknowingly bring about irritation and stereotyping. Recurring cultural and social clashes and tourism behaviour can cause irritation among the local people. Doxey's *Irridex* is a model that describes the changes in local people's attitude towards tourists at different phases of tourism evolution in a destination. It says there are four distinct stages and in each stage, local people behave differently. The stages are as follows:

- **Euphoria:** Soon after the initial development of tourism, visitors and investors are welcome; locals are excited over tourists' visit; little planning or control mechanism. Local people feel happy to welcome tourists.
- **Apathy:** Along with tourism development, visitors are taken for granted and contacts between residents and outsiders become more formal (commercial). Locals become more indifferent to tourists, and planning is directed towards marketing.
- **Annoyance:** As tourism gets established and saturation points approach, "hosts" have misgivings about tourism and get irritated with the tourists presence. Policy makers attempt solutions via increasing infrastructure (rather than limiting growth).
- **Antagonism:** Where residents became tourist averse and tensions, conflict and anti-tourism feelings became widespread. Irritations are openly expressed since visitors are seen as the cause of all problems. In this stage, planning turns to be remedial and promotion is increased to offset deteriorating reputation of destination (Doxey, 1976).

Overcrowding

In mass tourism destinations, crowding is a major issue. This affects the quality of tourist experience. Moreover, local people get suffocated and disturbed. Roads face congestion. Parking spaces get occupied by tourist vehicles. Traffic congestion is an inevitable consequence of some tourism activities, such as special events. A new project can increase traffic congestion in its vicinity.

Tourist intrusiveness and intensive interaction

Increasing tourism in a rural location can cause intrusion by foreigners into their privacy. Local people's social life can also be affected by regular tourism beyond a certain limit. Moreover, tourism of that kind can cause intensive interaction between tourists and local community. This can lead to some social and cultural consequences for local community.

11.4 CULTURAL IMPACTS

The sociocultural impacts of tourism is a subject drawing the attention of social scientists and planners, especially those responsible for developing tourism in the third world. Among the most debated issues pertaining to tourism in the third world are those related to the effects that tourists and the industry have on societies and the cultures of local communities. On the contrary to the benefits, tourism has severely affected indigenous customs and way of life. Any influx of tourism, however small, will make some impact on a region, but the extent of it is dependent on many factors. In the developed western countries, such impacts are considerably less in comparison with developing and undeveloped countries and the types of impact are also different to some extent. For many, tourism is, in fact, a bridge between people, fostering communication, mutual understanding and a desirable redistribution of wealth. To others, tourism is a negative factor destroying traditions, customs, manners, and environment. They view tourism as *cultural imperialism*. It has been proved that improperly planned tourism generates different sociocultural negative impacts in addition to the environmental hazards. Although it is difficult to generalize, sociocultural impacts will typically depend upon the degree of cultural similarity or dissimilarity between the tourists and hosts (UNWTO, 2011).

The major cultural impacts include:

- Commercialization
- Commoditization
- Staged authenticity and 'pseudo events'
- "Human zoo"
- Cultural changes and 'acculturation'
- Reduction in cultural diversity and homogenization of culture
- Cultural clashes

11.4.1 Commercialization

Tourism contributes in preserving the art and art forms. But at the same time, in some cases, it leads to mass commercialization of art and art forms. When a painter makes a painting, his mind fills with euphoria and he keeps a kind of sanctity in the same. When, opportunities for selling it in many numbers arise, the painter may forget, side line or avoid the sanctity and love towards the production of an art form, and may try to produce as many paintings in a short span of time. Hence, the profit he gets will be dominated by producing the art form. This is a simple example. But commercialization at large scale happens in relation to tourism. In one sense it is good that people get a livelihood, but on the other side, the art production loses its sanctity and perfection, which may lead to a distorted image of the art form. *Trivialization of culture* is another term used in this regard. It also means that the traditional ceremonies and rituals are shortened or modified to tourist products.

11.4.2 Commoditization

When a destination is promoted as a tourism product, the increasing demand for souvenirs, arts, entertainment and other commodities begins to exert influence, basic changes in human values may occur. It has been reported that, in many of the fragile and ancient cultures, indigenous people's art and culture have been over-commoditized. Culture becomes a commodity for financial transactions. It causes "the presentation of an entity as a market product available for sale. Problems occur when the entity was not intended to be sold, where there are non-market values attached to it, and where ownership does not lie with any individual or organizations" (Kelly and Nankervis, 2009). Mason (2008) defines *commoditization* as "demand for cultural aspects and performances has become packaged for convenient consumption by visitors." The traditional objects that are marketed as new products may not have the true value and meaning. *Reconstructed ethnicity* can be part of this. It happens when tourism turns local cultures into commodities when religious rituals, traditional ethnic rites and festivals are reduced and sanitized to conform to tourist expectations. Religious sites, objects, cultural features and rituals may not be respected when they are perceived as goods for trade.

11.4.3 Staged Authenticity and 'Pseudo Events'

Similar to commercialization, in order to attract tourists *cultural shows* are performed which are devoid of intrinsic meaning, and this is referred to as '*staged authenticity*'. It denotes adapting of cultural expressions and manifestations to the tastes of tourists or even performing shows as if they were "real life". Dean MacCannell introduced this concept in tourism with ample illustrations in his book, *The Tourist: A New Theory of the*

Leisure Class (1999). It has become a trend nowadays to organize such cultural shows for tourists, particularly when mass tourists arrive as part of package tours. Regular inauthentic performances can lead to forgetting true meaning and significance of the practice or event. *Pseudo events* are planned, rather than spontaneous, and designed to be performed at times that are convenient for tourists. They hold at best an ambiguous relationship to real elements on which they are based (Mason, 1995; Williams, 1998). Also, of particular concern, as Williams noted, is that these pseudo events eventually become the authentic events and replace the original events or practice.

11.14.4 "Human zoo"

This is another terminology used in similar context. Indigenous people displayed their customs and their attire: this was a practice, which was racial too, occurred in some parts of the world in the annals of history. People were kept in cages or inside fenced areas, and exhibited in the same way as animals. Others watched them with much enthusiasm due to the strangeness of colour, customs, costumes, traditions, and so on. The term *human Zoo* is used to refer to this barbaric form of entertainment of the so-called modern men of that era. In some locations, exhibitions of varying levels, similar to that primitive act are arranged to be exhibited before the tourists who get the pleasure of seeing the strangeness of some communities.

11.4.5 Cultural Changes and 'Acculturation'

The overall cultural features of a society can be influenced by continuous mass tourism for a long time. The reasons for that situation can be different. The society interested in tourism activities may adapt to new culture by which they can entertain tourism activities effectively. Such a change is often called *acculturation*. Williams (1998) define acculturation as: "When two cultures come into contact for any length of time, an exchange of ideas and products takes place that, through time, produces varying levels of convergence between the cultures; that is they become similar" (Williams, 1998).

11.4.6 Reduction in Cultural Diversity and Homogenization of Culture

Tourism services are now promoted in the same manner in most of the locations in the world. Many aspects of it are gaining homogenization. Hospitality is an example. The style of food serving, services offered, facilities, etc., are becoming similar everywhere in the world. Food sector is another example. Almost all the destinations have some of the same products available. *Homogenization* is all about the spread of western ideas and values into indigenous and rural communities across the world. Dressing styles and modern art forms are also getting homogenized. This results in reduction of cultural diversity in the world.

11.4.7 Cultural Clashes

Cultural clashes can take place as a result of differences in cultures, ethnic and religious groups, values and lifestyles, languages, and levels of prosperity. Tourism is a social process that leads to the mingling of different cultures. Moreover, when tourists do not respect the values and spirit of local cultures, the possibility of cultural clashes are high.

11.5 ENVIRONMENTAL IMPACTS OF TOURISM

The environment, whether it is natural or man-made, is the most fundamental ingredient of the tourism product. However, as soon as tourism activity takes place, the environment is inevitably changed or modified either to facilitate tourism or during the tourism process (Cooper et al., 2000). Different kinds of tourism activities affect the natural and built environment. There is a complex interaction between tourism and the environment. Many studies have shown that tourism has immense impact on the physical environment and that little has been done to correct or control the assault on ecology. The environment in which tourism takes place is important to the quality of tourist experience. Both natural environment in the form of land, water, plants and animals and manmade environment, which includes buildings and streets, form the foundation of the tourism industry. In the absence of an attractive environment tourism rarely succeeds, because it is one of the vital elements which tourists look for in a destination.

Environmental impacts of tourism are more site-specific. Yet, some of them are seen widely. There are some factors that act as determinants of environmental impacts of tourism. The following are some major ones.

- Location of tourism: where it takes place like urban or rural, etc.
- Type of tourism activities in the destination. Some cause more damage.
- Nature of tourist infrastructure: type and nature of tourist facilities in a destination.
- Extent of tourism development: vulnerability increases along with increase in tourism development.
- Time of activity like seasonal variations.
- Density of population.
- Duration of visitation: visits for longer periods may damage more.
- Duration of season: if the seasons are short, damage may be less.
- Fragility of location: the more fragile, the more vulnerable.
- Resilience of ecosystem to withstand and recover.

Much of the damage done to the environment as a result of tourism is caused simply by the volume of tourists arriving at the destinations which are not used to supporting people in great numbers and improper planning and infrastructure development. A variety of negative environmental effects are reported from tourism areas all over the world and the types of impacts vary. In general, the more ecologically fragile a destination is, more will be the chances for damage. *Fragility* and *environmental* (ecological) damage have a direct relationship. Like economic and sociocultural impacts, the environmental impacts of tourism development can generate indirect effects as well in addition to the direct effect. The following constitute some of the major environmental impacts of tourism:

- Pollution
- Physical damage
- Waste disposal and sewage
- Erosion
- Depletion of natural resources
- Loss of biodiversity
- Deforestation and disturbance to animals
- Emissions and climate change
- Aesthetic pollution/visual pollution/architectural pollution

11.5.1 Pollution

Mass tourism leads to different kinds of pollution. It affects the quality of water, air, and noise levels. The hotels' sewage disposal, disposal from boats and other motorized water transporting vehicles, etc. pollute the water. Vehicle emissions and others pollute the quality of air. Night camps, discos, transportation, etc. create noise pollution and when the destinations are in forest areas, these disturb the fauna in the forest. The following types of pollution take place due to tourism:

- Air pollution: from transport like cars, buses, etc.
- Water pollution: disposal from boats, waste, chemicals from gardens, airports, etc.
- Noise pollution: from airplanes, cars, and buses, as well as recreational vehicles such as snowmobiles and jet skiis, etc.
- Soil pollution: waste disposal, littering, chemicals from different sources, etc.

11.5.2 Physical Damage

Physical deterioration of both natural and manmade environments pose serious consequences. Attractive landscape sites, such as sandy beaches, lakes, riversides, and mountain tops and slopes, are often transitional zones, characterized by species-rich ecosystems. Landscape destruction and loss of natural beauty is a common impact world over. The development of tourism can involve sand mining, beach and sand dune erosion, soil erosion and extensive paving. Deterioration of the ecosystems is a common issue and contribution of tourism in the destinations is quite severe. Crowding and congestion is another issue that leads to damage of nature and ecosystems. Overuse of the infrastructure can also create problems. Hunting and fishing have obvious impacts on the wildlife environment. Sand dunes tend to damage by overuse.

11.5.3 Waste Disposal and Sewage

Waste disposal is a serious problem and improper disposal can cause further environmental issues. Tourist activities cause littering on rivers, scenic areas, and roadsides. Tourism industries like hotels and resorts too dispose of wastes of various kinds. Many of the destinations do not have effective and efficient waste mechanisms. Sewage is another issue. According to UNEP, "Wastewater has polluted seas and lakes surrounding tourist attractions, damaging the flora and fauna. Sewage runoff causes serious damage to coral reefs because it stimulates the growth of algae, which cover the filter-feeding corals, hindering their ability to survive. Changes in salinity and siltation can have wide-ranging impacts on coastal environments. And sewage pollution can threaten the health of humans and animals" (www.unep.org).

11.5.4 Erosion

Erosion takes place at different occasions. For instance, on coastal areas it is more as removal of vegetation covers expose the beach to sea storms. Construction activities of various kinds on different locations cause erosion due to rain. Overdevelopment may cause chances for landslides/slips, damage to riverbanks, sea coasts and increased soil erosion.

11.5.5 Depletion of Natural Resources

Large scale tourism activities create issues in relation to natural resources especially when resources are scarce. It has been reported that tourists' water consumption is much higher than that of local people. Overuse of water resources by hotels, golf courses and personal use by tourists can result in water shortages and degradation of water supplies, as well as generating greater volumes of waste water. Too much pressure can be exerted by tourism on local resources like energy, food, and other raw materials that may already be in short supply. Increasing transport needs for tourism can result in shortage of fossil fuels as well.

11.5.6 Loss of Biodiversity

This aspect is more serious in nature related tourism and tourism in forest areas. The rich natural resources attract more tourists and consequently, can severely affect the biodiversity there. Though at times large animals are protected, smaller living beings and floral diversity get neglected in many a cases. Regular tourist arrivals, constructions, facilities and services, souvenir collection, etc., can dampen the biodiversity richness.

Table 11.1: Potential impacts of tourism on the environment (Green's checklist)

Natural environment

A. Changes in floral and faunal species composition

- Disruption of breeding habits
- Killing of animals through hunting
- Killing of animals in order to supply goods for souvenir trade
- Inward or outward migration of animals
- Destruction of vegetation: gathering wood or plants
- Change in extent and/or nature of vegetation cover through removal or planting to accommodate tourist facilities
- Creation of wildlife reserves/sanctuaries

B. Pollution

- Water pollution through discharges of sewage, spillages of oil/petrol
- Air pollution from vehicular emissions
- Noise pollution from tourist transportation and activities

C. Erosion

- Compaction of soils causing increased surface run-off and erosion
- Change in risk of occurrence of land slips/slides or avalanches
- Damage to geological features (e.g., caves)
- Damage to riverbanks

D. Natural resources

- Depletion of ground and surface water supplies
- Depletion of fossil fuels to generate energy for tourist activity
- Change in risk of occurrence of fire

E. Visual impact

- Facilities (e.g., buildings, chairlift, car parking)
- Litter

Built environment

A. Urban environment

- Land taken out of primary production
- Change of hydrological patterns

B. Visual impact

- Growth of the built-up area
- New architectural styles
- People and their belongings

C. Infrastructure

- Overload of infrastructure (roads, railways, car parking, electricity grid, communication systems, waste disposal, and water supply).
- Provision of new infrastructure
- Environmental management to adapt areas for tourist use (e.g., sea walls, land reclamation)

D. Urban form

- Changes in residential, retail or industrial land uses (e.g., transition from houses to hotels/ boarding houses)
- Changes to the urban fabric (e.g., roads, pavements)
- Emergence of contrasts between urban areas developed for the tourist population and those for the host population

E. Restoration

- Reuse of disused buildings
- Restoration and preservation of historical buildings and sites
- Restoration of derelict buildings as second homes

F. Competition

- Possible decline of tourist attractions or regions because of the opening of other attractions or a change in tourist habits and preferences.

Source: Green & Hunter (1992).

Loss of biodiversity is more relevant when land and resources are strained by excessive use, and when impacts on vegetation, wildlife, mountain, marine and coastal environments and water resources exceed the carrying capacity. Moreover, tourism itself is affected by the loss of biodiversity when the place loses its charm due to the loss of biodiversity.

11.5.7 Deforestation and Disturbance to Animals

Forests, too, are vulnerable to the impacts of tourism. Mass movement of tourists is always a problem for the wildlife. It may cause disruption to breeding habitats especially in the cases of species which make breeding arrangements on land. Regular visitation of tourists may force animals to migrate to other places. The free movement of animals is also disrupted by tourist activities. Tourists are always fond of souvenirs, and when they are exotic, the attractiveness increases. In destinations closer to forests chances of souvenir makers to kill small or even big animals to make souvenir items using their skin or other parts increase. Some purely profit-minded tour operators practise unethical ways to attract animals to be shown to tourists and even provide hunting opportunities at times. Clearing land for roads and constructions, trampling by walkers, vehicle movement and plant souveniring are also common as part of tourism development. The following are some consequences:

- Disturbing species diversity : less resistant plants may be displaced by introduction of new plants.
- Disruption of habitats' equilibrium.
- Animal's foraging routes and feeding habits are disrupted.
- Breeding areas are abandoned as unsafe for some living beings.

11.5.8 Emissions and Climate Change

Tourism is a significant contributor of carbon emission. It also contributes to ozone layer depletion that eventually leads to climate change. Aviation sector contributes a large share in it.

11.5.9 Aesthetic Pollution/Visual pollution/Architectural Pollution

This is another impact of tourism on nature. Basically, it refers to the loss of natural beauty or traditional architectural aesthetics due to construction. Highrise hotels and resorts of disparate design can look out of place in any natural environment and may clash with the indigenous structural design. These are so common in coastal tourism as well as in hill stations. "*Visual pollution* generally refers to those elements of the landscape that the community finds unattractive, including badly maintained buildings, advertisements (hoardings), business signs, telephone and utility poles, weeds, garbage dumps and litter" (Albuquerqus Environmental Society/CPR Environmental Education Service). Tourism can cause all such aspects that lead to visual pollution. The effect of inappropriate development of buildings is also referred to as *architectural pollution*. Constructing highrise hotels on beaches, for instance, is considered an *environmental rape*.

11.5.10 Some Other Impacts include

- Geological formations are vulnerable to wear and tear.
- Skiing mountain slopes are subject to clearance and increased frequency.
- Some caves are damaged by fossicking, vandalism, chemical reactions.
- Trampling: Tourists using the same trail over and over again tramples the vegetation and soil.
- Anchoring, snorkeling, sport fishing and scuba diving, yachting, cruising, etc., can degrade marine ecosystems such as coral reefs.
- Erosion may also occur on river and lake banks.
- Swamp and lagoons are drained, landfilled/canalized for development.

11.6 CONCLUSION

Tourism, though perceived once as a *smokeless industry*, is no more a pure sector; rather it generates a wide range of impacts on economy, society, culture and environment. In the economy it causes inflation, migration of labour, overdependence on tourism, opportunity cost, seasonal character of jobs, economic inequality, and leakage of economic benefits. The impacts on the society include demonstration effect, changing attitudes of the host population, increasing social menace, displacement of local communities and irritation towards tourists. Cultural impacts are also diverse and include commercialization, commoditization, staged authenticity, human zooification, acculturation, reduction in cultural diversity and homogenization of culture, and cultural clashes. Environment is affected badly by tourism in many ways. Pollution is a common concern of tourism. Others include physical damage, waste disposal and sewage, erosion, depletion of natural resources, loss of biodiversity, deforestation and disturbance to animals and emissions contributing to climate change.

Key Terms

Inflation
Migration of labour
Overdependence on tourism
Opportunity cost
Seasonal character of jobs
Job level friction
Economic inequality
Leakage of economic benefits
Demonstration effect
Changing attitudes of host population
Change in hospitality
Pseudo behaviour
Removal of charity
Increasing social menace
Displacement of local community
Irritation within local community
Overcrowding
Tourist intrusiveness
Commercialization
Commoditization
Staged authenticity and pseudo events
Human zoo
Cultural changes and acculturation
Reduction in cultural diversity
Homogenization of culture
Cultural clashes
Pollution
Physical damage
Waste disposal and sewage
Erosion
Depletion of natural resources
Loss of biodiversity
Deforestation and disturbance to animals
Emissions and climate change
Aesthetic pollution
Visual pollution
Architectural pollution

Review Questions

Short Answer Type Questions.

1. Explain inflation due to tourism.
2. What do you mean by migration of labour due to tourism development.

3. Discuss overdependence on tourism.
4. Define opportunity cost.
5. Elucidate economic inequality as a result of tourism.
6. Discuss how leakage of economic benefits takes place.
7. Explain the demonstration effect of tourism.
8. What types of attitudinal changes take place in the host community due to tourism?
9. What are the various bad social impacts of tourism?
10. Write about displacement of local community from tourism destinations.
11. Explain Doxey's Irridex.
12. Elaborate commercialization in tourism.
13. What do you mean by commoditization in tourism?
14. Elucidate 'staged authenticity' in tourist destinations.
15. Define "human zoo", with respect to tourism.
16. Discuss about cultural changes as a result of tourism.
17. How reduction in cultural diversity and homogenization of culture take place as a result of tourism?
18. Discuss various kinds of pollution in tourism.
19. Write how flora and fauna are affected by tourism.
20. Define aesthetic pollution and write tourism's role in it.

Essay Type Questions

1. Explain economic consequences of tourism.
2. Discuss in detail the social issues due to tourism development.
3. Elaborate cultural impacts of tourism, citing suitable examples from Indian tourism.
4. Explain environmental impacts of tourism.

12 SUSTAINABLE TOURISM

Learning Outcomes

After studying this chapter, you will be able to:

- define sustainable tourism, ecotourism and responsible tourism;
- explain the concept and principles of sustainable tourism;
- elucidate different types of sustainable tourism;
- describe the concept and types of carrying capacities;
- explain environmental impact assessment; and
- comprehend other measures for sustainable tourism, such as environmental auditing, cost-benefit analysis, visitor management, recreation opportunity spectrum and limit to acceptable change.

12.1 INTRODUCTION

The tremendous and vigorous industrial developments in the last century generated many kinds of problems on the earth. This resulted in the growing environmental concerns of development. The origin of environmental consideration and social equity concerns can be dated back to the nineteenth century and the Garden city movement in the UK, which was formed in 1898, is an example for this. The idea of planning for development had begun from the starting of the last century and the environmental and land use considerations started soon after. The decades 1960s and 1970s have been marked by the intensification and spread of pollution—one of the primary issues development generates. 1960s witnessed the rebirth of environmentalism, not as a unitary movement, but sectionalized into diversity of groups and ideologies. Pollution and environmental changes were the main themes in all kinds of discussions and meetings in relation to development and its problems. But still, concrete steps and strategies to ameliorate the problems were not evolved.

The Stockholm conference on the human environment (1972) was a milestone in the history of international environmental protection summits and it resulted in the development of an international policy. Establishment of United Nations Environmental Programme was a big achievement of the conference and various national environmental protection agencies were created, especially in the northern developed countries. The US Global 2000 Report (formulated in 1980) appeared to confirm environmental declarations about the consequences of the neglect of the global common interest and overexploitation of open access of resources.

During this period, the case related to natural resource limitations was also put under discussion. Clark (1996) introduced the term, *bioeconomic equilibrium*, which emphasized this aspect. 1980s saw a reorientation of some environmentalist thinking. The term sustainability slowly emerged, initially in relation to the use of resources and then it appeared in a range of contexts (environmental and developmental) and probably, most prominently in publications like the World Conservation Strategy and the UK response to that document as set out by the conservation and development programme, UK, 1982.

Numerous reports warned that the future of the earth was under threat because of imbalances in the consumption of resources. One such important report, titled the World Conservation Strategy specified the concept of sustainable development as well. It was published in 1980 by the International Union for Conservation of Nature and Natural Resources. Another important event, the World Commission on Environment and Development, was held in 1987. It published a report named *Our Common Future*, otherwise known as Brundtland Report. The report gave a clear-cut definition for the term sustainability. It defines sustainability as "meeting the needs of the present without compromising the ability of the future generations to meet their own needs." This has been widely accepted as the basic principle and further developments were supposed to be based on the same.

12.2 SUSTAINABLE DEVELOPMENT

The historic evolution of the concept of sustainability appeared to be accepted as the mediating term designed to bridge the gap between the developers and the environmentalists. But later the concept of sustainability broadened from the idea of just intelligent use of resources to a wider aspect, which included a variety of interrelated factors. Turner (1988) describes sustainability as a broader phenomenon embracing ethical norms pertaining to survival of the living matter, to the rights of the future generations and to the institutions responsible for ensuring that such rights are fully taken into account in policies and actions. The Brundtland Report gave a clear direction for the consideration of the concept of sustainability in all kinds of sustainable developmental priorities all over the world. Murphy (1985) interpreted the Brundtland Report and summarized the components of sustainable development as listed below:

- Establishing ecological limits and more equitable standards for development.
- Redistribution of economic activity and reallocation of resources.
- Population control.
- Conservation of basic resources.
- More equitable access to resources.
- Carrying capacity for each sector has to be considered and sustainable yield is to be followed.
- Retention of resources.
- Minimizing adverse impacts.
- Community control over development decisions affecting the ecosystem.
- Broad national and international frameworks.
- Economic viability.
- Environmental quality.
- Environmental audit, etc.

The components given above clearly demonstrate the diversity in the concept of sustainability. The sustainable development concept was put under rigorous discussions and the beginning of the 1990s saw an increased need for more discussions and implementation of the principles in the industrial scenario. The most important milestone was the Rio Earth Summit. In 1989, the UN expressed deep concern at the serious degradation of the global life-support system and convened the United Nations Conference on Environment and Development in Rio de Janeiro in June, 1992. The purpose and content of the conference was to elaborate strategies and measures to halt and reverse the effects of environmental degradation in the context of strengthening national and international efforts to promote sustainable and environmentally sound development in all countries. The results of the conference were foreseen in six parts:

- The earth charter or declaration of basic principles.
- Agreement on specific legal measures
- New and additional financial resources
- Agenda for action- Agenda 21
- Transfer of technology
- Strengthening of institutional capacities and processes.

Among the parts given above, Agenda 21 is a comprehensive programme of action needed throughout the world to achieve a more sustainable pattern of development for the following centuries. The conference put forward some areas that needed to have particular consideration, like resource utilization, population growth, global atmosphere, fresh water, land use, wildlife and habitats, economic development and sustainability.

Different sections of international machinery were also established to follow up the agreements. A new UN Commission on Sustainable Development (CSD) was set up to monitor the programme, Agenda 21 and the first meeting was held in New York in 1993. Agenda 21 also called on the governments to prepare national strategies for sustainable development and to submit the reports to the CSD.

Afterwards, CSD held many meetings for pursuing the sustainable development of tourism. In addition to that many other meetings were also held later, like, Monterrey Conference on finance and development, Jakarta Mandate on marine and biological diversity, Doha Ministerial Conference, etc., which accept the principles of sustainable development. Another World Summit on Sustainable Development (WSSD) was held in Johannesburg later on. The Summit reaffirmed the stakeholders' collective responsibility to advance, strengthen the interdependent and mutually reinforcing pillars of sustainable development—*economic development, social development* and *environmental protection*—at local, regional and global levels. The committee, in addition to the commonly discussed areas, specifically mentioned commitments to ensure women's empowerment and emancipation and gender equality that are integrated in all activities, and the vital role of indigenous people in sustainable development. WSSD declaration in the section of challenges we face, says that the global environment continues to suffer and biodiversity depletion is one major threat.

12.3 SUSTAINABLE TOURISM DEVELOPMENT

Tourism is a phenomenon arising out of movements of people from their normal place of work and residence to another, their stay and engaging in activities over there. It has been proved that this phenomenon has significant role and relevance in the socio-economic scenario of the people world over. Tourism was initially promoted as a smoke-less and non-polluting industry. But now, it has been experienced that tourism is producing a variety of impacts, and at times the effects are much worse than the impacts generated by the other types of industries. Lot of discussions are being held everywhere in the world related to this. The intensity of the impacts forced the tourism sector to accept the sustainability principles. Increased tensions due to the negative impacts of tourism and the world level concerns about the tourism problems led to many discussions and summits, and they realized the importance of implementing the sustainable development principles in the tourism sector. In addition, the UN agencies concerned wanted the tourism sector also to adopt the sustainability principles. Later on discussions and conferences accepted the concept and adapted the same for applicability in tourism sector.

Giving an exact definition for sustainable tourism is difficult. When we consider the social, cultural and environmental elements of the tourism system, *sustainable tourism* can be defined as "the mass tourism which is economically viable, but does not destroy

Table 12.1: Sustainable development components

Establishing ecological limits and more equitable standards	It requires the promotion of values that initiate consumption standards that are within the bounds of the ecological limits possible and to which all can reasonably aspire.
Redistribution of economic activity and re-allocation of resources	Meeting essential needs depends partly on achieving full growth potential and sustainable development clearly requires economic growth in places where such needs are not being met. Though population control issue is not merely one of population, size of the distribution of resources. Sustainable development can only be pursued if demographic developments are in harmony with the changing productive potential of the ecosystem.
Conservation of basic resources	Sustainable development should not imperil the natural systems that support life on the earth: the atmosphere, the waters, the soils, and the living beings.
More equitable access to resources	Growth has no set limits in terms of population or resource use, beyond which lies ecological disasters. Yet, ultimate limits are there and sustainability requires that long before these are reached, efforts are made to ensure more unbiased access to resources.
Carrying capacity and sustainable yield	Most renewable resources constitute a great share of a complex and interlinked ecosystem, and maximum sustainable yield must be defined after taking into account system-wide effects of exploitation.
Retention of resources	Sustainable development necessitates that the rate of depletion of non-renewable resources foreclose as a few future options as possible.
Diversification of the species	Sustainable development should take care of the conservation of plant and animal species.
Minimize adverse impacts	Sustainable development states that adverse impacts on the quality of air, water, and other natural elements are minimized so as to sustain the ecosystem's overall integrity.
Community control	Community control with regard to development decisions affecting local ecosystems.
Broad national/international policy framework	Biosphere is the common home of all living beings on the earth and joint management of the biosphere is a prerequisite for global political security.
Economic viability	Communities have to pursue economic well-being while recognizing that [government] policies may set limits to material growth.
Environmental quality	Corporate environment policy can be treated as an extension of total quality management.
Environmental audit	An effective environmental audit system forms the core of good environmental management.

Source: Adapted from Murphy (1985), based upon the Brundtland Report, 1987.

the resources on which the future of tourism will depend, notably the physical environment and the social fabric of the host community" (Swarbrooke, 2002). The definition speaks of mass tourism, but sustainable tourism has to be ensured in all forms. Small scale, *niche tourism*, is also considered important in the realm of sustainable tourism. The UNWTO, a promoter of sustainable tourism world over, specifies it in this way: "*Sustainability principles* refer to the environmental, economic, and socio-cultural aspects of tourism development, and a suitable balance must be established between these three dimensions to guarantee its long-term sustainability" (www.unwto.org). According to WTO (1995), sustainable tourism is a model form of economic development that is designed to improve the quality of life of the host community, provide high quality experiences for the visitors, and maintain the quality of the environment on which both the host community and the visitor depend. This type of tourism has to be one sustaining for the future by considering the social, cultural, economical and environmental aspects. The needs and expectations of tourist community and the host community should be taken into consideration. The UNWTO specifies the following principles to be followed while promoting sustainable development in tourism.

- Make optimal use of environmental resources that constitute a key element in tourism development, maintaining essential ecological processes and helping to conserve natural resources and biodiversity.
- Respect the socio-cultural authenticity of host communities, conserve their built and living cultural heritage and traditional values, and contribute to inter-cultural understanding and tolerance.
- Ensure viable, long-term economic operations, providing socioeconomic benefits to all stakeholders that are fairly distributed, including stable employment and income-earning opportunities and social services to host communities, and contributing to poverty alleviation.
- Sustainable tourism development requires the informed participation of all relevant stakeholders, as well as strong political leadership to ensure wide participation and consensus building. Achieving sustainable tourism is a continuous process and it requires constant monitoring of impacts, introducing the necessary preventive and/or corrective measures whenever necessary.
- Sustainable tourism should also maintain a high level of tourist satisfaction and ensure a meaningful experience to the tourists, raising their awareness about sustainability issues and promoting sustainable tourism practices amongst them. (UNWTO/UNEP, 2005).

The principles of sustainable tourism, suggested by Bill Bramwel and others, are:

- The approach sees policy, planning and management as appropriate, and, indeed *essential responses* to the problems of natural and human resources misuse in tourism.

- The approach is generally *not anti-growth*, but it emphasizes that there are limitations to growth and that tourism must be managed within these limits.
- *Long-term* rather than short-term thinking is necessary.
- The concerns of sustainable tourism management are not just environmental, but are also *economic, social, cultural, political* and *managerial*.
- The approach emphasizes the importance of *satisfying human needs* and *aspirations*, which entail a prominent concern for equity and fairness.
- All *stakeholders* need to be consulted and empowered in tourism decision-making, and they also need to be informed about sustainable development issues.
- While sustainable development should be a goal for all policies and actions, putting the ideas of sustainable tourism into practice means recognizing that in reality, there are often *limits* to what will be achieved in short and medium terms.
- An understanding of *how market economies operate*, of the cultures and management procedures of private sector business and of public and voluntary sector organizations, and of the values and attitudes of the public is necessary in order to turn good intentions into practical measures.
- There are frequent *conflicts of interest* over the use of resources, which means that in practice tradeoffs and compromises may be necessary.
- The *balancing of costs and benefits* in decisions on different courses of action must extend to considering how much different individuals and groups will gain or lose (Bramwel et al., 1996).

12.4 COMPONENTS OF SUSTAINABLE TOURISM

The sustainability concept in tourism needs to have some basic areas to be taken under consideration. Sustainability has to be ensured in all the areas vulnerable to impacts. Tourism exerts impacts in the social, cultural and environmental arenas and hence the concept of sustainability has to be ensured in all these areas. Mowforth and Munt (1998) identified four different types of sustainability, such as ecological, social, cultural and economic.

- **Environmental sustainability:** It refers to the sustainability in the ecological and other environmental parameters. There are different dimensions like sustainable use of resources, elimination of impacts, creation of environmental awareness, maintenance and management of the natural features, etc., in a sustainable manner. Effective and efficient use of resources is the most crucial aspect in this. Natural resources need to be used in a minimum way with effective and efficient utilization. Possible impacts should be assessed at the stage of planning and effective measures have to be ensured to avoid these. Moreover, regular monitoring is inevitable once the project comes into effect.

- **Social sustainability:** Tourism causes diverse social impacts. Sustainable tourism should not lead to such impacts, rather it should enable in ensuring equitable distribution of economic benefits among all in the society. Harmony between tourism and the societal objectives and between tourists and the local people are to be initiated. A mutually beneficial tourism with zero impacts on society can endure for a long time. *Social disharmony* may cause barriers for tourism as well. Effective local community participation is essential for ensuring social sustainability.
- **Cultural sustainability:** Tourism has an incredible capacity to rejuvenate the dying arts and art forms, preserve heritage remains and protect the remains of the history. Moreover, tourism helps in *cultural exchange*. On the other hand, tourism can lead to excessive commercialization, commoditization, human zooification, trivialization of culture, etc. Properly planned tourism can enhance the positive effects and minimize the negative impacts. Cultural sustainability refers to ensuring sustainability in the cultural aspects related to tourism.
- **Economic sustainability:** Tourism has to be economically viable and survive for long at a destination. Moreover, it should ensure equitable distribution of economic benefits to each and everyone in the society. Leakage of income generated needs to be restricted, and small- and medium-scale businesses are to be promoted to ensure maximum local entrepreneurship and income generating opportunities for the local people. The benefitrs of tourism have to be enjoyed more by the local community, than the alien societies and large-scale investors from abroad.

Hence, sustainable development of tourism needs to ensure the above-mentioned sustainabilities. While UNWTO initiated sustainable tourism development at various locations in the world, it aims at the following to be achieved:

- **Economic viability:** To ensure the viability and competitiveness of tourism destinations and enterprises, so that they are able to continue to prosper and deliver benefits in the long term.
- **Local prosperity:** To maximize the contribution of tourism to the prosperity of the host destination, including the proportion of visitor spending that is retained locally.
- **Employment quality:** To strengthen the number and quality of local jobs created and supported by tourism, including the level of pay, conditions of service and availability to all without discrimination by gender, race, disability or in any other ways.
- **Social equity:** To seek a widespread distribution of economic and social benefits from tourism throughout the recipient community, including improving opportunities, income and services available to the poor.

- **Visitor fulfilment:** To provide a safe, satisfying and fulfilling experience to visitors, without discrimination by gender, race, disability or in any other ways.
- **Local control:** To engage and empower local communities in planning and decision making about the management and future development of tourism in their area, in consultation with other stakeholders.
- **Community well-being:** To maintain and strengthen the quality of life of local communities, including social structures and access to resources, amenities and life support systems, avoiding any form of social degradation or exploitation.
- **Cultural richness:** To respect and enhance the historic heritage, authentic culture, traditions and distinctiveness of host communities.
- **Physical integrity:** To maintain and enhance the quality of landscapes, both urban and rural, and avoid the physical and visual degradation of the environment
- **Biological diversity:** To support the conservation of natural areas, habitats and wildlife, and minimize damage to them.
- **Resource efficiency:** To minimize the use of scarce and non-renewable resources in the development and operation of tourism facilities and services.
- **Environmental purity:** To minimize the pollution of air, water and land and the generation of waste by tourism enterprises and visitors. (UNWTO/UNEP, 2005)

All these are essential in the sustainable development agenda of any project or region. These have to be followed by all nations and authorities who develop tourism.

12.5 CARRYING CAPACITY

We have already discussed the impacts of tourism. Furthermore, the alternatives for developing tourism in the form of sustainable tourism have also been introduced. Sustainable tourism development is possible not just through implementation, scientific planning and strategic development. A range of measures have to be undertaken to minimize impacts and aim at sustainability. Carrying capacity is one such measure commonly used during the planning and development stages of tourism of a destination. Nature of impacts may vary from one destination to another. The cities of western countries can accommodate more tourists without generating many impacts than cities of developing or undeveloped Asian countries. The rainforests will produce more environmental impact than other kinds of forests when tourism is introduced. Here, *fragility* comes into play. Impacts are quicker and deeper in highly fragile areas. The concept of *carrying capacity* has an important role in this context. Carrying capacity assessment (CCA) as a specific technique that came into being in the 1960s is a method of numerical/computerised calculation for prescribing land-use limits and development control (Clark, 1996). The term *carrying capacity* originated in range management, where it is used to refer to the number of stock that can be supported by a unit of land. As

Table 12.2: Types of carrying capacity

Physical capacity	Economic capacity
This relates to the number of tourists a place can physically accommodate.	The number of tourists that can be welcomed before the local community starts to suffer economic problems, e.g., increased housing values and land prices.
Environmental or ecological capacity	**Social capacity**
The number of tourists that can be accommodated before damage begins to be caused to the environment or ecosystem.	The number of people beyond which social disruption or irrevocable cultural damage will occur.
Infrastructure capacity	**Perceptual capacity**
The number of tourists that can be accommodated by the destination infrastructure.	The number of people a place can welcome before the quality of the tourist experience begins to be adversely affected.

Source: Swarbrooke, 2003.

per the carrying capacity, it can be inferred that every destination is subject to a carrying capacity.

Carrying capacity analysis is a basic technique used in tourism to determine the upper limits of development and visitors use and optimum exploitation of tourism resources. Within the country, carrying capacities need to be established generally for the planning area and calculated more precisely for each development site at the community planning level (Inskeep, 1991). The concept of carrying capacity has its base in resources and their management, and the carrying capacity of a site, resort or even a region refers to its ability to undertake tourism without deteriorating. Cooper et al. (1993) say that "there may be a threshold level of tourist presence beyond which the impacts become unacceptable or intolerable". It shows the level of tourism activity or some other similar parameters that can be sustained into long term without creating serious or irreversible changes to the destination. When carrying capacity is exceeded, it is reported that the negative impacts will increase and positive impacts will diminish.

Carrying capacity can be basically defined as "the amount of tourism a destination can handle" (Goeldner and Ritchie, 2006). UNWTO states that the carrying capacity of a tourist resort may be defined as: "the maximum number of people that may visit a tourist destination at the same time, without causing destruction of the physical, economic and socio-cultural environment and an unacceptable decrease in the quality of the visitors' satisfaction" (UNWTO, 1981). Wall and Mathieson (2005) explain carrying capacity as, "the maximum number of people who can use a site without an unacceptable alteration in the physical environment and without an unacceptable decline in the quality of experiences gained by visitors". Basically, carrying capacity is all about developing or promoting tourism without deteriorating the nature, culture and social fabric, focusing on the threshold limit of the site. Resources and resource management are primary aspects in this. The site should be developed adhering to its capacity, resources should not be overutilized.

Swarbrooke (2003) states that there are several types of carrying capacities in relation to a destination, and those include: physical carrying capacity, environmental carrying capacity, infrastructure capacity, perceptual capacity, and economic carrying capacity (Table 12.2). Cooper et al. (1993) have identified four categories such as physical, biological, psychological and social carrying capacities (Table 12.3).

A diverse range of factors play an important role in generating impacts in the destinations. Some of the factors which influence the carrying capacity of the destination are present in the destination and some are alien to the destination. All such factors that influence in determining the carrying capacity are classified into two categories, *viz.*, local factors and alien factors. The factors are listed in the table given below.

Table 12.3: Factors influencing carrying capacity

Local Factors	Alien Factors
Social structure: This factor has a role in determining carrying capacity of a destination. The social structure of, say, London is much more able to absorb and tolerate the presence of tourists than that of a city in Western Samoa in the South Pacific.	*Tourist characteristics:* The characteristics of tourists are an important factor in determining the social and cultural impact of tourism on the host community. In general, the greater the difference between the local and the visitor's social and cultural background the greater will be the impact and consequent changes.
Culture: It has a role in determining impact. The more unusual the cultural background, the more attractive a destination may become, but the more likely it is to be affected by the presence of tourists.	It also includes visitor expenditure patterns, mode of transport, party structure and size, age, educational background, income, purpose of visit, etc.
Environment: The environment will be changed by the presence of tourists. The more sensitively an environment is balanced, greater is the danger of irreversible environmental damage.	*Types of tourist activity*: The types of tourist activity will be closely linked to the characteristics of the tourists. The presence of certain activities such as gambling can bring social impacts which are far greater in magnitude. Gambling can bring increased risks to the host community in terms of exposure to prostitution, drugs and crime.
Economic structure: In general, the more developed and industrialized the economy, the more robust it will be and such economies are able to secure the maximum benefits from tourism.	
Political structure: Political structure often (not always) reflects the ideals and beliefs of the host community, and can actively encourage or hinder tourism development.	
Resources: When local resources are scarce including infrastructure, then competition will increase for use which will lead to many consequences.	

Source: Cooper et al., 1993.

Table. 12.4: Sample evaluation matrix for environmental impact

Type of Impact	Evaluation of impact				
	No impact	Minor impact	Moderate impact	Serious impact	Comments
Air quality					
Surface water quality					
Groundwater quality					
Road traffic					
Noise levels					
Solid waste disposal system					
Archaeological & historical sites					
Visual amenity					
Natural vegetation					
Wild animal life					

Note: This list of types of impacts is only a sampling. There may be additional or different factors in an actual environmental analysis.

Source: Inskeep, 1991.

12.6 ENVIRONMENTAL IMPACT ASSESSMENT (EIA)

Destination planning involves impact assessment also. *Environmental Impact Assessment* (EIA) was introduced as a tool in the planning process, as a part of environmental management initiatives. EIA procedure is being increasingly applied throughout the world to all types of development, including tourism projects, to ensure that any negative environmental impacts are identified in advance, analyzed and minimized. With the increasing concern about the environmental impacts of development, the EIA procedure has been set out to assess the impacts of the proposed development projects. EIA is considered one of the primary tools for the environmental manager and a useful guide for decision making (Khoshoo, 1991). It has been used by national decision makers in their efforts to prevent further environmental degradation (Sniffer, 1995). EIA process is seen as a means not only of identifying potential impacts but also of enabling integration of the environment and development (Green & Hunter, 1992). EIA is primarily undertaken to identify risks, minimize adverse impacts, determine environmental acceptability and obtain environmentally sound proposals through research, management and monitoring, and also to manage conflict public participation (Peiyi, 2000). According to Middleton and Hawkins (1998), EIA is designed to prevent environment degradation by giving decision makers better information about the likely consequences that developmental actions could have on the environment. It thus informs planning decision and ensures that decision makers take environmental issues into account when making development control decisions.

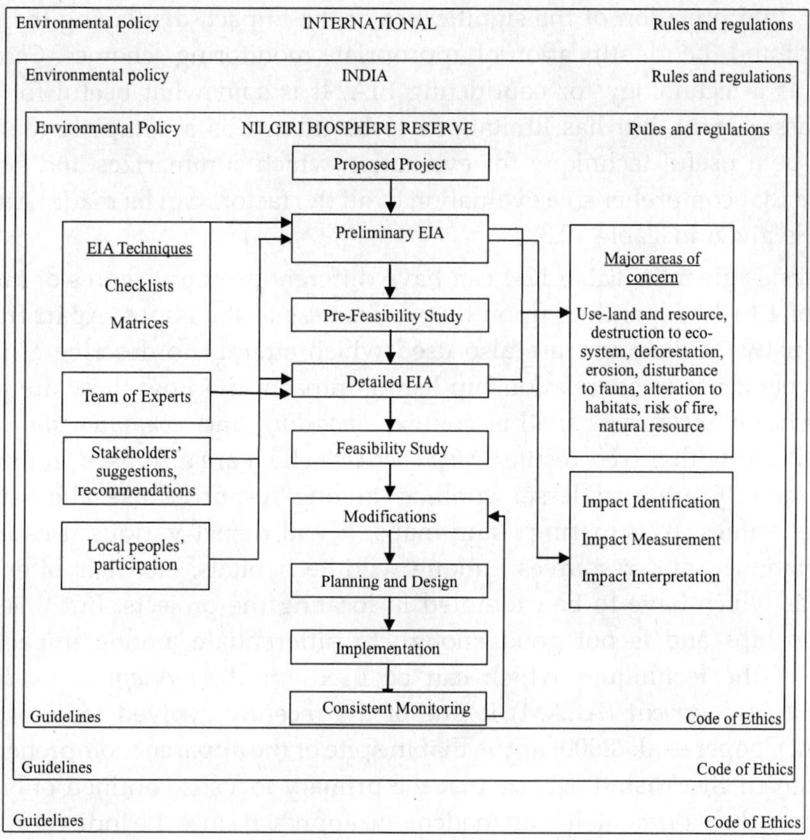

Source: Dileep, 2005.

Figure 12.1 A compact framework of EIA for Nilgiri biosphere reserve.

It is suggested that the assessment will be undertaken by the planner working for the relevant public state policy. The most significant benefit of EIA is the ability for inter-comparison of the developmental options and the screening of alternate sites for locating development projects. For getting maximum benefits, EIA must identify measures to minimize effects and evaluate both the beneficial and adverse environmental impacts of the development project (Khoshoo, 1991).

Generally, identification and measurement of potential impacts are assessed to varying degrees of precision, depending on the nature of the project and the data available. At the planning stage of a proposed project, the significant environmental impacts can be identified and examined, and measures are suggested for prevention or mitigation. There is no set structure for the EIA process, but it is generally assumed that EIAs have to assess future levels of noise pollution, visual impact, air pollution, hydrological impacts, land-use and landscape changes associated with the development. Holden (2000) states that most of the EIAs involve five stages, such as identification of the impact, measurement of the impact, interpretation of the significance of the impact, displaying the results of the assessment and the identification of appropriate monitoring schemes. *Checklists* are widely used as a technology for conducting EIA. It is somewhat useful for having a preliminary assessment, but has limitations to be treated as a complete tool for EIA. *Matrices* will be a useful technique for evaluation which summarizes and synthesizes the impacts so that comprehensive evaluation of all the factors can be made. An example for the same is given in Table 12.3.

The matrices as given in Table 12.4 can have different arbitrary scores of importance on the scale of 1 to 10 depending upon the seriousness of the issues. Apart from these, systems and network diagrams are also used which attempt to describe a little more comprehensively cause-effect relationship listing impacts and how these are generated through effects on resources. In this context, *modeling* and *computer simulation* are sometimes utilized with mixed results. *Map overlays* which are also used in this context, intended to identify areas of lesser conflicts among resources use alternatives and environmental values. By superimposing maps, it will depict various uses for values such as vegetation, water resources, unique wildlife habitats, etc. It is often possible to screen areas which have to be exempted in locating the projects. But this does not reveal relationships and is not good enough to differentiate among impacts. *Delphi study* is one of the techniques which can be used for EIA. *Adaptive Environmental Assessment and Management* (AEAM) is one of the recently evolved tools used in the context of EIA. Cooper et al. (2000) argue that in spite of the apparent comprehensiveness of the above given checklist, it is clear that the primary focus is confined only to direct effects of tourism development. It is an inadequate approach since the indirect approaches also have to be assessed. In considering such views, they formulated a process which consists of stages such as site selection and preliminary assessment, pre-feasibility report, detailed environmental assessment, feasibility study, modification of proposals to minimize impacts, projection of physical planning and design, implementation of environmental protection measures, project implementation, environmental monitoring, project monitoring and evaluation. They state that the process should examine the environmental auditing procedures, limitations to natural responses, environmental problems and conflicts that may affect the project viably and possible detrimental effects to people, flora and fauna, soil, water air, etc., that either within the proposed project area or will be affected by it. Figure 12.1 gives a comprehensive EIA for tourism development for a protected wildlife area.

12.6.1 Environmental Auditing

Environmental auditing can be defined as a process comprising a systematic, documented, regular and objective evaluation of the environmental performance of any aspect of an organization. The term *auditing* is generally referred to as a methodological examination involving analysis, tests and confirmation of a facility's procedures and practices with the goal of verifying whether they comply with legal requirements and internal policies and accepted practices—in the context of tourism, environmental performance and specific problems of an organization, and a ready means for self-regulation of its environmental performance. The essential purpose of environmental management systems in particular is to ensure that commitments made are implemented, that environmental standards are met, and that relevant procedures are in place and are being followed. The concept of environmental auditing is a relatively recent evolution and is a developing technique.

12.6.2 Cost-Benefit Analysis

Cost-benefit analysis is a technique for assessing the viability of new investments or expenditure programmes. It was developed as a decision-making tool in commercial organizations, but is used particularly in the public sector in developing countries. Costs include initial and replacement investments, working capital, and all operating cost items. Similarly, the estimated benefits arising from these expenditures are written out for each year of the project life. Each year, a comparison is made of the costs and benefits. Typically, these net benefits will be negative. Since investment is taking place, it will turn positive, shortly after operation commences. It can be used in three different situations:

- Study of a single proposed project.
- Comparison between alternative proposed projects.
- Study of an existing project or projects (Veal, 2002).

Cost-benefit analysis ensures a consideration of all the costs and benefits from an investment and their timing, and provides a clear decision-making criterion. In case of non-viability, cost-benefit analysis allows consideration of alternatives if it is not viable from all perspectives. Cost-benefit analysis of a tourism investment can play an important role in the decision making process. The anticipated costs and benefits of a new investment need to be related to a market analysis of the types of service and facilities tourists will demand and its duration. Particularly with the inclusion of infrastructure expenditures, the analysis needs to concentrate on the incremental effects of new projects on costs and benefits, and not just on the commercial effects for the operator. In relation to tourism, costs and benefits are to be assessed in many areas. Mainly, economic, physical and socio-cultural areas are considered for assessing costs and benefits in a destination region. Destination region is the most important geographical area and development and impacts are generally concentrated in it. Hence, a cost-benefit analysis is very important. In tourism, physical cost and benefit analysis is very important. Physical aspect includes environment. The environmental impacts of tourism are worse than others and generally, irreparable also. Hence, costs and benefits at the physical level have to be assessed and analyzed well for development. Costs and benefits can be identified in *Tourism Generating Regions* (TGR) and *Transit Route Regions* (TRR). But, as far as tourism development is concerned, costs and benefits at TDR are the most important and the rest don't have much importance. Preparing such lists of costs and benefits helps to look into cost and benefits of tourism development and to approach tourism development in the areas concerned.

12.7 VISITOR MANAGEMENT

Number of visitors is a cause of impact generation. When a destination has more tourists than its carrying capacity, it leads to increased impacts. In such cases, visitor management measures can be applied to minimize the impact of excess visitor concentration. These measures primarily focus on restricting and managing visitor flow and their activities. Visitor management measures are broadly classified into two as *hard measures* and *soft measures* (Page, 2007). The former places extensive and permanent restrictions on visitor activity. The latter involves improving marketing, interpretation, planning and visitor coordination. The variety of visitor management models include Recreation Opportunity Spectrum (ROS), Carrying Capacity Model, Visitor Activity Management Programme (VAMP), Visitor Impact Management Model (VIMM), Limit of Acceptable Change (LAC), and Tourism Optimization Management Model (TOMM) (Hall and Arthur, 1998).

12.7.1 Recreation Opportunity Spectrum (ROS)

This is a *land zoning system* identifying the environmental setting and offering guidelines for appropriate activities and visitor experience. It provides a framework that is widely used to guide outdoor recreation planning and management. Developed back in the 1970s, this helps to classify and monitor existing and desired recreation settings and in identifying and determining the diversity of recreation opportunities for a natural geographical location, based on the idea that quality of visitor services is best assured by offering a group of opportunities suited to the full range of expected tourists. From a visitor's perspective, the output is providing opportunities to participate in preferred activities in the appropriate physical, social, and managerial setting. Veal (2002) illustrates ROS as: "Classification of areas in which people might seek outdoor recreation along a continuum from the totally undeveloped, such as pristine wilderness (primitive), to the highly developed, such as a fully serviced camping site and recreation area (modern). Against this are set the sorts of activity which the management and users of these areas might engage in to maintain the appropriate ambience of the site and compatibility with visitor expectations." It provides a means for classifying the range of recreational opportunities and managing that range. It is a flexible and adaptable approach and valuable for integrated planning, particularly for analysis and planning in a region with a range of natural attractions. As an allocation and planning tool, it accounts for a variety of recreational opportunities and their relative scarcity or abundance. Moreover, it assists

Table 12.5: UNWTO global code of ethics for tourism

Article 1: Tourism's contribution to mutual understanding and respect between people and societies which focuses on the underlying principles of diversity and tolerance, harmony, mutual respect, ensuring the safety of visitors and risk minimization.
Article 2: Tourism as a vehicle for individual and collective fulfillment, should be a privilege and force for self-education while promoting human rights and combating the exploitation of persons, especially children.
Article 3: Tourism, as factor of sustainable development, indicating that all stakeholders involved in tourism should seek to safeguard the natural environment and strive towards sustainable growth.
Article 4: Tourism, as user of the cultural heritage of mankind and a contributor to its enhancement, so that the cultural heritage is preserved while cultural products are not degenerated, or standardised or commoditized.
Article 5: Tourism, a beneficial activity for host countries and communities, so that the standard of living of local populations is enhanced, especially in sensitive environments such as coastal, mountain and island communities.
Article 6: Obligations of stakeholders in tourism development, whereby suppliers need to act with honesty and integrity in terms of the information and services they provide while cooperating with the public sector to ensure the safety and security of visitors.
Article 7: Right to tourism, which is a universal right and the promotion of social tourism to assist the less privileged to access holidays should receive public support.
Article 8: Liberty of tourist movements, where tourists should have freedom to travel in accordance with Article 13 of the Universal Declaration of Human Rights.
Article 9: Rights of workers and entrepreneurs in the tourism industry, where the rights of workers need to be guaranteed including access to training opportunities.
Article 10: Implementation of the principles of the Global Code of Ethics for Tourism, which requires the cooperation of the public and private sectors for its effective implementation and the establishment of a world committee on tourism ethics for the settlement of disputes.

Source: United Nations World Tourism Organization/Global Code of Ethics.

in guiding allocation decisions so that individual recreation areas contribute to a more comprehensive system of recreation opportunities. Ultimately, an ROS enables a mechanism to invent the existing opportunities, analyzing the effects of other resource activities, assessing the consequences of management decisions on planned opportunities and in developing standards and guidelines for planned settings and monitoring activities.

12.7.2 Limit to Acceptable Change (LAC)

This focuses on the *management of visitor impacts* by identifying, first, desirable conditions for visitor activity to occur, and then how much change is acceptable. Basically, it is a framework for establishing acceptable and appropriate resources and social conditions in recreational settings (Stankey, 1984). This process identifies appropriate and acceptable resources and social conditions and the actions needed to protect or achieve those conditions. Its monitoring programme determines whether desirable conditions are within acceptable standards and also determines the management actions required to achieve the desired conditions. It is ideal for deciding the most appropriate and acceptable resources and social conditions in natural areas. Moreover, it incorporates opportunity classes based on the concepts of ROS. Ultimately, this provide a strategic and tactical plan for the area based on defined limits of acceptable change for each opportunity class, with indicators of change that can be used to monitor ecological and social conditions (Nilsen & Tayler, 1998).

12.7.3 Visitor Activity Management Programme (VAMP)

VAMP is a *planning system* which integrates visitor needs with resources to reduce specific visitor opportunities, and is designed to resolve conflicts and tensions between visitor, heritage and heritage managers. It requires the heritage manager to identify provider for and market to designated visitor groups.

12.7.4 Visitor Impact Management Model (VIMM)

VIMM focuses on *reducing or controlling the impacts* that threaten the quality of heritage and visitor experience. It is an eight-step sequential process for assessing and managing visitor impacts aimed at: identification of problem conditions (unacceptable visitor impacts); determination of potential causal factors affecting the occurrence and severity of the unacceptable impacts; selection of potential management strategies (Graefe, Kuss and Vaske, 1990). It uses explicit statements of management objectives and research. It also monitors heritage and social conditions and then generate a range of management strategies to deal with the impacts.

12.7.5 Tourism Optimization Management Model (TOMM)

TOMM focuses on achieving optimum performance by addressing sustainability of the heritage, viability of the tourism industry and empowerment of stakeholders. It covers environmental and experimental elements, characteristics of the tourist market, economic conditions of the tourism industry and socio-cultural conditions of the local community. It mainly contains three main parts: context analysis, monitoring programme and management response system (Hall and Arthur, 1998).

12.8 CONCLUSION

Sustainable tourism development is the need of the hour, less tourism will create impacts at an alarming rate. World over, there is increased pressure on planners, developers and industries to adhere to the principles of sustainable tourism. In fact, reducing the impacts of tourism and ensuring sustainability of resources necessitate a multi-pronged strategy. In addition to proper planning based on necessary research, a number of other measures have to be put in practice. Environmental impact assessment, carrying capacity analysis, environmental auditing and visitor management practices are some of the common measures to mitigate the effects of haphazard tourism development leading to severe impacts. Tourism is poised for further growth and hence it is inevitable to develop tourism sustainably.

Key Terms

Tourism
Sustainability
Sustainable development
Sustainable tourism
Economic sustainability
Social sustainability
Cultural sustainability
Environmental sustainability
Carrying capacity
Environmental impact assessment
Environmental auditing
Cost-benefit analysis
Recreational opportunity spectrum
Visitor management
Limit to acceptable change

Review Questions

Short Answer Type Questions

1. Define sustainability.
2. Narrate the history of sustainable development.
3. What do you mean by sustainable development?
4. Define sustainable tourism.
5. Discuss the need for sustainable development in tourism.
6. Write the principles of sustainable tourism.
7. Write short notes on tourism sustainabilities.
8. Examine the concept of 'carrying capacity'.
9. Discuss the relevance of carrying capacity in tourism development.
10. What are the various types of 'carrying capacities'?
11. Discuss some of the factors that determine 'carrying capacity' of a destination.
12. What do you mean by EIA?
13. Discuss the applicability of EIA in tourism.
14. Discuss the process of EIA in tourism.
15. Elucidate recreation opportunity spectrum.
16. Discuss community involvement in tourism.

17. What do you mean by environmental auditing?
18. Write a short note on cost-benefit analysis in tourism.
19. Define visitor management.
20. Discuss various visitor management practices.

Essay Type Question

1. Discuss the concept of sustainable tourism. What are the measures that can be taken while developing tourism in a sustainable manner?

13 ECOTOURISM AND RESPONSIBLE TOURISM

Learning Outcomes

After studying this chapter, you will be able to:

- describe the concept of ecotourism;
- identify the characteristics and principles of ecotourism;
- define responsible tourism; and
- comprehend various aspects associated with responsible tourism.

13.1 INTRODUCTION

Ecotourism, a 'buzzword' in recent tourism development, is a term which is widely used, but rarely defined. It is sometimes used interchangeably with other terms such as soft tourism, alternative tourism, responsible tourism and nature tourism. It is experimented as an efficient tool for sustainable tourism development since 1990. The year 2002 was declared *International Year for Ecotourism* (IYE). As part of promoting ecotourism and to spread the awareness of the necessity to improve the environmental performance of tourism, a world summit was organized in Qubec in Canada in 2002.

Viewed as being a newer form of tourism, it is often cited as one of the fastest growing forms of tourism. Though many activities in the name of ecotourism are happening throughout the world, only a proportion of it is true ecotourism. Ecotourism, or *sustainable tourism*, primarily focuses upon indigenous people, lands, ecosystems, and cultures. Ecotourism is more than just wildlife. Tourists generally appear to be more interested in watching animals than in meeting and seeking to understand people of different cultures. Ecotourism can lead to indigenous people being patronized by the tourists, often innocently.

Conceptually, ecotourism should not only look at protecting the environment and the biodiversity, it must also take into account protection of the cultural diversity, and other important views of the indigenous and local communities. As a sustainable form, it should ensure prior informed participation of all stakeholders and their equal, effective and active involvement. In addition, it has to promote processes for indigenous people and local communities to control and maintain their resources.

13.2 DEFINITION AND CONCEPT OF ECOTOURISM

The term *ecotourism* is usually attributed to Ceballos-Lascurain, who defined it as "tourism that consists of travelling to relatively undisturbed or uncontaminated natural areas with specific objectives of studying, admiring and enjoying the scenery and its wild plants and animals as well as any existing cultural manifestation found in these areas" (Quoted in Eplerwood, 2002). It is more than a marketing concept attached to any tourism product to attract those sympathetic to environmental causes. Ecotouirsm must contribute directly to the maintenance and enhancement of parks and protected areas, the well-being of resident communities and environmental education.

There are various definitions of ecotourism, most of which are concerned with environmental conservation and preservation. It is directed towards responsible travel that conserves ecosystems, preserves the local culture and benefits the local people. It is an enlightening and participatory travel experience to natural environments. Ecotourism ensures the sustainable use of environmental resources, while producing viable economic opportunities for the host communities. It is also defined as a responsible way of travelling that supports preservation of natural and cultural heritage and welfare of local communities. The International Ecotourism Society (TIES) defines it as "purposeful travel to natural areas to understand the culture and natural history of the environment taking care not to alter the integrity of the ecotourism while producing economic opportunities that make the conservation of natural resources beneficial to local people". Later, in 2015, TIES modified the definition of ecotourism as "responsible travel to natural areas that conserves the environment, sustains the well-being of the local people, and involves interpretation and education". Also it urges that those who implement and participate in ecotourism activities should follow the essential principles such as minimization of impacts, creation of environmental and cultural awareness and respect, providing positive experience for both visitors and hosts, direct financial benefits for conservation, financial benefits and empowerment for local people and raising sensitivity to host countries' political, environmental, and social climate. According to Swarbrooke (2002), ecotourism is seen to be:

- inherently small scale;
- more active than most other forms of tourism;
- less reliant on the existence of sophisticated tourism infrastructure;
- undertaken by tourists who possess awareness about the issues of environmental degradation due to tourism; and

- less exploitative of local cultures and nature than traditional forms of tourism.

According to Weaver (2001), ecotourism is "a form of nature based tourism that strives to be ecologically, socio-culturally and economically sustainable while providing opportunities for appreciating and learning about the natural environment or specific elements thereof." He suggests that ecotourism encompasses the following fundamental elements.

- Attraction of natural environments, hence ecotourism is nature based.
- Emphasizes on learning as an outcome of ecotourism for the tourist that differentiates from other hedonistic forms of "nature based" tourism, like, beach tourism.
- High desire for sustainability of the natural attraction and native people of the region.

The World Wildlife Fund, which has a vested interest in the ecotourism industry in terms of wilderness protection for habitats and various species, believes that "the term *ecotourism* refers to any travel to or through wilderness areas that has minimal impact on the natural environment and its wildlife while providing some economic benefits to local communities and the area's indigenous stewards". According the UNWTO, ecotourism has the following characteristics:

- All nature-based forms of tourism in which the main motivation of the tourists is the observation and appreciation of nature as well as the traditional cultures prevailing in natural areas.
- It contains educational and interpretation features.
- It is generally, but not exclusively organised by specialised tour operators for small groups. Service provider partners at the destinations tend to be small, locally owned businesses.
- It minimises negative impacts upon the natural and socio-cultural environment.
- It supports the maintenance of natural areas which are used as ecotourism attractions by:
  - generating economic benefits for host communities, organisations and authorities managing natural areas with conservation purposes;
  - providing alternative employment and income opportunities for local communities; and
  - increasing awareness towards the conservation of natural and cultural assets, both among locals and tourists. (The British Ecotourism Market/UNWTO, 2012)

Ecotourism can be a sustainable form of tourism. Its aim should be to manage ecotourism so that it is an enlightening nature travel experience that contributes to the conservation of the ecosystem while respecting the integrity of the host community. It is viewed as a complex phenomenon, involving integration of many actors including tourists, residents, suppliers, and managers and multiple functions (Ceballos-Lascurain, 1993). There are some classifications also seen in ecotourism. One of the most quoted is of *Lindberg typology of nature/ecotourism*. According to this, following are the types of ecotourism:

- **Hard-core:** Scientific researchers or members of tours specifically designed for education, environmental restoration, or similar purposes.
- **Dedicated:** People who take trips specifically to see protected areas and who want to understand local, natural and cultural history.
- **Mainstream:** People who visit the Amazon, the Rwandan Gorilla Park, or other such destinations primarily to take an unusual trip.
- **Casual:** People who partake of nature incidentally, such as through a day trip during a broader vacation. (Lindberg, 1991)

Ecotourism is also classified as soft and hard.

- **Hard ecotourism:** This type of ecotourism necessitates active involvement of tourists. It requires a lot of physical activities and hence health requirements are also high. Only those having good health and physical condition can participate. Most of such types may be adventurous as well, relatively. Participation is usually by less number of tourists.
- **Soft ecotourism:** Involvement of tourists is more passive and activities are less adventurous. More tourists may participate and health requirements are low, compared to that of hard ecotourism.

Ecotourism development should proceed adhering to the basic principles. Many experts have suggested principles in different ways, though with almost similar essence. The International Ecotourism Society (TIES) laid down the following principles:

- Minimize physical, social, behavioural, and psychological impacts.
- Build environmental and cultural awareness and respect.

Table 13.1: Benefits of ecotourism

Economic benefits	Increased employment opportunities (guides, transportation, construction; protected area employees; restaurants, motels, shops, retail, etc.) entrepreneurship, distribution of tourist revenues.
Infrastructure benefits	Access to goods and services, quality/access to healthcare; education, communication infrastructure, transportation infrastructure.
Social welfare benefits	The indirect benefits of improved infrastructure, and socio-economic status, status of environmental conditions, intercultural appreciation, strengthening of cultural heritage.

Source: Ross and Wall, 1999.

- Provide positive experiences for both visitors and hosts.
- Provide direct financial benefits for conservation.
- Generate financial benefits for both local people and private industry.
- Deliver memorable interpretative experience to visitors that help raise sensitivity to host countries' political, environmental, and social climates.
- Design, construct and operate low-impact facilities.
- Recognize the rights and spiritual beliefs of the indigenous people in your community and work in partnership with them to create empowerment. (TIES/ecotourism.org)

Government of India, Ministry of Environment and Forests suggests the following principles of ecotourism development in India:

- Adopt low-impact tourism that protects ecological integrity of wilderness areas, secures wildlife values of the destination and its surrounding areas.
- Highlight the heritage value of India's wilderness and protected areas.
- Build environmental and cultural awareness and respect.
- Facilitate sustainability of ecotourism enterprises and activities.
- Provide livelihood opportunities to local communities.
- Use indigenous, locally produced and ecologically sustainable materials for tourism activities.

In order to get a clearer picture about ecotourism and its implementation in the country, some essential details from the ecotourism guidelines and policy are given here.

Table 13.2: Government of India—Ministry of Environment and Forests: Ecotourism Guidelines—Excerpts

Guidelines for Ecotourism

It is important to involve all stakeholders in implementing ecotourism guidelines. Synergy and collaboration amongst the Central Government, State Governments, hospitality sector, State Forest Departments, Protected Area management, and local communities and civil society institutions is vital for ensuring successful implementation of the guidelines.

2.1 State Governments

The State Government must develop a State-level Ecotourism Strategy – a comprehensive plan to ensure, inter alia: Wilderness conservation in ecologically sensitive landscapes; local community participation and benefit-sharing; sound environmental design and use of locally produced and sustainable materials; conservation education and training; adequate monitoring and evaluation of the impact of ecotourism activities; and capacity building of local communities in planning, providing and managing ecotourism facilities.

Contd...

The State-level Ecotourism Strategy must be in tune with the framework of guidelines provided here. Ecologically sensitive land use policies should be prescribed for the landscape surrounding protected areas. Adequate provisions must be made to ensure that ecotourism does not get relegated to purely high-end, exclusive tourism, leaving out local communities. Relevant modifications in State rules and regulations must be carried out in order to ensure adherence to these standards by tourist developers and operators.

No new tourist facilities are to be set up on forest lands. This is in compliance with the Wildlife (Protection) Act, 1972, and the directives of the Honourable Supreme Court.

The State Government must develop a system by which gate receipts from Protected Areas should be collected by the Protected Area management, and not go as revenue to the *State Exchequer*. This will ensure that resources generated from tourism can be earmarked for protection, conservation and local livelihood development.

The State Forest Department should be the arbiter in case of any dispute regarding the ecological advisability of any tourism plans, whether protected area management, private entity, temple board or community, as the welfare of wildlife and protected areas/biodiversity takes precedence over tourism.

The *Chief Wildlife Warden* of the State must ensure that each Protected Area prepares an ecotourism plan, as part of the Management Plan/Annual Plan of Operation/Tiger Conservation Plan.

The Chief Wildlife Warden (CWLW) of the State shall develop a monitoring mechanism, estimate carrying capacity, delineate tourism zones, and decide the area open to tourism on the basis of objective, scientific criteria.

A *State Level Steering Committee* should be constituted under the chairmanship of the Chief Minister for quarterly review vis-à-vis the recommendations contained in the *State-level Ecotourism Strategy*. The Chief Wildlife Warden of the State shall be the Member Convener of the said committee. The State Government will decide its composition and rules of procedure. Each State should constitute State Level Steering Committees and the names of its members should be put in the public domain. The Committee should have representation from local communities that live in and around Protected Areas, tribal welfare department, Panchayati Raj Institution and Civil Society Institutions.

As part of the State-level Ecotourism Strategy, the State government should levy a "local conservation cess" as a percentage of turnover, on all privately-run tourist facilities within 5 km of the boundary of a Protected Area. The rate of cess should be determined by the State Government, and the monies thus collected should be earmarked to fund Protected Area management, conservation and local livelihood development, and not go to the State Exchequer as discussed above.

Financial assistance/incentives should be provided for communities/individuals who own revenue lands outside protected areas, to convert such lands to forest status. The value of such lands for wildlife will be enhanced, even as it improves the income of the landowner from ecotourism.

A *Local Advisory Committee* (hereinafter referred to as LAC) must be constituted for each Protected Area by the State government. The LAC will have the following mandate:

- To review the State Ecotourism Strategy with respect to the Protected Area and make recommendations to the State government.
- To ensure site specific restrictions on buildings and infrastructures in private areas in close proximity to core/critical tiger habitat/National Park/Sanctuary or buffer zone, keeping in mind the corridor value.
- To advise local and state government on issues relating to development of ecological tourism in non-forest areas of ecological tourism zones, etc.

- Regularly monitor all tourist facilities falling within 5 km of a Protected Area vis-à-vis environmental clearance, area of coverage, ownership, type of construction, number of employees, etc., for suggesting mitigation/retrofitting measures if needed.
- Regularly monitor activities of tour operators to ensure that they do not cause disturbance to animals while taking visitors into the Protected Area.

Composition of LAC:

District Collector (Chairman); PA Manager (Member Secretary); Local Territorial DFO; Honorary Wildlife Warden (if present); Official of State Tourism Department; Block Development Officer (1); Members of Local Panchayats (2); Wildlife Scientist (1); Local Conservationists (2); and Representative from Civil Society Institution (1). In case of North Eastern States, the traditional village councils should be recognized as equivalent to Panchayat Members, wherever such councils exist. For Tiger Reserves, the Tiger Conservation Foundation should be the overseeing authority and should include members that are not represented in the Tiger Conservation Foundation. The Detailed Terms of Reference of individual Local Advisory Committee will be determined at the State level.

2.2 Protected Area Management

Each Protected Area must develop its own *Ecotourism Plan,* as part of its Tiger Conservation Plan, Management Plan, or Annual Plan of Operation, and should be duly approved by the Chief Wildlife Warden of the State, and the National Tiger Conservation Authority (where relevant). The plan should be consistent with the State Ecotourism Strategy and must be approved by the LAC and the State Government.

The plan should:

i) Identify (using GIS) and monitor the ecologically sensitive areas surrounding PAs, in order to ensure the ecological integrity of corridor/buffer areas, and prevent corridor pinching/destruction.

ii) Assess carrying capacity of the Protected Area, at three levels: physical, real and effective/ permissible carrying capacity of visitors and vehicles.

iii) Set a ceiling level on number of visitors allowed to enter a Protected Area at any given time, based on the carrying capacity of the habitat.

iv) Indicate the area open to tourism in the reserves to be designated as *ecotourism zone.*

v) Develop a participatory community-based tourism strategy, in collaboration with local communities, to ensure long-term local-community benefit-sharing, and promotion of activities run by local communities.

vi) Develop codes and standards for privately-operated tourist facilities located in the vicinity of core/critical wildlife habitats, eco-sensitive zones or buffer areas, with a view to, inter alia, ensure benefit and income to local communities.

vii) Develop monitoring mechanisms to assess impact of tourism activities.

viii) Develop generic guidelines for environmentally acceptable and culturally appropriate practices, and for all new constructions.

ix) Do's and Don'ts for visitors:

In the case of human-animal conflicts, compensation should be paid within a period of 15 days apart from immediate payment of *ex gratia.* In case of North-Eastern States, the traditional village councils should be recognized and made responsible for this purpose, wherever such councils exist.

All ecotourism activities should take place only in *'ecotourism zones'* delineated in the ecotourism plan.

Contd...

Given that traditional tourism has been taking place in national parks/sanctuaries; many of which now form part of core/critical tiger habitat or critical wildlife habitat, and also taking note of the need to implement the provisions of the Wildlife (Protection) Act, 1972, the following norms maybe be adhered to in the context of ecological-tourism activities, and included in the ecotourism plan of the Protected Area. For critical wildlife habitats of national parks/sanctuaries and for core/critical tiger habitats of tiger reserves;

a) Larger than 500 sq. km, 20% of such areas may be permitted for regulated ecotourism access, subject to the condition that 30% of the surrounding buffer/fringe area should be restored as a wildlife habitat in 5 years.

b) Smaller than 500 sq. km, 15% of such areas may be permitted for regulated ecotourism access, subject to the condition that 20% of the surrounding buffer/fringe area should be restored as a wildlife habitat in 5 years.

Any core area in a Tiger Reserve from which relocation has been carried out, will not be used for tourism activities. Forest dwellers who have been relocated will be given priority in terms of livelihood generation activities related to ecotourism in the Protected Area from which they have been relocated. Protected Area Management will make a special effort in this regard.

In a phased manner (within five years), permanent residential facilities located inside core-critical tiger habitat/critical wildlife habitat, which are being used for wildlife tourism should be moved to revenue lands outside.

Protected Area authorities must ensure that all facilities within a 5 km radius of core/critical wildlife habitats/PAs/reserves must adhere to all environmental clearances, noise pollution norms, and are non-polluting, blending in with surroundings. Severe penalties must be imposed for non-compliance.

There shall be a complete ban on burying, burning or otherwise disposing of non-biodegradable or toxic waste in the tourism area.

In the case of number of visitors/vehicles exceeding carrying capacity, establish an advance booking system to control tourist and number of vehicles. Rules of booking must be transparent, and vehicles must strictly maintain a distance of 15 m from one another when stationary. Violators must be penalized, since congestion and overcrowding in this manner causes undue disturbance to wild animals that are being observed.

Protected Area authorities must delineate a minimum area for the visitor facility, which should be in a site-specific manner.

Residential tourist facilities (number of beds) should be in conformity with the carrying capacity of the PA.

In the case of Tiger Reserves, ecotourism should be under the oversight of the respective Tiger Conservation Foundations for each tiger reserve, to enable Eco Development Committees/Village Forest Committees/forest cooperatives to strengthen the institutional framework through a Memorandum of Understanding.

2.3. Tourist Facilities/ Tour Operators

Tourism infrastructure must conform to environment-friendly, low-impact architecture; renewables including solar energy, waste recycling, rainwater harvesting, natural cross-ventilation, no use of asbestos, controlled sewage disposal, and merging with the surrounding landscape.

All tourist facilities falling within 5 km of a protected area must be reviewed regularly by the Local Advisory Committee vis-à-vis environmental clearance, area of coverage, ownership, type of construction, number of employees, etc., for suggesting mitigation/retrofitting measures if needed.

All tourism facilities located within 5 km of a protected area must adhere to noise pollution rules under 'The Noise Pollution (Regulation and Control) Rules', 2000, and 'The Noise Pollution (Regulation and Control) (Amendment) Rules', 2010 issued by the Ministry of Environment and Forests.

All tourist facilities, old and new must aim to generate at least 50% of their total energy and fuel requirements from alternate energy sources that may include wind, solar and biogas.

There shall be a complete ban on burning or disposing non-biodegradable waste within the Protected Area or in surrounding eco-sensitive zone or buffer area.

The use of wood as fuel shall be prohibited, except for campfires for which wood must be procured from State Forest Department/Forest Development Corporation depots.

In order to allow free passage to wildlife, development should be sensitive to the conservation of flora and fauna, and the corridor value of the area.

Tourist facilities/tour operators must not cause disturbance to animals while taking visitors on nature trails.

2.4. Temple/Pilgrimage Boards

Pilgrim sites located inside Protected Areas must be designated as sacred grooves, with strict building and expansion controls, in accordance with the Forest Conservation Act, 1980 and the Environment Protection Act, 1986.

All transit camps and places of stay for such pilgrimage must be restricted to nominated days in a year.

All rules that apply to tourism facilities including noise, building design, use of alternate energy and free passage to wildlife will apply to such pilgrim facilities.

Temple boards must negotiate terms of revenue sharing with local communities, and channel a minimum of five percent of gross revenue collected into development of local communities through the Panchayat and Gram Sabha.

2.5. Local Communities

The first benefit from ecotourism must go to the local people, and in the long-run, capacity-building should be carried out to forge a sustainable partnership between the forest department, tourism professionals and local communities.

Soft loans may be provided for Community Credit Programmes/Special Trust Funds/Special Central Assistance/Developmental Schemes of Tribal Department/District level.

Integrated Developmental Programme/Tiger Conservation Foundation, to pre-identified local-community/beneficiaries for promoting ecotourism.

2.6. Public / Visitors

Public/Visitors must abide by the code of conduct, and 'Do's and Don'ts, as developed by the Protected Area Management.

Model Do's and Don'ts for Visitors:

- Appreciate the colours and sounds of nature.
- Treat the Protected Area/wilderness area with respect.

Contd...

- Dress in colours that blend with the natural environment.
- Take pictures, but without disturbing wildlife.
- Observe the sanctity of holy sites, respect local customs.
- Keep a reasonable distance from wild animals, and do not provoke them.
- Dispose of waste responsibly: carry back all non-biodegradable litter, and leave campsites clean before departing.
- When in a vehicle, remember wild animals have right of way.
- Keep to the speed limit, don't use the horn, and do not scare animals.
- Do not talk loudly or play loud music.
- Do not get out of the vehicle or approach wild animals.
- Do not approach animals closer than 15 m or disturb them while they are resting.
- Do not take away flora and fauna in the form of cuttings, seeds or roots.
- Do not feed wild animals.
- Do not light fires, or smoke inside protected areas. Accidental forest fires cause irreparable damage.
- Carrying of guns, firearms, inflammable materials are strictly prohibited, as per the provisions of the WildLife (Protection) Act, 1972, and is punishable by law.

Courtesy: Excerpts, adapted from Guidelines for Ecotourism in and Around Protected Areas (Draft, 2011), Ministry of Environment and Forests, Government of India, www.moef.nic.in/ (given for education purpose)

13.3 ECOTOURISM RESOURCES OF INDIA

Government of India, as part of ecotourism policy, identified the following resources for ecotourism development in India.

Biosphere Reserves

- Nilgiri
- Nanda Devi
- Nokrek
- Great Nicobar
- Gulf of Mannar
- Manas
- Sunderbans

Mangroves

- Northern Andaman and Nicobar Islands
- Sunderbans (West Bengal)
- Bhitarkanika and Mahanadi Delta (Odisha)
- Coringa, Godavari Delta and Krishna estuary (Andhra Pradesh)

- Pichavaram and Point Calimere (Tamil Nadu)
- Goa
- Gulf of Kutch (Gujarat)
- Coondapur (Karnataka)
- Achra/Ratnagiri (Maharashtra)
- Vembanad (Kerala)

Coral Reefs

- Gulf of Mannar
- Andaman and Nicobar Islands
- Lakshadweep Islands
- Gulf of Kutch

Deserts

- Thar desert
- Other little deserts in the north-western region of the country

Mountains and Forests

- The Himalayas and other mountain ranges
- Forests: The country has an area of about 752.3 lakh hectares notified as forest land and of this, about 406.1 lakh hectares are classified as reserve forests and 215.1 lakh hectares as Protected Forests. There are a total of 421 Wildlife Sanctuaries and 66 national parks.

Table 13.3 Predecessors of sustainable tourism

Alternative Tourism

It evolved during the period when criticism over mass tourism reached its peak and was in vogue during 1970s and 80s. The concept relies fundamentally on the desire to stop uncontrollable development of tourism and to evolve suitable tourism forms that will cause minimum impacts rather than severe effects on environment, society and culture. The concept is ambiguous and vague and a number of similar concepts are regarded as alternative tourism forms.

Green Tourism

Basically, it denotes *nature tourism,* considered to be environmentally compatible and with little or no ecological impacts on the destination. It is generally related to rural tourism and widely accepted as a form of alternative tourism. It was succeeded by ecotourism from the beginning of 1990s.

Nature Tourism

Nature in its pure form has been an attraction and a major travel motivator since ancient times. The goal of experiencing flora and fauna in natural setting is basically considered nature based tourism. The increasing awareness on environment and greater accessibility of wilderness and interior areas gave momentum to the growth of nature tourism. Visitors to rainforests, whale watching, bird watching, etc., constitute a few examples.

Source: Encyclopedia of Tourism, 2000.

Flora and Fauna

- India has 45,000 species of plants, a little over 65,000 known species of fauna, including 1228 of birds, 428 of reptiles, 372 of mammals, 204 of amphibians and 2546 of fish.

Water Resources

- The Arabian Sea, the Indian Ocean and the Bay of Bengal
- Rivers and lakes (Government of India, 1998)

13.4 RESPONSIBLE TOURISM

Tourism was once limited only to the rich and its associated activities remained isolated from the local community of the destination, particularly in the case of *enclave tourism*. In many places, members of local community were barred from entering tourism properties. They could view large hotels only from a distance, outside the fences. Instances are common where the local community was rehabilitated to other places while developing tourism infrastructure. Big businesses in a destination were owned and operated by bigwigs from outside the local economy, while the local community members were mere spectators.

Tourists spent money in establishments run by outsiders and hence they were the beneficiaries of tourism. Employees in those establishments were also mostly recruits from non-local areas. Circumstances were not conducive for local businesses to flourish. At the same time the resources used for development of tourism are actually of the local community, and visitors only arrive and consume the same. Visitors were also not exposed to the local community directly. Ironically, the negative impacts of tourism affected the local society, culture and environment, not the visitors. Vast majority of the economic benefits was not reaching the local community. The increasing menace of tourism created a sort of antagonism against the visiting community in many locations in the history of tourism.

Years went by and people began thinking about the disparity in income distribution and benefit sharing with the local community. A number of ideas, concepts as well as new forms of tourism emerged to develop and promote equitable tourism options. 1980s and 1990s have seen the emergence of major ideas and concepts in this direction. Ecotourism, alternative tourism, sustainable tourism and responsible tourism are the major ones among them. Responsible tourism is of more recent origin.

According to Husbands and Harrison (1996) *responsible tourism* is a way of carrying out tourism and not a tourism product or brand in itself. It is obvious that responsible tourism involves more than simply having the desire to do so. They further interpret that responsible tourism refers to "a way of undertaking tourism planning, policy and development to ensure that the benefits are optimally distributed, maximum among the impacted populations, governments, tourists as well as investors". Basically, it involves a framework and a set of practices that chart a sensible course between the fuzziness of ecotourism and the well known issues associated with conventional mass tourism. Husbands and Harrison further state that responsible tourism acknowledges that there is a place for well-conceived ecotourism products. However, it also recognizes that, drawing on experience, foresight, and new techniques, mass tourism itself can be practised in ways that minimize and mitigate its obvious pitfalls. Able and effective leadership is a necessity for practising responsible tourism in any destination. Resources are a crucial aspect and effective utilization of the resources is essential in sharing benefits equitably amongst the host population.

Responsible tourism demands utmost care in planning. When a tourism destination is developed, a number of important aspects have to be taken care of. The development of tourism should not lead to depletion of resources and the benefits have to be shared maximum among the local community. The development should not lead to impacts on society and environment. Promoting tourism based on the principles of responsible tourism would definitely help in generating more benefits than negative impacts. The first international conference was convened in Cape Town in South Africa in 2002. This was a landmark in the history of responsible tourism and the conference provided ample clarity to the concept of responsible tourism.

According to the *Cape Town Declaration on Responsible Tourism in Destinations* (2002), responsible tourism has the following characteristics:

- minimizes negative economic, environmental, and social impacts;
- generates greater economic benefits for local people and enhances the well-being of host communities, improves working conditions and access to the industry;
- makes positive contributions to the conservation of natural and cultural heritage, to the maintenance of the world's diversity;
- involves local people in decisions that affect their lives and life chances;
- provides access to physically challenged people;
- provides more enjoyable experience for tourists through more meaningful connections with local people, and a greater understanding of local cultural, social and environmental issues; and
- provides culturally sensitive, respect between tourists and hosts, and builds local pride and confidence.

Responsible tourism, in theory, consists of three important components—*economic responsibility, sociocultural responsibility* and *environmental responsibility*. Ensuring these responsibilities is essential for its promotion in any destination. Tourists too have to take care of a number of aspects. Some important aspects related to tourists that have to be considered are:

- Buy souvenir items produced locally and support local skills.
- Consume the local food and specialties.

- Value the host community's cultural features.
- Avoid buying products and similar products that may exploit wildlife.
- Be careful in generating waste and handling waste.
- Be careful in disposing of materials that may pollute soil and water.
- Use resources like water judiciously.
- Avoid disturbing the wildlife while travelling into a forest.

At the same time, it is very important to note that before expecting responsible behaviour from a tourist, one has to make sure that a tourist is aware of the facts. The tourist has to be provided information on levels of local poverty and the need for development at the local level. This will inspire him/her to spend money in the local economy.

According to *South Africa's Responsible Tourism Guidelines* developed in 2002 by the Department of Environmental Affairs and Tourism (DEAT), a number of measures have to be kept in mind while implementing and promoting responsible tourism in a country. In case of economic aspects of RT, it is essential to find out measures to minimize *leakage* from the local economy (leakage is referred to as the revenue leaking out of the economy for purchasing goods and services from outside the economy). Maximum number of employees have to be recruited from the locality itself. Locally produced goods and services have to be sold as part of tourism. In the case of social responsibility, it is important to involve local community in the development of tourism. This would develop a positive attitude towards tourism development among the community and can help in minimizing the impacts. Creating awareness and educating the host as well as the guest community would definitely help to generate cultural exchange and mutual respect between them. Environmental impact assessment, preservation and maintenance of the biodiversity and sensible utilization of resources are extremely important aspects to be taken care of in tourism development, particularly in environmentally sensitive areas. Cape Town Declaration on Responsible Tourism set essential guiding principles under each type of responsibility associated with tourism. They are enlisted below.

Economic Responsibility

- Assess economic impacts before developing tourism and exercise preference for those forms of development that would benefit local communities and minimize negative impacts on local livelihoods, recognizing that tourism may not always be the most appropriate form of local economic development.
- Develop quality products that reflect, complement, and enhance the destination.
- Maximize the local benefits by increasing linkages and reducing leakages, by ensuring that communities are involved and thereby benefit from tourism.

- Market tourism in ways which reflect the natural, cultural and social integrity of the destination, and which encourages appropriate forms of tourism.
- Provide appropriate and sufficient support to small, medium and micro enterprises to ensure that tourism related enterprises thrive and are sustainable.
- Adopt equitable business practices, pay and charge fair prices, and build partnerships in ways in which risk is minimized and shared, and recruit and employ staff recognizing international labour standards.

Environmental Responsibility

- Assess environmental impacts throughout the lifecycle of tourist establishments and operations—including the planning and design phase—and ensure that negative impacts are reduced to the minimum.
- Manage natural diversity sustainably, and where appropriate restore it. Consider the volume and type of tourism that the environment can support and respect the integrity of the vulnerable ecosystems and protected areas.
- Use resources sustainably, and reduce waste and overconsumption.
- Promote education and awareness for sustainable development for all stakeholders
- Raise the capacity of all stakeholders and ensure that best practice is followed; for this purpose consult environmental and conservation experts.

Social Responsibility

- Actively involve the local community in planning and decision making and provide capacity building to make this a reality.
- Endeavour to make tourism an inclusive social experience and ensure that there is access for all, in particular vulnerable and disadvantaged communities and individuals.
- Assess social impacts throughout the lifecycle of the operation—including the planning and design phases of projects—in order to minimize the negative impacts and maximize the positive ones.
- Combat the sexual exploitation of human beings, particularly of children.
- Endeavour to ensure that tourism contributes to improvements in health and education.
- Be sensitive to the host culture, maintain and encourage social and cultural diversity.

After a gap of five years, the proponents of responsible tourism have decided to convene the second international conference. Kerala, that has been pursuing the task to implement the concept of responsible tourism, was chosen to play the host. The event which was attended by more than five hundred delegates, was held at Cochin. The delegates were of the view that those involved in the responsible tourism movement have to share their experiences of what works and what doesn't, to redouble their efforts to use tourism to make better places for people to live in. Also, it is viewed that stress had been laid on the robust and transparent financial management of destinations, to empower the local community and ensure that the earnings are distributed equitably within the community. The conference emphasized the need to reduce carbon pollution from the tourism industry. The governments, tourism businesses, airlines, and other forms of transport and consumers must prioritize carbon reduction, reduce the usage of fossil fuels, increase energy efficiency and use renewable energy. The increased publicity and social, cultural as well as environmental concerns cause more entrepreneurs, policy makers and planners to think in terms of sustainable and responsible tourism. It is important to live to its spirit, rather than it being converted into a tourism brand as has happened to many other similar development strategies. Essentially, promotion of responsible tourism demands devotion, dedication and innovation.

13.5 CONCLUSION

Sustainable tourism, responsible tourism, ecotourism and other alternative types of tourism have almost similar principles and guidelines. Theoretically, they are flawless and immaculate, but practically they are intricate and challenging. Implementing any form of alternative tourism successfully is a daunting task demanding dedication from top to bottom of the organizations involved. Moreover, complete stakeholder involvement is inevitable in the exercise of implementation. Ensuring local community involvement and equitable distribution of economic benefits with the local community, along with ensuring socio-cultural and environmental sustainabilities remain vital determinants in the success of any such forms of tourism.

Key Terms

Ecotourism	Economic responsibility
Local community participation	Souvenir
Tourism stakeholder	Alternative tourism
Ecotourism resources	Green tourism
Responsible tourism	Nature tourism
Social responsibility	Hard ecotourism
Environmental responsibility	Soft ecotourism
Cultural responsibility	

Review Questions

Short Answer Type Questions

1. Explain the concept of ecotourism.
2. Define ecotourism.
3. Discuss the principles of ecotourism.
4. Write about some important ecotourism resources in India.
5. Differentiate between hard ecotourism and soft ecotourism.
6. Define alternative tourism.
7. What are the common characteristics of ecotourism?
8. How can we classify ecotourism activities?
9. Define responsible tourism.
10. Discuss the nature and characteristics of responsible tourism.
11. What are the points that tourists should take care of while visiting a destination?
12. Explain the concept and principles of responsible tourism.
13. Discuss how tourists can contribute to responsible tourism.

Essay Type Questions

1. Explain the concept, principles and guidelines of ecotourism.
2. Write about ecotourism in India.
3. Explain responsible tourism. Discuss how to promote responsible tourism in a destination.

14

TOURISM MARKETING

Learning Outcomes

After studying this chapter, you will be able to:

- define tourism marketing;
- conceptualize tourism product;
- understand the significance of marketing in tourism;
- identify the nature and characteristics of tourism products;
- comprehend tourist as a consumer;
- explain market segmentation in tourism;
- differentiate between the marketing mix elements in tourism sector; and
- use marketing mix in tourism industry.

14.1 INTRODUCTION

Tourism has experienced continuous growth over the last six decades to become one of the largest industries and the fastest growing economic sector in the world. Dynamic marketing has played a significant role in the phenomenal evolution of tourism to this level. Tourism, being a hyper competitive sector, every country with adequate tourism potential attempts to attract as many tourists as possible. The competition existing among various countries and destinations is on steady ascent and the successful destinations are those who could market and promote, in addition to the other essential aspects like planning and management, tourism features and services well in the national and international markets.

In fact, marketing has increased relevance for tourism since tourism has certain unique characteristics in addition to the common service features. Those unique characteristics include geographic fragmentation, immovability, seasonality, high fixed costs and the like. The scope and relevance of marketing is enhanced due to intangibility and perishability of most of the tourism products. Effective marketing of tourism needs constant gearing up of tourism facilities and services to international standards and presupposes its coordination with the tourism suppliers.

14.2 TOURISM MARKETING

Tourists, the ultimate consumers in tourism, are more sophisticated and informed due to the advancements in information technology and mobile technology, and hence they are aware of the increased choices. Tourists have plenty of options to choose the most suitable one according to their needs, and destinations are increasingly adopting a strong focus on customer satisfaction as it is vital in the competitive survival of the destinations and other tourism industries. Indeed marketing is a process involving a diverse range of activities and functions including *product/service development*, *place* (location and distribution), and *pricing*. Marketing is the management process responsible for identifying, anticipating and satisfying customer requirements profitably (UK Chartered Institute of Marketing). The American Marketing Association defines marketing as a process of planning and executing the conception, pricing, promotion, and distribution of ideas, goods, and services to create exchanges that satisfy individual and organizational goals. The basic focus for marketing is exchange, a way to satisfy a want. "Marketing is a social and managerial process by which individuals and groups obtain what they need through creating and exchanging products and value with others (Kotler and Armstrong, 2013). As a business philosophy, it states that business success will result from providing the customer with what the customer wants or needs – the customer is the most important part of the business. It is also an important business function which focuses on determining customer needs and then ensuring that the business delivers a product or service that meets those needs.

In tourism, the tourists visit and obtain experience by visiting the attractions and consuming various services and products offered by tourism industrial elements. Here an exchange of intangibles takes place, and that gives the remark for international tourism as '*invisible export*'. Table 14.1 describes the evolution of the concept of marketing through the stages of production, selling and marketing (Medlik and Middleton, 1973).

A number of agencies are involved in tourism marketing. In fact, tourism marketing takes place at different levels. National tourism authorities undertake destination marketing for the country as a whole. Authorities at regions, provinces and states also market their respective destinations. Tourism industries also undertake both destination marketing as well as product marketing at different levels. For example, hotels market both their products as well as destinations. Airlines also do the same. At the national level, National Tourist Office or National Tourism Organization (NTO) undertakes tourism marketing and promotion for the entire country. Destination marketing forms its quintessence. In tourism, it involves identification of target tourist markets;

Table 14.1: Evolution of marketing concept: Stages

Production orientation
This stage is characterized by a shortage of available goods and services, and is therefore a seller's market. The main problem is to increase the output. Until the 1950s tourism was, in general, at this stage.
Selling orientation
This occurs when technological progress enables mass production, leading to increased competition, lower prices and a supply in excess of demand. This is therefore a buyer's market with a sales orientation from the producer to sell the increased output. The development of wide bodied jets and large hotels in the 1960s and 70s are examples of the second phase in tourism.
Marketing orientation
Increased competition and sophistication of buyers in an affluent society leads to the recognition of the necessity to identify consumer needs. Selling will not be sufficient by itself since consumer needs become the starting point for what is produced. Of late, the aim is to achieve optimal satisfaction of the consumer and to do so at an appropriate return to the producer.

Source: Modified from Medlik and Middleton (1973).

Table 14.2: Tourism sector: Characteristics, trends and issues

- Industry is featured with low level of concentration with large number of small businesses, yet, relatively a few large firms have market predominance.
- The high ratio of fixed costs to variable costs, with significant implications for financial stability that dominates tactical and strategic operation.
- The high levels of customer contact, necessitating staff to be skilled in both operational aspects and customer care.
- The relatively low levels of technological adoption across most of the sector.
- The inadequate marketing and human resource management expertise remains a constraint in all sectors of tourism, albeit to varying degrees.
- The importance of location vis-a-vis access to markets.
- The perishable nature of the product for all tourism sectors demands continuous investment in reservation and yield management systems.
- The prevalence of seasonal and irrational demand patterns, involving enterprises in the use of promotional and pricing strategies.
- The inconsistent application of principles of sustainability, environmental auditing and EIA techniques.
- The increasing degree of vertical, horizontal and diagonal integration in almost all the sectors.
- The different outlook of service sector and, the so-called under-management of the tourism sector, which denotes that the sector as a whole is valuable to ideas and takeovers from other industrial sectors.
- Conversely, increasing professionalism of the sector.

(Cooper et al., 2008)

communication with the actual and potential tourists to ascertain and influence their needs, motivation and likes; and to design and initiate their tourist products so as to accomplish utmost tourist satisfaction. It is defined as: " the management process through which the national tourist organisations and/or tourist enterprises identify their selected tourists, actual and potential, communicate with them to ascertain and influence their wishes, needs, motivation, likes and dislikes, on local, regional, national and international levels, and to formulate and adapt their tourist products accordingly in view of achieving optimal tourist satisfaction thereby fulfilling their objectives" (Wahab et al., 1976). Tourist gains satisfaction from the visit, and it is very important in the overall success of the destinations. Marketing of destinations is done primarily by the *destination marketing/ management organizations* (DMO) at the individual destination level. As stated above, national level, regional level and state level tourism organizations also engage in destination marketing.

14.3 TOURISM: THE PRODUCT AND ITS CHARACTERISTICS

Definition of tourism product is highly volatile. Diverse concepts and definitions are given in tourism literature. Each of the views has contradictions, yet for understanding it as a product some of the definitions are discussed here. According to (Kotler, et al., 2013): "A product is defined as anything that can be offered to a market for attention, acquisition, use, or consumption that might satisfy a want or need. It includes physical objects, services, persons, places, organizations and ideas." This product has to be purchased from the market. For example, biscuits, mobile phones, a car, etc., are available in the market satisfying different needs and wants of the buyer. From that viewpoint, a tourism product can also be described as a service that can be enjoyed by tourists starting from the place of origin, while in a tourist destination and until returning back home. It is supported by natural and cultural attractions; facilities and services like hotel, transportation, food, entertainment, etc. The often remarked view about tourism product is the '*convenient view*', which considers that tourism product is "a group of components or elements brought together in a 'bundle' selected to satisfy needs of tourists" (Middleton and Clarke, 2001). This bundle is a combination of service delivery components, each of which can satisfy different needs of a tourist. An example of this is given in Table 14.4. On the other hand, '*overall tourism product view*' has a focus on tourist experience, and as per it "... the product covers the complete experience from the time a consumer leaves home to the time he returns to it" (Medlik and Middleton, 1973). The 'consumer benefit' concept of product argues that tourists as customers, who are buying leisure products, are buying 'benefits' not products. According to Bateson and Douglas Hoffman (1999), the consumer benefit will be a bundle of functional, effectual and psychological attributes. In fact tourist purchases a variety of things, like:

- Beautiful location with clean beaches
- Transport facilities within the town and links to surrounding areas

Table 14.3: Fundamental concepts of marketing

- Needs: The basic human requirements.
- Wants: Needs become wants when they are directed to specific objects that might satisfy the needs.
- Demands: Demands are wants for specific products that are bagged by an ability and willingness to buy them.

Source: Based on Kotler et al., 2009.

- Accommodation
- Catering products
- Access to visitor attractions
- Access to shopping for general and special purchases relating to the holiday
- Access to recreational facilities such as leisure parks, bars, nightclubs, cinemas, water sports, etc. (Horner and Swarbrooke, 2005)

These are purchased based on various needs and wants of the tourist as part of his/her journey. The products are offered by different sectors. Yet, consumer benefit concept has been distinguished from product concept. Tourism product is "composite in nature and includes everything that tourists purchase, see, experience and feel from the time they leave home until the time they return" (Collier, 1997). Collier further adds that tourism product is a combination of total "experiences and expectations which are not directly purchased but which nevertheless still form part of the overall package" and hence he ascertains that tourism is a "total experience". Tour operator sells a package tour which is an amalgam of variety of services and products that form an end experience often called *tourist experience.* This product is a combination of services offered by different industries like airlines, hotels, etc. Hotel industry product separately offers a bundle of experiences as shown in Table 14.4. Tourism products offered by tourism industry consist

Table 14.4 Hotel product: Components of product 'Bundle' consisting of 'service delivery experiences'

- Initial experience and reactions in selecting from a guidebook, brochure or website.
- Experience of the booking process.
- First impression on entering the hotel – design of physical evidence.
- Reception process on arrival – front of house staff contact.
- Standard of rooms and its range of en suite facilities.
- Experience of customers – staff interactions during the stay.
- Provision of meals and any ancillary services.
- Checking out process.
- Any follow-up, such as direct mailing, received subsequently.

Source: Middleton and Clarke, 2001.

of different services and other products, each of which must be brought together and presented to the customer by the various sectors of the industry. Tourism demand is first created and then satisfied by the concentrated marketing efforts of diverse range of organizers providing tourists the needed products. These altogether constitute the world's largest and fastest growing industry (Holloway, 2006). Though different sectors are involved, tourist ultimately gets an experience which encompasses the satisfaction and experience gained from all the sectors. Dissatisfaction from any sector can affect the total experience of the tourist as well. The factors that constitute visitor experience from the site are:

- Tangible elements of the product, like, retail outlets, cafes, toilet facilities, etc.
- Service delivery elements including the appearance, attitude, behaviour and competence of the personnel involved.
- The expectation, behaviour and attitude of the visitor.
- Other factors, like climatic conditions (Swarbrooke, 2002).

The concept of a product is also described as having different levels. Number and type of levels may vary according to different authors. Core, generic, expected, augmented and potential products constitute one classification in the marketing concept. *Core benefit or product* includes the fundamental service or benefit that the customer is really buying. In tourism, this can be different for different sectors. For a hotel industry, the core product can be comfortable stay and for an airline, it can be safe and smooth travel from one place to another. *Basic or generic product* is the next level. The hotel industry marketer has to convert the core benefit as a product to be marketed and sold in the market. Next level is the expected product, wherein the marketer prepares an expected product by incorporating a set of attributes and conditions, which buyers normally expect while purchasing this product. Hotel marketer adds features to the core product of accommodation, like ensuring friendly and prompt customer service; clean rooms and other facilities; security and a feeling of being safe; and so on. This level is followed by *augmented product*. At this level, the marketer prepares an augmented product that exceeds customer expectations. Customer may not expect these types of features, but the marketer incorporates some incredible features into the product. In a hotel, a range of extra features and services can be added to augment the product. The visitor gets exceeded customer satisfaction by the added features which are extra to the core and expected product. Next level is the *potential product* and it takes into account all the possible augmentations and transformations the product might undergo in the future. This level considers how the product can be modified into the future, primarily to generate future sales from the existing customers.

14.4 CHARACTERISTICS OF TOURISM PRODUCTS

Tourism products are unique in many ways. Though tourism encompasses a number of diverse products, many of them share some common characteristics. A few major products have been briefly described here.

14.4.1 Intangibility

Intangibility is one of the significant features of tourism products. They cannot be seen, tasted, felt, heard or smelt before they are consumed (Kotler, 2004). Unlike manufactured goods, most of the tourism products cannot be inspected or verified prior to purchase and therefore it is almost completely dependent on representations and descriptions to help consumers make a purchase (Sheldon, 2003). This denotes that it is rather difficult to judge the tourism products, as in the case of service products, before they are bought. For instance, prior to boarding an aircraft, airline passengers have nothing but a document showing confirmation of a seat or a boarding pass, and the promise and expectation of reaching the destination in a safe and comfortable manner. At the same time when one goes to purchase a car, for instance, he/she can have physical verification and even a test drive to see its various product features. Implications associated with intangibility in tourism industry are varied. The busy schedule of modern man makes it difficult for him to spare time as time is now becoming very precious and scarce. A holiday is a time consuming process, while tour is a discretionary product. This makes it more difficult for a tourist to take a decision, i.e., intangibility adds to the complexity of decision making of a potential tourist.

Table 14.5: Comparison between goods and services

Goods	Services
Goods are manufactured.	Services are performed.
They are made in premises normally not open to customers (separable).	They are performed on the producers' premises, often with full customer participation (inseparable).
Goods are delivered to places where customers live.	Customers travel to places where the services are delivered.
Purchase conveys ownership and right to use at own convenience.	Purchase confers temporary right of access at a prearranged place and time.
Goods possess tangible form at the point of sale and can be inspected prior to sale.	Services are intangible at the point of sale; often cannot be inspected (other than 'virtually').
Stocks of product can be created and held for future sale.	Perishable; services can be inventoried but stocks of product cannot be held.

Sources: Middleton & Clarke, 2001.

14.4.2 Perishability

Most of the tourism products are highly perishable. The *perishability* of tourism products results in the risk and uncertainty for the businesses and marketers. It leads to the fact that revenue lost from unsold tourism products is gone forever. Here, the most important aspect to be highlighted is the *time factor*. The product has a life period and the same has to be sold in the specific period of time. The lapse will cause the product to become obsolete. It denotes that the job of the marketer is more difficult as the products have to be sold within a time period.

14.4.3 Variability

Variability is another feature of tourism products. The product-consumer interaction is a unique experience that is influenced by a large number of unpredictable human element factors. Tourism being a service industry, presence of people is essential in due course of production and consumption of the products. The people involved in offering services have a great role to play in satisfying customer's needs and wants. The mood, nature, mental stress, etc., of the service delivery personnel have a role in the delivery of services. Generally, the success of the services varies according to those factors.

14.4.4 Inseparability

From a marketing perspective, *inseparability* pertains to the simultaneous production and consumption of the product. Manufacturing goods, usually, are produced at one point of time and consumed at the other at a different location. Geographical aspect is relevant here. But in the case of tourism, most of the products are produced and consumed simultaneously and at the same location. The consumer becomes inseparable in the production system, an integral part of the production process since he/she has to be physically present while the service is produced. For instance, the guest has to reach the hotel for the consumption of the product as it is generated in his/her presence only. If the guest does not reach, the product is not generated.

Apart from the above, as suggested by Middleton and Clarke (2001), tourism products and services have some other common characteristics, such as:

- Seasonality and other variations in the pattern of demand.
- High fixed costs of operations, allied to fixed capacity at any point in time.
- Interdependence of tourism products.

Most of the tourism industries are characterized by high fixed costs and low variable costs. Fixed costs do not vary according to output level or sales revenue, and include rent, buildings, machinery, etc. A firm which has large proportion of fixed cost in comparison with the total cost is said to have high fixed cost. Hotels, especially up-market hotels are featured with high fixed costs. The initial expenses for the buildings and arranging the required facilities are quite high. Tourism industry demand fluctuates greatly in different seasons in a year. As a result, the supply side also makes necessary adjustments to manage the demand fluctuations. Though a variety of reasons are responsible for this phenomenon in tourism, yet climate remains the cardinal reason. Institutional causes such as religious, public and school holidays also cause seasonal fluctuations in tourist arrivals. It affects the industry severely in the off seasons when tourist arrivals are very low. All these factors influence both supply and demand and consequently production, distribution and consumption are also affected. In addition to the economic aspects of seasonality, it has considerable impact on environment, society and culture as well.

Diversity is another feature of tourism industry as tourism products consist of varied components. Tourism products involve different elements. Most of the industries in the tourism sector depend on each other for their survival. The interdependence is more and many are complementary to each other. The dependency and interrelationship may vary, but the same need to be taken into consideration. The supply of one sector depends on the supply of another sector and they complement each other. A change or an issue in one industry can affect the supply and delivery of service in the other sector. For example, when airline sector suffers demand due to sudden increase in fuel prices and the corresponding price hike, it can impact the hotel located in a destination as number of travellers will reduce which will affect the occupancy level of the hotels. A crisis due to a cyclone can affect a destination, which will impact demand to the destination and consequently all tourism industries in that destination will also suffer. Similarly, the airline services to the destination will also face crisis. A tourist chooses a destination for a holiday, but it is not just the geographical location and the attractions involved. He/she chooses it together with the products of accommodation, transport, catering, etc.

Immovability is perhaps a unique characteristic of tourism industry. The industries and their products cannot be moved in order to make consumption possible. Instead, the consumer has to travel and consume the product where it is located. According to Collier (1997), "Tourism cannot be taken to consumer, the consumer must be taken to it." This denotes that the location of the industry is an important aspect in tourism and the tourist has to reach the location to consume the product. This is quite relevant in most of the tourism sectors, including attractions, hospitality, air transport, and the like. Elements of tourist attractions are also immovable. A destination is composed of immovable natural and cultural attractions. Beaches, mountains, lakes, monuments and similar elements are to be enjoyed by the tourists in locations where they are situated.

14.5 TOURIST AS THE CUSTOMER AND THE PURCHASE DECISION MAKING

A core aspect, i.e., learning about decision making in regard to buying, is important in the context of marketing. It has more significance particularly in product design and marketing mix strategy formation. Consumer behaviour concerns the way tourists, as purchasers of products and services, behave in terms of spending, their attitudes, and values toward what they buy. This is affected by demographic factors like age, gender, marital status, educational background, and other factors. For marketers who sell and promote tourism products and services, these factors are crucial to the way they divide tourists into groups so that they can provide products that appeal to each group. In short, it examines why people buy the product and how they make their decision (Horner & Swarbrooke, 1996). It, considered as a process, has been pointed out that the consumer makes judgements while choosing the right option (Peter & Olson, 1999; Loke, 1995). Schiffman and Kanuk (2009) consider buying behaviour as "the process of making purchase decisions based on cognitive and emotional influences such as impulse, family, friends, advertisers, role models, moods, and situations that influence purchase." The consumer itself is sometimes described from the perspective of information search and decision making aspects. Engel, Blackwell and Miniard (1995) are of the opinion that it is a process by which a consumer chooses to purchase or use a product or service. As stated earlier, buying behaviour has ideally been considered a process of sequential stages such as need recognition, search for information on various products according to these needs, formation of alternative choices, evaluation of alternatives, act of purchase and consumption and post-purchase behaviour (Horner & Swarbrooke, 2007). The number of stages may differ according to different authors. For instance, Schiffman and Kanuk (2009) distinguish consumer decision making into three distinct interlocking stages: the *input stage*, the *process stage* and the *output stage*. In this, the first stage deals with consumers' recognition of a 'need' for a product and the following stage focuses mainly on how consumers make decisions. The last stage includes the process of purchase behaviour and post-purchase evaluation. Lovelock and Wirtz (2007) have indentified the buying behaviour process into three stages such as *pre-purchase stage, service-encounter stage* and *post-encounter stage*. The pre-purchase stage deals with decision making, which involves awareness of need, information search, evaluation of alternatives and making choices. The next stage includes 'moments of truth' and most importantly, the service delivery. The third consists of evaluation of service performed during service delivery and further intention formation. Though, different authors have identified stages in different ways, almost all such concepts, in one way or other, focus on the same activities. It can be summed up that decision making of a tourist passes through a series of stages and following are the identifiable steps in it:

1. Need recognition
2. Information search
3. Formation of alternatives
4. Evaluation of alternatives and decision making
5. Act of purchase

6. Consumption
7. Post-purchase behaviour and analysis.

Tourists have to consider various aspects while taking a decision. When a tourist is in the stage of decision making, variety of factors should be taken care of. The experience of buying and consuming tourism products, especially a holiday package will be very different from the purchase of common products like car, food, etc. Horner and Swarbrooke (2007) further illustrate that, the decisions for a tourist include aspects related to: which destination (country, region, resort) to choose; which mode of travel (like scheduled air, charter air, ferry, rail, coach, car, bus) to use; which type of accommodation (e.g., serviced or non-serviced) to choose for stay; duration of the holiday; at which time of the year will the holiday be taken; deciding between package tour or independent travel, and if choosing package tour, which operator to contact. It is likely to dedicate much more time and involve more careful consideration and selection especially when the cost is very high. Consumer behaviour or buyer behaviour is influenced by several factors or forces, like: internal or psychological factors, social factors, cultural factors, economic factors, personal factors, environment factors and other similar factors. In addition to the determinants in buying behaviour of common products, tourist destination selection includes a number of other factors (Yale, 1995). For example, health status of the traveller as well as his/her family members may have to be considered by the potential tourist while he/she takes a decision for travel. VISA requirements for travelling to a foreign country can be considered another factor. Also the destination reflects the holidaymakers' personality, which may turn decision making further complex. Decision making in tourism is highly complex particularly because tourists are aware of significant differences among various choices, and are highly involved in a purchase which occurs when the product is expensive, bought infrequently, risky and highly self-expressive. Horner and Swarbrooke (2007) made an attempt to list the reasons for high involvement in purchase decision making in tourism and it involves:

- high consumer commitment;
- high levels of insecurity linked to intangibility;
- strong influence of other people in decision making (e.g., influence of family members);
- long-term decision (interval of time which elapsed between purchase and consumption);
- high level of information search; and
- high level of emotional significance.

'High cost of holiday', and difficulty of 'knowing what to expect' in a distant, unfamiliar place also increase the difficulty of tourists decision making.

14.6 MARKET SEGMENTATION AND TARGET MARKETING

Market segmentation is crucial in the success of tourism businesses. Product development, segmentation, and positioning techniques are linked to the techniques of segmentation. Basically, it is the segmentation or division of markets into various homogenous groups of customers, each of them reacting differently to promotion, communication, pricing and other variables of the marketing mix. By this process, the marketer gets meaningful groups that share some common characteristics and those groups form the base for target marketing. As per the latest concepts, it is better to identify market segments as small as possible so as to address every segment with an individually targeted marketing mix. The market segments identified should be measurable, obtainable, accessible, valid and relevant. It has characteristics summed up as 'SMART'. It represents:

- Specific
- Measurable
- Accessible
- Realistic (and substantial)
- Time limits

Market segments chosen become the target markets. *Target market* is the fundamental starting point for the creation of a successful marketing mix strategy. Some of the most commonly used targeting strategies include 'undifferentiated targeting' (also known as mass marketing), concentrated targeting (niche marketing) and multi-segment targeting (separate marketing strategies for separate market segments). The effectiveness of the marketing strategies, to be precisely the marketing mix, depends as much on the ability to select the right target market, as on the skill in devising which will generate high levels of satisfaction. Common market segmentation bases in tourism are:

- Geographic segmentation
- Socio-demographic segmentation
- Psychographic segmentation
- Behavioural segmentation

Geographic segmentation, widely used in tourism sector, is based on the source markets. This divides the market into different geographical units such as nations, states, regions, countries, districts, cities, localities, urban/rural, etc. In tourism, this type of segmentation is more focused on the generating region, population (market size), weather patterns, or rural/urban areas. *Socio-demographic segmentation* is another type in which, tourists are divided into different groups on the basis of demographic variables, social class and income. Large number of variables such as age, occupation, gender, ethnicity, income, family composition, lifestyle, education status, religion, marital or cohabitational status, social class, etc., are used in this segmentation. *Psychographic segmentation* is also undertaken using variables like attitudes, interests, values, personality traits, beliefs, etc. *Bhavioural segmentation* highlights markets deserving particular attention and enables one to prioritise market focus and expenditure. Some of the variables used in tourism are number of trips taken, expenditure and repeat visits.

14.7 MARKETING MIX FOR TOURISM

Competitive survival, growth of tourism and its various industries depend greatly on the effective and efficient use of marketing mix elements. *Marketing mix* refers to the set of actions, strategies or tactics, that a company uses to attract, influence and persuade customers. There are four basic marketing mix elements, called 4P's, that comprise four different categories of strategies related to product, price, promotion and place. Later, more elements were added to this. Organizing systematic process by adopting appropriate strategy for implementing marketing mix will help the organization influencing the demand for that product or services (Bakhshi, 2007). Booms and Bitner (1981) suggested three more P's for service marketing, i.e., people, physical evidence and process. Ensuring right combination of marketing mix elements is crucial in the success of the business. The following are a complete set of elements in marketing mix applicable in tourism:

- Product
- Price
- Promotion
- Place
- People
- Physical evidence
- Process

14.8 PRODUCT

Products are tangible and intangible elements that are offered in the market for tourism, consumer interest, purchase, use or their consumption that fulfil the consumer needs and provide satisfaction. They involve quality and performance levels that the consumer receives but in services, quality and high standards of delivery assure an advantage over the competitor. The tourism marketing mix elements must be chosen with greater care especially with the tourism product design, attachment to physical evidences and product delivery/distribution. It is also important for marketers to think about their *product* in terms of the benefits that it provides consumers with, rather than in terms of its physical attributes or features. Those firms that provide higher-quality service levels than their competitors are likely to be successful in gaining more customers. The product offered to the marketplace by the firm must be designed to ensure segmentation fit and the quality to achieve customer satisfaction. Range of tourism products offered by the same firm must ensure that each one provides value-added benefits to the customer and employ methods to assure the performance level convenience and the benefits they are expected to deliver. This is because much of the consumer decision making process is focussed on the benefits that the product or service will provide the consumer with – consumers buy benefits, not features. The designed tourism product feature should reduce the risk, be safe and secure, compatible, have value-added benefits (Cooper et al, 2008) and be less complex in nature to the consumer to provide product acceptability and branding with high satisfaction levels, image and added value to a product. The employees of the organization require definite skills and resources along with marketing in order to attract more tourists and earn revenue. Certain products like archaeological sites attract less tourists if the historical background is not known; therefore the firm must equip the employees with historical information and importance along with promotion adding to features and benefits to consumers to buy products.

Image too has significance in tourism as possessed by the potential travellers, are thus important in the destination selection process. Most of the tourism products often compete via images and according to Pike (2008), destination image is a repertoire of brand associations held in the mind of the traveller. **Branding** helps customers to decide which products to buy. Almost all sectors in tourism attempt to develop their own brands. Airlines and hospitality sectors have world renowned brands. *Product innovation* and *product development* are key activities in which any organization in tourism should be involved. New products have to be introduced regularly. *Packaging* is also relevant in tourism, by ensuring use of brand names, logos, attractive entrances, attractive merchandising materials, and the use of other organisations such as tour operators or ticket companies to sell the product as part of a package (Horner & Swarbrooke, 2005). *Product positioning* is considered to be significant as they reflect the attributes and occupy consumers' minds to purchase as per the needs. It is important in any industry which consists of close substitutes. In majority of tourism markets particularly those dominated by package deals and charter flights, competing destinations have close substitutes (Pike, 2008) and hence brand positioning is a potential source of competitive advantages for destinations. The correct product positioning will help the consumer to identify the uniqueness of the product and help the organization to differentiate the product from competitors for exploring the possibility of gaining the consumer. According Pike (2005), there are seven stages in destination positioning. They are:

- identifying the target market and travel context;
- identifying the competitive set of destinations in the target market and travel context;
- identifying the motivation/benefits sought by previous visitors and non-visitors;
- identifying perceptions of the strengths and weaknesses of each of the competitive set of destinations;

- identifying opportunities for differentiated positioning;
- selecting and implementing the position; and
- monitoring the performance of the positioning strategy overtime.

14.9 PRICE

To the consumer, price is considered to be cost; to the supplier, it is revenue, and hence pricing has utmost significance in business sectors. It is basically the amount of money charged by the organization from the tourism consumer for the product or service they consume. *Price* can also be explained as the sum of the values that consumers lose in exchange for using the benefits of having a product, item or a service (Kotler & Armstrong, 2013). When setting a price for a product or service the key factors to consider are pricing objectives, demand (what consumers are willing to pay), cost and the prices of competitor's products. *Pricing* is considered to be most sensitive element of marketing mix for competition. The price of the tourism product must be carefully decided as they directly link to the quality and delivery of product and services. Pricing decision of any tourism product needs to consider the value of the operation, delivery and quality of the product. The market price must be kept in mind to devise market strategy which includes image creation and branding. Pricing of tourism product includes accommodation, travel, food and many others based on the requirement of the customers. Different marketing techniques used for tourism pricing are as follows:

- The pricing strategy adopted is based on *matching the demand and supply* for particular destination. If the demand is high and supply is low, premium pricing can be charged or vice versa.
- Next, pricing strategy is based on *market competition* and the *acceptability of the organizational product* in the market among the consumers rather than competitors.
- Last but not the least, pricing strategy is based on *brand building, market positioning, sustainability, building consumer relationship, return on investments,* etc.

The most common pricing strategies applied in tourism sector are cost-oriented pricing and demand-oriented pricing. **Cost-oriented pricing** is based on the cost, and in cost pricing. It is one kind of cost-oriented pricing, wherein the seller's costs are calculated and the price is set by adding a margin. **Demand-oriented pricing** is based on the demand trends. Usually, when the demand is high, price will be higher and vice versa. Another type, rate of return pricing, focuses on the profits generated in relation to the capital invested (usually, not suitable to tourism as it sidelines the need to link the pricing policy to the creation of a sales volume).

Some of the derivatives of the above and others that are commonly applied in tourism are following:

- **Skimming pricing:** This is usually much high, goes to products that are fairly unique in a newer market offering new customer experiences. This method is

Table 14.6: Characteristics of travel and tourism services that influence pricing

- High price elasticity in the discretionary segments of leisure, recreation and vacation travel markets.
- Long lead times between price decisions and product sales. Twelve months or more are not uncommon lead times when prices must be printed in brochures to be distributed months before customer purchases are made, as is typically the case for tour operators.
- No possibility of stockholding for service products, so that retailers do not share with producers the burden and risk of unsold stocks and tactical pricing decisions.
- High probability of unpredictable but major short-run fluctuations in cost elements such as oil prices and currency exchange rates.
- Near certainty of tactical price cutting by major competitors if supply exceeds demand.
- High possibility of provoking price wars in sectors such as transport, accommodation, tour operation and travel agencies, in which short-run profitability may disappear.
- Extensive official regulation in sectors such as transport, which often includes elements of price control.
- Necessity for seasonal pricing to cope with short-run fixed capacity.
- High level of customers' psychological involvement, especially with vacation products, in which price may be a symbol of status as well as value.
- The high fixed costs of operation, which encourage and justify massive short-run price cuts in service operations with unsold capacity of perishable products.
- High level of vulnerability to demand changes reflecting unforeseen economic and political events.

Source: Middleton and Clarke, 2001.

utilized when there is shortage of supply of the product and where demand will not be dampened by charging premium price. For example, luxury villas with pools set in good location are normally priced with higher margins.

- **Penetration pricing:** This is aimed at maximum distribution in a new market with price at a lower level to get maximum sales and market share. This is adopted when an organization wants to establish itself in a marketplace.
- **Discriminatory pricing:** This means that the organization is selling a product or service at two or more prices to suit different customers, products, locations and times, despite the fact that the product costs are the same.
- **Backward pricing or intuitive method:** This is a market-based method of pricing that focuses on what the consumer is willing to pay.
- **Competition-oriented pricing:** The prime concern of pricing shall be the prices of the competing products.
- **Strategic and tactical pricing:** Prices are set a long way in advance, based on the long-term view of corporate strategy, product positioning and value for money in the marketplace.
- *Premium pricing* must be based on quality, brand and significance of delivery.

It is important to know that the right price set for the tourism product creates positive impact and ease to market the product and services to the people.

14.10 PROMOTION

Simply, it is the process of promoting, communicating to inform, remind or persuade the consumer to buy the product and services offered by the organization. Organisations often use a variety of methods and techniques at the same time to meet their marketing objectives. Promotion is used by organisations to affect the way in which consumers behave and is therefore a vital motivator for any tourism organization. The role of promotion is to convince potential customers of the benefits of purchasing or using the products and services of a particular organisation. Through promotion, tourism organization communicates in an effective way with its target customers. It can influence consumer attitude and behaviour that creates interest, desire and attention to purchase the product at a particular price. It is basically marketing communication. Advertising is an ideal tool for promotion of any form of business. The methods of marketing communication that tourist business uses depends on the type of product, the aims of the campaign and market characteristics. The different ways in which a business may communicate with its target market(s) is known as the *promotional mix*. It includes a number of elements, like:

- Advertising
- Public relations
- Sales promotions
- Personal selling

Promotional mix media include word of mouth, television, magazine, telemarketing, exhibition, travel newsletter, publicity, billboards and more that offer and showcase the product and create desire in the potential customer to purchase the product. Selection of media must incorporate the budget, frequency and the visibility of the promotion.

Advertising is considered a non-personal communication from the firm to the mass to attract the customer and create interest to buy the product. The message and choice of media are two important aspects of promotion. Other forms of promotion include sales promotion and public relations. *Sales promotion* includes the activities that create sure sales and achieve desired outcomes to attract the potential customers, traders and other intermediaries. According to Kotler (2004), sales promotion is short-term incentives to encourage purchase or sales of a product or service. Different sales promotion techniques are used by tourism companies according to seasons and occasions. *Public relation* creates a positive image of the firm and opportunity to create brand image through news and media coverage. *Publicity* is also used by the tourism sector which represents non-personal communication in news story form about an organization on its products, transmitted through the media for no charge. Organizations need to build good relationship with media to obtain mass media coverage and reduce the risk of damaging news. Brochure is one of the main forms of marketing communication in tourism sector, particularly due to the tourism industry characteristics such as intangibility, inseparability and immovability. Nowadays, digital brochures are also available. Print brochures are an inevitable tool for many of the tourism industries, particularly tour operators and hospitality industries. The last form of promotion is through personal selling. It is all about persuading customers to purchase products and services in a personal face-to-face situation. It includes face-to-face communication like telephone, email, etc., to gain benefits and information. Apart from e-Marketing techniques using internet based platforms for promoting tourism products, the industry also use mobile platforms to communicate effectively and efficiently with the customers. Promotion supports the organization and consumer to maximizing benefits, frequency, innovation of offering, duration, backing diverse areas, exploring niche areas, etc. The tourism organization is required to explore various promotional mix mechanisms to secure large number of tourists and attract new users to purchase tourism products and services.

14.11 PLACE

Place is all about *channel strategies* used by industries that enable easy and smooth delivery of tourism products and services to the customer at specific location and time (Alvedari, 2005). Channel selection needs to consider the number of levels and types for effective delivery and feedback. The upcoming tourism based firms may face difficulty in positioning their product and services to the channel members due to low awareness. Therefore, new firms in travel and tourism business must consider strategies for distribution very carefully to ensure success. Distribution is all about *"down stream"* section of the supply chain and the players involved in it are also called *marketing channel partners*. Distribution is getting increasing relevance in this hyper competitive environment due to a myriad of factors like threat of disintermediation and direct distribution at the global level and increasing competition. This makes tourism firms depend on distribution channels. *Perishability* is another factor. Many industries are engaging in alliances at the global level. Distribution channel is primarily meant for making available the product or services to the consumer in a convenient manner. There exists, as pointed out by Kotler et al. (2010), fundamental difference between distribution of goods and services. According to them, "distribution systems are traditionally used to move goods (tangible products) from the manufacturer to the consumer. In hospitality and travel industries, distribution systems are used to move the customer to the product: the hotel, restaurant, cruise ship, or airplane". Channel of distribution in tourism is described as "an operating structure, system, or linkage of various combinations of organizations through which a producer of travel products describes, sells, or confirms travel arrangements to the buyer" (Goeldner and Ritchie, 2003). As stated before, in tourism also, direct, indirect as well as hybrid types of distribution are commonly seen. The trend of disintermediation is increasing, yet many industries still find comfort with the intermediary involved distribution. In tourism, distribution channels ensure the following functions:

- Provision of market intelligence
- Promotion and marketing communication
- Interactive communication
- Negotiation with suppliers
- Packaging/consolidation
- Reservation, confirmation, selling
- Distribution
- Risk taking on behalf of principals
- Payment collection
- Representative of the payment
- Customization
- Stock and inventory management

There are different levels observed in tourism distribution. *One level distribution* denotes direct selling by the supplier to the consumer. 'Walk-in' in a hotel is an example of direct distribution. Through this, the supplier enjoys a range of benefits. Since it is direct selling, channels of communication substantially reduce which saves time and *minimize chances of making mistakes*. Maximum direct interaction is possible and the supplier has *control in distribution and sale of the product*. In addition, the supplier has maximum liberty to be flexible to change plans. Since the commission need not to be given to the intermediaries, direct distribution benefits more, along with increased profit levels. Apart from them, there can be *flexibility on distribution and maintaining stock*, etc. Yet there are disadvantages as well. The company has to *set up a distribution system* which needs capital investment as well. In addition, the *existing intermediaries become hostile* since they lose the business and rival actions can be expected. Suppliers and intermediaries can be geographically dispersed, which makes *distribution complicated*.

Two-level system involves one intermediary, usually a retailer. The product moves from supplier to the retailer and the retailer sells it to the final consumer. It also occurs when the wholesaler acts as a bridge between for the consumer and supplier. For example, an IATA recognized travel agent can sell the ticket of an airline, where airline is the supplier and the travel agent is the retailer. Or, a tour operator can sell a hotel room to a tourist. Here, hotel is the supplier and the tour operator is the wholesaler. There are advantages like responsibility of selling will be taken care of by the retailer and the cost needed for distributing directly can be saved. The customer is benefitted greatly since the product can be accessed easily and gets diverse options to choose from the most suitable. Also, the intermediary acts as a one-stop shop for many of their travel requirements. *Intermediary* is usually more professional in dealing with the customers. This makes the distribution more efficient. In addition, payment and feedback are collected by the intermediary and it gives more freedom to the supplier. At the same time, commission has to be paid for distributing the product. Control in distribution reduces and the supplier lacks interactive communication with the customer.

Three-level system involves two intermediaries, usually a wholesaler and a retailer. For instance, a tour operator buys hotel rooms in bulk, splits into single units to include in a package tour and finally distributes the package to a travel agent for sale to the final consumer. Here, travel agent acts as a retailer. The advantages and disadvantages are similar to the two-level system, but the customer may have more benefits, since due to the presence of a wholesaler, the price to be paid for consuming the product will be much less compared to purchasing those products separately. The customer can enjoy the benefit more, yet the professional ability of the intermediaries gives advantages and benefits to the supplier by making the process of distribution more efficient and effective without investing capital for establishing its own system of distribution. In addition to intermediaries such as travel agents and tour operators, tourism industry has IT based exclusive distribution systems like *Global Distribution Systems* that play a significant role in the distribution and promotion of travel and tourism products.

14.12 PEOPLE

People involved in tourism provide solutions to satisfy consumer needs and provide value for money. Employees, especially the operational and delivery personnel contribute directly to the effectiveness and consumer satisfaction levels. The selection, training and motivation of employees can contribute to customer satisfaction. The employees should exhibit competence, caring attitude, responsiveness, initiative and problem-solving abilities. Many services like hotel, restaurant, airlines, etc., have direct interaction with clients and firms' employees, which strongly influences how customers perceive service quality. The frontline employees must be presented with utmost care and etiquettes while representing the organization.

14.13 PHYSICAL EVIDENCE

The service provider must ensure tangible evidence of a firm's service quality that have a deep impression on customers (Lovelock and Wirtz, 2007). The service quality can be enhanced through proper physical evidence and presentation. A hotel can be good looking with observable style of dealing with the customers that carry out its intended customer value proposition in cleanliness, speed or other benefits. The environment, physical layout, décor, employee's appearance, equipment used, ambience, background, and other services contribute significantly to the customer's quality judgement, experience, satisfaction with a service, and expectations of the service.

14.14 PROCESS

The set of procedures, measures, activities in sequential order for service delivery and operation can be termed *process*. The process implements, controls and assures the flow of activities to achieve desired results. Unlike product, services are inseparable along with variability characteristics, the services delivery need to be standardized for achieving quality for each customer. Therefore, the process used in the service industry especially in tourism should follow specific processes for operation, pricing, promotion, distribution and delivery. The processes of delivery must be based on customer choice and different service brands with which consumers compare and assess the quality of the services of that of the competitor services. Process allows service differentiation, provides customers' attributes and supports branding and brand building. Service companies can choose among different processes to deliver their service. Restaurants develop fast-food counters, cafeteria sections, buffet corners. Product elements and process can support service delivery and operating systems for employees to build and develop customer perception.

14.15 CUSTOMER RELATIONSHIP MANAGEMENT (CRM)

It is inevitable for the business entities to create and maintain close and cooperative relationship with customers to remain competitive in this modern business environment (Parvatiyar & Sheth, 2003). Cano & Prentice (1998) have stated that from the part of service providers, customers are seeking more intimate relationship. Now, it is important to create and maintain long-term, mutually beneficial relationships with customers and also with business intermediaries. Acquiring new customers is six to nine times as expensive as keeping a new customer (Pepper & Roger, 1993). Hence, keeping a customer for future sale has become very important and has necessitated generating loyalty among customers. It was due to these business pressures that concepts such as *relationship marketing* and *customer relationship management* (CRM) evolved and constitute some of the new thrust areas of business. A competitive environment has always made businesses to change and improve their process of working. Focus on cooperative and collaborative relationship between the firm and its customers, and/or other marketing actors is the main theme in CRM and relationship marketing programmes. (Parvatiyar & Sheth, 2003). After MRP (Manufacturing Resource Planning), TQM (Total Quality Management), QFD (Quality Function Deployment), EDI (Electronic Data Interchange), BPR (Business Process Reengineering), ERP (Enterprise Resource Planning), SCM (Supply Chain Management), the next three lettered mantra has rewritten the marketing lexicon through a paradigm shift from traditional transactional marketing to web enabled interactive relationship marketing in CRM.

CRM can be defined as "the infrastructure that enables the delineation of and increase in customer value and the correct means through which to motivate valuable customers to remain loyal, indeed to buy again"(Dyche, 2003), whereas relationship marketing is defined as an integrated effort to identify, maintain and build up a network with individual consumers and continuously strengthen the network for mutual benefit of both sides, through interactive, individualized and value added contacts over a long period of time (Shani & Chelsani, 1992). For generating loyal customers and to keep customers for a long time, Pine et al. (1995) suggests that learning relationship with the customers has to be evolved which demands 'an ongoing connection that becomes smarter as the customer and the organizations interact with each other, collaborating to meet the consumer's needs overtime'. Mass customization strategy was changed to individual customization and individual or one-to-one relationship building became one of the main strategies.

14.16 CONCLUSION

Marketing is one of the most important functions of tourism organisations. Along with destination organisations and national tourism authorities, various tourism industries are also engaged in tourism marketing. Tourism product, defined in diverse ways, is unique to a certain extent and hence marketing of them necessitates care and diligence. Employing most appropriate marketing mix is crucial in the success of tourism industries. Tourism organisations have to consider each element of the marketing mix separately and use of right mix of elements for competitive survival and growth of the businesses. Moreover, marketers have to ensure that the different components of the marketing mix interact effectively to produce the desired effect on the target consumers and their behaviour patterns.

Key Terms

Marketing
Product
Need
Want
Service
Marketing mix
Price
Place
Promotion
Marketing communication
People
Physical evidence
Process
Demand oriented pricing
Cost oriented pricing
Target marketing
Market segmentation
Buying behaviour
Purchase decision making
Intangibility
Perishability
Inseperability
Variability

Review Questions

Short Answer Type Questions

1. Define tourism marketing.
2. Discuss the importance of marketing in tourism.
3. What do you mean by tourism product?
4. Explain tourism product concepts from different angles.
5. What are the elements of tourism product?
6. What do you mean by tourist/visitor experience?
7. What are the factors that influence tourist/visitor experience?
8. Write the characteristics of a tourism product.
9. What do you mean by tourist buying behaviour?
10. What are the factors that determine tourist buying behaviour?
11. Discuss why tourist purchase decision making is a difficult process.
12. Discuss market segmentation in tourism.
13. Write different market segments in tourism.
14. What do you mean by marketing mix?
15. Write how tourism product can be enhanced using product mix.
16. What are the product strategies that can be used in tourism?
17. Write the significance of pricing in tourism.
18. Discuss various tourism pricing strategies.
19. Explain the promotion tools used in tourism.
20. Elucidate the channel strategies applied by tourism industries.
21. Explain CRM in tourism sector.

Essay Type Questions

1. Explain marketing mix in tourism.
2. Write the importance of marketing in tourism.

15 TOURISM INFORMATION TECHNOLOGY

Learning Outcomes

After studying this chapter, you will be able to:

- explain the role of IT in tourism;
- define e-Tourism and distinguish it from e-Business in tourism;
- conceptualize cyber tourism;
- describe the applications of IT in air transport and its benefits;
- elaborate how travel intermediaries make use of IT;
- explain the impact of online sales on travel intermediaries;
- identify global distribution systems and their products and services;
- comprehend IT applications in the hospitality sector; and
- explain how destinations make use of IT for their competitive survival.

15.1 INTRODUCTION

Tourism and information technology (IT) are intricately interdependent as both share a symbiotic relationship. International travel industry is a major user of data and information of all kinds. Developments in computing and telecommunication technology have radically altered the way in which multinational organizations operate their businesses. Some of the elements in tourism, like airlines, are the pioneers in business application of information technology. Sheldon (2003) opined that *information technology* is the life blood of tourism industry as its components are at the forefront of users of modern information and communication technology. Tourism is a consumer of a diverse range of information, and IT has been immersed deeply into the whole system of tourism. Technology in the tourism industry is undoubtedly having an impact on tourism operations. The success of tourism industry to a great extent relies on its ability to efficiently deliver accurate, up-to-date and relevant information to various stakeholders with information and communication technology. According to Benchendorff et al. (2005), in tourism, technology has two main types of roles in the creation and enhancement of tourist experience. One is its use behind the curtains and the other is in the front stage which helps in creating as well as enhancing tourist experiences. Industry players and tourists have an important role in the use of the technology and their attitude and familiarity are relevant in this context. Technology, particularly Information Technology plays a number of roles in tourism. Of them, the major are:

- Technology contributes to the growth of tourism.
- Technology as creator of the tourism experience.
- Technology as protector of the tourism experience.
- Technology as an enhancer of the tourism experience.
- Technology as focal point of the tourism experience.
- Technology as tool of tourism industry.
- Technology as destroyer of the tourism experience.

15.2 SIGNIFICANCE OF INFORMATION TECHNOLOGY IN TOURISM

In this modern competitive business environment, as in other sectors, information is one of the most valuable and important resources (Ralph & Reynolds, 2001). Tourism is not an exception and, all the players involved such as producers, suppliers, intermediaries as well as consumers are in need of latest and most accurate information in a big manner. Information must be able to flow quickly and accurately between the client, intermediaries and all tourism suppliers involved in servicing the client's needs. As a result, *information and communication technology* (ICT) has become an almost universal feature of the tourism industry. Its power allows information to be managed more effectively, and transported worldwide almost instantly. As a result, it has had (and continue to have) a major effect on the methods of operation of the tourism industry. However, it has not affected all functions and sectors equally. It has the greatest impact on marketing and distribution functions, while leaving others which need more human contact relatively untouched. Similarly, certain sectors such as the airlines have been keen adopters of technology, using it to help to manage and streamline their operations and to gain strategic advantage. Others, in particular the hotel sector, were less enthusiastic, but are gradually waking up to the benefits. However, given the way in which ICT is reshaping the basic structure of both commerce and society in general, and consumers increased demand for information, its importance to the success of a tourism enterprise can only grow in the coming days. The need for information for the tourists is manifold as compared to common consumers. It is heightened by certain characteristics of the tourism product. Tourists need information before going on a trip to help them plan and choose options, and also increasingly need information during the course of the journey as the trend towards more independent travel increases. Tourists undertake extensive information search before they make a trip.

Tourism products are mostly service products and hence need for latest and accurate information is very essential. The reasons why tourism industry needs information intensively are due to its own characteristics like intangibility and inseparability. Due to these, pre-demonstration or testing may not be possible. Travellers have to take a decision before neither experiencing nor seeing the product. Therefore, since travellers cannot pre-test the product or easily get their money back if the trip does not meet up to their expectations, access to accurate, reliable, timely and relevant information is essential to help them make an appropriate choice. It is notable that greater the degree of perceived risk in a pre-purchase context, greater is the consumer propensity to seek information about the product. Some of the tourism products are highly perishable. Due to this peculiarity, need for information by those industries is very high. Latest information is needed to sell the products in time. Tourism products are volatile in that if they are not sold, they represent lost revenue. Tourist's presence is essential in the production process. Here also, there is much need for the information at the right time. Majority of the industries are located in the Tourist Destination Regions (TDR), which are usually away from the markets. This necessitates increased need for information for both tourists as well as industrial components. For the tourist, the destination and the industry elements may appear strange and hence information search will be very crucial. Most of the tourism products are immobile, so that the customers have to experience what they are buying. IT helps in this regard by providing information in various forms to get a clearer picture. Tourism is a heterogenous sector. The industry is an amalgam of many industries and the products being produced by them are also different. Two other characteristics are its complexity and its interdependence. In addition, tourism products are rarely bought individually, and the endless combinations and permutations of alternative travel routes, transportation modes, time and lodging accommodation make travel decisions difficult even for the initiated. Suppliers therefore, face a challenge, which is described as trying to gain identity among millions of potential customers covering the whole spectrum of incomes, interests, knowledge sophistication and needs. Increasingly, consumers can undertake their entire tourism product search and booking online and, therefore, they require flexible, specialized, accessible, interactive products and communication with tourism organizations. Thus, both tourism destinations and enterprises increasingly need to adopt innovative methods and enhance their competitiveness. Moreover, tourists are increasingly sophisticated and demand latest tools for booking, consuming the products and for enhancing their experience.

15.3 IT APPLICATION IN TOURISM

Before going into the details of IT applications in each sector, its overview in tourism is given below.

All kinds of computer hardware in one form or other have some usage in tourism sector. PCs, minicomputers and mainframes are commonly used in reservation as well as operational functions, in different segments of tourism industry. CD-ROMs gave way to diffusion of multimedia technology for individual users. In addition to its usage as data storage device, they are used extensively in tourism promotion. Self-service terminals or kiosks are used as points of information and sale. Information kiosks are another technology used in tourism sector to disseminate information particularly when tourists arrive at the destination. Many of the systems incorporate a computer, a credit card reader, printer, modem, and a cash receiver, and in certain cases they are used to sell tickets/travel documents or keys. Stand-alone as well as systems connected to reservation facilities are also available.

Information technology application on destinations is of great benefit for tourism enterprises and destinations as they increase their distribution networks, labour efficiency and ubiquity. *Automated travel machines* (ATMs) are a tool for consumers to access travel databases, installed in strategic areas where travellers can access information/other services. Videotext systems are used extensively in some European countries to offer information access to masses, particularly people at home inexpensively. Travel information is transmitted rigorously through videotext systems. Interactive TV is another media used by travellers to access travel information and databases.

As computer networking technology progressed and the coming together of computer and telecommunication took place, the scope of ICT in tourism increased tremendously. Internet based inter-organizational networking on a global scale emerged which enhanced effective communication in tourism. The usual kind of networking, intra-organizational, helped tourism industry in a big manner. The Internet or stakeholder wide systems help tourism organizations in selling and undertake e-commerce, brand building, in generating loyalty clubs, affiliations, and communication and interaction with all stakeholders. The *extranet/partner systems* enable the organizations to communicate and interact with partners effectively to interact with all stakeholders smoothly and to ensure e-Business functions like eSales and marketing, eProduction and manufacturing, eProcurememt, eAccounting and eFinance, as well as electronic HR outsourcing. These help tourism organizations greatly in remaining competitive in the modern world. The *intranet/internal systems* enable organizations for better operational processes that involve control inventory, dynamic pricing, check-in and billing procedures, routing and scheduling and coordination of production. Such systems also help in undertaking e-Business functions like eProduction and manufacturing, eProcurement, eAccounting, eHR and eManagement (Buhalis, 2003). Knowledge management is another usage of these systems. These benefits are applicable to almost all sectors of the tourism industry, including transportation, hospitality and food and beverage sector.

Electronic Data Interchange (EDI) is also used in tourism industry. It is defined as the electronic transmission of structured business documents in a predefined, machine-readable format between trading partners' internal computer systems. It involves capture and creation of documents in electronic form and their transmission electronically along with organization, retrieval, synthesis, printing and display (Sheldon, 2003). *Electronic Fund Transfer* (EFT) enables electronic transfer of money from customers to service providers' accounts through credit and debit card transactions.

Mobile devices are used by tourism industries in a variety of ways. Wireless applications are incorporated in ICT and devices like cellular phones, smart phones, pagers, GPS, codeless computer peripherals, home-remote control and monitor systems are examples of it. Communication between consumers and tourists has improved greatly due to mobile telephony. The advent of mobile telephony over global system for mobile communication (GSM) enabled communication of voice and data over mobile phones. Third generation mobile phones and services are in use in some countries. Personal Digital Assistants (PDAs) and 4G mobile phones with Geo Positioning Systems (GPSs) help travellers retrieve travel related information without time and geographic constraints. Mobile devices are also used by principals and suppliers to reserve rooms, book tickets, car rentals, retrieve information on transportation schedules, etc. Mobile networks and Wireless Local Area Networks (WLANs) enable users to connect devices to the Internet through a wireless radio connection (WiFi), while Bluetooth connects PDAs, cell phones, smart phones, computers' mice and other peripherals over short distances. Mobile Apps are also of much use in the tourism sector. *WiMax* (Worldwide Inter-operatability for Microwaves access) is an emerging technology that promotes conformance and inter-operatability of the IEEE 802.16 standard and provides wireless data over long distances. This will help the users to browse the Internet without physically connecting the computer to a wall jack and is expected to offer the highest possible coverage up to 30 miles.

Newsgroups, Electronic Bulletins Boards (EBB), and chat rooms are important services on the Internet that enable travellers to research travel products and destinations, though commercial flavour may lack in them, rather with focus on particular interest groups. Newsgroups, accessible through Usenet are virtual communities where users are more interested in specific topics to store and share information and commentary. EBBs also offer similar services, though the information is not replicated on different servers. Chat rooms offer different services as the information exchange is in real-time, where real-time discussions take place.

Travel industry involves networks to connect together computer systems of travel firms to enable smooth flow of data and information. The basic networks such as WAN and LAN are created for the exchange of information in the organizations. All the industries in tourism sector are interlinked and hence the need for smoother flow of data and information is inevitable. Airlines constitute one sector that introduced communication networks for the first time. Aeronautical Radio Incorporated (ARINC) was formed by a number of airlines to provide communication and information processing services for the aviation and travel industries. SITA, claimed to be the largest global data and voice communication network covering numerous travel industries, spans over 225 countries in the world.

Travel industry also has a number of switches, which are basically communication facilitating measures to enable the industry to translate the data before it is received at the other end. Majority of the switches are formed to enable travel firms to communicate with GDSs in their unique protocol (Sheldon, 2003). Ultra switch, Wiscom, and THISCO (The Hotel Industry Switching Company) are examples of switches. Ultra Switch helps travel agents to make hotel bookings on-line through their GDS terminals and receive rapid communication. THISCO was set up to provide accurate and rapid information on room availability, rates, and confirmation number to travel agents through GDS terminals and to encourage electronic booking of hotel rooms worldwide by travel agents. Terminal emulation systems, protocol converters and/or gateways are also used in certain contexts in the travel industry.

Information technology helps the organizations perform operational, managerial and strategic functions efficiently. Advent of IT in the tourism industry influences almost all the functions involved in the travel and tourism industry. According to Buhalis (2002), the various functions empowered by ICTs can be categorized under two broad classes such as key strategic functions and key operational functions. They are as follows:

Key Strategic Functions

- Enhance organizational efficiency and effectiveness.
- Improve quality of services.
- Diversify to new products and services or new markets.
- Formulate new combinations of tourist products.
- Undertake strategic research for new markets and products.
- Follow up competition.
- Penetrate existing and new markets and expand market share.
- Differentiate and personalize products and add value at all stages.
- Reduce cost and achieve cost competitive advantage by creating value for money.
- Constantly reinvent new and innovative business practices.
- Outperform competition in the long run.
- Achieve time competitive advantage by maximizing efficiency for consumers and creating value for time.
- Re-engineer business processes and rationalize operations.
- Develop partnerships and explore virtual corporations.

Key Operational Functions

- Information distribution and reservation process.

- Production and delivery of tourism products.
- Organization, management and control of tourism enterprises.
- International tourism management and marketing.
- Facilitation of producer, intermediary and consumer interaction.
- Front office: reservations, check-in, billing, communication.
- Back office: accounting, payroll, procurement, administration.
- React to unexpected events and adopt flexibility and reflective procedures.
- Dynamic yield management and adjust price and capacity.
- Customer entertainment and service.
- Communicate with consumers and partners.
- Monitor performance and build feedback mechanisms.
- Control and administration (Buhalis, 2002).

15.4 e-TOURISM

The advent and tremendous development of the Internet over the last three decades paved way for doing business through it. e-Tourism is a concept coined recently to reflect the changes, modifications and value addition in tourism due to profound influence of IT. Online platform enables direct booking, payment for end-user, and business-to-business trading for principals, suppliers and intermediaries. e-Tourism is simply referred to as digitization of all processes and value chains in tourism, travel, hospitality and catering industries (Buhalis, 2003). Basically, it represents the paradigm shift experienced in the tourism industry due to the adoption of ICTs and the Internet. e-Tourism has only become possible through the spread of information and communication technologies (ICT). The Internet played a crucial role by changing the distribution of tourism sales and information. e-Tourism is an umbrella term for e-Marketing, e-Finance, e-Accounting, e-HRM, e-Procurement, e-HRD, e-Production, e-Strategy, e-Planning, e-Management and e-commerce for all subsectors of the tourism industry. e-Tourism is a conglomeration of three fundamental disciplines such as business management, information systems and management, and tourism. The broader dimensions of e-Tourism with impact of IT are:

- **Tactical level:** in this level, e-Tourism includes e-commerce and applies ICTs for maximizing efficiency as well as effectiveness of tourism organizations.
- **Strategic level:** at strategic level, e-Tourism changes all business processes, the entire value chain as well as the strategic relationships of tourism organizations with various stakeholders (Buhalis, 2003).

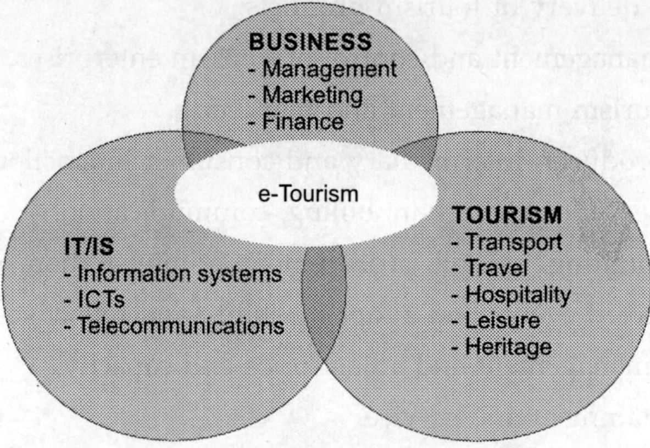

Source: Buhalis, 2003.

Figure 15.1 e-Tourism in tourism.

15.5 e-BUSINESS IN TOURISM

The Internet is increasingly bridging the gap between consumers and businesses enabling interactive communication and trade. E-commerce is a growing sector. Many tourism businesses, like traditional travel agents, tour operators, national tourist offices, airlines, hotels and other accommodations, providers and car hire firms, are involved in developing their Internet services. For every tourism destination and supplier, whether it is large or small, electronic business on the platform of the Internet offers the opportunity to undertake their business in new and more cost-effective ways (WTOBC, 2001). In general, under the banner of e-commerce, there are three kinds of business applications over the Internet: *business-to-business*, *business-to-customer* and using *digital middleman*. The first one refers to the company selling or buying from other companies. Here, the company communicates with other companies by electronic means. The next is the transaction of products/services by the businesses to the customer, in parlance of tourism-tourists. e-mediaries constitute the third category.

The Internet supports electronic commerce in four major areas such as *attracting new customers* via marketing and advertising; *serving existing customers* via customer service and support functions; *developing new markets* and distribution channels for the existing products; and *developing new information based products*. E-business impacts all types of communication and business processes, internally and externally, and requires new ways of thinking and working. A new phenomenon is evolving proving that nearly everything can be found on the Internet, breaking boundaries between the buyers and sellers. With geographical barriers disappearing, a customer is able to compare products from various manufacturers and make a more informed choice. In the digital marketplace, it is the educated customer who holds absolute power. Not only do customers demand

Table 15.1: e-commerce applications by segments of the tourism industry

Functions	Visitor Attractions	Travel Agencies	Hospitality/Accommodation sector	Tour Operators
Front office	Catalogue referencing	Catalogue referencing		Package lists on travel marts
Marketing Promotion	online previews	affiliate programmes	Individual website, DMS	Package customization
Customer Relationship Management	Automate guidance	Client profiles	Front desk automation	Call centres
Distribution Channels	Inclusion in packages	Network based portals	Inclusion in packages	Direct access for agencies
Loyalty Programmes	Frequent client points	Customized deals	Frequent client points	Over-commissions
Reservation & Payment	Online ticketing	Reservation systems	Online accounts	Payment processing
Back office				
Supply Chain Mgmt.	e-Procurement	Reservation systems	e-Procurement	Inventory management
Human Resources	Online recruitment, IT training services	IT training services	Online recruitment, IT-training services	IT training services
Enterprise Resource Planning	Customized accounting systems	Customized accounting systems	Customized accounting systems	Customized accounting system
Operational Control	Attraction management systems	Agency management systems	Property management systems	Package assembly
Product Development	Content production	Package assembly	Room technology	Package assembly

Source: WTOBC, 2001.

the best price, but they also want the best services regardless of the type of product category. Thus, there is a high imperative for quality IT integrated services and support.

An Internet-based tourism service sector is developing IT based networks that links producers and users effectively. This has resulted in a shift away from traditional supply chains and communication channels to new forms. As in other components of tourism industry, e-business has much importance on tourism destinations. The most important benefits of the Internet based business can be summarized, as per WTOBC, as it opened opportunity to establish electronic links to tourism suppliers within the destination, to enable them to maintain their own product information and availability, act as an intermediary in consolidating the full range of destination products (particularly the small and medium size enterprises, which need DMO support the most), and distributing it electronically to travel giants (online or otherwise) and other players in the travel trade, perhaps even to the GDS.

e-commerce has applications in all the functional areas of a business. As discussed earlier, *marketing* is one area where the influence of e-commerce is extensive. The benefits include new channels of distribution, new means for customer retention and relationship marketing, cost-effective ways for selling and making transactions, easier way for global distribution, etc. Tourism industry is being benefited in many ways by the advantages of using Information Technology supporting e-commerce. Internet based business enables to have more cost-effective communication with target markets, quicker and easier for the customer to buy and thereby increasing conversion and levels of spending, improved customer service and retention as well as reduced costs through more efficient internal operations and purchasing processes.

15.6 CYBER TOURISM

Cyber tourism that will provide an experimental alternative to physical travel, is likely to be a major tourism growth area as we move towards 2020. In the future, people can interact with synthetic computer generated characteristics in a context not bound by time and space. Cyber tourism may be able to create an electronic authentic experience that may be little different from similar physical experience, at least in the conscious mind of the user (Prideaux & Singer, 2005). In the near future, cyber tourism may rely on an advanced form of 'tele-immersion' that will offer users immense scope for visiting remote and exotic places in this world or others using eternally projected stimuli. It enables curious people to enjoy tourism experience in a simulated environment. Cyber tourism experience is said to possess the ability to transport an individual from everyday monotonous, personal limitations inherent in being a tourist and the petty exigencies. Cyber tourism, due to its inherent potential in many forms, is regarded as both a vehicle in the promotion of tourism as well as the means for experiencing destinations (Ross, 2005). A range of new technologies are emerging. Experts are of the view that further developments in technology related to it and the convergence of these technologies at some time in the future, cyber tourism will have the potential to take tourist experiences from the physical realm defined by specific parameters of time, place and space into a cyber world that is inevitably boundless.

15.7 IT APPLICATION IN TRANSPORT SECTOR

Accessibility is a determining factor in the success of a tourist destination. In general, the more accessible a destinations, the greater will be the possibility for its success.

Transportation is the essence of 'accessibility'. Transport simply means to carry goods or people from one place to another whereas transportation refers to the means or system for the same. Generally, transportation is classified into three: air, water and land, on the basis of the medium in which it takes place. Travel involves the act of moving from one place to another. Application of information technology is as prevalent in the transportation sector as in other sectors and it has been experiencing the influence of IT for the efficient and smooth functioning in this modern competitive environment.

Airlines are pioneer in using IT for operations. An airline offers services to passengers or freight, generally with a recognized operating certificate or licence. Airlines vary widely in size, from small companies with only one or two planes to huge multinational companies. Operation of an airline involves a range of complex operations and thousands of passengers or tonnes of cargo. This necessitates utmost care, efficiency and competitiveness in operations and services. Airports also have to deal with a large quantity of information daily as large number of passengers pass through the airports and a number of aircraft land and take off daily. In catering to the comfort and convenience people who use airports, the authorities aim at ensuring best possible solutions to operate and manage airport functions. A simple mistake will end up in big issues. It is in this circumstance that the role of IT and information systems comes into play. A range of similar technological systems are used by airlines and at airports mainly with the objective to make the operations efficient. The major systems used in air transportation, mainly from a commercial perspective are as follows:

- Baggage and cargo handling systems
- Baggage handling systems
- Cargo movement systems
- Systems used in aircraft
- Safety systems
- Systems for flight scheduling and planning
- Crew scheduling and management
- Gate management and departure control system
- Automated ticket machines (ATMs)
- Flight information display systems
- Immigration control systems
- Global distribution systems

Baggage and cargo handling as part of air transportation is a complex process and hence different systems are used. Baggage handling system helps improve movement of bags from check-in area to the departure gate, from one gate to another during transfers and to move bags from arrival points to baggage claim area. IT solution systems are also used in cargo movement as well. They are often referred to as *automated cargo movement systems*. Expert systems that use the knowledge base and software module, act as an expert consultant to users. Tourism industry has begun using expert systems, particularly airlines are using these systems to deal with many of the functional applications. Inside the aircraft also, different systems are used. *Point-of-sale systems* are used while selling food and souvenir items in the aircraft. *Visual graphic information systems* are used inside aircraft as interpretation tool for the passengers. Airlines commonly use *safety systems* to avoid accidents and increase safety while flying. Flight scheduling and planning is another area where airlines use systems. These systems support the entire flight scheduling activities of an airline, from strategic planning to tactical adjustments. Crew scheduling and management is a complex task as the possibility for unanticipated incidents is high. Crew scheduling systems are used in airline operations widely. Gate management systems enable airlines to coordinate with airports in obtaining details on flight landing. Airports use *departure control systems* also for making the operation more smooth and efficient. Automated ticket machines (ATMs) that offer travel database to travellers are also installed at various locations, particularly check-in areas of the airports. Automated check-in kiosks are also present at airports. Airports also have passenger information display systems which show information on flight departures and arrival schedules, gate assignment and the like. Immigration and customs department to a great extent depends on information systems to make travel document verification and the related activities fast and smooth. Global distribution system is the primary distribution mechanism of airlines, which is discussed later in this chapter.

Though not extensively as in air transport, road and water transport modes also use information systems considerably. Some of the systems used from a tourism point of view are:

- Intelligent transportation system
- Route guidance system
- Automated vehicle location system
- Fleet management system
- Automated traffic management system

Intelligent transport system is the most commonly used system in road transportation. This includes different systems like car navigation system, container management system, traffic signal control system, etc. *Route guidance system*, also called in-vehicle navigation system, helps drivers to determine the best route to a given location while they are in the vehicle. *Automated vehicle location system*, equipped with sensors that communicate with a GPS, helps monitor the location of a vehicle. Large transport operators use *fleet management systems* which represent a combination of technologies to manage their fleet of vehicles. *Automated traffic management systems*, aimed at managing the flow of road traffic, are also used by large-scale operators. Information on delays, congestion, accidents, speed limits, etc., can be given to the drivers who use this system. Car rental companies, railways, cruise operators also use a range of systems for smooth and competitive functioning and management.

15.8 INFORMATION SYSTEMS IN TRAVEL INTERMEDIARIES

Travel agencies and *tour operators* are the major intermediaries involved in the distribution system of travel products. Travel agents basically offers a convenient location for the purchase of travel products (Holloway, 1989). They act as a distributor, retailer or a broker on behalf of the suppliers (Werthner, 1999). Their services also include provision of information on travel products, destinations, schedules, fares, rates and availability.

A traveller approaching a travel agent enquires about a wide range of information including rates, schedules, location, climate, facilities, availability, booking procedures, issuing of tickets, currency, travel insurance, transfers and local transportation, etc. Provision of accurate, timely and precise information as per their request seems essential for the success of any travel agency business and remain competitive. According to Sheldon (2003), the more information the travel intermediary can access electronically, the more timely, efficient and accurate service can be offered to the client. Here, in this particular context, the role of information systems is very important.

Agencies sometimes establish extranets to access dedicated parts of principals or intermediaries systems (Buhalis, 2003). This helps them reduce cost of booking, improve communications and efficiency, increase speed of booking procedures and enhance customer service. Similar extranets are also developed with corporate clients. This helps the clients to utilize specialized sections of their on-time provisions. Travel agents can expand their value chains to provide tools for their corporate customers to undertake part of the process themselves.

A range of information systems are used by travel agents. The systems used in large travel agencies are:

- Global distribution systems
- Front office systems
- Travel agency bank office systems
- Video text systems and interactive TV systems
- Travel agency systems
- Agency management systems
- Customer relationship management systems
- Supply chain management (SCM)

- Management information systems
- Decision support systems
- Systems for corporate travel planners

Most of these systems are used by tour operators as well. Yet, they use tour planning software in addition to these.

15.9 INFLUENCE OF TECHNOLOGY IN THE DISTRIBUTION OF TRAVEL PRODUCTS

Indeed, travel industry is a major user of data and information of all kinds. Travel and tourism industry owes its phenomenal expansion to the *development of the jet engine* that substantially improved aircraft productivity by increasing the number of passengers carried over a greater distance. Experts are also of the view that the second development which has the potential of making an equally significant impact on productivity in the travel industry is the *computer reservation systems* (CRSs), which have become critical marketing components of the travel industry. CRSs became an essential component of travel distribution system (Buhalis and Licarta, 2002). Computer reservation systems (CRSs) were accorded as *Transaction Processing Systems* (TPS). The influence of IT continued, which led to the expansion of scope and functioning of CRSs. They have been transformed into *Global Distribution Systems* (GDS). SABRE, AMADEUS, GALILEO and WORLSPAN are the leading GDSs in the world, which are also referred to as *travel supermarkets* (Go, 1992). Meanwhile, other technology solutions like Videotext systems entered the scene. Altogether, it was seen that tourism industry distribution system had expanded including new e-Mediaries.

The Internet, being a universal as well as interactive means of communication, has influenced the electronic travel distribution system dramatically, especially since consumers could undertake their entire tourism product search over the Internet and booking online. The Internet offer up-to-date information. This created lot of opportunities for businesses. Many examples can be cited for e-Mediaries in tourism. British Airways (www.britishairways.com) and Marriott Hotels (www.marriot.com) constitute examples for single supplier provision. Examples for multi-supplier web pages emerge to support airlines like intermediating travel agencies such as www.opodo.com and www.orbitz.com. Destinations also distribute information and products using exclusive systems. Destination management systems are comprehensive systems that are developed by NTOs/DMOs. TISCover (www.tiscover.com) and DMS of Holland (www.holland.com) are some typical examples of these.

The increasing scope of product transaction and distribution led to the formation of web based travel agencies. An online travel agency specializes in online sources and online bookings. Expedia (expedia.com) and ebookers (ebookers.com) are some examples. A few major travel agencies also developed their own online travel distribution systems (e.g., www.thomascook.com and www.lunnpoly.com). The Internet portals also developed online travel distribution, often by sourcing their travel context from external online agents and suppliers (Buhalis, 2003). Even media has come up with providing travel options. For example, the famous Telegraph newspaper (http://travel.telegraph.co.uk) and CNN TV channel (www.cnn.com/travel) have a provision for travel. The travel product distribution poised for further advancements due to the increasing application of IT.

CRS is often used as an umbrella term to include the entire variety of the information systems used for bookings. In general, CRS refers to computerized system set up for booking of services/facilities offered by businesses. Many sectors are incorporating such systems mainly for making booking/selling of the services/facilities. CRS is basically a computerized system which can process the reservations through a database which handles details of inventory, schedules and prices among other details. Airlines, hotels, railways, etc., are the best examples of sectors which use CRS. CRS runs on mainframes, minicomputers or microcomputers and are usually connected through data communication links to terminals within various branches of the company. Airlines industry is the pioneer who used similar systems. These systems were emerged as *Transaction Processing Facility/System* (TPF/S) which could handle large volumes of data as part of the transactions in the business. In tourism and travel industry, CRSs are extensively used. Airlines use CRS to allow direct access through terminals for intermediaries to check availability, make reservation and print tickets (Buhalis, 2003). According to Foster (1994), CRS is a computer system designed for use by booking agents to facilitate the sale of travel products and services of participating vendors. Original purpose of CRS was simply to provide an automated means for managing data about flights, available seats and fares and were controlled by their airlines.

15.10 GLOBAL DISTRIBUTION SYSTEM

The term *Global Distribution System* (GDS) refers to a network of one or more CRSs for distributing product offers and functionalities of the participating organizations in different countries across the world (Werthner & Klein, 1999). CRS and GDS form one of the major players in the value chains. They provide the main electronic link between big supplier groups and the travel agent/tour operator community. The major functions of a GDS include:

- Maintenance and search facilities for flight schedules and availability.
- Information on other travel and tourism products and their availability, like package holidays, car rentals, ferries, etc.
- Seat reservation and selling.

- Ticketing
- Maintenance of user information based on passenger name record (PNR).
- Maintenance of search facilities for fare quotes and rules.
- Management functions both for intermediaries like travel agents and for airlines (Vialle, 1995).

A GDS will have a large number of interconnected systems and firms from the supply side as well as from the demand side. Details of some major GDSs are as follows.

15.10.1 Galileo

Galileo, formerly a subsidiary of Cendant Corporation, is a high-end technology solution that basically connects travel buyers and sellers through computer reservation systems. Galileo as a Global Distribution System (GDS) claims to have better content, control and cost reduction. Galileo, according to them, offers significant quantity of global content, with more depth and breadth in all dimensions of a GDS. A large number of hotels, airlines, car rentals, etc., are linked through Galileo. They can connect customers to 470 airlines, 57 hotel properties and 23 car rental companies worldwide. Galileo with more control offers technology solutions to ensure data integrity and quality. Moreover, it offers financial resources through cost reduction, stability and negotiating leverage to continue to deliver best-in-clan solution along with a diversified revenue stream to weather industry shocks and cycles (www.galileo.com). The history of Galileo dates back to 1971 when United Airlines of America introduced the *Apollo*, a computer reservation system (CRS) for their own use. Apollo Travel Service (ATS) division was created later and Apollo CRS was marketed to travel agencies in North America and Japan. Over the years, Galileo expanded its operations and became one of the leading GDSs in the world.

15.10.2 Amadeus

Amadeus is another leading provider of technology solution to the travel and tourism industry with its corporate headquarters in Madrid (Spain). Airlines such as Air France, Lufthansa, Iberia and SAS founded Amadeus as a Global Distribution System (GDS) company in 1987. The diverse range of products and services of Amadeus are specially designed to facilitate the making of travel arrangements for both leisure and corporate travel including booking solutions for car, hotel and flight; solutions for business travel management for corporations; and information provision for the travellers at destinations. Some other airlines like British Airways, Finn Air and Qantas Airways joined Amadeus for certain services through agreements for a period. Many other corporations and travel suppliers have been getting services of Amadeus mainly for sales, reservations and e-ticketing systems, corporate self-booking tools and customer management solutions for airlines.

Table 15.2: Products and services of Amadeus

The main products and services of Amadeus can be categorized into four.
Distribution and Context
This GDS provides a comprehensive information service and other contents to the users. Also it offers means to optimize content distribution through extensive point-of-sale network.
Sales and e-Commerce
The GDS provides ability to access, market and sell content across all channels. This allows for easier workflow, profitability and customer service throughout the sales process.
Business Management
Amadeus offers different means to optimize customers, business operations, process and administration and maximize customer relations.
Service and Consulting
This is a specialized area by which customers can get services and consulting solutions by which they can leverage the full value of their business processes and IT investments.

Source: www.amadeus.com

15.10.3 SABRE

SABRE aims to connect people with the world's travel possibilities, merchandises and travel products. It offers distribution and technology solutions for the travel industry. It was in 1960, SABRE offered the first passenger reservation system. SABRE airline solutions pioneered technological advances for the industry in areas including revenue management, pricing, flight scheduling, cargo, flight operations and crew scheduling. Development of SABRE (*Semi-Automatic Business Research Environment*) was initiated by American Airlines to replace handwritten passenger reservation system with IBM by the late 1950s. They are the pioneers in computer reservation system agencies. SABRE Holdings support travel agents, corporations, travel suppliers and travellers. With headquarters in South Lake, Texas (US), it offers its products and services in three forms, such as Travelocity, SABRE travel network and SABRE airline solutions (www.sabre-holdings.com). *Travelocity* is an online travel agency in Europe, which can fulfill the travel needs of customers. It allows travellers to book more rewarding and affordable trips. Travelocity now powers websites in many languages across four continents with 24 hour customer support. In US also, Travelocity is a major travel intermediary.

15.10.4 World Span

World Span, founded in early 1990s by Delta Airlines, Northwest Airlines, and TWA, intended to serve the customers through sophisticated global communication systems and networks. With its headquarters in Atlanta, World Span primarily offers technology solutions to deal with travel related products globally. In mid 2003, World Span was sold by its owner airlines to Citigroup Venture Capital and Ontario Teachers' Pension

Fund. It is now a part of the Travelport GDS business. It was in December, 2006, that Travelport agreed to acquire World Span, but did not decide to merge it with Galileo. The acquisition was completed on August 21, 2007. On September 28, 2008, the Galileo and Apollo GDS systems were moved from the Travelport data center in Denver, Colorado to the World Span data center in Atlanta, Georgia (although they continue to be run as separate systems). As a leading global distribution system (GDS), World Span provides travel distribution, technologies and services for thousands of travel companies worldwide, including travel agencies, corporations, travel suppliers and travel websites.

15.10.5 Abacus

Abacus is one of the leading travel facilitators in the Asia and Pacific region with more than 15,000 travel agency locations in 24 markets. Incorporated in 1989, this Singapore based system is technically owned by SABRE and a consortium of Asia's leading airlines including All Nippon Airways, Cathay Pacific, China Airlines, EVA Airways, Garuda Indonesia, Dragonair, Philippine Airlines, Malaysia Airlines, Royal Brunei Airlines, SilkAir and Singapore Airlines. Singapore Airlines and Cathay Pacific are its first founding partners.

15.10.6 SITA: Largest Travel Industry Communication Network

Airline was one industry that recognized the importance of telecommunications from early times and communication networks were formed to help transmit industry messages to different parts of the world. First such network created was *Aeronautical Radio Incorporated* (ARINC) developed in 1929 mainly for communication in the US. Following ARINC, *Society for International Telecommunications Aeronautique* (SITA) was established in 1949. SITA is claimed to be the largest global data and voice communication network, spans across the travel industry in 225 countries. Started by ten IATA airlines with the objective to provide airline communication services to its members, SITA has grown to include a membership of around one thousand agencies situated in different countries across the world, and provide data communication services to firms in the travel industry.

15.10.7 New Distribution Capability (NDC)

IATA is initiating an NDC (*New Distribution Capability*) with a claim that it will enable the travel industry to transform the way air products are distributed to corporations, leisure and business travellers. According to them, it can help in overcoming the industry's current distribution limitations. The following assurances are being offered by IATA:

- Product differentiation and time-to-market
- Access to full and rich air content
- Transparent shopping experience (www.iata.org)

NDC is an innovative approach to the way airlines' products and services are being distributed, by enabling them to fill the capability gap between their direct and indirect channels and offering identical retail capabilities across all channels, while facilitating product differentiation and customer personalization. IATA points out that they intend to offer passengers with more choice of products and services, more personalization, more transparency, and indeed increased competition among the airlines.

15.11 m-COMMERCE DISTRIBUTION

Mobile devices have now formed a new platform for transactions. Increasingly smart phones are being used for payments, transactions and for selling goods and services. *m-Commerce* has its own role and relevance in the travel and tourism sector. Tourism providers already use WAP and SMS for distributing information, allowing consumers to check flight arrivals and departures and for checking-in. Mobile Apps are now a trend, along with using mobile based virtual communities. Tourism organizations are expanding their Internet provisions to support mobile devices since technology is in place. Perhaps, mobile devices are now increasingly useful to frequent business travellers and to people who purchase familiar tourism products. m-Commerce is also claimed as a good opportunity for last minute sales as well as a medium enabling consumers to make and change reservations nearing departure or arrival time.

15.12 DISINTERMEDIATION AND REINTERMEDIATION

The Internet based distribution of travel products became harmful to the intermediaries, as their primary role was being taken over by the Internet. The role of traditional intermediaries has changed in recent years due to the introduction of the Internet and e-commerce technologies. Emerging tourism e-Mediaries, rising along with the growth of Internet and electronic commerce, has changed the entire "Business to Business (B2B)" and "Business to Consumers (B2C)" relationships, and at the same time, it changed consumer behaviour and attitudes. Independent search and booking travel products over the Internet have become common. The broad application of the Internet also creates a new travelling market on the Net. Due to the increasing scope of direct sale of products, suppliers depend on the Internet more to sell their products. Airline is an example that depends on the Internet more for direct distribution. Also as part of airline's drive to reduce costs, airlines are seeking more direct contact with their clients, and technology providing the possibility for a direct channel between the airlines and their customers. This results in elimination of intermediaries from the distribution products and it is often remarked as *disintermediation*. Disintermediation refers to the elimination of intermediaries from the distribution of products and trying to sell maximum products with the help of the Internet. Direct marketing on the Internet is cutting into the traditional intermediaries business. Industries now try to reduce costs at all levels in the distribution system through disintermediation and direct compensation or commission cuts, where these cuts can be rationalized. This has led to an increasing intermediary elimination at all levels; suppliers now strive to get closer to their customers and rebel against the insulation imposed by distributors. Due to the increasing rate of disintermediation, the role of intermediaries has changed to a great extent (Buhalis, 2003). However, travel agencies now look out for a consumer's best interest by using IT to help them find the best products.

Another trend that emerged recently is *reintermediation*. Variety of online platforms has emerged due to the scope of distributing and selling products over the Internet. Reintermediation represents the emergence of new forms of intermediaries, commonly called *e-Mediaries*, using the capability of the Internet. Now, such online intermediaries are playing an increasing role in distributing and selling travel, tourism and hospitality products.

15.13 IT APPLICATION IN HOSPITALITY INDUSTRY

Hospitality industry is now using information technology extensively for its various activities and functions. IT has significant influence on almost all the functions of a hotel. Correspondingly, a diverse range of IT tools are used in the hotels. The major IT systems in hospitality sector are:

- Property management system
- Back office system
- Front office system
- Guest rooms system
- Integrated property system (IPS)
- Food and beverage system
- Restaurant management system
- Computer reservation system
- Customer relationship management system
- Central reservation system
- Marketing information system
- Decision support system.
- Revenue management system
- Yield management system
- Point-of-sale system
- Electronic locking system

- Guest information and entertainment system
- Call accounting system
- Energy management system
- Self-service kiosk
- Voice messaging system
- Self check-in machine
- Building management system (BMS)
- Guest management software
- Attendance monitoring system (Dileep, 2011).

Property Management Systems (PMSs) are the most crucial systems used in hotels. It is the hub of information processing in hotels. The functions of PMS can be summarized as: room availability, capacity management, operational leverage, facilitate central room inventory control, offer yield management, better database access for managers, support extensive marketing and sales reports, facilitate market research and planning, offer travel agency trading and commission payments, track frequent flyers and repeat guests, direct marketing and personalized services, and enhance efficiency in handling group bookings.

A PMS has interfaces with almost all other systems used in hotels like central reservation system, call accounting system, energy management system, back office system, point-of-sales system, guest room management system, etc. A PMS consists of different modules. *Reservation module* handles reservation at the property level. *Registration module* deals with registering a guest on his arrival. *Check-in module* enables hotels make the process more efficient and fast. *Guest accounting module* helps increase the hotel's control over accounts and compliments the night accounting process. Processing of a good guest history database is a feature of a PMS. *Rooms management functionality* of PMS helps the housekeeping department to function efficiently whereas a *maintenance module* streamlines the processing of work orders.

Integrated property systems are used in large hotels, particularly in chain hotels. *Revenue management systems* are used by large hotels mainly to bring in sophisticated tools for forecasting analysis and rate quotations in a fully integrated, easy to use format. *Yield management system* is used as a tool for demand forecasting to maximize rooms' revenue. Also, PMS has a module for revenue management function. Back office of a hotel is a crucial department and there are comprehensive systems for back office functions.

In the guest room, a range of systems are used. *Electronic locking system* increases the safety and security of guests. Hotel rooms usually have IT enabled entertainment enhancing systems. In rooms, systems that help guest to access various communication facilities are also there. *Call accounting systems,* basically used to monitor to and from calls that are being used by the guests, are beneficial for hotels to account guest telephone usage. *Point-of-sales systems* are common in hotels. These are used wherever supply of services or products takes place. In hotels, these are used in restaurants, gift shops, telephone call centres, etc. Food and beverages department, in certain cases, also have exclusive systems for their efficient functioning.

Restaurant management system, which has functions such as purchasing and inventory control of food items, menu and recipe control and food costing, are used in restaurants. In kitchen also, different systems are used like kitchen display system, back of the house systems, etc. *Centralized reservation systems* are used in the central reservation offices of the hotels, where the reservation of the hotel at individual level takes place.

As in other industries, sales and marketing systems are also crucial in the hotel industry as well. Apart from PMS modules, hotels may use exclusive systems in the areas of marketing and sales. *Guest management software* is also used as a tool for mangers to manage various activities like guest requests and complaints and similar jobs. Many other systems are also used in the hospitality industry like energy management systems, customer relationship management systems, building management systems, attendance monitoring systems and the like. All of these benefit the hotels to have more efficient functioning, increase in customer service thus enhancing customer satisfaction.

15.14 DESTINATION'S USE OF ICT FOR COMPETITIVE ADVANTAGE

Information is crucial in the success of a destination. Tourists require up-to-date information on destination in all the stages of tourism process. The accessibility of true, proper and relevant information about facilities, attractions, events and others is important in this modern tourism environment. Tourists require information before they travel as well as during the course of their journey. As far as a destination is concerned, quality information is provided by its official tourism promotion agency. Realizing the importance of providing quality information to the tourists, destinations are now coming up with IT tools and measures. They use technology in order to improve their functions and performance as well as communicating marketing messages globally. Latest information should be available through the more accessible media.

National tourist offices have a variety of options to process and disseminate information to various end users, intermediaries, principals as well as other stakeholders in the tourism industry. Electronic processing and dissemination of information is a suitable option and *destination information systems* (DISs) are developed with this objective. They are considered very comprehensive and integrated option to process and disseminate information in the most efficient and economical manner. Destination management systems (DMSs), destination marketing systems, etc., are some of the terminologies used interchangeably in this context, though the functions may vary slightly. These systems also offer technology solutions for destination marketing and promotion. In general, destination information systems can handle pre-trip and post-arrival information requirements of tourists. Furthermore, it can also offer reservation/ booking facilities as well. DMS/DIS can be set up at the national, regional or local level with the required database. National, regional or local authorities are responsible for establishing DMSs and the financial expenditure is met by them. In some cases, the capital requirement is shared by private industries as well.

Destination information/management system is defined as a *comprehensive electronic database* of a destination's facilities that can be accessed by travel counsellors and/or travellers themselves, either in the destination or in the region (Sheldon, 2003). A DMS has the ability to represent a destination in a well organised manner in the marketplace. It can distribute efficiently and economically the information across the tourism industry spread in different geographical locations. It is considered a cost effective and comprehensive medium for the dissemination of information. The DMS functionalities are seen much more than that of a GDS as the latter focuses mainly on the established industries and may not be able to reach up to the local level agencies. It can handle pre-trip, post-arrival information requirements of tourists and in many cases, it offers reservation/booking facilities as well. In addition, it can offer facilities to the tourists of the local and ancillary services. Usually, DMS includes information on public sector services like museums, parks, recreation centres, monuments, historical sites, etc. These make the DIS more relevant to the destination and distinguish it from GDSs. More advanced systems are developed at the destination level by the concerned national tourist offices (NTOs) or destination management organizations (DMOs). Establishing a business system by the DMO to utilize the potential of the Internet would be inevitable for the destination to remain popular. Such a system can offer the following services:

- Information search – by category, geography (using GIS), keyboard, etc.
- Itinerary planning
- Reservations
- Customer/contact database management (which would cover registration, membership and grading management)
- Customer relationship management (CRM) functions
- 'Push' marketing
- Market research and analysis
- Image library
- Publishing in electronic and traditional channels
- Event planning and management
- Marketing optimization and yield management
- Data editing and management
- Financial management

- Management information systems and performance evaluation
- Economic impact analysis
- Access to third party sources, such as weather, transport timetables and travel planning, theatre and event ticket reservations (Buhalis, 2003; WTOBC, 2001).

The history of application of IT by destinations in managing and marketing destinations is not very old. The IT enhanced intra-, inter- and open communication were established rather very late. Though destination oriented system emerged in the late 1960s, it had experienced sluggish growth since then. DMS gained prominence only in the 1980s. *Dandata* in Denmark or TIS in Tyrol (TIS Cover), Austria are the examples of such systems that were established in 1980s. *TIS Cover* is an advanced destination oriented system, operated by the TIS company, a subsidiary of the Tyrol Tourist Board (Austria).

Austria's National Tourist Office has been using a decision support instrument since 1984 called *Tour MIS* (Tourism Marketing Information System). The system developed by Austrian Society of Applied Research in Tourism (ASART), started the project in 1982 with the aim of optimal information supply and decision support for the tourism industry. In the beginning it consisted of a database installed in a host system of Scientific Computer Centre, Vienna and now it has an extensive database to tourism managers. Further development took place by 1999 when the Internet version was introduced which enabled Tour MIS to supply information area-wide for top managers in the tourism industry. Free access to overall data and functions of Tour MIS is available since 2000.

Along with the advancements in IT, the scope and functionalities of destination systems expanded. Now more comprehensive and substantial systems that can modernize various aspects of destination management along with integrating all tourism actors at the local level, have emerged, called *Destination Integrated Computerized Information Reservation Systems* (DICIRMSs). Many other latest technologies have been incorporated in information systems that are used in tourism sector. *Artificial Intelligence* (AI) is applied in some of the systems used in the tourism information systems. Expert systems and neural networks are areas where increased system intelligence is used. *Multimedia information* is another emerging area, which tourism information systems accept and use. Websites are utilized maximum for incorporating with most modern Information Systems, which will make the systems more effective and efficient. Applying *semantic web technologies* is one of the methods where semantic web technologies are considered the next generation web, which has the vision of having background knowledge about the meaning of web sources stored in a machine-processable and interpretable way. GIS (geographic information system) based tourism information systems are introduced now and such systems are built mainly for giving information to the tourists and for planning and development of tourist destinations. Recommender systems are also used at the destination level.

Table 15.3: Major applications of GIS in tourism

• Developing tourism resource inventories
• Tourism planning while safeguarding the environment
• Identifying location suitability under conflicting demands
• Monitor and control tourism activities
• Tourism marketing
• Providing information about tourist destinations over the Internet
• Simulation and model spatial outcomes or visual impact analysis
• Tourist time-space analysis
• Community involvement and participation
• Providing information for decision making for managers as well as consumers.

Source: Farsari & Prastacos, 2004.

15.15 MOBILE APPLICATIONS

Value-added mobile services through destination management organizations should be strategically developed to enhance awareness of a destination, satisfy travel experience, and create destination loyalty. Large and mid-sized travel suppliers and intermediaries are likely to launch mobile services in order to stake a claim for their brand in the mobile sphere. Mobile Apps are the most popular applications now. They are used to describe software that runs on smart phones, palmtop or personal digital assistant (PDA) and tablet computers. Mobile applications are designed to educate, entertain, or assist consumers in their daily lives. These are available from various application distribution platforms, designed by a certain mobile operating system such as Apple App Store, Blackberry App World, Google Play, Windows Phone Store, etc. It is accessible through iPhone, Blackberry, Android or Windows phone, and other mobile devices such as iPads, Samsung Galaxy Tabs and others. These are usually aimed at managing specific tasks and provide its user context specific data just when the user needs it and limits choices to the tactical needs of the moment. The following are some application areas connected to mobile technology:

- **Navigation** : GPS, Augmented reality, Way Finder
- **Social** : Social networks, communication
- **Mobile Marketing**: Contests/Awards, Alerts, Discounts
- **Security/Emergency**: Medical, Emergency, Information (weather forecasts, etc.)
- **Transactional** : Auctions, Financial/Banking, Tickets/Reservations, Shopping
- **Information** : General travel information, city guides, event schedules, translators
- **Entertainment** : Games, video/TV, music, E-reader, photographs, fantasy sports

Benefits of integrating mobile applications include:

- Easy booking and reservation
- Easy finding of tourism services and facilities
- Worldwide access
- Provision of latest and accurate information
- Customer relationship management
- Enhancing tourist experience
- Increased safety and security provisions, etc.

15.16 e-MARKETING IN TOURISM

The advent and developments in information technology has influenced tourism marketing significantly. As a result of IT influence, new marketing tools have emerged, new distribution channels have sidelined the traditional ones and customer relationship practices have gained different dimensions.

Due to the increasing role of the Internet in marketing, online marketing practice has gained momentum. Companies, both large as well as small, are rapidly integrating online marketing into their marketing strategies and policies, due to reasons such as increased cost effectiveness, increased accessibility, availability of real-time information, increased interactivity, and the like. The Internet based marketing encompasses all the activities associated with usual marketing like activities to reach the target market, attract visitors, encourage them to purchase the products/services and retain the customers for ever.

Websites are the focal point of Internet marketing. Websites have been turned into channels of sales and customer relationship activities. They are used for market segmentation and for similar activities associated with tourism marketing. Electronic marketing has *three* basic *principles* such as build and actively manage customer database, develop a clear concept on how the company could take advantage of the Internet and be easily accessible and quick in responding to customer calls. Business to business, customer to customer, customer to business and business to customer are the four online marketing domains.

Due to the tremendous application of IT and dependency on the Internet in tourism marketing, companies have started distributing products online. The new channels developed due to the usage of the Internet for product distribution are called *e-Mediaries*. Airlines, car rentals, hotel chains, etc., the have already developed e-Commerce applications and products are transacted through the Internet. Now there are a number of Internet based full-fledged travel agencies. Online marketing involves a range of tools. Online advertising is an essential tool in online marketing. Advertisements of different forms can be undertaken on the Internet. Banner ads are a dominant ad format in use on the web. The expandable ads, animated ads, and banner ads containing embedded

HTML are the common forms seen in practice. Classified ads, commercial links and mailing lists are some other online ad forms. Rich media ads, more digital interactive media, are also used by marketers and floating ad and snap back are some forms of rich media advertisements. Pop-up ads are very popular. Interstitial ads, active ads and landing pages are some other online ad tools.

A number of newsgroups, a form of web communities, are there and majority of them are functioning as specialized areas. These are basically discussion groups on the Internet that focus on specific subjects. These facilitate fast and reliable communication to a large community. Emails are also widely used by marketers to initiate more personalized communication with the customers. *Permission marketing* is also an associated term which focuses on sending email messages to people who request/or interact to have information on a particular topic. Signature files are similar to business cards, which give a short message given at the end of the email message that will help attract a customer to a company's website.

Affiliate programme is a programme that allows companies to market other firms' products or services for a commission fee per item sold. For the affiliate organizer, it is a way to attract traffic and business from a number of other sites and for the affiliate it adds to the service the site provides, by offering convenient links to beneficial, complementary services or products. There are different types of affiliate programmes. *Viral marketing*, a 'word of mouth' type of marketing technique promoted through the Internet is in fashion nowadays. This helps in rapid and economical communication of messages to thousands of people. Virtual tours, calendar of events, web rings, virtual world, etc., are some other common online marketing tools used by tourism industries. The Internet is used as a tool to differentiate their brands and to fortify brands further. Mobile devices are also used extensively in tourism marketing. Mobile TV, m-Commerce, Satnav, Podcasting, Digital TV, Web TV, Smart TV, search related ads, etc., are some other measures used in marketing of tourism products using information technology.

Mobile devices are used in tourism marketing and it could be greater in the next five to ten years than that of the desktop PC, website and fixed link broadband which has been over the past 10 years (UNWTO and ETC, 2008). The term *mobile* in this context refers to various electronic equipment that are used for communication. It includes mobile phones, personal digital assistants such as Palm Pilots or Blackberrys, MP3 players such as iPods, and satellite navigation devices like Tom Toms. According to World Tourism Organization, the reasons for the growth of mobile marketing are that mobiles:

- are going to be the most convenient channel for most of the communication, which visitors and destinations want to maintain with each other;
- have already become indispensable as personal companion, throughout the day, throughout the world;

- are useful and comfortable and hence, they could overcome the resentment that many people have felt about its intrusiveness for young and old alike;
- are personal;
- can be used anywhere, in the street, hands-free in car, etc.;
- are used by almost every tourist in contrast with PC Internet access;
- can work fully across frontiers and contact can be made before, during and after the trip; and
- offer the opportunity to send content to mobile phones of tourists, that it is tailored to the subscribers' database (UNWTO and ETC, 2008).

Industries are now using the Internet and other latest technology solutions for customer relationship management as well. Web enabled services of CRM constitutes eCRM. It enables the firms to take care of the customers via the Internet.

15.17 CONCLUSION

IT influenced the tourism sector greatly, to remain competitive and to transform it into a modern industry. Economic reasons, rapid advances in technology, increase in cost effectiveness of using IT tools, increasing rate of technology awareness among consumers, growth in the Internet usage, globalization and rising consumer expectations to have more sophisticated services are the major reasons why IT is an integral part of tourism industry. Information and communication technology (ICT) application in tourism involves a variety of tools and measures including computer systems, mobile devices, standard software, system architecture and network, different types of media, telecommunication tools, interactive communication technologies, and networking and IP based networks. In fact newer and advanced technologies are entering every now and then and the industry has to be dynamic enough to adapt to those developments.

Key Terms

Information and Communication Technology	Tour operation
Tourism	e-Ticketing
Tourism industry	e-Tourism
Key strategic functions	e-Business
Key operational functions	e-commerce
Air transportation	m-Commerce
Intermediaries	e-Marketing
	Global distribution systems

Computer reservation systems
Destination management systems
Destination
Hotels
Information
Property management system
Information technology
Distribution channels
Communication
Front office
Back office

Review Questions

Short Answer Type Questions

1. ICT has become an integral part of strategy of all the tourism industries. Discuss the reasons.
2. Write a brief account on application of IT in tourism.
3. What are the IT tools used in travel and tourism industry.
4. Discuss the advantages of IT based networking in tourism.
5. What are the latest ICT tools used in travel industry?
6. Discuss how ICT helps tourism organizations strategically as well as in performing operations more efficiently.
7. Give a summary of cost-benefit analysis of ICT applications in tourism industry.
8. Which are the areas in air transportation where ICT is used extensvely?
9. How does IT help commercial operations of airlines?
10. What are the airline strategic business functions supported by ICTs?
11. What are the functional activities supported by ICT in airline business?
12. How does ICT help airline industry in dealing with customers?
13. Give a brief account of SITA.
14. Discuss how do travel agencies use ICT.
15. What do you mean by online travel agency?
16. Discuss the influence of IT in tour operation business.
17. What are the advantages of using IT in tour operation business?
18. What are the critical factors that are supported by ICT in hotels?
19. What are the front office applications of IT?
20. What are the benefits of using IT in hotels?
21. Give a brief account of Ultra Switch.
22. Discuss the use of IT in destinations.
23. Discuss how DMOs make use of IT tools for effective functioning as well as for promoting destinations internationally.
24. What are the various IT tools used in land transportation.

25. Which are the different information systems used by travel agencies?
26. What are the information systems used in air transport?
27. Give a brief account of DMS.
28. What are the applications in property management systems?
29. Write short notes on major GDSs.

Essay Type Questions

1. Discuss in detail the IT applications in tourism industry and its benefits.
2. Discuss how airline industry is making use of ICT for efficient strategic management.

16

THE FUTURE OF TOURISM

Learning Outcomes

After studying this chapter, you will be able to:

- understand contemporary issues in tourism;
- explain the challenges of tourism; and
- elucidate the future of tourism in the decades to come.

16.1 INTRODUCTION

Tourism is gaining popularity among all sections of societies and communities. Earlier, this was limited to the 'rich and the aristocratic' societies alone. The tremendous developments in transportation, communication technology, information technology and economic conditions have paved the way for phenomenal transformation of tourism into this modern form involving billions of people. In fact, almost 9 billion people, including international and domestic tourists, are taking part in tourism. As of now, tourism has shown remarkable growth and the forecasts of tourism are quite promising. The official statistics of tourism for the year 2015 by the UNWTO shows record of arrivals and earnings. While international tourist arrivals register a record of approximately 1.2 billion with a remarkable receipt of US$ 1.4 trillion. Compared to the previous year, some 50 million more tourists travelled to international destinations last year, making the total to 1184 million. International tourism receipts in destinations around the world grew by 3.6% in 2015, with a share in world's exports to 7% in 2015. Growth in tourist arrivals has been observed in the 6th consecutive year of above-average growth, with international arrivals increasing by 4% or more every year since the post-crisis year of 2010 (UNWTO Barometer, March 2016).

The UNWTO further reveals that the income generated from visitor expenditure on accommodation, food and drink, entertainment, shopping and other goods and services is US$ 1232 billion and an amount of US$ 210 billion is generated in exports through international non-resident passenger transport services. That makes the total value of tourism exports up to US$ 1.4 trillion. This constitutes 7% of the total world exports and 30% of services exports, with a global rank of three, after fuels and chemicals. In terms of tourist arrivals, Europe, the Americas and Asia and the Pacific all recorded around 5% growth, and the Middle East has grown by 3%. As per the available statistics, Africa points to an estimated 3% decrease. In terms of earnings, the Americas, Asia and the Pacific and the Middle East all grew by 4%, while Europe and Africa grew only by 3% and 2% respectively. The United States, China, Spain and France remain the world's top tourism destinations. The earnings from tourism are: United States (US$ 178 billion), China (US$ 114 billion), Spain (US$ 57 billion) and France (US$ 46 billion).

China remains the number one tourism market with a double-digit growth in expenditure. Chinese visitor expenditure increased by 25% in 2015 to reach US$ 292 billion, as total outbound travellers rose by 10% to 128 million. United States is the second largest source market and it registered a growth of 9% with an expenditure of US$ 120 billion by US residents in foreign countries. Other leading source markets include the UK (+6), Germany, Italy and Australia (growth rate 2%), and Canada and France. Travel propensity in Russian Federation and Brazil declined significantly, reports the UNWTO Barometer of March 2016.

The above statistics reveal the economic significance of tourism as well, along with various aspects associated with the consistent growth in tourist arrivals in major destinations in the world. The future of tourism, its growth potential and challenges are discussed in detail later in this chapter. Before that, some of the significant issues seen in contemporary tourism are discussed below.

16.2 UNETHICAL TOURISM PRACTICES

Tourism is being used as a veil for many unethical practices. The latest that marks the goodwill of tourism is the ill-intended *Birth tourism*, which is totally unacceptable by any means. Recently, the USA made a massive attempt to foil illegal birth tourism practices at different locations. Federal agents stormed 37 locations in Southern California, gathering evidence about illegal "birth tourism" businesses for wealthy Chinese women. The raid took place in several homes and apartment complexes where pregnant Chinese women on fraudulent visas paid up to $80,000 so their babies would be born as U.S. citizens. As per some reports, in what appears to be a growing trend, thousands of wealthy Chinese families are willing to pay tens of thousands of dollars to have an American-born baby. The customers, in the disguise of tourists, give their babies U.S. citizenship, which is bequeathed to anyone born there regardless of their parents' citizenship. The lure of gaining a foothold in the USA goes deeper. Many rich Chinese are looking for an insurance policy for their children against financial and lifestyle risks in their own places.

All such happens in the name of tourism which defames tourism immensely. As per the existing laws in the United States, though controversial, coming to the country to give birth is not illegal. But here, the issue is about motivation and the purpose of travel. The law of a country with all good intention should not be exploited with wrong intentions. The intended visitors lie on their visa applications about reasons to travel to America. The marketing and promotion of birth tourism primarily take place over the Internet. The proponents and doers of unethical practices find lot of freedom on the Internet platforms. Birth tourism is relying on the concept of travelling to another country with the intention of giving birth to a child in the visiting country. There are many factors that inspire the people for engaging in this activity. Conceptually, it may be better healthcare system within an affordable range. To a certain extent, it can be considered a part of health tourism. Hence, birth tourism, in theory, is an accepted practice. But in many cases, the reality is the opposite. Getting citizenship in a foreign country, especially in a developed country is the most predominant reason seen nowadays. The United States and Canada are popular destinations for birth tourism. Hong Kong, where the right of abode is awarded at birth instead of citizenship, is also a popular spot for such tourists. With regard to citizenship, some countries give it to babies being born there regardless of the citizenship of parents. The US still follows it. Realizing the wrong intentions many countries have now changed the rules. For instance, Australia, France, Germany, Ireland, New Zealand, South Africa, and the United Kingdom now grant citizenship by birth only when at least one parent is a citizen of the country or a legal permanent resident who has lived in the country for several years.

16.3 SEX TOURISM AND CHILD SEX TOURISM

Sex tourism is a menace of modern tourism. Though, tourism, being a multifaceted one, does not just depends on sex trade, yet the grave impetus it provides in luring the new generation to indulge in commercial sex trade is something that has to be pondered at various levels as the social, cultural and health ramifications are alarming. Countries are knowingly or unknowingly promoting sex tourism. Both men and women are involved in it. Millions of women are trapped as part of sex tourism. *Sex tourism* is not a type of tourism seen classified in tourism literature and official promotion of it is rarely seen. But the sector gets indirect promotion either by legalizing sex trade or by keeping a closed eye, legally by the authorities, to the propagation of sex trade, particularly in the tourism centres.

Sex tourism represents those kinds of tourism activities which are hedonistic in nature, with the primary objective of seeking sexual pleasures from commercial sources. In the western societies, sex tourism involves gay tourism, lesbian tourism, heterosexual tourism as well as child abuse category, apart from indulging in other sexual recreational activities. Women, men and children from poorer societies become a commodity for consumption by those who are economically richer, and their nil/pseudo sexual desire is a feature of sex tourism. The economic disparity and inequality, in different terms including age, caste, creed and colour, between the service provider and the consumer is one of the major concerns in the tourism associated with sex trade. It is a tendency that the wealthy and the not so wealthy seek recreational breaks from the busy schedules in order to seek hedonist pleasures and the poor find jobs by renting out their bodies, as commodities. A number of countries are popular for sex tourism, and those may include Thailand, Indonesia, Philippines, Brazil, Costa Rica, Cuba, Dominican Republics, Columbia, Caribbean Islands, Morocco, Mexico, Ecuador, Peru, Fiji, Netherlands, and many other African countries.

Casinos, which emerged as a recreation centre for the rich, are too seen promoting sex trade widely. Having hundreds of casinos, Nevada, located in the US, is very popular world over for such hedonistic recreational activities. It is also home to hundreds of brothels and approximately five thousand strip clubs. As per an estimate, a good functioning strip club makes profit between $ 5,00,000 and 50,00,000 annually.

Many destinations are notorious for sex tourism. Of the sex tourism, child sex tourism is the nastiest and most worrisome. In fact, the tourists who take part in child abuse are not just *pedophiles* alone as this category consists of those who have clinical disorder with affinity for sex with children. Child sex tourists involves another category of tourists who do not have a clinical disorder, but find pleasure by engaging in such activities according to the situation where they get an opportunity to do so. This is a commercial activity with a massive customer base and there is a set of businesses that provides these services. The product offered is the service provided by the suppliers by supplying children below 12 years of age, mainly, for sexual satisfaction. This is mostly observed in some hotels, resorts, brothels, massage parlours, casinos and other similar establishments in many tourism locations across the world. Large-scale child trafficking is taking place as part of this from the poorer countries/regions. The Code, an agency that works against such practices, defines child sex tourism as "acts perpetrated by those who are travelling or using their status as tourists in order to sexually exploit children. It is considered to be a sub-type of child prostitution with clear links to the tourism industry" (www.thecode.org). They also remind us that there are different types of offenders who utilize the tourism industry and infrastructure in order to contact children at destinations and that makes it important for the tourism companies to be alert and to take part in proactive measures to combat child sex exploitation.

According to ECPAT, another agency acts against CST, and it "involves the exchange of cash, clothes, food or some other form of consideration to a child or to a third party for sexual contact. CST occurs in multiple venues, from brothels in red-light districts to beaches or five-star hotels and in urban, rural or coastal settings"(www.ecpat.net). The child sex marketing is expanding and simultaneously, child trafficking is on the steady increase. As stated before only part of child sex tourists seek sex with children specifically, but the rest are situational abusers who do not usually have a sexual preference for children, but take advantage of a situation in which a child is made available to them.

Though it varies, child sex tourism occurs in almost all the tourist regions. *Commercial Sexual Exploitation of Children* (CSEC) is a growing crime world over and tourism becomes a catalyst and facilitator for its expansion.

A comprehensive statistics on child sex tourism is not available. A rough estimate says that more than 2 million boys and girls were involved in child sex tourism directly, until a decade ago. Some statistics as quoted by ECPAT based of some studies are given here. In Mexico, 20,000 minors were involved in prostitution by 2005. Columbia has up to 35,000 child victims. Up to 30,000 girls between ages 12 and 14 are exploited in tourism industries in Kenya. In Asia, particularly Southeast Asia and certain countries in South Asia, have long been the target of child sex tourists. In Philippines, an estimated 100,000 child victims are involved. In Moscow, estimates of children victimized in prostitution have reached 20,000 to 30,000 (ECPAT, Child sex tourism document). If you take the figures including common prostitution and sex work using children, the number will be quite voluminous. For example, in India, the UNICEF has estimated that around 1.2 million children are exploited in prostitution, in general. According to government information there are at least 100,000 children exploited through prostitution every year in the United States (www.ecpat.net/resources).

16.4 TERRORISM AND POLITICAL CRISIS

Terrorism is turning out to be a villain of tourism. Recurring terrorist attacks can ruin a tourist destination. Even a bomb blast can dampen tourism in a place temporarily or even permanently. In 2002, Bali, an island tourist destination in Indonesia was struck by massive bomb blasts killing more than 200 people. It led to the dampening of tourism for a couple of years; many people lost jobs and the economy was shattered. France is suffering from recurring terrorist attacks. Egypt has lost its tourism charisma due to the terrorist activities. One Russian flight was crashed by a blast. Later another flight was crashed down to the sea, resulting in loss of life of all those onboard in Egypt. Travellers are now scared to travel to Egypt, Syria, Tunisia, Turkey and some other Middle East countries due to terrorism.

Apart from terrorist attacks, the advancement of this multi-billion people involved phenomenon has halted at different occasions due to various unforeseen political havocs. The political deadlock that happened in Thailand in 2015, one of the leading leisure tourist locations in Asia, resulted in the decline of tourism there for a short period. Moreover, the Russia-Ukraine and Russia-Turkey issues created havoc in International tourism. New threat is the ongoing internal war in Iraq and Syria which has left tourism to doldrums.

Of course, political chaos that had significant bearing on the tourism sector popped up many a times in the history of tourism. But, of late, it is like a chain, emanating *ad infinitum*, though it gets shifted from one location to another. The aftermath of the *Jasmine*

Revolution that occurred in the beginning of this decade and the ongoing political turmoil that is being embroiled in the Middle East is something that has already caused much worry to the tourism sector. A couple of years ago, some of the countries in Europe and Africa too faced political and economic hurdles which hampered tourism. Many other instances can be cited, with varying impact magnitudes. Tourism industry in Egypt, one of the oldest tourist locations in the world, has been battling to recover from the worst ever fall in tourism as millions of tourists were put off visiting Egyptian resorts and heritage sites in 2013 due to the prolonged civil unrest. The crisis which began in 2011 dampened tourism by then itself. But the issues continued over there. The repercussions of the nose-dive of this largest industry has taken a disastrous toll on the economy, starving the country of income and the much needed foreign currency.

16.5 CLIMATE CHANGE AND TOURISM

Tourism too is a contributor in *climate change*. According to NASA, climate change is change in the average or typical climate of a region or city, or even that of the earth's surface. Due to climate change, extreme variations in climate can occur at some occasions. Increase in average temperature of earth's surface is a phenomenon that has been happening over several centuries, and is called *global warming*. Effects of climate change can be summed up under the following titles:

- Rising of average global temperature
- Rising sea levels
- Increasing frequency of extreme climatic events.

Depletion of ozone layer is a prime reason behind these phenomena. Excessive emission of greenhouse gases leads to the depletion of ozone layer and climate change, in general. Burning of fossil fuels emit greenhouse gases in large quantities. Many of the tourism activities also lead to emission of gases causing ozone layer depletion. Transportation sector contributes to the largest share in it. Of the transport forms, aviation is blamed for maximum contribution.

Apart from its contribution, tourism may face a number of consequences of climate change. Increasing temperature is going to create many issues for tourism. The seasons can be extended in some locations, whereas some other locations may have shortened seasons. Due to temperature variations, some communicable diseases may become widespread. Polar regions may face melting of ice. As a consequence, more water will flow to sea. Sea levels may increase. Flow of more water can lead to floods as well. Increasing sea level may lead to submerging of some islands under sea. Beach tourism may also be affected by climate change. Rising sea levels can affect beaches severely. Erosion can occur in large quantities. Reduced water supply, and increase in sand storms can be some other effects. Coral reef may face increasing levels of bleaching and extinction due to global warming. Beach spaces may shrink. Decreasing snow cover and shrinking glaciers can cause many other issues. Winter tourism can be affected badly due to lack of snow in winter sport destinations with increased snow-making costs, shorter winter sports seasons and loss of aesthetic value of landscapes. Due to loss of snow and ice on lower regions, pressure may be more at higher altitudes which may cause more visitors to flock there.

Seasonality in the destinations can also be affected. Altered seasonal variations in destinations can cause social and economic impacts. Shortage of seasons may cause economic problems. Increasing frequency and intensity of extreme storms can pose risk to tourism facilities, increased insurance costs/loss of insurability, and business interruption costs. Climate changes like torrential rain, cyclones, flood, tsunami, etc., can affect tourist arrivals to a large extent. Also they can affect the natural and cultural heritage. Damages can occur to monuments, etc., due to flood and rains. More frequent and larger forest fires; loss of natural attractions; increase in flooding risks; damage to tourism infrastructure, soil changes (e.g., moisture levels, erosion and acidity); loss of archaeological assets and other natural resources, with impacts on destination attractions, etc., are some other impacts of climate change over tourism (UNWTO-UNEP-WMO, 2001).

16.6 GLOBALIZATION AND TOURISM

We are living in the era of globalization, which is commonly used to refer to a world that is on its way to becoming borderless and an interdependent whole. It primarily aims at the elimination of obstructions to trade, such as tariff and non-tariff barriers. It ensures economic, social, cultural, political and technological interdependence among nations which allows increasingly smoother and freer flow of goods, services, money, labour, and ideas across national borders. Integration of markets in the world is also taking place with the support of a wide range of agendas and strategies along with ample brace from technological forces. From a business perspective, it is all about the complete internationalization of markets as it creates a spatial level of international trade. Practically, it enables the convergence of buyer preferences in markets world over and hence the firms get advantage by reduction in marketing cost due to standardization of related activities. New markets can be easily explored. Moreover, since there are markets in many countries, seasonality consequences of the demand can be minimized by redistribution of products in different locations. Another business aspect is the *globalization of production*, which refers to the production of products or parts of the same product in different locations wherever cost effectiveness and efficiency is felt maximum. Capitalism and globalization have a mutual coexistence and share a symbiotic relationship. Capitalism is a social, political and economic system in which the trade and industry are controlled by private entrepreneurs with the primary objective of earning maximum profit.

General Agreement on Tariffs and Trade (GATT) was the pioneer force that paved way for modern corporate globalization. GATT is a multilateral agreement that came into force on 1 January 1948. The World Trade Organization (WTO) was formed as a result of the Uruguay Round of Negotiations during 1986-94 and earlier negotiations under the General Agreement on Tariffs and Trade (GATT). It came into force from 1st January 1995. International Monetary Fund (IMF) is another organization that fosters globalization. It was established at the Bretton Woods Conference and came into existence in 1945. World Bank is another financial agency, but with more focus on the economic reconstruction of weaker countries. It was instituted to support reconstruction of Europe initially, later it emphasized on provision of finance for national economic developmental initiatives.

While globalization opens up new vistas for entrepreneurs, its consequences are also in wide discussion world over. A plethora of concerns, in fact, mark the glory of globalization as they pose irreversible damage to the society, culture and environment. Globalization is widening the gap between the poor and the rich; and brings in increased inequality among the people inside nations, between nations, and globally as well. As part of eliminating trade barriers, a slow process of denationalization is also taking place along with the loss of sovereignty of many nations. Surprisingly, some of the transnational corporations are financially more powerful than some of the sovereign countries. The existing traditional economic sectors are in deep trouble, and the international firms take advantage and exploit resources and labour for making profit. Capital gains extreme significance and even countries are in a race to lure investors. Excessive resource utilization from the third world countries became a serious issue. The environmental consequences of globalization form a serious concern. Moreover, many traditional societies are experiencing fast disappearance of indigenous cultural values and diversity, and instead the western culture is spreading which is heading towards a homogenization of culture and society. Hence, new globalization, a double-edged sword, can be considered a socio-economic trend of the new era in which utmost internationalization is there, and with a wide range of social, cultural and environmental ramifications.

In tourism, globalization has immense impact, both directly and indirectly. Instead of GATT, tourism is being affected by GATS, the General Agreement on Trade in Services, which entered into force on January 1995 as a result of the Uruguay Round. The GATS applies in principle to all service sectors, except a couple of areas. In fact, globalization benefited tourism greatly. The GATS has enabled international development by removing barriers of overseas investments, contributing to the foreign ownerships of tourism businesses. It spurred *business travel* across the world. The fast spread of privatization and liberalization impacted the economic growth of many countries and that resulted in newer tourism markets by increasing travel propensity among the populations. According to Mowforth and Munt (2009), today's society's *post-fordism movement* ended up in transformations in the way goods and services are produced and consumed and as a result, it leads to the emergence of segmented and niche markets. Consequently, newer destinations are benefited by *distinctiveness.* Countries are now focusing more on developing tourism, and the increasing competition results in *dynamism* and *diversification.* Moreover, multinational tourism organizations are now entering into almost all countries wherever tourism is being developed. Hotel chains are expanding their business horizons to newer areas. Overall *enhancement of quality* and *professionalism* along with *increased employment opportunities* are obvious benefits. Global tourism market is open for all and destinations are now expected to compete on an equal basis.

On the other hand, globalization damages local tourism entrepreneurial potential and employment opportunities. Globalised transnational firms overpower the local entrepreneurs with their capital power, top quality human resource, knowledge and technology advantages. Ultimately, it ends up in massive 'leakage' as well. Ill effects of demonstration effect, commercialization, commoditization and acculturation can be much more due to the effects of globalization. Moreover, cultural habits are getting homogenized. For instance, the widespread of *pizza* food culture is more in tourism areas. Cultural shows are also getting homogenized which dampens the indigenous cultural varieties. Global tourism threatens indigenous knowledge, social structures and relationships. Unfair competition kills the smaller organizations with less capital power. Eventually, it results in *income inequality, economic dependency* on large corporations, tourism *expenditure leakages, destruction of local industries* and *unfair competition.* Moreover, international firms have much less environmental concern for the local natural heritage and hence the possibility of increased environmental impacts is very high due to globalization effects on tourism. The above are just a few implications of globalization on tourism.

16.7 GROWTH OF TOURISM AND THE CHALLENGES

In fact, tourism is growing at an amazing pace. Indeed tourism is faced with barriers very often. Yet it shows extreme resilience to bounce back. The following are the challenges of tourism as of now.

16.7.1 Terrorism

Terrorism is a very serious issue for tourism. Tourism is a highly sensitive sector. A terrorist attack or a fear of a possible attack can elude tourists from visiting those places. Many destinations are already facing the issue of terrorism in a big way. Even European tourism, particularly France, is facing the issue of terrorism badly. Turkey and Egypt are already suffering from the ill effects of terrorism for several years. The increasing terrorism possibilities certainly curb tourism's remarkable growth potential at different points of time.

16.7.2 Communicable Diseases

Spread of communicable diseases is a major issue in the parlance of tourism. At regular occasions, the threat of such diseases halted the progress of tourism. SARS curbed tourist flow to the Asian countries for a short period. The spread of Ebola virus in Africa barred tourists from visiting many of the African countries for a while. Currently, the tourism in Latin American countries is being threatened by the scare of Zika virus. Similar incidents can be there in the future as well.

16.7.3 Political Instabilities

Political issues are always serious issues in tourism. Intervention of political issues has stalled the evolution of tourism on many occasions in the history of tourism. After the world wars, political instabilities occurred at different junctures at different locations in the world. The nature and degree of political issues can be varying. Yet, in spite of the nature and depth, any issue can pose threat to tourism. There are plenty of examples in contemporary history of tourism as well. Currently, tourism in Syria, Iran, Turkey, Tunisia, and Egypt are facing the issue of political turmoil to a large extent. Thailand faced the issue of political unrest, though short lived, in its recent history of tourism.

16.7.4 Economic Downturns

Since 2008, for more than a couple of years, the world reeled under an economic depression. It impacted tourism directly. The rate of growth in number of tourist arrivals decreased considerably. Similar occurrences happened at many occasions. Tourism's progress is directly linked to the economic progress as well. As economic downturns are prone to occur and in future also tourism can be challenged.

16.7.5 Climate Change

Climate change can be a major challenge for tourism in the future. Increasing temperature, rising sea levels and unpredictable climatic conditions can harm tourism at any point of time. Changes in the seasonality, threat to winter tourism and beach tourism, increase in temperature further in warmer destinations, etc., are the major challenges tourism is going to face in the future. Indeed, destinations and countries have to keep an eye on this futuristically and prepare long-term plans in advance itself.

16.7.6 Crisis Management

Recurring crises of large scale trouble tourism often. Natural calamities are frequent nowadays. Manmade issues are also occurring quite often. Tourism sector at all levels, from the national level to the local level and industry levels, have to be ready to tackle the issues as and when they occur. For it, anticipatory mechanism and crisis management plans are necessary. Preparing efficient crisis management mechanism is a challenge for the agencies involved in tourism management.

16.7.7 Potential of Tourism

The advancements of tourism can be due to many reasons. Some of the major reasons are listed below.

- Tremendous developments in information and communication technology
- Advancements in transport technology, particularly the aviation related
- Incredible dynamism and new product development in niche tourism segment
- Emergence of new tourism markets
- Decreasing fuel prices and consequent reduction of travel costs
- Emergence of new destinations
- Progressing economic and social status of the populations
- Emergence of new economic powers
- Increased urbanization
- Increasing affordability for air transport
- Enhancement in the health status of people
- Growing awareness on travel opportunities
- Rising interest of governments in developing tourism
- Influence of social media and mobile applications in inducing travel propensity
- Globalization, privatization and liberalization, etc.

16.8 THE FUTURE

Global tourism is facing a paradigm shift in its geographical focus; the dominance of the West is being challenged; and the emerging economies are forecast to lead world tourism soon! The epicentre of its evolution, undoubtedly, was Europe, though America had substantial contribution into it at later stages. These two regions together had the hegemony over global tourism for a long period. As international tourism progressed to new heights, by the end of the last century, its dominance began to dwindle and as per the current forecasts, the other regions together may have more share in international tourism soon.

Asia is already one of the fastest growing regions in the world. China has become the number one source market, surpassing the USA, for international tourism. World Travel and Tourism Council (WTTC) predicts that by 2020, Asian travellers will account for nearly one-half of all global tourism expenditures and out of the 70 million new jobs the industry will create globally in the next ten years, about two-thirds (47 million) will be in Asia. Experts are of the opinion that within the next few years, Asians will comprise two out of five international travellers and that China will overtake the United States to become the world's largest travel and tourism economy by 2023. An analysis of international tourist arrival statistics clearly reveals the dwindling hegemony of Europe and America in Tourism. In 1950, when modern tourism was taking off as a significant economic force, the number of international tourist arrivals was merely 25.3 million. Of them, vast majority travelled to European countries and the American continent, particularly to the US. Europe received 16.8 million and Americas received 7.5 million tourists, and that constituted 96% of the total tourist arrivals. Africa, Asia and the Pacific, and the Middle East received only a marginal share during then. By 2000, tourist arrivals rose to 687 million, of which Europe received 395 million and America got 128 million. This constituted 76%, a drop from 96%. According to the UNWTO, in 2014, 1133 million tourists visited foreign countries. Of them, 581.8 million travelled to Europe which is 51% of the total. Asia and the Pacific countries received 263 million tourists (23%). Americas, which includes South, North, and Central Americas was visited by 181 million (16%). There were 56 million (5%) tourist arrivals to the Africa and 51 million (4.5%) to Middle East countries. Still the Americas and Europe together received the majority of international tourists, but the share had decreased to almost 67% in 2014 from the share of 76% in 2000.

Growth rate too is on a descending trend in comparison with the rest of the regions. From 1950s to 2000, the world has grown with an average rate of 6.8%. Europe and the Americas grew at rates such as 6.5 and 5.8 percentages respectively. At the same time, Asia and the Pacific recorded the highest rate (13.1%), followed by Middle East (10.1%) and Africa (8.3%). From 1950s to 60s, America and Europe grew at an average rate of 8.4 and 11.6 percentages. But when it turned to 1990s to 2000, the rates decreased to 3.3 and 4.1 percentages respectively. Other regions had been growing at much faster rates compared to these.

The forecasts too reveal the same trends. The UNWTO Tourism Towards 2030, a forecast for 20 years from 2010, shows that by 2020 the international tourist arrivals may reach 1.4 billion and in 2030 the figures may go up to 1.8 billion. It further shows that the share of Europe and America will decrease to 63 per cent of the whole tourist arrivals in 2020. While countries in Asia, Middle East, Africa, Central and Eastern Europe, eastern Mediterranean is estimated to grow faster than the remaining countries; the advanced nations will have a moderate growth rate (approximately 2.2%) only. Asia and the Pacific region countries may continue with the highest growth rates till 2030's.

The UNWTO report reveals the growth potential of tourism in the following way:

"Global growth in international tourist arrivals to continue, but at a more moderate pace, from 4.2% per year (1980–2020) to 3.3% (2010–2030), as a result of four factors:

- The base volumes are higher, so smaller increases still add substantial numbers

- Lower GDP growth, as economies mature
- Lower elasticity of travel to GDP
- Shift from falling transport costs to increasing ones.

Tourism Towards 2030 shows that there is still a substantial potential for further expansion in the coming decades. Established as well as new destinations can benefit from this trend and opportunity, provided they shape adequate conditions and policies with regard to business environment, infrastructure, facilitation, marketing and human resources. Along with opportunities, challenges also arise in maximising social and economic benefits and minimizing negative impacts. Long-term tourism growth patterns are more moderate, sustainable and inclusive (UNWTO, Tourism towards 2030).

While European destinations, particularly in the developed countries, stare at saturation levels, many new destinations are emerging. The phenomenal rise of the East in tourism is due to a range of reasons. Many of the Asian destinations have seen incredible economic progress and consequent changes in the lifestyle, education and health conditions, during the last couple of decades. China and India have advanced greatly and these countries are becoming important source markets. Tourism development has become a priority for many countries. Countries like China, Malaysia, Thailand, Singapore, Turkey, UAE, India and Indonesia have become major international destinations within a short span of time.

16.9 CONCLUSION

Tourism is poised for further growth. Yet, a range of issues cause disruptions in its smooth development. As always, tourism will certainly demonstrate its strong resilience to come back whenever hit by external forces of various kinds. There are a large number of reasons on the anvil to facilitate the evolution of tourism to greater heights. Whatsoever, it is inevitable to develop tourism adhering to the sustainable developments in the most possible manner and to minimize its impacts to the lowest levels.

Key Terms

Contemporary tourism
Birth tourism
Unethical tourism
Sex tourism
Child sex tourism
Terrorism
Political instability
Climate change
Globalization
GATS
Challenges of tourism
Communicable diseases
Political instability
Economic recession
Crisis management

Review Questions

Short Answer Type Questions

1. Write some of the unethical practices in tourism.
2. What do you mean by sex tourism?
3. Discuss child sex tourism.
4. Write how terrorism can affect tourism.
5. Explain the issue of political instability for tourism.
6. Discuss how climate change can affect tourism.
7. Write the advantages and disadvantages of globalization on tourism.
8. Discuss how economic recession impacts tourism.
9. Write in brief on the challenges for tourism in its growth.
10. What factors can stimulate the growth of tourism?

Essay Type Questions

1. Write an essay on the current tourism scenario.
2. Discuss in detail the future of tourism.

REFERENCES AND BIBLIOGRAPHY

Aggarwal, R.D. (1993). *Organization and Management*. New Delhi: Tata McGraw Hill.

Airbus (2003). *Global Market Forecast (2003-2022)*. Bagnac, France's Airbus, SAS.

Akhtar, J. (1990). *Tourism Management in India*. Delhi: Ashish Publishing House.

Albuquerqus Environmental Society/CPR Envtl. Edn. Service: Visual Pollution, www.cabeq.gov, quoted in http://cpreec.org/161.htm

Allerton, C. (2003). Authentic Housing, Authentic Culture: Transforming a Village into a 'Tourist Site' in Manggarai, Eastern Indonesia. Indonesia and the Malay. *World*, 31: 119-128.

Alvedari, H. (2005). *Marketing and Market Management*. Payam Noor University. Tehran. analysis/

Andereck, K.L. & Caldwell, L.L. (1993). The influence of tourist characteristics on ratings of information sources for an attraction. *Journal of Tourism Marketing*. 2(2/3): 171-189.

Andersons, L.T. (1995). *Guidelines for Preparing Urban Plans*. Chicago: Planners Press.

Andreasen, A.R. (1965). Attitude and consumer behaviour: A decision model in new research. In: L.E. Preston (Ed.). *Marketing*. pp. 1–16. Berkeley, CA: Institute of Business and Economic Research, University of California.

Archer, B. (1977). Tourism Multipliers: The State of the Art. Bangor Occasional Papers in Economics. No. 11. University of Wales Press.

Archer, B. (1987). Demand forecasting and estimation. In: *Travel, Tourism, and Hospitality Research: A Handbook for Managers and Researchers*. J.R.B., Ritchie & C.R. Goeldner (Eds.). New York: John Wiley & Sons.

Ashley, C., Roe, D. & Goodwin, H. (2001). Pro-poor Tourism Strategies: Making Tourism Work for the Poor: A Review of Experience. http://r4d.dfid.gov.uk/PDF/Outputs/Mis_SPC/R7557-ppt_report.pdf (19 August 2013).

ATC/Breeze Robertson, on behalf of Australian Tourism Commission, 2011. Aboriginal tourism in Australia, *Year Book Australia: 2004*, Australia Bureau of Statistics.

Bakhshi, A. (2007). The Impact of Tourism Marketing Mix on Attracting Domestic and Foreign Tourists in Kish Island. Masters Thesis, Islamic Azad University, Tehran.

Bateson, J.E.G. & Douglas Hoffman, K. (1999). *Managing Services Marketing: Text and Readings*. 4th Edition. USA: The Dryden Press.

Baud-Bovy, M. (1982). New concepts in planning for tourism and recreation. *Tourism Management*, 3(4): 308-313.

Becheri, E. (1989). From thermalism to health tourism. *Revue de Tourisme*. 44(4): 15-19.

Beeton, S. (2005). *Film-Induced Tourism*. Clevedon: Channel View Publications.

Benchendorff, P., Noscardo, G. & Murphy, L. (2005). High tech versus high touch: Visitor responses to the use of technology in tourist attractions. *Tourism Recreation Research*. 30(3): 37-47.

Bezbaruah, M.P. (1999). *Indian Tourism: Beyond the Millennium*. New Delhi: Gyan Publishing House.

Bhatia, A.K. (2006). *The Business of Tourism: Concepts and Strategies*. New Delhi: Sterling Publishers.

Biederman, S.P. (2007). *Travel and Tourism: An Industry Primer*. Upper Saddle River. New Jersey (USA): Prentice Hall.

Bisht, S.S., Mishra, V. & Fuloria, S. (2010). Measuring accessibility for inclusive development: A census based index. *Social Indicators Research*. 98: 167-181.

Blank, U. (1989). *The Community Tourism Industry Imperative: The Necessity, the Opportunities, its Potential*. State College. PA: Venture.

Boeing, 2003. *Current Market Outlook 2003*, Seattle, Boeing Commercial Airplanes, Marketing.

Boniface, C. & Cooper, C. (2002). *Worldwide Destinations Casebook: The Geography of Travel and Tourism*. Oxford: Butterworth-Heinemann.

Booms, B.H. & Bitner, M.J. (1981). Marketing strategies and organizational structures for service firms. In: *Marketing of Services*. J. Donnelly and W.R. George (Eds.). Chicago: American Marketing Association, pp. 47-51.

Bramwel, B., Henri, I., Jackson, G., Prat, A. G., Richards, G., & Vander Straaten, J. (Eds.) (1996). *Sustainable Tourism Management: Principles and Practices*. Tilburg, Netherlands: Tilburg University Press.

Brotherton, B. & Himmetoglu, B. (1997). Beyond destinations: Special interest tourism. *Anatolia*. 8(3): 11-30.

Brundtland World Commission on Environment and Development (1987). *Our Common Future*. New Delhi: Oxford University Press.

Buckley, R.C. (2006). *Adventure Tourism*. Oxford: CABI.

Buckley, R.C. (2009). *Ecotourism: Principles and Practices*. Wallingford: CABI. p. 368.

Buhalis, D. & Licata, M. (2002). The future of e-Tourism intermediaries. *Tourism Management*. 23: 207-220.

Buhalis, D. (1998). Strategic use of IT in the tourism industry. *Tourism Management*. 19(3): 409-423.

Buhalis, D. (2002). *e-Tourism: Information Technology for Strategic Tourism Management*. London: Pearson Education.

Buhalis, D. (2003). *e-Tourism: Information Technology for Strategic Tourism Management*. Essex: Prentice Hall.

Buhalis, D. (2004). eAirlines: Strategic and tactical use of ICTs in the airline industry. *Information and Management*. 41(7): 805-25.

Buhalis, D. (2008). IT and management information systems in tourism. In: Bech J. and Chadwick S. (Eds.). *The Business of Tourism Management*. Pearson.

Buiatti, S. (2011). Food and tourism: The role of the "Slow Food" Association. In: Katia Laura Sidali, Achim Spiller and Birgit Schulze (Eds.). *Food, Agriculture and Tourism*. London, New York: Springer Heidelberg Dordrecht.

Burkart, A.J. & Medlik, S. (1980). Tourism: Past, present and future. Seminal Studies, reported in S. Page (2003). *Tourism Management, Managing for Change*. Oxford: Butterworth-Heinemann.

Burns, A. & Burns, R. (2008). *Basic Marketing Research* (Second Ed.). New Jersey: Pearson Education.

Burns, P. & Holden, A. (1995). *Tourism: A New Perspective*. London: Prentice Hall.

Burns, P.M. (1999). *An Introduction to Tourism and Anthropology*. London: Routledge.

Butler, R. & Hinch, T. (1996). *Tourism and Indigenous People: Issues and Implications*. Butterworth-Heinemann.

Butler, R. (1990). "The influence of the media in shaping international tourist patterns." *Tourism Recreation Research*. 15(2): 46-53.

Butler, R. (1993). Tourism development in small islands. In: Lockhart, D., Drakakis-Smith, D. and Schembri, J. *The Development Process in Small Island States*. Great Britain: Routledge.

Butler, R.W. (1980). The concept of tourism area life cycle of evolution. *Canadian Geographer*. 24: 5-12.

Cano, V. & Prentice, R. (1998). Opportunities for endearment to place through electronic 'Visiting'. WWW Home Pages and the Tourism Promotion in Scotland. *Tourism Management*. 19(1).

Capella, L.M. & Greco, A.J. (1987). Information sources of elderly for vacation decisions. *Annals of Tourism Research*. 14(2): 148-151.

Cape Town Declaration (2002). First International Conference on Responsible Tourism, held in Cape Town, South Africa. www.icrtourism.org

Ceballos-Lascurain, H. (1993). Ecotourism as a worldwide phenomenon. In: K. Lindberg & D. Hawkins (Eds.). *Ecotourism: A Guide for Planners and Managers*. pp. 12-14. North Bennington: The Ecotourism Society.

Chadwick, R. (1994). Concepts, definitions and measures used in travel and tourism research. In: J.R.B. Ritchie and C. Goeldner (Eds.). *Travel Tourism and Hospitality Research: A Handbook for Managers and Researchers*. 2nd Edn. New York: Wiley.

Choi, C.K.B & Pak, W.P.A. (2006). Multidisciplinarity, interdisciplinarity and transdisciplinarity in health research, services, education and policy. Definitions, objectives, and evidence of effectiveness. *Clin. Invest. Med.* 29(6): 351-64.

Christaller, W. (1963). Mountain bike management: Rescue, protection and social conflicts. *Trends*. 34: 36-40.

Christos, S. (1982). Trends in tourism planning and development. *Tourism Management*. 3(4): 314-318.

CIA (2013). The World Fact Book of Central Intelligence Agency of the US. Accessed from https://www.cia.gov/library/publications/the-world-factbook/fields/2053.html

Clark, J. R. (1996). *Coastal Zone Management Handbook*. Boca Raton: Lewis Publishers.

CLIA (2012). The Overview: 2010 CLIA Cruise Market Overview. <http://cruising.org/regulatory/clia-statistical-reports> (9 December 2013).

Cliff, A. & Ryan, C. (2002). Vital Encounters: When Tourists Contact Travel Agents. In: Chris Ryan, *The Tourist Experience*. London: Thomson.

CNBC. http://www.cnbc.com/2015/10/01/tourism-to-replace-oil-economy-in-saudi-arabia.html

Cohen, E. (1972). Towards a sociology of international tourism. *Social Research*. 39(1): 164-182.

Collier, A. (1997). *Principles of Tourism: A New Zealand Perspective*. 4th Edn. Auckland: Addison Wesley Longman.

Colton, J. & Bissix, G. (2005). Developing agritourism in Nova Scotia: Issues and challenges. *Journal of Sustainable Agriculture*. 27(1): 91-112.

Connell, J. & Reynolds, P. (1999). The implication of technological developments on tourist information centres. *Tourism Management*. 20: 501-509.

Cook, A.R. & Yale, J.L. (2006). *The Business of Travel*. New Delhi: Pearson Education.

Cook, A.R., Yale, J.L. & Maryna, J.J. (2002). *Tourism: The Business of Travel*. 1st Edition. New Jersey: Prentice Hall.

Cooke, K. (1982). Guidelines for socially appropriate tourism development in British Columbia. *Journal of Travel Research*. 21(1): 21-28.

Coombera, L. & Limb, C. Farm Tourism: A Preliminary Study of Participants' Expectations and Perceptions of Farm Tours. Data accessed from www.iemss.org/iemss2004/pdf/ecotourism/coomfarm.pdf

Cooper, C. & Hall, M. (2008). *Contemporary Tourism: An International Approach*. Oxford: Butterworth-Hiememan.

Cooper, C., Fletcher, J. Gilbert, D., Wanhill, S. & Fyal, A. (2004). *Tourism: Principles and Practices*. New Delhi: Pearson Education.

Cooper, C., Fletcher, J., Fyal, A., Gilbert, D. & Wanhill, S. (2008). *Tourism: Principles and Practice*. London: Pitman Pearson Education Ltd.

Cooper, C., Fletcher, J., Gilbert, D. & Wanhill, S. (1993). *Tourism: Principles and Practices*. London: ELBS-Pitman Publishing.

Cooper, C., Fletcher, J., Gilbert, D. & Wanhill, S. (2000). *Tourism: Principles and Practices*. London: Prentice Hall.

Cooper, C., Fletcher, J., Gilbert, D. & Wanhill, S. (2008). Information Technology. In: Shepherd Rebecca (Ed.). *Tourism Principles and Practices*. 2nd edition. England: Longman/Pearson Education Ltd.

Costal and Marine Tourism Activities, International Coastal and Marine Tourism Society (ICMTS), Data available at www.coastalmarinetourism.org (data accessed on 21-03-2016).

Craik, J. (1997). The culture of tourism. In *Touring Cultures: Transformations and Theory*. C. Rojek and J. Urry. (Eds.). pp. 113-136. London: Routledge.

Crandall, R. (1980). Motivations for leisure. *Journal of Leisure Research*. 12: 45–54.

Crompton, J.L. (1979). An assessment of the image of Mexico as a vacation destination and the influence of geographical location upon that image. *Journal of Travel Research*. 17(4): 18-23.

Dalkey, N.C. (1972). The Delphi method: An experimental study of group opinion. In: N.C. Dalkey, et al. (Eds.). *Studies in the Quality of Life: Delphi and Decision-making*. Lexington, MA: Lexington Books.

Daley, B. (2010). *Air Transport and the Environment*. London: Ashgate.

Dann, G.M.S. (1981). Tourist motivation: An appraisal. *Annals of Tourism Research*. 8(2). pp. 187-219.

David, L.E., DelMastro, M., Smith, G. & Swanson, J.R. (2008). *Tourism Policy and Planning*. Oxford: Butterworth-Heinemann.

Davidson, R. (1989). *Tourism*. London: Pitman.

Davidson, R. (1996). The impacts of tourism. In: *Tourism Destinations*. Rob Davidson and Robert Maitland (Eds.). London: Hodder Education.

Davis, G., Wanna, J., Warhurst, J. & Weller, P. (1993). *Public Policy in Australia*. St Leonards: Allen and Unwin.

De Kadt, E. (1979). *Tourism: Passport to Development*. Oxford: Oxford University Press.

Deleche, J. (1994). *Transport and Communications in India: Prior to Steam Locomotion*. Vol II. New Delhi: Oxford University Press.

Diamantis, D. (1999). The concept of ecotourism: Evolution and trends. *Current Issues in Tourism.* 2(2/3): 93-122.

Dileep, M.R. (2005). Environmental impact assessment and tourism: A framework for Nilgiri biosphere reserve. In S.C. Bagri (Ed.). *Ecotourism Development: Strategies and Management.* Uttaranchal: HNB Garhwal University.

Dileep, M.R. (2011). *Information Systems in Tourism.* New Delhi: Excel Books.

Dodds, R. & Joppe, M. (2001). Promoting urban green tourism: The development of the other map of Toronto. *Journal of Vacation Marketing.* 7(3): 261-267.

Douglas, C., Frechtling, C.D. & Horvath, E. (1999). Estimating the Multiplier Effects of Tourism Expenditures on a Local Economy through a Regional InputOutput Model. *Journal of Travel Research.* 37(4): 324-332.

Doxey, G.V. (1976). When enough's enough: The natives are restless in Old Niagara. *Heritage Canada.* 2: 26-28.

Dunn, H. (1959). High-level wellness for man and society. *American Journal of Public Health.* 49(6): 786-792.

Duval, D. (2007). *Tourism and Transport: Modes, Network and Flows.* Clevedon: Channel View.

Dyche, J. (2003). *The CRM Handbook: A Business Guide to Customer Relationship Management.* Delhi: Pearson Education (Singapore).

Dye, T. (1992). *Understanding Public Policy.* Prentice Hall.

D'Aveni, R. (1998). Hyper Competition Closes, *Financial Times,* 4 Feb. New York: John Wiley.

Eckman, C.A. (1983). Development of an instrument to evaluate intercollegiate athletic coaches: A modified Delphi study. Unpublished doctoral dissertation, West Virginia University, Morgantown.

EdCaN - learning resources - Australia (http://edcan.org.au/edcan-learning-rcsources/supporting-resources/aboriginal-and-torres-strait-islander-peoples/cultural-safety/cultural-appraisal).

Edwards, D., Griffin, T. & Hayllar, B. (2008). Urban tourism research: Developing an Agenda. *Annals of Tourism Research.* 35(4).

EIA (2011). United States Energy Information Administration. *Country Analysis Briefs-Oman.* Data accessed on 25 March 2012, from http://www.eia.gov/EMEU/cabs/Oman/pdf.pdf

Ellis, S. (2013). The Global Wellness Tourism Economy. Presentation in the Global Spa and Wellness Summit. ITB Experts Forum 2013.

Encyclopedia of Tourism (2007). Jafar Jaffari (Ed.). London: Routledge.

Engel, J.F., Blackwell, R.D. & Miniard, P.W. (1995). *Consumer Behavior.* 8th Ed. Forth Worth, TX: The Dryden Press.

Eurostat, in McIntosh, R.W. & Goeldner, R.C. (1990). *Tourism Principles, Practices and Philosophies*. New Delhi: John Wiley and Sons.

FAA (Federal Aviation Administration) (2015). Airport Categories. Data accessed from http://www.faa.gov/airports/planning_capacity/passenger_allcargo_stats/categories/

Fakeye, P.C. & Crompton, J.L. (1991). Image differences between prospective, first-time, and repeat visitors to the Lower Rio Grande Valley. *Journal of Travel Research*. 30(10): 10-16.

Farsari, Y. & Prastacos, P. (2004). "GIS applications in the planning and management of tourism." In: Lew, A., Hall, M. & Williams, A. (Eds.). *Tourism Companion*. pp. 596-607. UK: Blackwell.

Fayos-Solà, E. & Marín, C. (2009). *Tourism and Science Outreach: The Starlight Initiative*. UNWTO Papers. Madrid: UNWTO.

Foster, L.D. (1993). *An Introduction to Hospitality*. Singapore: McGraw Hill International Edition.

Foster, L.D. (1994). *First Class: An Introduction to Travel and Tourism*. Singapore: McGraw Hill International Edition.

Foxall, G.R. & Goldsmith, R.E. (1994). *Consumer Psychology for Marketing*. London: Routledge.

Gee, Y.C., Makens, C.J. & Choy, J.L.D. (1997). *The Travel Industry*. 3rd Ed. New York: Van Nostrand Reinhold.

Getz, D. (1987). Tourism Planning and Research Tradition: Models and futures. In: Hall, C.M. (Ed.) (2000). *Tourism Planning, Policies, Processes and Relationships*. England: Pearson Education.

Getz, D. (2008). Event tourism: Definition, evolution, and research. *Tourism Management*. 29: 403-428.

Gilbert, D.C. (1991). An examination of the consumer decision process related to tourism. In: Cooper, C.P. (Ed.). *Progress in Tourism, Recreation and Hospitality*. Upper Saddle River. NJ: Prentice Hall.

Go, F.M., Milne, D. & Whittles, L.J.R. (1992). Communities as destinations: A marketing taxonomy for the effective implementation of the tourism action plan. *Journal of Travel Research*. 30(4): 31-37.

Godfrey, K. & Clarke, J. (2000). *The Tourism Development Handbook*. London: Continuum.

Goeldner, R.C. & Ritchie, J.R.B. (2006). *Tourism: Principles, Practices and Philosophies*. New Jersey (USA): John Wiley and Sons.

Goeldner, R.C., & Ritchie, B.R.J. (2003). *Tourism: Principles, Practices, Philosophies*. New Jersey: John Wiley and Sons Inc.

Goossens, C.F. (1994). External information sources search: Effects of tour brochures with experimental information. *Journal of Tourism Marketing*. 3(3): 89-107.

Government of India (1998). Ministry of Tourism. *Ecotourism in India: Policy and Guidelines*.

Graefe, A.R., Kuss, F.R. & Vaske, J.J. (1990). *Visitor Impact Management: The Planning Framework*. Washington DC, USA: National Parks and Conservation Association.

Graham, A. (2003). *Managing Airports: An International Perspective*. 2nd Edition. Oxford: Butterworth-Heinemann.

Gray, H.P. (1970). *International Travel-International Trade*. Brooke: Lexington.

Green, H. & Hunter, C. (1992). The environmental impact assessment of tourism development. In: P. Johnson and B. Thomas (Eds.). *Perspectives in Tourism Policy*. London: Mansell.

Grozeva, M. (2009). Bulgarian-Greek Cultural-Historical Tourism Corridors. East-Central European Regional Seminar, Gyula Discussion Papers, pp. 71-78. <http://discussionpapers.rkk.hu/index.php/DP/article/view/2346/4386> (5 August 2013).

Guidelines for Ecotourism in and Around Protected Areas (Draft, 2011). Ministry of Environment and Forests, Government of India. www.moef.nic.in (given for education purpose)

Gunn, C. & Targut, V. (2002). *Tourism Planning: Basics, Concepts, Cases*. London: Routledge.

Gunn, C.A. (1979). *Tourism Planning*. New York: Crane Russam.

Gunn, C.A. (1994). *Tourism Planning: Basics, Concepts, Cases*. London: Taylor & Francis.

Gursoy, D. & Mc Cleary, K.W. (2004). An integrative model of tourist information search behaviour. *Annals of Tourism Research*. 31(2): 353-373.

Haahti, A. & Komppula, R. (2006). Experience design in tourism. In: *Tourism Business Frontiers: Consumers, Products and Industry*. D. Buhalis & C. Costa (Eds.). Oxford: Elsevier Butterworth-Heinemann. pp. 101-10.

Hadjiphanis, L. & Christou, L. (2006). The role of e-commerce on consumer behaviour. *Journal of Business Administration Online*. 5(1). Data accessed from www.atu/business/spring2006/ on 10/12/2011.

Haigh, R. (1995). *Backpackers in Australia*. Bureau of Tourism Research, Canberra.

Hall, C., Sharples, L., Cambourne, B. & Macionis, N. (Eds.). (2000). *Wine Tourism Around the World*. Oxford: Butterworth-Heinemann.

Hall, C.M. & Arthur, S. (1998). *Integrated Heritage Management*. London: The Stationery Office.

Hall, C.M. & Page, S. (2006). *The Geography of Tourism Recreation: Space, Place and Environment*. London: Routledge.

Hall, C.M. & Sharples, L. (2003). The consumption of experiences or the experiences of consumption? An introduction to the tourism of taste. In: C.M. Hall, E. Sharples, R. Mitchell, N. Macionis & B. Cambourne (Eds.). *Food Tourism Around the World: Development, Management and Markets*. Oxford: Butterworth-Heinemann.

Hall, C.M. (1991). *Tourism in Australia: Impacts, Planning and Development*. Melbourne: Longman.

Hall, C.M. (1992). *Hallmark Events: The Impacts, Management, and Planning of Event Tourism*. New York: Belhaven Press.

Hall, C.M. (1992). Sex Tourism in South East Asia. In: *Tourism in the Developing World* (D. Harrison, Ed.). Chichester: John Wiley and Sons.

Hall, C.M. (1994). *Tourism and Politics: Policy, Power and Place*. Christoester: John Wiley.

Hall, C.M. (2000). *Tourism Planning: Policies, Processes and Relationships*. Harlow, UK: Prentice Hall.

Hall, C.M. (2008). *Tourism Planning: Policies, Processes and Relationships*. Harlow, UK: Prentice Hall.

Hall, D., Roberts, L. & Mitchell, M. (2003). *New Directions in Rural Tourism*. Aldershot: Ashgate.

Hall, M., & Tucker, H. (Eds.). (2004). *Tourism and Postcolonialism: Contested Discourses, Identities and Representations*. London: Routledge.

Harmsworth, S. (2004). The latest trends and developments in health and spa market. *Insights*. 15(2): 173-178.

Hensher, D. & Brewer, A. (2001). *Transport: An Economics and Management Perspective*. New York: Oxford University Press.

Higginbottom, K. (2004). *Wildlife Tourism: Impacts, Management and Planning*. Altona: Common Ground Publishing. (Edited)

Hill, K.Q. & Fowles, J. (1975). The methodological worth of the Delphi forecasting technique. *Technological Forecasting and Social Change*. 7: 179-192.

Hills, J.M.M. (1965). *The Holiday: A Study of Social and Psychological Aspects with Special Reference to Ireland*. London: The Tavistock Institute of Human Relations.

Hojo, Y. (2002). The expansions of the essays on tourism multiplier model. *The Economic Journal of Takasaki City*. University of Economics. 45(1): 15-33.

Holden, A. (2000). *Environment and Tourism*. London: Routledge.

Holloway, J.C. (1989). *The Business of Tourism*. 4th Edition. London: Longman.

Holloway, J.C. (1994). *The Business of Tourism*. London: McDonalds and Evands.

Holloway, J.C. (1996). *The Business of Tourism*. 4th edition. England: Longman.

Horner, S. & Swarbrooke, J. (1996). *Marketing Tourism, Hospitality, and Leisure in Europe*. London: International Thomson Business Press.

Horner, S. & Swarbrooke, J. (2003). *The Business of Travel and Tourism*. Oxford: Butterworth-Heinemann.

Horner, S. & Swarbrooke, J. (2005). *Leisure Marketing: A Global Perspective*. Elsevier: Butterworth-Heinemann.

Horner, S. & Swarbrooke, J. (2007). *Consumer Behaviour in Tourism*. 2nd edn. Oxford: Butterworth-Heinemann.

Howard, A.J. & Sheth, N.J. (1969). *The Theory of Buyer Behaviour*. New York: Wiley.

Howie, F. (2003). *Managing the Tourist Attractions*. Continuum/Thomson Learning. New York: John Wiley & Sons.

Hunt, J.D. & Lsayne, D. (1991). Evolution of travel and tourism terminology and definitions. *Journal of Travel Research*. 29(4): 7-11.

Hunzicker, W. (1951). *Social Tourism: Its Nature and Problems*. Berne: International Tourists Alliance Scientific Commission.

Hunziker, W. & Krapf, K. (1941). Grundriß Der Allgemeinen Fremdenverkehrslehre (in German). Zurich: Polygr. Verl.

Hunziker, W. & Krapf, K. (2005). Definition quoted in TS-1, Tourism Phenomenon, IGNOU Foundation Course in Tourism.

Husbands, W. & Harrison, L. (1996). *Practicing Responsible Tourism*. New York: John Wiley & Sons.

ICAO, 2009. International Civil Aviation Organization: Review of the classification and definitions used for civil aviation activities. Data accessed from http://www.icao.int/Meetings/STA10/Documents/Sta10_Wp007_en.pdf

ICAO, 2014. Facts and Figures: Statistics of International Civil Aviation Organization. Data accessed from http://www.icao.int/sustainability/pages/factsfigures.aspx

ICAO, 2015. Continuing Traffic Growth and Record Airline Profits Highlight 2015 Air Transport Results, ICAO Press release, dated 22/12/2015.

IEMR (1977). *Tourism in India: A Perspective to 1990*. Ahuja, S.P. & Sarna, S.R. (Eds.). The Institute of Economic and Market Research (IEMR), New Delhi.

Incredible India.org., incredibleindia.org/.../rural-tourism/rural-guideline.pdf

India Tourism Statistics (2014). *Tourist Statistics: Incredible India*. Ministry of Tourism. Government of India.

India Tourism Statistics (2014). Ministry of Tourism, Govt. of India, New Delhi.

Inskeep, E. (1991). *Tourism Planning: An Integrated and Sustainable Development Approach*. New York: Van Nostrand Reinhold.

International Air Transport Association, IATA-UFTAA Study Material (2002). Montreal.

IPCC, Intergovernmental Panel on Climate Change. (www.ipcc.ch)

Iwashita, C. (2006). Media representation of the UK as a destination for Japanese tourists. *Popular Culture and Tourism*. 6(1).

Jacobs, J.M. (1996). *Essential assessment criteria for physical education teacher education programs*: A Delphi study. Unpublished doctoral dissertation, West Virginia University, Morgantown.

Jafari, J. & Xiao, H. (Eds.) (2016). *Encyclopedia of Tourism*. New York: Springer.

Jafari, J. (Ed.) (2000). *Encyclopaedia of Tourism*. London: Routledge.

Kalakota, R. & Whintson, B.A. (2004). *Electronic Commerce: A Manager's Guide*. Delhi: Pearson Education.

Kamra, K. (2000). Hotel and Hospitality. In: Kamra, K., Mill, C.R. & Kaushil, S. (Eds.). *Hospitality Operations and Management*. New Delhi: Wheeler Publishing.

Kazada, A. & Caves, R. (2000). *Airport Design and Operation*. New York: Pergamon Press.

Kelly, C. & Smith, M. (2009). *Holistic Tourism: Integrating Body, Mind, Spirit*. In: *Wellness and Tourism: Mind, Body, Spirit, Place*. R. Bushell and P. Sheldon, Eds., pp. 69-83. New York: Cognizant.

Kelly, I. & Nankervis, T. (2001). *Visitor Destination*. Australia: John Wiley & Sons.

Khoshoo, T.N. (1991). *Environmental concerns and strategies*. New Delhi: Ashish Publishing House.

Klein, N.M. & Yadav, M.S. (1989). Context effects on efforts and accuracy choice: An enquiry into adaptive decision making. *Journal of Consumer Research*. 15(4): 411-421.

Knowles, T., Diamantis, D. & El-Mourhabi, J.B. (2001). *The Globalization of Tourism and Hospitality*: A Strategic Perspective. London: Continuum.

Koth, B., Kreag, G., Sem, J. & Kjolhaug, K. (1991). *Rural Tourism Development Training Guide*. St. Paul: Tourism Center, University of Minnesota.

Kotler, P. & Armstrong, G. (2013). *Principles of Marketing* (Global Edition). 15th Ed. Harlow: Pearson Education.

Kotler, P. & Gertner, D. (2004). Country as brand, product and beyond: A place marketing and brand management perspective. In: Morgan, N., Pritchard, A. and Pride, R. (2004). *Destination Branding: Creating the Unique Destination Proposition*. 2nd edition. Burlington, MA: Elsevier.

Kotler, P., Bowen, J. & Makens, J. (2003). *Marketing for Hospitality and Tourism*. London: Prentice-Hall, Inc.

Kotler, P., Bowens, J. T., & Makens, J. (2010). *Marketing for Tourism and Hospitality*. London: Prentice Hall.

Kumar, J., Hussain, H. & Kanna, S. (2015). Positive vs negative economic impacts: A review of the economic impact studies. In: the proceedings of *Developments of the New Tourism Paradigm in the Asia Pacific Region*. Malaysia.

Lansing, J. & Lilienstein, E. (1957). The Travel Market 1955: The Report to the Travel Research Association. Ann Arbor: University of Michigan Institute for Social Research.

Lascurian, C. (2002). Definition quoted in Eplerwood. Ecotourism: Principles, Practices and Philosophies for Sustainability. UNEP Programme.

Latham, J. (1989). The statistical measurement of tourism. In: C.P. Cooper (Ed.). *Progress in Tourism, Recreation and Hospitality Management*. Vol. 1. London: Bethaven.

Laws, E. (1995). *Tourist Destination Management: Issues, Analysis and Policies*. London: Routledge.

Laws, E. (1997). *Managing Packaged Tourism*. London: International Thompson Business Press.

Lawson, R. (1997). Consumer decision making within goal driven framework. *Psychology and Marketing*. 14(5): 427-449.

Leiper, N. (1979). The Framework of Tourism. *Annals of Tourism Research*, Oct-Dec, pp. 390-407.

Leiper, N. (1990). Tourism system. Massey University, Department of Management Systems. Occasional Paper 2, Auckland, New Zealand.

Li, Y., Hu, Z.Y. & Zhang, C.Z. (2010). Red tourism: Sustaining communist identity in a rapidly changing China. *Journal of Tourism and Cultural Change*. 8(1–2): 101–119.

Lickorish, L. (1994). *Introduction to Tourism*. London: Sage.

Lindberg, K. (1991). *Policies for Maximizing Nature Tourism on Ecological and Economic Benefits*. Washington D.C.: World Resources Institute.

Loke, W.H. (1995). Models of judgement and decision making: An overview. *Perspectives on Judgement and Decision Making*. Lanham (USA): Scarecrow Press Inc.

London Tourist Board (1990). At Cross Roads: The future of London's Transport.

Long, L.M. (1998). Culinary tourism: A folkloristic perspective on eating and otherness. *Southern Folklore*. 55(3): 181-204.

Lovelock, C. & Wirtz, J. (2007). *Services Marketing: People, Technology, Strategy*. 6th Edn. New Jersey: Pearson Prentice Hall.

Lundberg, E.D. & Lundberg, B.C. (1993). *International Travel & Tourism*. New York: John Wiley and Sons.

Lunt, N., Smith, R., Exworthy, M., Green, T.S., Horsfall, D. & Mannion, R. (2011). Medical Tourism: Treatments, Markets and Health System Implications: A scoping review, OECD. https://www.oecd.org/els/health-systems/48723982.pdf

MacCannell, D. (1999). *The Tourist: A New Theory of the Leisure Class*. New York: Schocken Books.

MacKay, K.J. & Fesenmaier, D.R. (1997). Pictoral element of destination image formation. *Annals of Tourism Research*. 24(3): 537-565.

Marlina, A., Gomez, M. & Consuegra, D.M. (2010). Tourism Marketing Information and Destination Image Management. *African Journal of Business Management*. 4(5): 722-728.

Mason, P. (1995). Tourism: Environment and Development Perspectives. WorldWide Fund For Nature. UK: Godalming.

Mason, P. (2008). *Tourism Impacts, Planning and Management*. Oxford: Butterworth-Heinemann.

Mathieson, A. & Wall, G. (1982). Tourism: Economic, Physical and Social Impacts. London: Longman.

Mayenes, E.S. (1976). Decision Making for Consumers: An Introduction to Consumer Economics. New York: McMillan Publishing Co. Inc.

McIntosh, R.W. & Goeldner, R.C. (1990). Tourism Principles, Practices and Philosophies. New Delhi: John Wiley and Sons.

McIntosh, R.W., Goeldner, R.C. & Ritchie, J.R.B. (2003). Tourism Principles, Policies and Practices. New Jersey: John Wiley and Sons Inc.

Medlik, S. & Middleton, V.T.C. (1973). The tourist product and its marketing implications. *International Tourism Quarterly*. 3: 28-35.

Medlik, S. (2003). Preface. In: *Dictionary of Travel, Tourism and Hospitality*. Oxford: Butterworth-Heinemann.

Michael, P. (1969). International Tourism. London: Hutchinson.

Middleton, V. (1994) Marketing in Travel and Tourism. London: Routledge.

Middleton, V.T.C. & Clarke, J. (2001). Marketing for Travel and Tourism. 3rd edition. Oxford: Butterworth-Heinemann.

Middleton, V.T.C. & Hawkins, R. (1998). Sustainable Tourism Making Perspective. Oxford: Butterworth-Heinemann.

Mill, C.R. (1990). Tourism: The International Business. New Jersey: Prentice Hall.

Mill, R.C. & Morrison, A.M. (1992). The Tourism System: An Introductory Text. 2nd Edn. Englewood Cliffs, N.J.: Prentice Hall.

Miller, M. (2016). www.pressofatlanticoncity.com. Data accessed from http://www.pressofatlanticcity.com/news/breaking/cape-population-shrinks-as-tourism-thrives/article_af70ce72-2861-11e6-9621-d3d55be37897.html

Mills, S. (1995). National and regional tourism planning – Methodologies and case studies. *Tourism Management*. 16(4): 328-329.

Milman, A. & Pizam, A. (1995). The role of awareness and familiarity with destination: The Central Florida case. *Journal of Travel Research*. 33(3): 21-27.

Minnaert, L., Maitland, R. & Miller, G. (2011). What is social tourism? *Current Issues in Tourism*. 5: 403-415.

Moore, R.S. (1995). Gender and alcohol use in a Greek tourist town. *Annals of Tourism Research*. 22(2): 300-313.

Morinis, A. (1992). *Sacred Journeys: The Anthropology of Pilgrimage*. Santa Barbara: Praeger.

Morrison, J. (2006). *International Business Environment: Global and Local Marketplace in a Changing World*. London: Palgrave Macmillan.

Moss, S. (2004). *A Bird in the Bush: A Social History of Bird Watching*. London: Aurum.

Mowforth, M. & Munt, I. (1998). *Tourism and Sustainability: New Tourism in the Millennium*. London: Routledge.

Mowforth, M. & Munt, I. (2009). *Tourism and Sustainability: Development, Globalisation and New Tourism in the Third World*. 3rd Edition. Oxon: Routledge.

Muller, H. & Kaufman, E.L. (2000). 'Wellness tourism'. *Journal of Vacation Marketing*. 7(1): 5-17.

Muller, M. (1882). INDIA - Lecture 1. What can India teach us? A Course of Lectures delivered before the University of Cambridge, Project Gutenberg. Data available online at https://www.gutenberg.org/files/20847/20847-h/20847-h.htm (accessed on 15-02-2017).

Murcott, A.G. (1986). Review of S. Mennell. All manners of food: Eating and taste in England and France from the middle ages to the present. *Sociology*. 20: 645–646.

Murphy, P.E. (1985). *Tourism: A Community Approach*. NewYork: Methuen.

Nankervis, T. & Kelly, I. (2001). Visitor Destination. Australia: John Wiley & Sons.

NASA, Airplanes and Parts, data accessed from https://www.grc.nasa.gov/www/k-12/airplane/airplane.html

Nash, R. (2001). Wilderness and the American Mind. New Haven: Yale University Press.

National Geographic, http://travel.nationalgeographic.com/travel/geotourism/about/).

Nilsen, P. & Tayler, G. (1998). A comparative analysis of protected area planning and management frameworks. In: McCool, S.F. & Cole, D.N. (Compilers). *Limits of Acceptable Change and Related Processes: Programs and Future Directions*. Proceedings of Conference, 1997 (May 20–22), Missoula, MN. U.S. Department of Agriculture, Forest Service, Rocky Mountains Research Station, Ogden, UT, USA.

NZTPO, 1976, in Pike, S. 2008. *Destination Marketing: An Integrated Marketing Communication Approach*. London: Elsevier.

OECD (1973). OECD Expert Committee, Tourism Policy and International Tourism in OECD Countries. Paris: OECD.

OECD (2010). Health Accounts Experts' Progress Report. Trade in Health Care Goods and Services Under the System of Health Accounts. Paris: OECD.

OECD (2012). Food and the Tourism Experience: The OECD-Korea Workshop. Paris: The Organization for Economic Co-operation and Development.

Official website of Indian Railways/luxury trains, data available from http://www.indianrail.gov.in/luxury_Train.html (accessed on 23-03-2017).

Oona, S. & Michai, T. (2011). Consumer behaviour in different sectors of tourism. *Studies in Business Economics*. Data accessed from http://eceesf.ulbsibiu.ro/RePEc/blg/journal/5319 standard tichindelean.pdf, on 10/12/2011.

Orams, M.B. (1999). *Marine Tourism: Development, Impacts and Management*. London: Routledge.

O'Connor, E.W. (2001). *An Introduction to Airline Economics*. Santa Barbara, CA: Greenwood Publishing Group.

Page, S. (2003). *Tourism Management: Managing for Change*. Burlington: Butterworth-Heinemann.

Page, S. (2005). *Transport & Tourism Global Perspectives*. 2nd Edition. Harlow: Pearson Education.

Page, S. (2007). *Tourism Management: Managing for Change*. Oxford: Butterworth-Heinemann.

Parvatiyar, A. & Sheth, N.J. (2003). Conceptual Framework of Customer Relationship Management. In: Sheth, J.N., Parvatiyar, A. and Shainesh, G. (Eds.). *Customer*

Relationship Management: Emerging Concepts, Tools and Applications. pp. 3-25. New Delhi: Tata McGraw Hill.

Pearce, D.G. (1995). *Tourism Today: Geographical Analysis*. 2nd Edn. Harlow: Longman.

Pearce, D.G., Reid, L. & Schott, C. (2009). Travel arrangements and the distribution behaviour of New Zealand outbound travelers. *Journal of Travel and Tourism Marketing*. 26(1): 80–97.

Pearce, P. (1991). Analysing tourist attractions. *Journal of Tourism Studies*. 2(1): 46-55.

Pearce, P.L. (1982). *The Social Psychology of Tourist Behaviour*. Oxford: Pergamon.

Peiyi, D. (2000). Environmental impact assessment. In: Jaffer Jafari (Ed.). *Encyclopaedia of Tourism*. London: Routledge.

Pelsmacker, P.D. & Janssens, W. (2007). A model for fair trade buying behaviour: The role of perceived quantity and quality of information and of product-specific Attitudes. *Journal of Business Ethics*. 75(4): 361-380.

Pepper, D. & Rogers, M. (1993). *One to One Future Building Relationships: One Customer at a Time*. New York: Doubleday.

Peter, J.P. & Olson, C.J. (1999). *Consumer Decision Making, Consumer Behaviour and Marketing Strategy*. Boston: Irwin/McGraw Hill.

Peter, M. (1969). *International Tourism*. London: Hutchinson.

Philip, L., Murphy, L. & Brymer, E. (2009). Evolution of the backpacker market and the potential for Australian tourism: Sustainable Tourism Cooperative Research Centre (STCRC). National Library of Australia (Cataloguing-in-Publication Entry)

Pike, S. (2005). *Destination Marketing Organisations*. Oxford: Elsevier.

Pike, S. (2008). *Destination Marketing: An Integrated Marketing Communication Approach*. London: Elsevier.

Pine, B.J., Peppers, D. & Rogers, M. (1995). Do you want to keep your customers forever? *Harvard Business Review* (March-April). pp. 103-113.

Pitts, B.G. (1997). From leagues of their own to an industry of their own: The emerging lesbian. *Women in Sports and Physical Activity Journal*. 6(2): 109-139.

Plog, S.C. (1974). "Why destination areas rise in popularity and fall in popularity?" *Cornell Hall and Restaurant Quarterly*. 14(4): 55-58.

Poetschke, B. (1997). Key success factors for public/private sector partnerships in Island tourism planning. In: M.V. Collin and T. Baum (Eds.). *Island Tourism*. John Wiley & Sons.

Poon, A. (1993). *Tourism, Technology and Competitive Strategies*. Oxford: CABI.

Prentice, R. (1993). *Tourism and Heritage Attractions*. London: Routledge.

Prezbórska, L. (2003). Relationships between rural tourism and agrarian restructuring in a transitional economy: The case of Poland. In: D. Hall, M. Mitchell, & L. Roberts (Eds.). *New Directions in Rural Tourism*. pp. 203-222. Aldershot: Ashgate.

Pridaeux, B. (2007). Echoes of war: Battlefield Tourism. In: Chris Ryan (Ed.). *Battlefield Tourism: History, Place and Interpretation*. New York: Elsevier.

Prideaux, B. & Singer, P. (2005). Space Tourism—A future dream or a cyber-tourism reality? *Tourism Recreation Research*. 30(3): 27-35.

Prideaux, B. (2000). The role of the transport system in destination development. *Tourism Management*. 21:53-63. CrossRef producing the 2013 WTTC/Oxford Economics Travel & Tourism Economic Impact.

Rafiq, M. & Ahmed, P.K. (1995). Using the 7Ps as a generic marketing mix: An exploratory survey of UK and European marketing academics. *Marketing Intelligence & Planning*. 13(9): 4-15.

Ralph, S. & Reynolds, G. (2001). *Principles of Information System*. Thomson Learning. Singapore.

Redclift, M. (1987). *Sustainable Development: Exploring the Contradictions*. London: Methuen.

Reid, D. (1995). *Sustainable Development: An Introductory Guide*. London: Earthscan.

Reid, D.G. (2003). *Tourism, Globalization and Development: Responsible Tourism Planning*. London: Pluto Press.

Reisinger, Y. (2009). *International Tourism: Cultures and Behaviour*. Oxford: Butterworth-Heinemann.

Rengaraj, N. & Reghuram, G. (2007). *Viability of Inland Water Transport in India*. Asian Development Bank. India Resident Mission. New Delhi.

Richards, G. (1996). *Cultural Tourism in Europe*. Wallingford: CABI.

Riley, M., Ladkin, A. & Szivas, E. (2002). *Tourism Employment Analysis and Planning*. Clevdon: Channel View Publications.

Ritchie, B., Tkaczynski, A. & Faulks, P. (2010). Understanding the motivation and travel behaviour of cycle tourists using involvement profiles. *Journal of Travel and Tourism Marketing*. 27:409-425.

Ritchie, J.R. & Goeldner, C.R. (1994). *Travel, Tourism and Hospitality Research: A Handbook for Managers and Researchers*. New York: John Wiley & Sons.

Roberts, L. & Hall, D. (2001). *Rural Tourism and Recreation: Principles and Practices*. Oxford: Wallingford.

Robinson, M. & Andersen, H. (Eds.). (2003). *Literature and Tourism*. London: Thomson Learning.

Ross, F.G. (2005). Cyber-tourism and social capital: Ethics, trust and sociability. *Tourism Recreation Research*. 30(3): 87-95.

Ross, S. & Wall, G. (1999). Ecotourism: Towards congruence between theory and practice. *Tourism Management*. 20: 123-132.

Sadry, B.N. (2009). Fundamentals of Geotourism: With emphasis on Iran. Tehran: SAMT Organization. p. 220. (English Summary available online at: http://physio-geo.revues.org/3159?file=1).

Samuelson, P. (1972). "*L Economique, introduction analyse economique.*" 1(4): 458.

Saur, L. (1999). Norske Ski – For Pleasure and Hassle. Finnmark: Finnmark University College.

Scheyvens, R. (2007). Poor cousins no more: Valuing the development potential of domestic and diaspora tourism. *Progress in Development Studies.* 7: 307-25.

Schiffman, L.G. & Kanuk, L.L. (2009). *Consumer Behaviour.* 9th Edn. New Jersey: Pearson Prentice Hall.

Shani, D. & Chelsani, C. (1992). Exploiting niches using relationship marketing. *Journal of Consumer Marketing.* 9(3): 33-42.

Sharpley, R. & Sharpley, J. (1997). *Rural Development.* London: International Thomson Business Press.

Sheldon, P. (2003). *Tourism Information Technology.* Oxford: CABI.

Simon, R. (1997). Studying public policy. *Canadian Journal of Political Science.* 9: 558-590.

Singh, K.P. (1998). *Fifty Years of Indian Tourism.* New Delhi: Kanishka Publishers.

Sinha, P.C. (1997). *International Encyclopedia of Tourism Management.* New Delhi: Anmol Publishers.

Smith, J.S. (1995). *Tourism Analysis: A Handbook.* England: Longman Group Ltd.

Smith, V. & Eadington, W. (Eds.). (1994). *Tourism Alternatives: Potentials and Problems in the Development of Tourism.* Chichester: Wiley.

Smith, V. (1977). *Hosts and Guests: The Anthropology of Tourism.* Philadelphia: University of Pennsylvania Press.

Snepenger, D. & Snepneger, M. (1993). Information Search by Pleasure Travellers. In: M. Khan, M. Olsen & T. Var (Eds.). *VNR's Encyclopaedia of Hospitality and Tourism.* New York: Van Nostrand Reinhold. pp. 830-853.

Sniffer, J. (1995). UNEP Impact Assessment Meetings.

Solomon, M.R. (1996). *Consumer Behaviour.* 3rd Ed. NJ: Engle-Wood Cliff.

space-india.com, http://www.space-india.com/astrotourism.html

Stankey, G.H. (1984). Carrying capacity in recreational settings: Evolution, appraisal, and application. In: *Leisure Science,* 6(4): 453-473.

Subramoniam, S., Al-Essai, A.N.S., Al-Marashadi, M.A.A. & Al-Kindi, A.M.A. (2010). SWOT analysis on Oman tourism: A case study. *Journal of Economic Development, Management, IT, Finance and Marketing.* 2(2): 1-22.

Sue, B. (2005). *Film-Induced Tourism.* Bristol (UK): Channel View Publications.

Swarbrooke, J. (1995). *The Development and Management of Visitor Attractions.* Oxford: Butterworth-Heinemann.

Swarbrooke, J. (2002). *The Development and Management of Visitor Attractions.* Oxford: Butterworth-Heinemann.

TCIL (2012). Thomas Cook India Ltd. Corporate Travel: Convergence of Travel and Technology 2012. Report in Voyagers World, June 2012. Data accessed from http://voyagersworld.in/content/thomas-cook-india-launches-whitepaper-corporate-travel.

Teagasc Fact Sheets (2006). Adventure Tourism. Data accessed on 24, May 2016, from https://www.teagasc.ie/media/website/publications/2006/23_AdventureTourism.pdf

The British Ecotourism Market/UNWTO, 2012. Data accessed from http://sdt.unwto.org/content/ecotourism-and-protected-areas

TIES (2009). The International Ecotourism Society (http://www.ecotourism.org)

TIES press release, January 7, 2015, https://www.ecotourism.org/news/ties-news/ties-press-release

Timothy, D.J. (1998). Cooperative tourism planning in a developing destination. *Journal of Sustainable Tourism*. 6(1): 52-83.

Timothy, D.J. (2005). *Shopping Tourism, Retailing and Leisure*. UK: Channel View Publications.

Tirmizi, A.M., Ur-Rehman, K. & Saif, M.I. (2009). An empirical study of consumer impulse buying behaviour in local markets. *European Journal of Scientific Research*. 28(4): 522-532.

Tosun, C. & Jenkins, C.L. (1998). The evolution of tourism planning in third world countries: A critique. *Progress in Tourism and Hospitality Research*. 4(2): 101-114.

Tourism Concern, https://www.tourismconcern.org.uk/displacement-caused -by-tourism/

Tourism Policy, 2002, Ministry of Tourism, Government of India. Data available online at http://tourism.gov.in/sites/default/files/policy/National%20Tourism%20Policy%202002.pdf (accessed on 15-01-2016).

Tribe, J. (2008). The *Economics of Recreation, Leisure and Tourism*. Oxford: Butterworth-Heinemann.

Tuman/Tartu Ulikool. (2013). A Framework for Health Tourism. Data accessed from www.pc.ut.ee/sites/default/files/h_tooman.pdf

Turban, E., Leidner, D., Melean, E. & Wetherbe, J. (2008). *Information Technology for Management-Transforming Organizations in the Digital Economy*. 6th edition. New Delhi: John Wiley and Sons.

Turner, K. (1988). *Environmental Management*. London: West View Press.

UFI (2007). The World Map of Exhibition Venues and Future Trends. www.ufi.org/pages/publicationspress/surveys.asp (6 May 2008).

UK Musica and Visiti Britain, (2012). 'WISH YOU WERE HERE, MUSIC TOURISM'. Contribution to the UK Economy: October 2013. Data accessed from www.ukmusic.org/.../music-tourism-wish-you-were-here-2015.

Ullman, E. (1980). *Geography on Spatial Interaction.* University of Washington Press.

UN & UNWTO (2008). *International Recommendations for Tourism Statistics.* Department of Economic and Social Affairs: Statistics Division, United Nations Publications.

UN & WTO (1994). *Recommendations on World Tourism Statistics.* United Nations Department for Economic and Social Information and Policy Analysis Statistical Division and World Tourism Organization. New York.

UNEP/PAP/RAC (2009). *Sustainable Coastal Tourism: An Integrated Planning and Management Approach.* UNEP Sustainable Consumption and Production Branch and Priority Actions Programme-Regional Activity Centre, Croatia.

UNESCAP (1996). Guidelines on Integrated Tourism Planning in Pacific Island Countries. United Nations Economic and Social Commission for Asia and Pacific. Available at: http://www.unescap.org/ (accessed in July 2007).

United Nations Environment Programme (2001). Data accessed from http://www.unep.org/resourceefficiency/Business/SectoralActivities/Tourism/FactsandFiguresaboutTourism/ImpactsofTourism/Socio-CulturalImpacts/TourismandSocio-CulturalConservation/tabid/78782/Default.aspx

United Nations Environment Programme (2017). http://www.unep.org/resource efficiency/Business/SectoralActivities/Tourism/FactsandFiguresaboutTourism/ImpactsofTourism/EconomicImpactsofTourism/NegativeEconomicImpactsofTourism/tabid/78784/Default.aspx

United Nations World Tourism Organisation/Global Code of Ethics, (2001). http://www.unwto.org/ethics/full_text/en/full_text.php?subop=2

UNWTO & ETC (2008). *Practical Guidelines for Destination Management and Marketing.* WTO, Madrid.

UNWTO & WYSE Travel Confederation (2011). The Power of Youth Travel. Madrid, Spain. http://dtxtq4w60xqpw.cloudfront.net/sites/all/files/pdf/the_power_of_youth_travel.pdf (14 December 2013).

UNWTO (1981). *Saturation of Tourist Destinations: Report of the Secretary General.* World Tourism Organisation, Madrid.

UNWTO (2003). *Proceedings of 1st International Conference on Climate Change and Tourism.*

UNWTO (2003). *Tourist Barometer.* Madrid.

UNWTO (2008). *Tourism Barometer.* Vol. 3, Madrid.

UNWTO (2009). *Handbook of Destination Branding.* Madrid.

UNWTO (2011). *Policy and Practice for Global Tourism.* Madrid.

UNWTO (2012). *Asia/Pacific Newsletter* Issue 25. <http://asiapacific.unwto.org/en/newsletter/2012-04-10/unwto-asiapacific-newsletter-issue-25>(9 December 2013).

UNWTO (2012). *Methodological Notes to the Tourism Statistics Database.* Madrid.

UNWTO (2012). *Tourism in the Green Economy: Background Report*. Madrid.

UNWTO (2013). *Tourism Highlights*. <http://mkt.unwto.org/en/publication/unwto-tourism-highlights-2013-edition.

UNWTO (2016). Exports from international tourism rise 4% in 2015. UNWTO press release-PR No.16033. 06 May, 2016.

UNWTO (2016). *Tourist Statistics*. Madrid.

UNWTO, (2016). Tourist Statistics (Highlights) 2015. Madrid: United Nations World Tourism Organization (UNWTO).

UNWTO-UNEP-WMO (2007). Climate Change and Tourism: Responding to Global Challenges. Data accessed on 25th Nov, 2016, from sdt.unwto.org/sites/all/files/docpdf/summarydavose.pdf

UNWTO. *Tourism Towards 2030: Global Overview*. Madrid.

UNWTO/STEP-Sustainable Elimination: Elimination of Poverty (STEP) , http://step.unwto.org/content/tourism-and-poverty-alleviation-1

UNWTO/UNEP (2005). *Making Tourism More Sustainable: A Guide for Policy Makers*. United Nations Environment Programme and World Tourism Organization. Madrid, Spain.

UNWTO Barometer, March 2016. United Nations World Tourism Organisation, Madrid (Spain).

UNWTO Statistics (2014). *Tourist Statistics*. Madrid.

UNWTO Tourism Policy. http://cooperation.unwto.org/technical-product/tourism-policy

Urry, J. (1990). *The Tourist Gaze*. London: Sage.

UTSOA's Top 10 Reasons to Book a Tour in 2013. https://www.ustoa.com/files/Top_10_Reasons_to_Book_a_Tour_in_2013.pdf.

Uysal, M. (1998). The determinants of tourism demand: A theoretical perspective. In: Loamides, D. & Debbage, K. (Eds.). *The Economic Geography of the Tourist Industry: A Supply Side Analysis*. London: Routledge.

Van den Berghe, P. (1992). Tourism and the ethnic division of labor. *Annals of Tourism Research*. 19: 234-249.

Veal, A.J. (2002). *Leisure and Tourism Policy and Planning*. Oxfordshire (UK): CABI.

Vialle, O. (1995). *Global Distribution Systems in the Tourism Industry*. WTO, Spain.

Wahab, S., Crampon, L.J. & Rothfield, L.M. (1976). *Tourism Marketing*. London: Tourism International Press.

Wall, G. & Mathieson, A. (2005). *Tourism: Change, Impacts and Opportunities*. New Jersey (USA): Prentice Hall.

Wall, G. (2000). Travel. In: *Encyclopedia of Tourism*, J. Jafari, (Ed.). pp. 600-601. London: Routledge.

Wanhill, S. (1994). The measurement of tourist income multipliers. *Tourism Management.* 15(4): 281-283.

Wearning, S. & Neil, J. (1999). *Ecotourism: Impacts, Potentials and Possibilities.* 2nd Edn. Routledge.

Wearning, S. (2001). *Volunteer Tourism: Experiences that Make a Difference.* Wallingford: CABI.

Weaver, D.B. (2001). Ecotourism or mass tourism: Contradiction of reality. *Cornell Hotel and Restaurant Quarterly.* 42: 1040-112.

Weaver, Glenn D. (1991). *Tourism USA.* Washington DC: U.S. Travel and Tourism Administration.

Weed, M. (2008). *Olympic Tourism.* Oxford: Elsevier.

Wells, T.A. (1998). *Air Transportation: A Management Perspective.* California: Wadsworth.

Werthner, H. & Klein, S. (1999). *Information Technology and Tourism: A Challenging Relationship.* New York: Springer Wien.

Weston, R. (2011). Being there and being then: Ideal presence and historical tourism. *New Zealand Journal of Public History.* 1: 84-96.

Whittaker, A. (2008). Pleasure and pain: Medical tourism in Asia. *Global Public Health: An International Journal for Research, Policy and Practice.* 3(3): 271-290.

Wight, P.A. (1992) "Tourism-Recreation EIAS in Alberta: A Need for an Integrated Approach in Legislation, Environmental Assessment, and Development Planning." 12th International Seminar on Environmental Assessment and Management. University of Aberdeen, Scotland, U.K.

Wilkes, W.L. (1994). *Consumer Behaviour.* New York: Wiley.

Williams, S. (1998). *Tourism Geography.* London: Routledge.

World Commission on Environment and Development (WCED). (1987). *Our Common Future.* Oxford: Oxford University Press.

WTO (1991). *International Conference on Travel and Tourism Statistics: Resolutions.* Madrid.

WTO (1994). *National and Regional Tourism Planning: Methodologies and Case Studies.* London: Routledge.

WTO (1995). *Concepts, Definitions and Classifications of Tourism Statistics.* Madrid.

WTO (1995). *Tourism to the year 2000 and Beyond*: The World. Vol. 1. Madrid.

WTO (2001). *Tourism 2020: Vision-Global Forecasts and Profiles of Market Segments.* Madrid.

WTO (2005). *Tourist Statistics: Overview.* Madrid.

WTO and UNSTAT (1994). *Recommendations on Tourism Statistics,* WTO, Madrid and UN, New York.

WTOBC (2001). *E Business for Tourism: Practical Guidelines for Destinations and Businesses*. Madrid.

WTTC (2013). *World Travel and Tourism Council. Annual Report on Country Economic Analysis of Tourism*. Data accessed from https://www.wttc.org/research/economic-research/economic-impact-analysis/

WTTC (2015). *Travel and Tourism Economic Impacts 2015*. London.

WTTC (2016). *Travel & Tourism Economic Impact: Annual Update Summary*. Data accessed from http://www.wttc.org/research/economic-research/economic-impact-

Yale, P. (1995). *The Business of Tour Operation*. Essex: Longman.

Yale, P. (2001). *The Business of Tour Operations*. UK: Longman.

Young, B.S. & Wells, T.A. (2004). *Airport Planning and Management*. 5th Edition. New York: McGraw Hill.

Yuan, Y.L., Gretzel, U. & Fesenmaier, D.R. (1999). The use of Internet and Internet in American Convention and Visitor Bureaus. In: Buhalis, D. (Ed.). *Information & Communication Technologies in Tourism*. Vienna: Springer Verlag. pp. 361-375.

Zaichkowsky, J.L. (1991) Consumer behaviour: Yesterday, today and tomorrow. *Business Horizons*. 34(5): 51-58.

Websites

- www.icao.int
- www.pata.org
- www.uftaa.org
- www.unwto.org
- www.unwto.org
- www.wtttc.com
- www.dgca.nic.in
- www.tourismconcern.org.uk
- www.amadeus.com
- www.thecode.org
- www.ecpat.ne

Official websites and published materials of tourism organizations such as Ministry of Tourism, Ministry of Civil Aviation, Ministry of Railways, ITDC, AAI, **ASI,** IRCTC, TFCI, TAAI, IATO, TAFI, **ADTOI,** ATTOI, ATOAI, IMTA, FICCI, CII, ICPB, RTDC, DTTDC, GTDC, UTDB, KTDC, and HPTDC.

INDEX